THE EMERGING REPUBLICAN MAJORITY

KEVIN P. PHILLIPS

THE

EMERGING REPUBLICAN

MAJORITY

ARLINGTON HOUSE   NEW ROCHELLE, N. Y.

This book is respectfully dedicated to the emerging Republican majority and its two principal architects: President Richard M. Nixon and Attorney General John N. Mitchell.

Library of Congress Catalog Card Number 76-79602

SBN 87000-058-6

MANUFACTURED IN THE UNITED STATES OF AMERICA

Contents

Charts

Maps

PREFACE

I N PURSUIT OF A LONGTIME AVOCATION, I WROTE MOST OF THIS book between November, 1966, and November, 1968. The first date signaled the emergence of a Republican majority. The second —when 57 per cent of the nation's vote was won by Richard Nixon and George Wallace—confirmed the upheaval and indicated its direction. Although a preliminary draft of the book was completed by Christmas, 1967, it seemed wiser to postpone publication until 1968's election results were in hand. This also allowed me time to rewrite the book with considerably more clarity and detail, for which I am retrospectively grateful.

Because of my position in the Nixon campaign as special assistant to national campaign manager John Mitchell, I want to make one point completely clear. This book is a study of American voting patterns and of their changing course. It does *not* purport to set forth the past strategies or future intentions of Richard M. Nixon, his campaign organization or administration. The analysis set forth here is simply my view of what has happened—and what is likely to happen. The perception or effrontery is mine alone.

In light of the complexity of the subject matter, some observations on the approach and method of the book seem in order. First of all, persons who advance a theory inevitably try to squeeze facts into it, often creating an element of distortion in the process. It is as a lawyer rather than an academician that I have propounded my theory—the beginning of a new cycle of national Republican hegemony. I do not pretend to have sought out every statistical, theoretical and historical loose thread which may or may not have been left hanging.

Secondly, some readers may be surprised by the extent to which I have sketched the historic, geographic, ethnic and cultural settings for seemingly contemporary political behavior. Yet one has to understand the origins, location and intensity of traditional political loyalties in order to understand fully the significance of their erosion or reversal. The framework of American politics being highly rational, an extraordinary amount of ballot behavior can be explained by detailed analysis.

Besides the relative abundance of this background material, I have also presented a multitude of statistics, in the simplest possible presentation. Often, a few numerical comparisons are worth a paragraph of explanation. While much of the data has been taken from Richard Scammon's excellent compilation, *America At The Polls*, no small part of it has been gleaned from newspapers, periodicals and semi-official vote canvasses. Since none of these latter statistics are wholly reliable, especially those for 1968, some figures quoted below may be slightly inaccurate in either percentage or raw numbers. It is unlikely that such discrepancies would be of sufficient size to affect trend validities, however.

This book includes one hundred forty-three charts. I believe that they are a useful—and often necessary—supplement to the narrative. Often reference is made to a county or political subdivision as an indicator, say, of Italian, German or Southern trends. Since no county or unit is homogeneous, the trend of the group in question has generally been diluted or modified by other voting groups. For example, if three largely German counties show a 10 per cent to 20 per cent Democratic trend, the German trend—the subject of interest—was probably even larger.

Few people realize the extent of ethnic influences in American politics. Historically, our party system has reflected layer upon layer of group oppositions: Irish against Yankee, Jewish against Catholic, French against English and so forth. Racial and ethnic polarization has neither stopped progress nor worked repression on the groups out of power.

One thesis of this book is that the South is turning into an important presidential base of the Republican Party. I would like to state clearly my opinion that this will *not* result from Republican civil rights law enforcement procedures—the laws undoubtedly will be fully enforced—but from erosion of the now meaningless Southern Democratic tradition.

Lastly, in saying often and emphatically that 1968 marks the beginning of a new Republican cycle comparable in magnitude to the New Deal era which began in 1932, I have doubtless indicated my own hopes and sympathies. But while I believe that a new era is now getting underway, I do not want to create a picture of great change or imminent solution of even the simpler problems facing the United States. Cyclical changes in American political history have been evolutionary, not revolutionary, as I hope this book will show. It will be some time before the new forces in control of the American government produce even some of the changes optimists expect overnight.

While the analyses and theories of this book are mine alone and have had no outside perusal—the material was neither publicized nor openly circulated during the pre-election period of 1968—I would like to extend my general appreciation to all those people in the Nixon organization whose insights and criticism polished or tempered my ideas. I would like to extend more specific thanks as follows: to my editor, David Franke, who went to bat for my thesis when the next Republican President was only a hope; to John Mitchell, Richard Nixon's 1968 national campaign manager, whose keen strategic sense literally made history; to Len Garment, Nixon law partner and campaign media chief, for his support and encouragement; to fellow Nixon aide and voting buff Jeff Bell, for incessant conversation, insight and enthusiasm; and to my wife Martha, for putting up with this book, its charts, maps and theories, at innumerable difficult moments.

KEVIN P. PHILLIPS

St. George,
Grenada, W.I.
November, 1968

I. INTRODUCTION

ᗞᗞ ᗞᗞ ᗞᗞ ᗞᗞ ᗞᗞ ᗞᗞ ᗞᗞ ᗞᗞ

Fᴀʀ ꜰʀᴏᴍ ʙᴇɪɴɢ ᴛʜᴇ ᴛᴇɴᴜᴏᴜꜱ ᴀɴᴅ ᴜɴᴍᴇᴀɴɪɴɢꜰᴜʟ ᴠɪᴄᴛᴏʀʏ suggested by critical observers, the election of Richard M. Nixon as President of the United States in November, 1968, bespoke the end of the New Deal Democratic hegemony and the beginning of a new era in American politics. To begin with, Nixon was elected by a Republican Party much changed from that deposed in 1932; and such party metamorphosis has historically brought a fresh political cycle in its wake. Secondly, the vastness of the tide (57 per cent) which overwhelmed Democratic liberalism—George Wallace's support was clearly an even more vehement protest against the Democrats than was Nixon's vote—represented an epochal shifting of national gears from the 61 per cent of the country's ballots garnered in 1964 by Lyndon Johnson. This repudiation visited upon the Democratic Party for its ambitious social programming, and inability to handle the urban and Negro revolutions, was comparable in scope to that given conservative Republicanism in 1932 for its failure to cope with the economic crisis of the Depression. And ironically, the Democratic debacle of 1968 followed the Party's most smashing victory—that of 1964—just as the 1932 toppling of the Grand Old Party succeeded the great landslide of 1928. A comparison of the two reversals is apt:

CHART 1

The Great Upheavals: 1928-32 and 1964-68

SHARE OF THE TOTAL VOTE FOR PRESIDENT

	1928	1932
Republican	58%	40%
Anti-Republican Left		
(Democrat & Socialist)	42%	60%

	1964	1968
Democratic	61%	43%
Anti-Democrat Right		
(Republican and American Independent)	39%	57%

The changed makeup and outlook of the GOP reflects its switch-over, during the 1932-68 span of the New Deal era, from orientation towards the establishmentarian Northeast—especially the Yankee and industrial bailiwicks of New England, upstate New York, Michigan and Pennsylvania—to representation of the rising insurgency of the South, the West, the New York City Irish and middle-class suburbia. At the same time, while the New Deal institutionalized into a nationally-dominant liberal Establishment, the Democratic power base shifted to the Northeast, historically the seat of America's dominant economic, social, cultural and political elite. By 1964, the transition was reasonably obvious; whatever the strategic ineptitude of the Goldwater candidacy, it was not a geopolitical fluke. As Chart 2 shows, the Republican Party had been moving its reliance South and West since the beginning of the New Deal cycle in 1932. The 1968 election confirmed the general Southern and Western impetus of 1964—only the Deep South parochialism had been an aberration—and set a cyclical seal on the partisan re-alignment.

Maps 1-4 illustrate the regional tides at work and Chart 3 estimates the group voting currents of 1960-68. In 1968, only six states and the District of Columbia gave the Democratic presidential nominee a majority of the vote; seven other states produced Humphrey pluralities in the face of Nixon-Wallace majorities. In thirty-seven other states, Nixon-Wallace majorities divided in such a way as to award victory to either the Republican candidate, who

CHART 2

*The Metamorphosis of the Republican Party's
Regional Support Base, 1932-68*

REPUBLICAN SHARE OF THE TWO-PARTY PRESIDENTIAL VOTE

1932		*1936*	
Northeast	48%	Northeast	42%
Heartland and West	43%	Heartland and West	40%
South	19%	South	19%

*1948**		*1952*	
Heartland and West	48%	Heartland and West	58%
Northeast	47%	Northeast	56%
South	27%	South	48%

1960		*1964*	
Heartland and West	52%	South	49%
South	48%	Heartland and West	39%
Northeast	47%	Northeast	32%

*1968***	
Heartland and West	53%
South	53%
Northeast	46%

*The regional figures represent the GOP share of the Republican-Democratic-
Dixiecrat presidential total.
**The regional figures represent the GOP share of the Republican-Democratic
vote only. (The Wallace vote has been excluded.)

carried thirty-two states, or Wallace, who carried five. Most of
the Democratic states were Northeastern—Maine, Massachusetts,
Rhode Island, Connecticut, New York, Pennsylvania, Maryland
(as well as the District of Columbia)—or (West Virginia excluded)
they were states—Michigan, Minnesota, Washington and Hawaii
—which had been heavily settled or influenced by Yankees or
Scandinavians. In light of its concentration in an area which had
been the prime sociological core of post-Civil War Republicanism,
1968 Democratic strength was peculiarly ironic.

The forces shaping this parochialism are clear enough; they
explain why, even as 1968 saw the nation turning against the

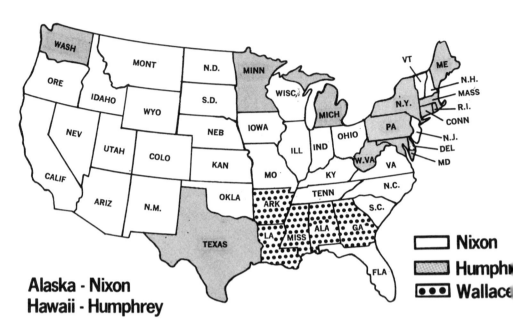

Alaska - Nixon
Hawaii - Humphrey

Nixon
Humphr
Wallace

ALASKA—12%

HAWAII—1%

WALLACE VOTE

0—5

5—1

10—

20—

OVER

*Ranked by Humphrey share of the total vote for President

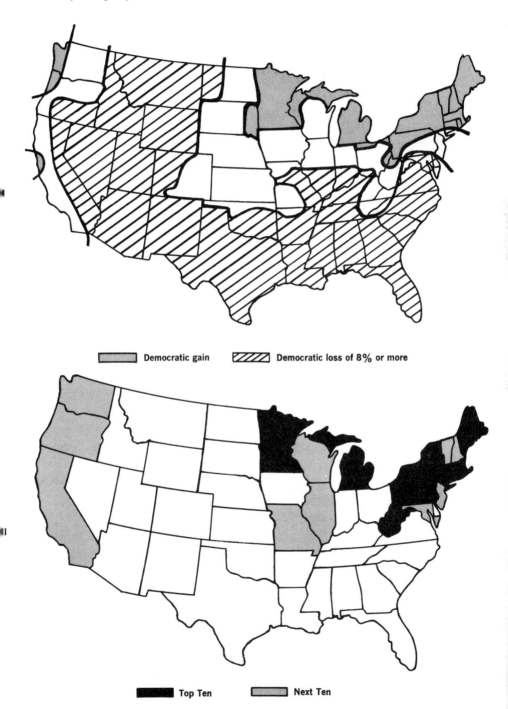

Democratic gain   Democratic loss of 8% or more

Top Ten   Next Ten

CHART 3

Gallup Poll Presidential Voting Analysis, 1952-68

VOTE BY GROUPS IN PRESIDENTIAL ELECTIONS
(1952-1968)

	1952		1956		1960		1964		1968		
	Dem. %	Rep. %	Dem. %	Rep. %	Dem. %	Rep. %	Dem. %	Rep. %	Dem. %	Rep. %	Wallace %
NATIONAL	44.6	55.4	42.2	57.8	50.1	49.9	61.3	38.7	43.0	43.4	13.6
Men	47	53	45	55	52	48	60	40	41	43	16
Women	42	58	39	61	49	51	62	38	45	43	12
White	43	57	41	59	49	51	59	41	38	47	15
Non-white	79	21	61	39	68	32	94	6	85	12	3
College	34	66	31	69	39	61	52	48	42	54	9
High School	45	55	42	58	52	48	62	38	42	43	15
Grade School	52	48	50	50	55	45	66	34	52	33	15
Prof. & Bus.	36	64	32	68	42	58	54	46	34	56	10
White Collar	40	60	37	63	48	52	57	43	41	47	12
Manual	55	45	50	50	60	40	71	29	50	35	15
Farmers	33	67	46	54	48	52	53	47	29	51	20
Under 30	51	49	43	57	54	46	64	36	47	38	15
30-49 years	47	53	45	55	54	46	63	37	44	41	15
50 years & older	39	61	39	61	46	54	59	41	41	47	12
Protestant	37	63	37	63	38	62	55	45	35	49	16
Catholic	56	44	51	49	78	22	76	24	59	33	8
Republicans	8	92	4	96	5	95	20	80	0	96	5

Democrats, a handful of the New England and above-mentioned states swam against the current and gave the Democrats a higher vote share than in 1960. First of all, no other part of the United States shares the historical penchant of the Northeast for supporting the politics and ideology of a hitherto nationally dominant, but fading, group of interests. The Jeffersonian, Jacksonian and New Deal upheavals *all* captured the White House against ballot opposition centered in the Northeast. And on top of growing national Democratic Party identification with Northeastern interests, another major fulcrum of 1968 upheaval was the erosion of Civil War political traditions which had been the source of American sectional politics and partisanship for a century. Because of loyalties formed in the crucible of slavery and civil war, Yankees and Scandinavians in New England, upstate New York, Pennsylvania, Michigan, Ohio, Minnesota, Iowa, Wisconsin and the Pacific Northwest were the

---

1960-68 Trends (Chart 3 on facing page)

Men showed a strong anti-Democrat trend between 1960 and 1968; women showed considerably less change. Historically, men have spearheaded political upheaval while women have given greater backing to *status quo* politics (since 1964, the Democratic Party).

In the eight years, the Democrats lost heavily among white voters, but fashioned much increased support among non-whites. The new popular majority is white and conservative.

Vocationally, the Democrats lost ground with almost every group, but their loss was greatest among farmers. On the plane of education, the Democrats scored a gain among the college-educated elite, but slipped badly among the country's huge high-school-educated middle spectrum.

The relative age profiles of the two parties did not change much, although Wallace scored his greatest inroads among young people.

Between 1960 and 1968, Nixon lost a large bloc of Protestants— mostly Southerners, Borderers and other conservatives temporarily switching to Wallace. Nixon gained sharply among Catholics, many of whom are leaving the Democratic Party. These statistics indicate Nixon's 1972 opportunity—acceleration of the Catholic GOP trend and recapture of the conservative Protestants who backed the Republicans in 1960 but bolted to Wallace in 1968.

driving force and numerical bulwark of a Republican Party they had principally created. But as a result of the social upheaval of the Nineteen-Sixties, these were the groups and states among whom and which the Democrats gained (or suffered only minimal losses) in 1968. In many of the same areas where the Civil War had ingrained the most intense Republicanism, Democratic identification with the Negro social and economic revolution precipitated that party's best gains a century later.

On the other side of the coin, the conservative and Republican alliance of 1968 mobilized in areas with an insurgent record—the South, the West and the Irish sidewalks of New York (as well as the emerging tax-revolt centers of middle-class suburbia)—and a record of support for popular movements like those of Thomas Jefferson, Andrew Jackson, William Jennings Bryan and Franklin D. Roosevelt. These voting streams were inclined to move away from, rather than towards, the emerging Negro-Establishment entente; and harkening back to the Civil War, the new conservatism was generally taking shape (there were exceptions, of course) in areas where Civil War feeling had been secessionist, divided or ambiguous, as in the South, Heartland, West, Border and German-Irish urban centers. Persistent ethnicultural cleavages were prompting a turnabout of partisanship.

But at this point it is necessary to lay down a few *caveats*. Granted that the Democrats were making their greatest strides among silk-stocking voters and Yankees, the two groups remained (diminishingly) Republican; and even though the Democrats were losing strength among Northern Catholics, the blue-collar Poles, Slavs, French-Canadians, Italians and Irish of industrial cities from Saco to Sault Ste. Marie (but excluding New York City) remained the bulwark of Northeastern Democratic hegemony. However much the trends of the Nineteen-Sixties foreshadowed the upcoming cycle, the raw statistics of group voting were a weakening link to the New Deal cycle. In the United States, political change is evolutionary rather than revolutionary.

Back in 1960, Richard Nixon had run for President as the candidate of a Republican Party still at least partly controlled, as Henry Cabot Lodge's vice-presidential nomination bore witness, by its traditional Yankee bastion. By 1968, however, things had changed. Not only had the civil rights revolution cut the South adrift from its Democratic moorings and drawn the Northeast towards the Democrats, but it had increased the Southern and Western bias of the GOP to a point—the 1964 Goldwater nomination—where the party had decided to break with its formative antecedents and make an ideological bid for the anti-civil rights South. Goldwater's extraordinary Deep South success, together with the unprecedented party defeat in Yankee and silk-stocking areas, speeded re-alignment already on its way. By dint of the 1964 election, the Republican Party shed the dominion of its Yankee and Northeastern Establishment creators, while the Democrats, having linked themselves to the Negro socioeconomic revolution and to an increasingly liberal Northeastern Establishment shaped by the success of the New Deal, sank the foundations of their future into the Northeast.

As of 1968, the Democratic and liberal record was one of failure—in global diplomacy, Asian warfare, domestic economics, social and welfare policy, and law enforcement—and the Republicans, together with third-party presidential candidate George Wallace, rode a wave of popular desire for change. The GOP swept the Farm Belt and Rocky Mountains; more narrowly carried the Great Lakes, Pacific and Border states; split the South with George Wallace; and lost only the Northeast. With a united rather than Civil War-divided conservative power base, centered in the great interior Heartland and peripheral South, a new political alignment and cycle began.

Despite George Wallace's grandiose dreams of achieving an ideologically compelling balance of power between the two major parties, he proved unable to reach beyond the electoral votes of the Deep South. More important, his popular support beyond Dixie followed contours of conservative Southern Democratic tradition (Delaware Bay to Nevada), William Jennings Bryan-era Democratic populism (the Plains and Rockies) or urban Catholic upheaval (cities where Negroes or other minority groups are taking over the Democratic Party). Where these trends were not present, Wallace showed negligible strength in either heavily unionized areas —Scranton, Fall River or Duluth—or among poverty-stricken whites (West Virginia). Some of Wallace's support came from aroused conservative Republicans, but most of it represented Democratic voting streams quitting their party. Among major Democratic electoral groups, only those already in revolt backed Wallace. The Alabaman tapped rather than shaped a protest; his party represents an electorate in motion between major parties rather than a new, permanent entrant into the national presidential arena.

Presumably Wallace's realization of this failure underlay his post-election comment—recognition of the GOP future was implicit—that he had swung the Republican Party to the right and simultaneously diverted enough votes to make Nixon's victory possible. But whatever Wallace's ideological influence, his vote diversions certainly did not help Richard Nixon. On the contrary, Wallace split the conservative electorate, siphoned off a flow of ballots that otherwise would have gone heavily for Nixon, and garnered many of his backers—Northern or Southern, blue-collar or white-collar—from the ranks of supporters of 1964 GOP presidential nominee Barry Goldwater.

As Chart 4 shows, Wallace's strength proved to be negligible—and he diverted few votes—in the states which found the national Democratic Party most appealing. Of the Alabaman's nine worst showings, six came in the nine best Humphrey states (including the District of Columbia, where Wallace was not even on the ballot). The *best* Wallace vote came in states where conservatism was powerfully emergent; states where Wallace lured unhappy Republicans or tapped a trend which otherwise would have aided the GOP. Even in liberal states like New York, the Wallace vote was drawn from a usually Republican—given a conservative nominee—electorate. Four of the five states backing Wallace had been among the six to

CHART 4

*The Inverse Relationship of Democratic Strength and
    Wallace Support, 1968*

Nine Top Democratic States	Nine Worst Wallace States
District of Columbia (82%)	District of Columbia (0%)**
Rhode Island (65%)	Hawaii (1%)
Massachusetts (63%)	Maine (2%)
Hawaii (60%)	Vermont (3%)
Maine (55%)	New Hampshire (4%)
Minnesota (54%)	Rhode Island (4%)
New York (50%)	Minnesota (4%)
West Virginia (50%)	Massachusetts (4%)
Connecticut (50%)	New York (5%)

*Humphrey and Wallace shares of the three-party vote.
**Wallace was not on the ballot in the District of Columbia.

back Barry Goldwater in 1964, and all across the nation, most Wallace supporters would have chosen Nixon in 1968 over Democratic nominee Hubert H. Humphrey. The probable inability of the Wallaceites to take the field in 1972, given the parochialism of their 1968 popular and electoral vote pattern and their vulnerability to a relatively conservative 1968-72 Republican administration, should add an important national bloc of popular votes and a key Deep Southern group of electoral votes to the barebones Republican triumph of 1968.

Despite his skimpy electoral vote, George Wallace had come tantalizingly close to holding the 1968 balance of power. Throughout election night, an apprehensive nation watched and listened to reports that perhaps neither candidate could command the clear electoral vote majority needed to win the presidency. What only a few weeks earlier had looked to be a Nixon landslide tightened into a close race, as once-dissident liberals rallied behind Humphrey and Democratic union leaders whipped their pro-Wallace rank and file back to the party line. If Humphrey had proved just a little stronger, the election might have been stalemated as the Wallace forces had hoped.

On the other hand, Wallace's vote would probably have dipped much lower had Richard Nixon chosen to rally aberrant multitudes of 1964 Goldwater backers by sounding the anti-Great Society clarion which had so successfully served as a fulcrum of re-alignment in the 1966 off-year elections. But, reflecting his confidence and a desire to avoid divisiveness, the Republican candidate maintained a mild campaign stance. Nixon, however, cannot be too easily faulted for the course he successfully steered between the Scylla of losing too many moderates to Hubert Humphrey and the Charybdis of leaving too many conservatives in the camp of George Wallace. He won enough moderates to overcome the division in his conservative support base, even as he took a sufficiently conservative stance to minimize the Wallace vote and undermine the third party's future. Under these circumstances, the vast significance of his victory lay in its occurrence and not in its magnitude. Observations that Nixon won no mandate were at odds with the verdict rendered on the Democratic administration by 57 per cent of the nation's voters—an obvious inchoate Nixon constituency.

Little credence can be given to the allegation that the Republican failure to make large gains in Congress bespoke public confidence in national Democratic Party programs and policy; nor did these results indicate continuation of the New Deal cycle in the face of a mere fluke on the presidential level. The ideological reaction against Democratic liberalism had come in 1966, so that there were not many Northern constituencies left for the Republicans to gain in 1968. But much more important was the fact that Congress *already* had a conservative majority—Republicans from all corners of the country and traditional Democrats from the South and Border. All fourteen Southern and Border states—Virginia, North Carolina, South Carolina, Georgia, Florida, Alabama, Mississippi, Tennessee, Louisiana, Arkansas, Texas, Oklahoma, Kentucky and Missouri—cast a majority of their vote against the national Democratic Party's presidential candidate but elected a vast preponderance of conservative Democrats at traditionalist odds with the ideological stance of the national party. Only by this anomaly of nomenclature, which cannot long survive the evolution of the national Democrats into the party of the Establishmentarian Northeast and Negro South, did the Great Society maintain the image of public support. The presidential election of 1968 marked a historic first occasion— the Negrophobe Deep South and modern Outer South *simultaneously* abandoned the Democratic Party. And before long, the conservative cycle thus begun ought to witness movement of congressional, state and local Southern Democrats into the ascending Republican Party.

Considerable historical and theoretical evidence supports the thesis that a liberal Democratic era has ended and that a new era of consolidationist Republicanism has begun. To begin with, the 1932-68 Democratic reign spanned thirty-six years and a social revolution. History indicates that this is the usual longevity of an American political cycle. For example, the modern American political system dates from the election of Andrew Jackson in 1828, which precipitated a Democratic predominance lasting until Lincoln's triumph in 1860. Contrary to general legend, the Civil War did not seat the Republicans firmly in the national saddle, however effectively it unseated the hitherto predominant Democrats. As a matter of fact, once the Southern states had returned to the Union, things settled into something of a stalemate. No president elected between 1876 and 1892 won a majority of the popular vote. Finally, in 1896, the Bryan-McKinley contest tarred the Democrats with the brush of agrarianism and revivalism, thus cementing Republican rule based on the populous, industrial Northeast and Great

Lakes. Thereafter, except for the eight-year Wilson Administration, the GOP held national sway until the advent of the Great Depression and the election of Franklin D. Roosevelt in 1932. Actually, the coming of age of urban America had begun to swing the pendulum towards the Democrats even before the Depression, as witness Al Smith's 1928 breakthroughs in the Northeast; however, many Republicans blamed Franklin Roosevelt's personal popularity and refused to face the socioeconomic fact that a new Democratic majority had come into being. Thirty-six years later, it too gave way to change.

To structure a mathematical perspective reaching back to 1828, political history divides into four cycles: 1828-60, 1860-96, 1896-1932 and 1932-68. All four cycles lasted thirty-two or thirty-six years, and all four included steady rule by one party, with an interregnum of just eight years when the lesser party held power. The interregnums were: (1) the tenures of Whig generals Harrison and Taylor amidst the otherwise Democratic span of 1828-60; (2) the two Grover Cleveland administrations in the 1860-96 post-Civil War era; (3) the two Woodrow Wilson administrations amidst the 1896-1932 rule of industrial Republicanism; and (4) the Eisenhower years in the middle of the 1932-68 New Deal Democratic cycle. The Nixon administration seems destined by precedent to be the beginning of a new Republican era.

Another bulwark of cyclical change is the obsolescence of the prevailing ideology or impetus of the dominant party. The principal force which broke up the Democratic (New Deal) coalition is the Negro socioeconomic revolution and liberal Democratic ideological inability to cope with it. Democratic "Great Society" programs aligned that party with many Negro demands, but the party was unable to defuse the racial tension sundering the nation. The South, the West and the Catholic sidewalks of New York were the focal points of conservative opposition to the welfare liberalism of the federal government; however, the general opposition which deposed the Democratic Party came in large part from prospering Democrats who objected to Washington dissipating their tax dollars on programs which did them no good. The Democratic Party fell victim to the ideological impetus of a liberalism which had carried it beyond programs taxing the few for the benefit of the many (the New Deal) to programs taxing the many on behalf of the few (the Great Society).

Back in 1932, the Democratic Party took office with a popular mandate to develop a new governmental approach to the problems of economic and social welfare which the Depression had brought into painful focus. Basically, Roosevelt's New Deal liberalism invoked government action to deal with situations from which the government had hitherto remained aloof; i.e., the malpractice of corporations, unemployment, malnutrition, lack of rural electricity, collapsed farm prices and managerial intolerance of organized labor. But in the years since 1932, federal interventionism has slowly changed from an innovative policy into an institutionalized reflex. Great Society liberalism propounded federally controlled categorical grant-in-aid programs and bureaucratic social engineering as the answer to crises big and little just as inevitably as Calvin ("The business of America is business") Coolidge sermonized laissez faire economics during the formative period of the Depression. And just as the political inability of laissez faire Republicanism to handle the post-1929 economic crisis signaled the end of one cycle and the beginning of another, so did the breakdown of New Deal liberalism in the face of a social and urban crisis which clearly demands its own ideological innovation. In all likelihood, 1968 marks the beginning of an era of decentralizing government, whereby Washington can regain the public confidence necessary to mobilize the inchoate American commitment to housing, education and employment opportunity.

Gone are the days when a conservative Establishment—Wall Street, the Episcopal Church, the great metropolitan newspapers, the U.S. Supreme Court and Manhattan's East Side—harassed Franklin D. Roosevelt and his fledgling New Deal. Today, these same institutions, now liberal, vent their spleen on populist conservatism. The contemporary Establishment reflects the institutionalization of the innovative political impetus of thirty years ago: the middle-aged influence and affluence of the New Deal. This is a good sign of change. By the time a once-popular political upheaval has become institutionalized in the partners' rooms of Wall Street and the salons of Fifth Avenue, a counter-movement has invariably taken hold in the ordinary (now middle-class) hinterlands of the nation.

A fourth and last theory on which a new political cycle can be predicated rests on the post-1945 migration of many white Americans (including many of the traditionally Democratic white ethnic groups) to suburbia and the Sun Belt states of Florida, Texas,

Arizona and California. This trend parallels, and is partially a result of, concurrent Southern Negro migration to the principal cities of the North. The Negro problem, having become a national rather than a local one, is the principal cause of the breakup of the New Deal coalition.

Previous American population shifts have generally triggered major political changes: (1) The rise of the trans-Appalachian "New West" in the early Nineteenth Century overpowered the conservatism of the Eastern Seaboard and provided the base of Jacksonian democracy. (2) The admission of California, Oregon and the Yankee-settled Farm states to the Union tipped the balance against the South and subsequently buoyed the Republicans throughout the post-Civil War era. (3) The expansion of the United States across the plains and Rocky Mountains added new Republican states to the Union, while the vast influx of European immigrants whose sweat ran the mills and factories of the Northeast laid down a vital foundation for the 1896-1932 era of industrial Republicanism. And (4) the coming of age of urban and immigrant America, rendered more painful by the Depression, established a national Democratic hegemony rooted in the cities which lasted from 1932 to 1968. Today, the interrelated Negro, suburban and Sun Belt migrations have all but destroyed the old New Deal coalition. Chart 142 vividly illustrates the declining population and power of the big cities. Some Northern cities are nearly half Negro, and new suburbia is turning into a bastion of white conservatism; moreover, growing Northern-based Negro political influence has prompted not only civil rights measures obnoxious to the South but social legislation and programs anathema to the sons and daughters of Northern immigrants. As in the past, changing population patterns have set the scene for a new political alignment.

American voting patterns are a kaleidoscope of sociology, history, geography and economics. Of course, the threads are very tangled and complex, but they can be pulled apart. The "science" in political science is not entirely a misnomer; voting patterns can be structured and analyzed in such a way as to show an extraordinary amount of social and economic behaviorism at work. Once the correct framework has been erected, national voting patterns can be structured, explained, correlated and predicted to a surprising degree. The trick is to build the framework.

For a century, the prevailing cleavages in American voting behavior have been ethnic and cultural. Politically, at least, the United States has not been a very effective melting pot. In practically every state and region, ethnic and cultural animosities and divisions exceed all other factors in explaining party choice and identification. From New York City, where income level has only minimally influenced the mutual hostility of Jews and Irish Catholics; to Wisconsin, where voting analysis requires an ethnic map of the state's Welsh, Belgian, French, Swiss, Finnish, Polish, Dutch, German, Danish, Swedish, Norwegian and Yankee populations; to Missouri, where partisanship has long pivoted on Virginian, New England, hillbilly and German settlement patterns and ensuing Civil War sympathies —everywhere ethnic, regional and cultural loyalties constitute the principal dynamics of American voting. Inasmuch as most of the Catholic ethnic groups live in Northern states where the rural Protestant population—their obvious political opposition—has been Republican, they have generally voted Democratic. Today these loyalties are ebbing along with the Republicanism of the Yankee countryside.

Beneath the checkerboard of ethnic settlement which extends from Maine's French Catholic Aroostook Valley to the Norwegian fishing villages of Alaska's Inland Passage—the South, except for its Negroes and Latin fringe, is largely Anglo-Saxon—the basic roots of American voting patterns have long rested in the regionalism of Civil War loyalties. And these in turn have reflected patterns of Yankee, Middle Atlantic and Southern settlement. During the hundred years after the founding of the Republican Party in 1854, GOP strength was principally rooted in Yankee New England and its outliers from upstate New York to Oregon. Democratic voting, based on Southern antecedents and Civil War sentiment, prevailed from Delaware west through Kentucky, Missouri, Oklahoma and the Southwest, as well as the eleven states of the old Confederacy. The two cultures met in the Missouri, Mississippi and Ohio valleys, though the "border" was irregular and outposts of one group sometimes pushed into the general territory of the other. For example, Virginian settlements were made in north-central Ohio and New England-planted towns can be found in northern Missouri.

Given the extent to which Civil War loyalties underlay the Republican-Democratic party alignment until the end of the New Deal era, the contemporary ebb of Republicanism in its bailiwicks of Yankee tradition and the more striking disintegration of the Democratic Party in its former Southern and Border fiefs suggests that a full-scale delineation of the scope and spread of both behavioral streams can shed real light on the forces and prospects of the emerging conservative and Republican majority. To a degree little appreciated by most Americans, the cultural patterns of the Northeast and the coastal South traveled due west across the pre-Civil War Mississippi Valley so that the county-by-county partisanship of, say, Indiana, can be largely explained in terms of Yankee, Middle Atlantic or Southern settlement. A number of pre-Civil War travelers and observers discussed this phenomenon, and one of the best descriptions is that written in 1834 by a contemporary emigration counselor named Baird:

> The emigration to the Valley of the Mississippi seems to have gone in columns, moving from the East almost due west, from the respective states . . . From New England, the emigrant column advanced through New York, peopling the middle and western parts of that state in its progress; but still continuing, it reached the northern part of Ohio, then Indiana and finally Illinois. A part of the same column . . . is diverging into Michigan . . . The Pennsylvania and New Jersey column advanced within the parallels of latitude of those states in west Pennsylvania, and still continuing, advanced into the middle and southern parts of Ohio, and extended even into the middle parts of Indiana and Illinois. The Virginia column advanced first into the western part of the state and Kentucky—which was long a constituent part of it—thence into the southern parts of Indiana and Illinois, until it had spread over almost the whole of Missouri. The North Carolina column advanced into East Tennessee, thence into West Tennessee, and also into Missouri. And the South Carolina and Georgia column has moved upon the extensive and fertile lands of Alabama (and Mississippi) . . . In Arkansas, the emigrating columns of Kentucky and Tennessee predominate.
>
> The above mentioned fact furnishes a better key than any other that I know of, to furnish a correct knowledge of the diversity of customs and manners which prevail in the Valley of the Mississippi. For if one knows what are the peculiarities of the several states east of the Allegheny mountains, he may expect them, with some shades of difference occasioned by local circumstances, in the corresponding parallels of the West. Slavery keeps nearly within the same parallels and so does nearly every other peculiarity.*

*R. Baird, *View of the Valley of the Mississippi* (Philadelphia, 1834), pp. 100-101.

Thus, what seems like uselessly remote historical data— the details of the peopling of the United States—is actually quite vital to understanding the dynamics of the upcoming political cycle. On the one hand, the Democrats are scoring gains in Yankee and Scandinavian areas of Civil War-era Republican tradition; yet on the other hand, they are suffering a much greater loss in Southern-oriented territory reaching beyond Dixie to Delaware Bay, the Ohio and Missouri valleys and the far Southwest. Map 3 shows the geographic scope of both (1960-68) trends. Not only is the Democratic Party's loss more extensive than its gain, but the loss is occurring in those sections of the nation—Florida, the Gulf Coast, Texas, Arizona and Southern California—where population growth is centered. The Yankee countryside and the old Northeastern cities are losing both people and political power. A century ago, for example, Maine had more congressmen than Texas; Rhode Island more than Florida. The 1970 Census is expected to award Texas and Florida thirty-nine to Maine and Rhode Island's collective four.

The best structural approach to the changing alignment of American voters is a region-by-region analysis designed to unfold the multiple sectional conflicts and group animosities in a logical progression. The key region—in past years it has been the seat of the prevailing national establishment and thus the *provocateur* of resentment elsewhere—is the Northeast. Next in order is the South, historically the leading political rival of the Northeast. The American interior or "Heartland," settled by the westward movement of both Northerners and Southerners, reflects the voting patterns of its two parent regions and as a result has historically divided along a trans-Appalachian extension of the Mason-Dixon line. The last region, of course, is the Pacific, which combines the people and traditions of all three regions in a fast-growing—California is the pacesetter—and decreasingly ethnic-minded middle-class tomorrowland. As for sequence, the best procedure is to begin where the United States first took (Anglo-Saxon) shape and Democratic liberalism is presently strongest—in the Northeast—and swing south and west with history, population migration and the coming conservative cycle of American politics.

II. THE NORTHEAST

ⵛⵛ ⵛⵛ ⵛⵛ ⵛⵛ ⵛⵛ ⵛⵛ ⵛⵛ ⵛⵛ

SINCE THE EIGHTEENTH-CENTURY BEGINNINGS OF THE UNITED States, the Northeast, as the seat of national wealth, power, population and culture, has more often than not dominated American politics. The exceptions to this hegemony have been periods of popular rule—the Jeffersonian, Jacksonian and New Deal eras— during which Southern, Western and urban working-class upheaval displaced the party of powerful Northeastern interests. More than any other region, the Northeast can be relied upon to defend the politics of the past and the interests of the dominant American "Establishment." Such persisting loyalty produced nationally atypical support for the fading regimes and impetus of John Adams, John Quincy Adams and Herbert Hoover.

In George Washington's day, the contemporary Northeast—the Middle Atlantic states and New England—was a heterogeneity of regional entities. New York, Boston, Philadelphia and Baltimore were centers of distinctive cultural and economic patterns. The first establishmentarian party, the Federalists, spoke for New England and the Seaboard mercantile aristocracy; they were followed by the Jeffersonians, whose popular politics gave way to a broader grouping of vested interests, only to be overturned in 1828 by the popular Jacksonians. After 1860, a new, powerful Northeastern Establishment of Boston and New York financiers, railroaders, New

England manufacturers and Pennsylvania mine-owners and iron-mongers, in control of the Republican Party, fought the South and won, profited extraordinarily and set a new course for the nation.

The Northeastern Establishment—those ruling powers which have historically played such an important national role—is not a fixed geographic, sociological, economic or ideological entity; it is a changing aggregation of vested interests, and Northeastern politics have shown a considerable tendency to change in its wake.

After the Civil War, the Northeastern industrial and commercial establishment espoused laissez faire and the locally controlled Republican Party, giving each more support than did any other part of the nation. Finally, the New Deal triumph of 1932 overthrew the old establishment, enthroning a new liberal impetus of expansive government. At first, the New Deal was Western, Southern, urban Catholic and anti-establishment, but as liberalism and the New Deal institutions took firm hold, they gave rise to a new establishment in the Northeast and became vested interests themselves. By 1968, there was a very real Northeastern Establishment centered on the profits of social and welfare spending, the knowledge industry, conglomerate corporatism, dollar internationalism and an interlocking directorate with the like-concerned power structure of political liberalism. Ever the mirror of establishmentarianism, the Northeast of 1968 was the most liberal and Democratic section of the United States (just as it was the most Federalist, anti-Jacksonian and anti-New Deal in bygone days). A new political cycle is beginning, and it is entirely commensurate with past history that loyalty to the existing order of things should be centered in the Northeast.

But if Northeastern politics flow onward in a dynamics of establishmentarianism, they do so with steadily less power to sway the nation. Every passing decade has shrunk the Northeast's share of United States population. Chart 5 shows the steady decline in the percentage of the electoral vote for president cast by the Northeastern states in the century after the Civil War. Liberalism does not face a bright national future as a Northeastern-based establishmentarian impetus.

Given the establishmentarianism of the Northeast, it is fitting that the Northeast should be delineated by the Megalopolis, seat of the liberal Establishment. Thus drawn, the Northeast encompasses the eleven states north of the Potomac and east of the Appalachians, all of which save Vermont are traversed by the Megalopolis. As ana-

CHART 5

Northeastern Electoral Vote Strength, 1860-1970

State	1860	1870	1880	1890	1900	1910	1920	1930	1940	1950	1960	1970
Vermont	5	5	4	4	4	4	4	3	3	3	3	3
New Hampshire	5	5	4	4	4	4	4	4	4	4	4	4
Maine	7	7	6	6	6	6	6	5	5	5	4	4
Massachusetts	12	13	14	15	16	18	18	17	16	16	14	14
Rhode Island	4	4	4	4	4	5	5	4	4	4	4	4
Connecticut	6	6	6	6	7	7	7	8	8	8	8	8
New York	33	35	36	36	39	45	45	47	47	45	43	42
Pennsylvania	26	29	30	32	34	38	38	36	35	32	29	27
New Jersey	7	9	9	10	12	14	14	16	16	16	17	17
Maryland	7	8	8	8	8	8	8	8	8	9	10	10
Delaware	3	3	3	3	3	3	3	3	3	3	3	3
Northeast	115	124	124	128	137	152	152	151	149	145	139	136
Total United States	315	369	420	447	483	531	531	531	531	531	535	538
Northeastern Percentage of Total	37	33	30	29	29	29	29	29	28	27	26	25

lyzed by geographer Jean Gottman, the Megalopolis is the massive urban-suburban corridor stretching from Washington, D.C. to Portland, Maine.* It is no exaggeration to say that the Megalopolis is the sociocultural spinal column of the Northeast and the prime shaper of the region's outlook. Even as the national power of the Northeast is on the wane, the Megalopolis' share of the population within the region is growing. However, the Megalopolis is not everywhere dominant; part of the Northeast remains small-city and rural. Non-Megalopolitan politics are particularly influential in the six states of Maine, Vermont, New Hampshire, Delaware, Pennsylvania and Maryland. Prior to the midcentury emergence of the Megalopolis, the true Northeast was more limited in geopolitical scope, pivoting as it did on Northern Civil War tradition.

In the years between the Civil War and the New Deal (and especially between the war and 1896), two different traditions relating back to the fratricidal conflict divided the area now spanned by the Megalopolis. The division was regional rather than sociological. Maryland, Delaware and much of southern New Jersey and Pennsylvania looked to the South while New England, upstate New York and northern Pennsylvania were Yankee by culture and Republican by politics. Map 5 shows the contemporary Megalopolis-defined Northeast, together with the two rural sections of disparate tradition. However, the rise of the Megalopolis has withered the partisan Mason-Dixon line and Megalopolitan social conflicts are structuring a new era. Given the impact of the Megalopolis, the best way to fathom Northeastern political trends is to tear apart the regional political fabric and examine the many strands—rural Yankee, Negro, urban Catholic, silk-stocking and suburban—rather than discuss states or sections. But first a historical sketch is in order.

The Civil War period was a decisive one for the Northeast. For many years the South and the Northeast had been rivals for the nation's future, and as the two competing socioeconomies moved west, they jealously divided the United States into slave and non-slave spheres of influence. Finally, the peace of Appomattox resolved the issue in favor of Yankeedom. Subsequent decades saw Northern industry expand, Northern capital multiply and Northern interests rule the country through the Republican Party which, having been

---

*Jean Gottman, *Megalopolis* (New York, 1961). Gottman defines his Megalopolis to include rural outliers like Cape Cod, western Maryland, Delaware and Pennsylvania Dutch country. Politically, these areas are not Megalopolitan.

The non-Yankee Northeast is essentially that part of the Northeast which was settled by non-New Englanders prior to the American Revolution. It included Hudson Valley Dutch, Schoharie Germans, Pennsylvania Germans, Scotch-Irish Appalachian uplanders, Quakers and the Southern-leaning inhabitants of Delaware Bay and Chesapeake Bay. New England is the cradle of the Yankee Northeast, but this latter section also includes most of upstate New York and part of Pennsylvania settled by New Englanders after the Revolution. Almost entirely Anglo-Saxon, the Yankee Northeast was the Nineteenth-Century seedbed of both the Civil War and the Republican Party, while the non-Yankee Northeast viewed both the war and the party with considerably less favor.

Since World War II, a number of Northeastern coastal cities and suburbs have fused into a practically contiguous corridor often called "Megalopolis." The new sociological oppositions attendant upon the rise of this Megalopolis have blurred the rural cleavage stemming from Civil War traditions and cultural oppositions. Democratic traditions are fading in the non-Yankee Northeast and Republican traditions in the Yankee bastions.

born in the pre-war sectional struggle and baptized in wartime strife, was virtually an arm of Northern hegemony. By 1929, the laissez faire of Northern industrialism and Republicanism was obsolescent, it was no longer needed for nation-building, but history could not have been written so boldly by a lesser drive.

Throughout this entire period, non-Yankee and non-Republican traditions prevailed through considerable sections of the Northeast; areas that had neither sought the Civil War nor shared in its political and industrial fruits. Most of today's history books oversimplify the Civil War; the loyalties of the time were quite complex. To many Northerners, the Civil War was a Yankee war, not a Northern war. Not only Border Marylanders and Delawareans, but a sizeable number of Pennsylvania Germans, Southern New Jerseyans, New York Irish, Hudson Valley landed conservatives and Ohio Valley farmers, feeling that none of their own interests were at stake in a war against the South, strongly objected to fighting a war for New England manufacturers and Pennsylvania ironmongers. To some of these groups, the South was their principal trade and produce outlet. For economic reasons, the New England states were the only bloc solidly behind the war. Beyond the boundaries of rabid New England, Northeastern war support was overwhelming only in upstate New York, northern Pennsylvania and the Great Lakes, all areas settled by New Englanders. The Civil War *was* principally a Yankee war and the party that fought it was principally a Yankee party. As the victors, the Northeast and the Republican party shared the spoils.

Contrary to public impression, the Civil War did not really create a Republican majority. As a matter of fact, once Northern military-supported Reconstruction governments surrendered their hold on the South, the GOP all but became a minority again, a *détente* which persisted through 1896. The base of Republican power was exactly those Yankee districts where Civil War support had been greatest— New England, upstate New York, machine-run Pennsylvania and the Great Lakes. (In Ohio, Indiana and Illinois there were close fights, because Great Lakes Republicanism was counterbalanced by Democratic voting in the Southern-settled Ohio Valley.) Voting patterns tended to refight the Civil War.

In the years between the Civil War and 1896 (when William Jennings Bryan's agrarian radicalism prompted conservative Democrats to flee to the GOP), Northeastern presidential preference divided along quite predictable lines. Maryland, Delaware and New

Jersey—much of southern New Jersey lay below the Mason-Dixon line—normally voted for Democratic presidents; Vermont, Maine, New Hampshire, Massachusetts, Rhode Island and Pennsylvania always voted for the Republican nominee; and New York and Connecticut were highly marginal. In Delaware, Maryland, Pennsylvania and New Jersey, Democratic strength occurred in rural and Southern-leaning areas, but from New York north, Democratic support in Yankee country was principally Catholic. Charts 6 and 7 illustrate the presidential partisanship of the eleven Northeastern states between 1860 and 1896, together with the post-Civil War Republican dependence on the Yankee states.

CHART 6

Northeastern Presidential Voting, 1860-92

SUPPORT OF THE REPUBLICAN PRESIDENTIAL NOMINEE

State	1860	1864	1868	1872	1876	1880	1884	1888	1892
Vermont	x	x	x	x	x	x	x	x	x
New Hampshire	x	x	x	x	x	x	x	x	x
Maine	x	x	x	x	x	x	x	x	x
Massachusetts	x	x	x	x	x	x	x	x	x
Rhode Island	x	x	x	x	x	x	x	x	x
Pennsylvania	x	x	x	x	x	x	x	x	x
Connecticut	x	x	x	x		x			
New York	x	x		x		x		x	
Maryland		x							
Delaware					x				
New Jersey					x				

Two sets of urban-rural opposition characterized post-Civil War politics in the area which now may be defined as Northeastern. In Pennsylvania, southern New Jersey, Maryland and Delaware, then something of a "Border," Republican support often centered in GOP machine-controlled cities. Philadelphia, Camden, Wilmington and Baltimore were usually more Republican than the nearby countryside; Catholic urban voters were similarly more Republican than sub-Mason-Dixon line farmers. Farther north, in the genuine North-

CHART 7

The Yankee Seats of Republican Power, 1856-1932

The Leading Republican States (Number of Times Supporting
Party Presidential Nominee in the Twenty Elections between
1856 and 1932)

Vermont	20
Maine	19
New Hampshire	18
Pennsylvania	18
Michigan	18
Iowa	18
Rhode Island	17
Massachusetts	17
Ohio	17
Minnesota	17*
Wisconsin	17**

*Minnesota was not yet admitted to the Union and did not vote in 1856.
**Wisconsin's seventeen include support of maverick Progressive Republican
LaFollette in 1924.

east of the Civil War era, the stereotyped pattern took over: Yankee
and Republican town, rural, urban middle-class and silk-stocking
precincts generally stood against strongly Democratic Catholic working-class districts.

This Catholic-Protestant cleavage was a deep-rooted one, reaching back to the days when Catholic immigrants walked off their
ships to be welcomed by the Tammanyites or Jacksonians—the local
anti-establishment—but disdained by the Protestant gentry and some
of their nativist working-class cousins. The first post-Revolution
Catholic immigrants were predominantly Irish and German, arriving in great waves during the late Eighteen-Forties and thereafter.
In reaction to the anti-Catholicism of the Protestant ruling classes,
both in Europe and America, Northeastern Catholics were inclined
to join the party opposed to the local Protestant Establishment.
When the "better element" of New York and New England enthused
over the Civil War, the Germans and Irish followed the other tack.
New York City's pro-Southern Irish rioted against both Negroes
and military conscription. In later years, they voted staunchly
Democratic. Philadelphia was something of an exception: its very

effective Republican machine mobilized working-class Catholics in support of a party dedicated to the economics of the Protestant industrial baronage. (It may have helped that the Pennsylvania Democratic Party was essentially rural.)

In New York, Catholic strength was sufficient by the second half of the Nineteenth Century to make the Protestant political hold on the state—first Whig and then Republican—tenuous or inadequate. New York's Irish were vehemently anti-Yankee; not only did they riot against the Civil War draft in 1863, but they elected a number of congressmen who were thorns in the side of the Republican administration's war effort. After the Civil War, New York's large and crucial bloc of electoral votes often teetered between the Republican North and the Democratic South, prompting the national Democratic Party to run New York governors (or former New York governors) for the presidency five times between 1868 and 1892. Grover Cleveland, the only Democratic President between Lincoln and Woodrow Wilson, was an Empire State chief executive, as were the party nominees in 1868 (Horatio Seymour) and 1876 (Samuel Tilden).

New York's swing position was a function of Tammany Hall's frequent ability to marshall a large enough Democratic vote in New York City to offset the rural, Protestant vote upstate. Ethnic and religious differences between the parties were so strong that when in 1884 an upstate New York Protestant minister labeled the Democrats the party of "Rum, Romanism and Rebellion," he was not so much inaccurate as tactless. However, his loose talk cost the Republicans New York State's electoral votes and the election, although the party nominee, James G. Blaine, was the son of an Irish Catholic mother and had been expected to win a substantial Irish Catholic vote.

Not all Northeastern Catholics were German and Irish. Sizable numbers of Quebec French drifted southward during the second half of the Nineteenth Century to work in New England's mills. Portuguese fishermen came to coastal Massachusetts. And beginning in the Eighteen-Eighties, many southern and eastern European immigrants began arriving. A large number of these became Republicans, some because their towns were under the thumb of Yankee mill owners, but others because they did not like Irish control of the local Democratic Party. In most New England states and in New York, the Irish ran the Democratic Party for their own benefit, and the non-Irish Catholics often preferred the Yankee Republicans (whose exclusionism they could tolerate more easily than that of the Irish). The German and Irish immigrants maintained their numerical predominance in New York until the turn of the century, and likewise the state remained politically marginal. But in Massachusetts and Rhode Island a sufficient number of the growing non-Irish Catholic group backed the Republicans so that neither of those leading Catholic states cast a Democratic presidential majority vote throughout the three quarters of a century after the Civil War.

Republican hegemony in the non-Yankee Northeast received a considerable boost in 1896, when the Democrats nominated William Jennings Bryan for President. Bryan, whose Great Plains agrarian radicalism antagonized conservative Eastern Democrats and whose Protestant revivalist oratory and tone did not sit well with urban immigrants, represented an impetus newly come to power within the Democratic Party. Since the Civil War, the party had nominated New Yorkers in its effort to win the electoral votes of New York, Connecticut and New Jersey. In choosing Bryan, the Democrats simultaneously repudiated the philosophy of incumbent President Grover Cleveland and opted to redirect party attentions to an agrarian alliance of South and West. The bold gamble failed, although narrowly. Not enough Western states joined the South, and for the first time since the Civil War, all eleven Northeastern states backed the Republican presidential nominee. Powerful local commitments kept a bare majority of New York's and Boston's Irish vote behind the Democratic nominee, but the Republicans were able to swing the growing Jewish and Italian votes behind their orthodox nominee, William McKinley. Hitherto marginal New York, New Jersey and Connecticut became normally Republican in presidential elections and stayed that way until 1932. Democratic Maryland and Delaware became marginal. Chart 8 shows the Republican 1892-96 gain by state and Chart 9 illustrates the increased 1896-1928 Republican bias of the Northeast. As a result of this re-alignment, Republican strength in the Northeast and Great Lakes allowed the Democrats to elect but one President during the 1896-1932 political cycle; and Woodrow Wilson's years in the White House were less the result of positive Democratic appeal than the division which split the GOP into two presidential candidacies—those of William Howard Taft and former President Theodore Roosevelt—and enabled a minority Democratic victory in 1912.

CHART 8

*The Impact of William Jennings Bryan on
Northeastern Presidential Voting, 1892-96*

State	Democratic Percentage of Total Vote for President, 1892	Democratic Percentage of Total Vote for President, 1896
Vermont	29%	17%
New Hampshire	47	26
Maine	41	29
Massachusetts	45	29
Rhode Island	46	27
Connecticut	50	33
New York	50	39
New Jersey	51	36
Pennsylvania	45	36
Maryland	53	42
Delaware	50	40

CHART 9

Northeastern Presidential Voting, 1896-1928

State	Support of the Republican Presidential Nominee								
	1896	1900	1904	1908	1912*	1916	1920	1924	1928
Vermont	x	x	x	x	x	x	x	x	x
New Hampshire	x	x	x	x			x	x	x
Maine	x	x	x	x		x	x	x	x
Massachusetts	x	x	x	x		x	x	x	
Rhode Island	x	x	x	x		x	x	x	
Connecticut	x	x	x	x		x	x	x	x
New York	x	x	x	x		x	x	x	x
New Jersey	x	x	x	x		x	x	x	x
Pennsylvania	x	x	x	x	x	x	x	x	x
Maryland	x	x	x	x			x	x	x
Delaware	x	x	x	x		x	x	x	x

*Woodrow Wilson (D) opposed William Howard Taft (R) and former President
Theodore Roosevelt, running as a third-party Progressive. Wilson won a plurality
in most of the Northeastern states. Taft won Vermont and Roosevelt took
Pennsylvania.

During the heyday of industrial Republicanism, the bulwark of the Northeastern Democratic Party was Irish—the Tammany Hall of "Mister" Murphy, the Brooklyn of "Uncle John" McCooey, the Bronx of Ed Flynn, the Jersey City of Frank "I am the Law" Hague and the Boston of James Michael Curley and John "Honey Fitz" FitzGerald. Party hierarchies in these fiefdoms read like the Limerick telephone directory; most non-Irish were excluded from power. Yet the Italians, Jews and others were implausible socioeconomic allies of the Republican Establishment, and constituted the potential base the Democrats needed to become a majority party.*

By 1920, immigration had wrought a great change in the Northeast of 1896. Irish and German arrivals were still numerous, but the massive tide of 1890-1920—the largest of all American immigration waves—had come from Southern and Eastern Europe. Whereas Italians and Jews had been only a small minority of New York City's population in 1890, by 1920 they accounted for 40 per cent of the city's residents. Other cities—Boston, New Haven, Springfield, Buffalo, Newark, Philadelphia and Baltimore—were similarly influenced, although on a smaller scale. This immigrant flood was pregnant with political potential. First, it created a vast new bloc of urban voters whose interests (social, economic and labor reform), ethnic antecedents and religious backgrounds were dissimilar to those of the Calvinist, Yankee and Republican Establishment. Secondly, it suggested an end to the Irish machine stranglehold on Democratic politics.** Together, these developments could remake the Northeastern political structure.

The old order took a dim view of the burgeoning power of the cities. Throughout the first quarter of the Twentieth Century, the national Democratic and Republican parties regarded the Northeastern immigrant blocs as something of a *Lumpenproletariat* and

---

*Of course, there were numerous exceptions. Under the guidance of Governor Alfred E. Smith, New York's Tammany Hall utilized Jewish and Italian talents and won considerable support in return.

**Most of the Irish machines were essentially ethnic institutions. Inasmuch as the Irish machines were not courting change—a national progressive upheaval would have displaced the Irish within the Democratic Party—they tended to be instruments of the status quo. Locally, they despised socialists and other leftist minor parties. And within the halls of Congress, congressmen and senators controlled by the Catholic machines of Northeastern states were regarded as "safe" by the conservative Republican leadership during the Nineteen-Twenties because they rarely made cause with the bipartisan minority of Western progressives.

sociopolitical under-class. Even President Wilson, a onetime history professor, was so inclined: in some of his earlier books, he had made derogatory remarks about Eastern and Southern European ethnic groups. Well into the Nineteen-Twenties, the Democratic Party was substantially swayed by Southern and Western agrarianism, Protestantism and prohibitionism—the impetus which thrice nominated William Jennings Bryan for President and which beat down a proposal to condemn specifically the Ku Klux Klan in the 1924 party platform. The Klan was strong in both parties and all but ruled a few states. As the party of the Yankee Establishment of the North, the Republicans were no more pro-Catholic than the Southern and Western Democrats. Thus, neither party was nationally in tune with immigrant aspirations. Local loyalties prevailed, since there was no national appeal by either party to overcome attraction to or revulsion from a specific local machine or alliance.

The years between 1896 and 1932 were a period of national Republican hegemony rooted in the Civil War traditions and industrial and financial might of the Northeast and kindred Great Lakes. Democratic President Woodrow Wilson was a fluke, a scholarly, naive and progressive internationalist, out of place in a contrary-minded Republican era; William Jennings Bryan was a Bible Belt anachronism whose percentage of the national vote decreased in each of his three presidential campaigns (1896, 1900 and 1908). Other names summed up the new era: William McKinley, Mark Hanna, J. P. Morgan, William Howard Taft, John D. Rockefeller, Henry Cabot Lodge, Warren Harding, Boies Penrose, Calvin Coolidge, Andrew Mellon and Herbert Hoover. The government was run less in Washington than in Boston, New York, Philadelphia, Pittsburgh and Cleveland—seats of the predominantly Yankee Republican oligarchy.* Many Democrats also danced to the tune of the financial and industrial Establishment, and by the early Nineteen-Twenties, the national Democratic Party was sufficiently captivated to nominate a Wall Street corporation lawyer, John W. Davis, as the party presidential candidate. This kind of mimicry was

---

*Three-quarters of the leaders of post-Civil War finance and industry were Yankees: Huntington, Stanford, Crocker, Hopkins and Hill (railroads); Holley (steel); Rogers and Rockefeller (oil); Armour and Swift (meat-packing); Pillsbury and Washburn (flour-milling); Morgan, Cooke, Drew, Gould and Fiske (finance). Although most of the power lay in the East, some of its practitioners headquartered in Chicago, Minneapolis and San Francisco.

particularly prevalent in the Northeast, where it helped win some local contests. However, the real party opportunity lay in another direction.

The Democratic presidential candidacies of 1920 and 1924 did nothing to achieve the needed party breakthrough. Ohio Governor James Cox, the 1920 presidential candidate, was obliged to shoulder the cross of Woodrow Wilson's foreign policy, namely, United States intervention in the First World War and the unpopular attempt to involve the country in the League of Nations. Wilson's memory was anathema to the Irish, who resented fighting a war alongside a Great Britain which was engaged in crushing Irish independence. And it was anathema to the Germans, who were naturally disturbed by what many considered to be a useless war against their ancestral homeland. Both groups were further angered by the terms of peace agreed on at Versailles: Germany was dismembered and Irish independence was ignored (although Wilson lavished marked attention on the mosaic of Eastern European nationalities). When the Irish and the Germans, bulwarks of the Northeastern Democratic Party, shunned Cox's candidacy in resentment of Wilsonian policies, the Republican sweep was vast. Harding carried every assembly district in New York City save Al Smith's own "Gas House" bailiwick; he likewise swept Irish Boston and Jersey City, as well as German Baltimore. In 1924, John W. Davis, a compromise nominee, selected when the party convention deadlocked between urban and rural forces, did little to recoup party strength among the immigrant ethnic groups. He too was badly beaten by the Republican candidate, although "Silent Cal" Coolidge was a remote and uninspiring figure to the urban masses.

But the urban bloc captained by New York Governor Alfred E. Smith had almost won the presidential nomination in 1924, and the scope of Davis' defeat, together with the growing strength of the immigrant-filled cities, served to accelerate the party changeover. And almost as if they sensed the rise of the cities and the emerging redefinition of their party's philosophy, a number of traditionally Democratic Northeastern rural counties were simultaneously trending toward the GOP.* Re-alignment was in the air. Then in 1928,

---

*Schoharie County, New York, is one example. Democratic in every presidential election from 1856 to 1916, it turned Republican in 1920. Not only did Schoharie County remain Republican in 1924 and 1928, but it continued to support the GOP during the depression of the Nineteen-Thirties.

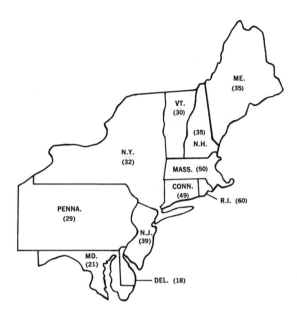

Al Smith easily won the presidential nomination which had been denied him four years earlier. The cities had found their champion.

In addition to being a successful state administrator, Al Smith was very much a man of the city sidewalks along which he had been raised. Although he was an Irish Catholic, he enjoyed considerable popularity among all immigrant groups. His brown derby, cigar and rasping New York accent—he went to school, he said, in Fulton Fish Market—made him a symbol of the entire immigrant quest. In retrospect, Al Smith was too much, too soon. He was too much a caricature of the Tammany politician, too much like the stereotype against which rural Protestant America held deep prejudice. Smith did little to mute the stridency of his origins and behavior patterns, and if this aided his cause in the Catholic cities, it somewhat unnecessarily damned it in the Protestant boondocks. As Barry Goldwater was to do a cycle hence, Al Smith played the cards of the political future prematurely. Still, it was unlikely that any Democratic presidential candidate could have beaten Republican tradition and prosperity in 1928, and even in losing, Al Smith forged part of the coalition that was to elect a Democratic President in the more opportune year of 1932.

Al Smith mobilized the hearts and the minds of the Catholic Northeast under the Democratic banner; not just the Irish and Germans, but the Italians, Poles and French Canadians. Dozens of Catholic counties hitherto Republican voted Democratic.* Until 1928, the two most heavily Catholic states in the Union—Rhode Island and Massachusetts had Catholic majorities—had never cast a majority of their votes against a Republican presidential nominee. However, Herbert Hoover lost both states to Al Smith. Thus, even before the Great Depression, Smith sparked a revolt of the urban ethnic groups which foreshadowed the make-up of the New Deal coalition, although the meaning of Smith's breakthrough was ignored because of his national defeat.** Map 6 shows the relative Catholicism of the Northeastern states, while Chart 10 enumerates the large gains that Smith achieved over Davis' 1924 levels. Delaware was the only state where Smith ran behind Davis. There was little anti-Smith voting in the rural Yankee bastions; their overwhelming GOP percentages of 1924 left small room for improvement. Such anti-Catholic voting as occurred in the Northeast in 1928 was concentrated in the non-Yankee rural areas where Protestant Democrats abrogated past ballot traditions.***

One can only guess what the Democrats would have achieved in 1932 without the intervention of the Depression. With it, they won the White House by capturing five of the eleven Northeastern states and all of the other thirty-seven. Franklin D. Roosevelt won most of Smith's Catholic vote in 1932, and he was thus able to win Rhode Island, Massachusetts, New York and New Jersey even though the Protestant Northeast still cast a majority of its vote for Herbert

*Smith carried dozens of counties which had gone Republican in both 1920 and 1924. Much more important, he carried a number of counties which had been Republican since 1896—all of them strongly Catholic. Among these counties were Elk, Luzerne and Lackawanna, Pennsylvania; Clinton and Franklin, New York; and Chittenden, Vermont.

**Two such assessments—that the 1928 election foreshadowed the Democratic majority which emerged in 1932—are Samuel Lubell's book, *The Future of American Politics* (New York, 1956) and David Burner, *The Politics of Provincialism* (New York, 1967).

***The counties showing the strongest anti-Smith trend were those in traditionally Democratic sections of Maryland and Pennsylvania. Monroe, Cumberland, Juniata and Columbia counties, Pennsylvania, produced 25 per cent Democratic declines; York County, Pennsylvania and Dorchester County, Maryland, lagged only slightly with 23 per cent Democratic losses between 1924 and 1928. At the other extreme, rural but Catholic Elk County, Pennsylvania showed a 31 per cent gain between 1924 and 1928. By and large, the anti-Smith counties showed the largest 1928-32 Democratic gains in the Northeast (25 per cent to 30 per cent); Elk County, however, was 6 per cent more Republican in 1932 than 1928.

CHART 10

The Revolt of the Cities—Northeastern Presidential Voting, 1920-32

	Democratic Share of the Total Vote for President			
State	1920	1924	1928	1932
Vermont	23%	16%	33%	41%
Maine	30	22	31	43
New Hampshire	39	35	41	49
Massachusetts	28	25	50	51
Rhode Island	33	37	50	55
Connecticut	33	28	46	47
New York	27	29	47	54
Pennsylvania	27	19	34	45
New Jersey	28	27	40	50
Delaware	42	37	34	48
Maryland	42	41	42	62

Hoover. Some measure of the intensity of 1928 Catholic voting can be gleaned from the fact that Roosevelt won fewer votes in Irish Boston in mid-Depression 1932 than Smith had in 1928. The entire state of Massachusetts showed only the slightest Republican presidential vote share decline between 1928 and 1932. On the other hand, Maryland Delaware and Pennsylvania, where rural anti-Catholic voting had been widespread in 1928, showed the strongest Democratic gains in 1932 (see Chart 10). Recoupment of Protestant support returned Maryland to the Democratic column in 1932.

Notwithstanding Roosevelt's gains, the Northeast was by far the most Republican section of the nation at the beginning of the New Deal. Roughly half of the Northeastern electorate voted for Herbert Hoover in 1932, and the GOP carried six of the eleven Northeastern states. Elsewhere in the country, Hoover won only one-third of the vote and no states. Even in the face of the Depression, the rural Yankee counties and urban silk-stocking precincts remained loyal to the party of their Establishment.* The Democratic victories in New York and Massachusetts, for example, were the product of

*All of the leading New England Yankee counties voted for Hoover in 1932. See Chart 26.

urban Catholic voting. In Pennsylvania and Delaware, Republican machines were able to keep much of the urban vote in line for Hoover. Du Pont-run Wilmington and machine-ruled Philadelphia both cast Republican presidential majorities.

Nationally, the Northeastern Establishment had been dethroned by urban Catholic machines allied with the Border, the South and the progressive West. Not that most Republicans understood the way in which the wheels of history were turning: they thought that Democratic power was a temporary phenomenon rooted in the popularity of "that man," Roosevelt. This bespoke a lack of perceptive behavioral analysis. In the South and West, the Democratic upheaval came in 1932, coinciding with F.D.R., but in the Northeast, the patterns of 1932 reflected the earlier breakthrough of 1928. Chart 10 shows how small the 1928-32 Democratic gain was in the strongly Catholic states of the Northeast. The sociology of caste and class, not reaction to post-1929 economic vicissitudes, was the denominator of Northeastern politics in the New Deal era. Chart 11 illustrates the minimal 1932-44 fluctuations—on a statewide basis— of these sociologically deep-rooted voting patterns. If Maine and Vermont were the only two Northeastern states to vote for each GOP presidential nominee between 1932 and 1944, Maryland was the only state in which any of them received less than 40 per cent of the two-party vote.

But although Northeastern fluctuations were less than those of other sections of the country—areas where the New Deal was shaping rather than ratifying a re-alignment—there were some important trends and counter-trends. First of all, the full ideological thrust of the New Deal had not been spelled out in 1932; by 1936 it was quite clear. Yankee and Establishment support for Hoover in 1932 had been loyalty to one's own Republican Party rather than intense opposition to the Hudson Valley squire who had often sounded budget-minded and orthodox. With the 1936 display of the New Deal colors in bold, anti-Establishment hue, the rural counties— Southern-leaning and Yankee alike—and the silk-stocking districts trended way from the urban and welfare-oriented Democrats. Whereas in 1932, bankers had furnished one-third of the Roosevelt war chest, they gave him practically nothing in 1936. Nevertheless, Roosevelt gained in most Northeast states between 1932 and 1936. The small Republican gains in the countryside were easily outweighed by Democratic urban strides. Roosevelt carried cities like

CHART 11

Northeastern Voting in the Roosevelt Era

	Republican Percentage of the Major-Party Vote for President			
State	1932	1936	1940	1944
Vermont	58%	57%	55%	57%
Maine	56	57	51	53
New Hampshire	51	49	47	48
Massachusetts	48	45	47	47
Rhode Island	44	43	43	41
Connecticut	51	42	46	47
New York	43	40	48	48
New Jersey	49	40	48	49
Delaware	51	45	45	45
Pennsylvania	53	42	47	49
Maryland	37	37	41	48

Philadelphia, Wilmington and Springfield which GOP machines had been able to control in 1932. No machines could fend off the urban appeal of the New Deal in 1936.*

This urban-rural split continued in 1940; as in 1936, only Maine and Vermont backed the Republican presidential nominee. But the pattern of partisanship was not quite the same. World War II loomed dangerously on the American horizon. Down East Maine, Cape Cod, other sections of Yankee New England and Anglophile silk-stocking precincts generally favored the Roosevelt Administration's policy of aid to embattled Britain. German, Irish and Italian voters, on the other hand, took an entirely different view. Many Irish disliked the idea of aiding the British, while some Italians and Germans feared that Roosevelt's policies were courting war with Italy and Germany. All three groups were inclined to argue that the Russian and Communist threat was a greater menace. As a result, many Irish, German and Italian urban precincts showed a decided

*Although Philadelphia's Republican machine was able to keep itself in municipal power until 1951, Franklin D. Roosevelt carried the city easily in 1936, 1940 and 1944.

CHART 12

A Profile of Northeastern Voting Behavior in 1940 (Change in the Republican or Democratic Share of the Total Vote for President)

Republican Gains		No Trend		Democratic Gains	
County	GOP Gain 1936-40	County	GOP Gain 1936-40	County	Demo. Gain 1936-40

Republican Gains

Irish

Suffolk (Boston) Massachusetts—12%

Hudson (Jersey City) New Jersey—12%

German-Irish

Queens, New York—20%

Italian

Richmond, New York—18%
Bergen, New Jersey—14%
Erie, Pennsylvania—14%

No Trend

Non-Yankee Protestant Rural

Schoharie, New York—4%
Otsego, New York—1%
Columbia, Penna.—3%
Frederick, Maryland—1%
Salem, New Jersey—0%
Wicomico, Maryland—1%
State of Delaware—0%

Democratic Gains

Yankee Rural

Hancock, Maine—6%
Lincoln, Maine—4%
Orange, Vermont—5%
Nantucket, Mass.—1%
Barnstaple, Mass.—0%
Washington, Rhode Island—1%
Essex, New York—0%

French-Canadian

Aroostook, Maine—6%
Coos, New Hampshire—3%
Franklin, Vermont—3%
Grand-Isle, Vermont—4%
Franklin, New York—2%
Clinton, New York—1%
Windham, Connecticut—2%

Republican trend between 1936 and 1940, while Yankee and silk-stocking precincts gave FDR higher vote shares than previously, as did Polish and Jewish districts. As a piece of neutral litmus paper, one can hold up the behavior of ethnically uninvolved rural Delaware and Maryland. Neither Anglophile nor Anglophobe, they showed no trend to speak of between 1936 and 1940. Chart 12 illustrates the crucial importance of ethnic voting in the 1940 election.

Few observers grasped the real significance of the 1940 election: that only foreign policy-prompted ethnic shifting differentiated Northeastern vote patterns from those of 1936. There was no domestic policy-rooted trend away from Roosevelt. Proof suggests itself in the fact that opposition to the New Deal did not increase over 1936 in just those rural areas where one would look for it, given the increasing urban, labor and minority group orientation of the Democratic Party; nor is there real evidence that the supposedly important third-term issue had much effect on Roosevelt's fortunes. While many GOP leaders still ignorantly dismissed Democratic success as a product of the President's personal popularity, the fact of the matter was that a new Democratic majority—in the Northeast and in the nation—had coming into being by 1936. Rooted in class and sociological conflict—urban-rural and (usually) Protestant-Catholic—the new political alignment favored the Democrats. The only reliably Republican Northeastern states were those of rural and Yankee upper New England. Elsewhere, Catholics and non-Yankee Protestants (in Maryland, Delaware or southern Pennsylvania) produced Democratic majorities, although New York Democrats could not have won their state without the New Deal-forged loyalties of New York City's large Jewish bloc.

A half-century earlier, the Catholic cities could not have exercised

---

Any profile, necessarily involving a selection process, is liable to criticism for subjectivity; however, this profile centers on banner counties of the several categories. As for the areas of Republican gain, Boston and Jersey City are the leading Irish cities of the Northeast; Queens County had more German and Irish Catholics for its size than any other with a substantial German population; Richmond, Bergen and Erie have higher Italian population ratios than any other counties in their states. The non-Yankee Protestant rural counties include many of the barometric counties of Democratic tradition described in subchapter 5. They are useful for showing that counties not swayed by the ethnic tugs of the threatening war in Europe showed very little change between 1936 and 1940. The Yankee counties include most of the banner Republican (and thus banner rural Yankee) counties used as examples of Yankee voting behavior in subchapter 2. The French-Canadian counties, save for Windham County, Connecticut, are those stretching along the New York-Vermont-New Hampshire-Maine frontier with French Catholic Quebec.

CHART 13

The Rise of the Urban and Suburban Electorates in New York State, 1924-68

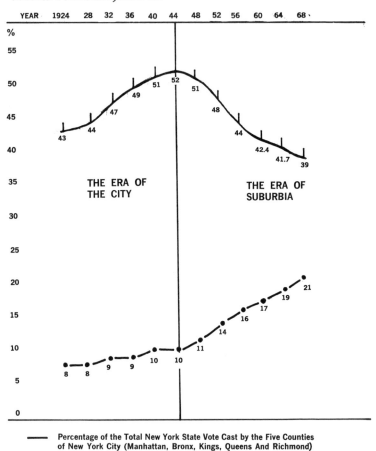

YEAR 1924 28 32 36 40 44 48 52 56 60 64 68

THE ERA OF THE CITY

THE ERA OF SUBURBIA

——— Percentage of the Total New York State Vote Cast by the Five Counties of New York City (Manhattan, Bronx, Kings, Queens And Richmond)

●-●-● Percentage of the Total New York State Vote Cast by the Three Principal Suburban Counties (Nassau, Suffolk and Westchester)

such sway, but the urban Northeast had experienced rapid growth since McKinley's day. Chart 13 shows the evolution of the percentage of the New York state vote cast by New York City. After rising throughout the Nineteen-Twenties and -Thirties to a point where it dominated the statewide balloting, New York City voting strength peaked during World War II; thereafter the five boroughs exercised steadily decreasing numerical muscle in state politics. And although the Democratic era launched in 1928 and 1932 persisted for more than twenty years after the World War II zenith of urban power, it took its impetus, shape and direction from the pre-war rise of the immigrant cities.

The 1944 presidential election followed very much in the tracks of the 1940 contest. Franklin D. Roosevelt was elected to a fourth term, losing only Maine and Vermont among the Northeastern states. The President died in 1945, and a postwar reaction enabled the GOP to recapture Congress in 1946, ending fourteen years of Democratic control. With the Eightieth Congress to reinforce their conviction that all would be well now that Roosevelt was dead, many Republican leaders looked forward to recapturing the White House in 1948. More than a few top Republicans wrote and spoke on how the normal Republicanism of the United States was about to reassert itself.

This proved to be wishful thinking. The New Deal coalition held together in the Northeast and in the nation, returning Harry S. Truman to the presidency for a full term in his own right. Truman knew what the Republicans did not: that a normal Democratic majority now existed in the country. Much of his campaign strategy pivoted on inflaming the social and regional animosities which had served Roosevelt so well. Trundling out the old lexicon of anti-establishmentarianism, the irascible Missourian called the GOP "gluttons of privilege," "princes of privilege" and "bloodsuckers with offices in Wall Street." In North Carolina, Truman said that Republican rule "treats the South and West as colonies to be exploited commercially and held down politically." These tactics worked. Not only did Truman win most of the South and West, but he also did well in the Northeast.

At first blush, the Republicans looked to have recaptured the Northeast (only Rhode Island and Massachusetts voted for Truman). However, this electoral vote sweep was deceptive. Several of the Republican victories were mere pluralities—minority successes dependent on the fact that the normal Democratic vote was slightly reduced by the inroads of Henry Wallace's Progressive Party candidacy.* New York and Maryland were thus captured. The vote in

*Most of the support Wallace won came from Jewish voters; thus Wallace ran his best race in the heavily Jewish areas of New York City, taking enough normally Democratic votes from Truman to give Dewey a plurality in New York

New Jersey and Pennsylvania was extremely close, and it can fairly be said that the GOP triumph in the Keystone State was rooted in a kind of "last hurrah" on the part of the fading Philadelphia party machine.* Much of the limited Republican gain in the Northeast came in rural Yankee counties and silk-stocking suburbs, while the Democratic strides came in the Irish, German and Italian urban centers. Consider the tides at work in Massachusetts: between 1944 and 1948, the GOP presidential vote share fell 10 per cent in Irish Boston and rose 12 per cent in sea-sprayed Yankee Nantucket. Elsewhere the trends were not so clear, but overall it is not unreasonable to suggest that wartime vagaries were ironing themselves out. The pattern of 1948 set forth a much clearer—and more New Deal-based—cleavage between Yankee countryside and Catholic cities than had prevailed in 1940. Chart 14 sets forth the very slight *statewide* 1944-48 trends in the major Northeastern states.

CHART 14

Change in the GOP Share of the Total Vote for
President in the Northeast, 1944-48

Connecticut	plus	2.6%
Pennsylvania	plus	2.5%
New Jersey	plus	1.3%
Maryland	plus	1.3%
New York	minus	1.3%
Massachusetts	minus	3.8%

Thus, even in the Northeast, the Republicans achieved no significant breakthrough as a result of FDR's death. Because of the New Deal revolution in the cities, there was no Republican majority to restore. The strongly Republican countryside was outnumbered; the silk-stocking Establishment precincts were weak in ordinary ballot resources; and the great postwar suburban boom was only

---

State. Fewer than 10 per cent of the state's voters backed Wallace, but many solidly Jewish precincts gave him better than a third of their vote. The Progressive Party was leftist and vaguely pro-Soviet. However, its anti-fascist stance appealed to Jewish liberals (who were also unhappy with President Truman's hesitant policy towards Israel). Very few Protestants and fewer Catholics supported the Progressive candidate.

*The GOP finally lost Philadelphia's City Hall in 1951.

beginning. But although the GOP percentage slipped below wartime levels in the Irish, German and Italian urban districts, it did not retreat to 1936 levels. Many Catholics were uneasy about Democratic foreign policy and social liberalism; others were prospering and moving to the suburbs. The Republicans would doubtless have done better in Northeastern Catholic neighborhoods if Truman had not been inadvertently helped by Henry Wallace, whose leftist, occasionally pro-Soviet and anti-Truman campaigning impelled many conservative Democrats to turn to Truman. Moreover, Republican nominee Thomas E. Dewey—the Governor of New York —was somewhat negatively viewed as priggish and establishmentarian.

For all of Truman's baiting of Wall Street, the Democratic national administration included quite a few leaders of the business and financial community, many of them men who had been brought into government during World War II. This *rapprochement* had begun prior to the war when Franklin Roosevelt's pro-British foreign policies appealed to the Anglophile Northeastern Establishment. (By 1940, the *New Yorker* magazine no longer cartooned Park Avenue types "going down to the Trans-Lux to hiss Roosevelt.") In the years after the war, many Northeastern business and financial leaders began to feel a greater empathy with the internationalist Democratic administration than with the conservative and isolationist Midwestern GOP congressional leadership. (Isolationist Republicanism had burgeoned in the Middle West between 1938 and the war's end.) Partly in reaction to this, the Northeastern Republican Establishment—conservative back in the Nineteen-Twenties when conservatism was in power—edged towards liberalism and internationalism. Pragmatically drawn to the ideology of power, the Northeastern Establishment was moving towards liberalism, albeit at first in the context of the Republican Party. By 1948 liberal Republicanism was headquartered in the party's Northeastern wing while conservatism ruled elsewhere. This marked a complete turnabout from the Nineteen-Twenties, when progressive Republican politics had been Western, and Northeastern Republicans stood for industrial and financial conservatism.

Despite their 1948 defeat, the Northeastern GOP Establishment was able to capture the 1952 presidential nomination for their candidate, General Dwight D. Eisenhower, by overcoming the Southern and Western strength of conservative Ohio Senator Robert A. Taft.

But paradoxically, Eisenhower's best gains in the general election were scored in anti-Establishment bailiwicks: the South, the isolationist West and Catholic sections of the Northeast, where a conservative and isolationist trend was at work. All eleven Northeastern states voted for Eisenhower—including Massachusetts and Rhode Island which had not voted for a Republican President since 1924. The most vivid Republican improvement came in the anti-Communist and pro-McCarthy Catholic strongholds. Some lower-middle-class Catholic precincts in Massachusetts gave Eisenhower 20 per cent to 30 per cent more of their vote than they gave Dewey in 1948. The Massachusetts counties showing the largest Republican gains were Suffolk (Boston) and Bristol (Fall River and New Bedford), where Catholic support enabled Eisenhower to lead Dewey by 13 per cent and 15 per cent.

At the same time, Eisenhower did not elicit any substantial party vote increase in the already arch-Republican Yankee rural counties, urban silk-stocking districts or old-line suburbs.* Although Eisenhower was the candidate of the Northeastern Republican Establishment, the new votes he won for the party came from non-Establishment sources. The largest Northeastern 1948-52 Republican increment came in New England and New York. The less Catholic states of Pennsylvania and Maryland produced smaller GOP gains. Perhaps the best proof of the religious specificity of the Eisenhower tide came in overwhelmingly Protestant Delaware, where the party presidential vote climbed only 1.8 per cent above 1948 levels. This is not to say that the Protestant Northeast did not support Eisenhower. There were no stauncher Republican counties than the leading Yankee bastions which Eisenhower carried by four-, five- and six-to-one margins; the point was that Republican strength in these areas had already approached its maximum in 1948, so that the crucial party advance of 1952 came in Catholic cities and suburbs.

The 1952 election confirmed the tentative beginning of a new era in Northeastern politics—the rise of suburbia. In the wake of World War II and the increased prosperity which it had engendered, many urban Northeasterners looked around for new housing in the suburbs. At first, only the affluent were able to move, but by mid-century, a great new middle-class trek was also under way. This trend caused the big city impetus to lose headway. For fifty years,

---

*The General did not run much ahead of Dewey's 1948 levels in Philadelphia's Main Line suburbs or in the fashionable suburbs of New York City.

the percentage of the New York State vote cast by New York City had been rising. In 1944, as Chart 13 shows, it had reached 52 per cent; now that percentage began to decline as suburban power fattened on the exodus from the central cities. Both trends accelerated in 1956.

Much of the new suburban middle class was Catholic: the sons and daughters of Al Smith supporters. Their larger numbers usually reduced the power of old-guard suburban GOP machines; however, they were ardent supporters of President Eisenhower. Chart 15 illustrates Eisenhower's tremendous appeal to the Catholic Northeast. Once Eisenhower had proved that a Republican administration did not jeopardize the economic gains of the new middle class—most of whom had risen under the auspices of the New Deal and World War II—the party was able to profit enormously from Catholic preference for Republican anti-communism abroad and social conservatism at home in contrast to the suspect "egghead" liberalism of Adlai Stevenson. Eisenhower won landslide victories in the eleven Northeastern states in 1956 (see Chart 15). He exercised such a strong Republican sway over Jersey City, for example, that the Irish of Boss Hague's old citadel almost elected themselves a young Republican congressman.

Most of Eisenhower's 1948-52 strides were attributable to Catholic behavior; this was even truer regarding his gains of 1952-56. Such was Eisenhower's Catholic strength in 1956 that for the first time a half-dozen of New York City's middle-class Catholic assembly districts turned in a higher GOP vote share than the fashionable silk-stocking districts. Actually, in some of the rural counties, small towns and silk-stocking precincts, the Republicans were starting to slip. Not a few small Yankee towns and wealthy Manhattan precincts gave Eisenhower a slightly lower vote share in 1956 than in 1952. Then in 1958, Vermont elected its first Democratic congressman since the Civil War. And in that same year declining majorities brought about the retirement of the conservative Republican congressman from New York's silk-stocking district.* Things were changing.

But the important Catholic GOP trend was disrupted. The Democrats were well aware of the need to recapture Catholic support, none more so than the supporters of Massachusetts' Senator John F.

---

*A liberal Republican took over the district.

CHART 15

Northeastern Voting in the Post-War Era

State	Republican Percentage of the Total Vote for President			
	1948	1952	1956	1960
Vermont	62%	72%	72%	59%
Maine	57	66	71	57
New Hampshire	52	61	66	53
Connecticut	50	56	64	46
Rhode Island	41	51	58	36
Massachusetts	43	54	59	40
New York	46	56	61	47
Pennsylvania	51	53	57	49
New Jersey	50	57	65	49
Delaware	50	52	55	49
Maryland	49	55	60	46

Kennedy, a vice-presidential aspirant in 1956 and a seeker of the presidency by 1960. Connecticut Democratic State Chairman John Bailey wrote a study suggesting that a Catholic on the Democratic presidential ticket—he meant Kennedy—could help the party win back large numbers of Catholic voters in key big-city states. Senator Kennedy won the Democratic presidential nomination in 1960, and much of the wayward 1952-56 Catholic vote returned to the Democratic fold. Partly with the help of this religious support, John Kennedy carried eight of the eleven Northeastern states. Only Maine, Vermont and New Hampshire endorsed Richard Nixon. Just as John Bailey had predicted, the Catholic vote proved decisive. Throughout the Northeast, the Democrats peeled away the Catholic adherents with whom Eisenhower had won his massive victories of 1952 and 1956. The Protestant vote showed little change; Kennedy made small gains in the Yankee counties of his native New England, but some rural counties of central and southern Pennsylvania showed 2 per cent to 4 per cent Republican trends (over Eisenhower's 1956 levels) probably of religious origin. Nor did the Jews evidence much of a Democratic trend. The 1956 Eisenhower vote had suffered in Jewish precincts as a result of the Suez controversy, besides which some Jews disliked the idea of a Catholic president.

Chart 16 illustrates the strong religious overtones of the 1960 presidential vote pattern in the Northeast. As a result of the Catholic return to the Democratic Party, together with the general post-New Deal Republican thrust of the South and West, the Northeast—in 1932 the most Republican section of the nation—was the most Democratic region of the United States in 1960.

CHART 16

Catholicism and the 1960 Presidential Vote

State	Democratic Gain, 1956-60	Catholic Percentage of Population (1960)
Rhode Island	22%	60%
Massachusetts	19	50
Connecticut	18	49
New Jersey	16	39
Maine	14	35
New York	14	32
Maryland*	14	21
New Hampshire	13	35
Vermont	13	30
Pennsylvania	8	29
Delaware	6	18

*Democratic gain enlarged by heavy Negro trend.

Within the Northeast, the pattern of 1960 voting was approximately the same as that of 1948. The GOP received nearly the same percentage of the vote in most urban and rural counties; the exceptions occurred in the suburbs—much more Catholic in 1960 than in 1948—where the Republican support level declined, as well as in rural Catholic counties and in some rural Protestant sections of Maryland, Delaware, Pennsylvania and New Jersey. In short, the election of 1960 reiterated the New Deal cleavage hacked out in 1936 and modified thereafter by GOP rural resurgence, suburban growth and Catholic foreign and social policy resentments. By and large, the Italo-Irish-German Catholic vote which had remained Republican after World War II stuck with Nixon in 1960 and it was the normally Democratic pro-Eisenhower Catholics who responded to Kennedy's ethnic and religious appeal.

Without a Catholic candidate, this vote would not have slipped back into place. In New York, for example, Democratic polls showed that no non-Catholic could have taken a majority of the Catholic vote away from Nixon. Electing a Catholic president, however, was part of the status quest which was otherwise leading many Catholics towards Republicanism. There was very little "liberalism" about the Kennedy majorities, depending as they did on large-scale Catholic ethnocentricity and religious identification. John F. Kennedy's huge Catholic vote was a milestone on the road to Catholic Republicanism, not liberalism. As later years were to show, the voting patterns of the Eisenhower era had been pregnant with prophecy.

Catholic appreciation of Republican anti-Communist foreign policies was not the only factor at work. Irish, Italian and German social conservatism was feeling increasingly ill at ease in a Democratic party under growing minority-group and silk-stocking control. The great political forces of the Nineteen-Sixties pivoted on the crisis of the cities—and on the mounting urban racial turmoil. By the early Nineteen-Sixties, cities like New York, Newark, Philadelphia and Buffalo had large enough non-white populations (see Chart 28) to cause considerable racial friction. Most Northeastern

CHART 17

Catholicism and the Vote in New York, 1960

DEMOCRATIC PRESIDENTIAL VOTE GAINS IN
NEW YORK COUNTIES, 1956-60

Catholic % of Total Population	Democratic % Gain, 1956-60
0-9%	up 9.5%
10-19%	up 11.7%
20-29%	up 14.3%
30-39%	up 16.5%
40% or more	up 20.7%

Brooklyn figures are omitted because of Jewish population size and resultant trend distortion.

CHART 18

Profile of 1960 Northeastern Presidential Voting

CHANGE IN PARTY SHARES OF THE TOTAL VOTE FOR PRESIDENT, 1956-60 (BY COUNTIES)

Small Republican Gain

Nor-Yankee Protestant*
York, Penna.—3%
Columbia, Penna.—2%

*Only a few Pennsylvania
counties showed actual
GOP gains.

Small Democratic Gain

Yankee
Hancock, Maine—9%
Carroll, N.H.—5%
Orange, Vermont—8%

Jewish**
Bronx 2nd A.D., N.Y.—3%
Brooklyn 21st A.D., N.Y.—4%

Negro**
Manhattan 14th A.D., N.Y.—7%
Brooklyn 6th A.D, N.Y.—9%

**New York City Assembly Districts

Large Democratic Gain

Irish
Suffolk County
    (Boston), Mass.—21%
Hudson County
    (Jersey City), N.J.—23%

Italian
Richmond, N.Y.—20%

French-Canadian
Clinton, N.Y.—26%
Coos, N.H.—23%

Negroes and Puerto Ricans adhered to the Democratic Party, weakening the control of Catholic machines and generating sociopolitical demands unpopular among Catholic Democrats. Many Irish, Italians and Germans responded by edging towards suburbia and Republicanism, separately or together. At the same time, the fashionable Northeastern Establishment moved towards liberalism, maintaining its historic opposition to the trend of the blue-collar and lower-middle-class Catholics. Throughout the fashionable sections of New York City, for example, the Democratic Party was on the rise —not the Democratic Party of Carmine DeSapio or the Irish bosses, but a (Reform) Democratic Party led by Protestant socialites and Jewish intellectuals. The old conservatism of the Establishment was giving way to a new liberalism; an institutionalization of New Deal attitudes up and down Manhattan's once-hostile East Side. Just as the Nineteen-Twenties had seen an alliance between a conservative Establishment and many Northeastern minority group members (Negroes and Jews), the early Nineteen-Sixties saw a similar alliance begin to take shape on behalf of a liberal Establishment.

This liberal Establishment became anathema to many Catholics and other conservatives, Democratic and Republican. In New York State, a Conservative Party was formed to protest liberal Establishment (Rockefeller) domination of the Republican Party. Within a few years, the Conservative Party—based largely in blue-collar and lower-middle-class Catholic precincts—grew into a major political force. Most of the Conservative leaders were Irish; some were ex-Democrats fleeing the minority-group and silk-stocking conquest of the party. Each year saw these many trends intensify; as urban Negro and Puerto Rican populations continued to grow, the exodus to suburbia increased, the liberalism of the Republican Establishment accelerated, and the Democratic Party came more and more under minority-group and Establishment domination.

In 1964, the national Republican Party, reflecting its growing Southern and Western makeup and orientation, broke with the Northeastern Republican Establishment and nominated Barry Goldwater for President, spurning the candidacies of such Northeastern liberal Establishment luminaries as Nelson Rockefeller, William Scranton and Henry Cabot Lodge. The animosity of the Establishment persisted throughout the campaign and the election, devastating Goldwater throughout the Northeast. Chart 19 sets forth the extent to which Goldwater slipped below Nixon's 1960 levels. But

CHART 19

A Profile of the Northeastern Anti-Goldwater Trend, 1964

DECLINE IN THE REPUBLICAN SHARE OF THE TOTAL VOTE
FOR PRESIDENT, 1960-64

Rural Yankee Counties[1]
Hancock, Maine—32%
Orange, Vermont—36%
Yates, New York—32%
Nantucket, Mass.—31%

Silk-Stocking
9th Assembly District of Man-
    hattan (Park and Fifth Ave-
    nue)—29%
Ward 5 of Boston
    (Beacon Hill)—25%

Suburban Counties[2]
Westchester, New York—19%
Morris, New Jersey—21%
Montgomery,
    Pennsylvania—18%
Montgomery, Maryland—15%

Urban Negro[3]
14th Assembly District of
    Manhattan (South
    Harlem)—14%
11th Assembly District of
    Manhattan (Central
    Harlem)—18%

Urban Jewish[4]
3rd Assembly District
    of the Bronx (Grand
    Concourse)—3%
4th Assembly District of
    Manhattan (Lower
    East Side)—4%
19th Assembly District
    of Brooklyn (Boro
    Park)—4%

Urban Italian[5]
Ward 1 of Boston
    (North Boston)—3%
10th Assembly District
    of the Bronx (Throgs
    Neck)—4%
8th Assembly District
    of Brooklyn (Park
    Slope)—4%

Urban Irish[6]
Ward 6 of Boston
    (South Boston)—2%
Ward 7 of Boston
    (South Boston)—2%
8th Assembly District
    of the Bronx
    (Fordham)—3%

1. Banner Yankee counties (see subchapter 2 and chart 26).
2. These prosperous and predominantly suburban counties include a cross-section of silk-stocking (high Democratic trend) and middle-class (low Democratic trend) voters.
3. Harlem's two solidly Negro assembly districts.
4. Banner Jewish Assembly Districts of New York City (see subchapter 4 and chart 35).
5. These districts are among the most heavily Italian in New York and Boston. At the precinct level, especially in areas nearly 100 per cent Italian, Goldwater often *improved* 1960 levels.
6. Same phenomena as in Italian districts.

the slide was by no means uniform among the major Northeastern voting streams. Contrary to most analyses, the Republican slippage was not centered in the cities, but in establishmentarian precincts (urban and suburban) and in rural areas, especially those Yankee areas of staunch Republican tradition. Many Catholic precincts actually showed Goldwater running stronger than had Nixon; and although the Arizona Senator ran well behind Nixon in Jewish and Negro precincts, the 1960-64 decline was not large either in percentage points or actual ballots. Goldwater's overwhelming 1960-64 losses were the result of ballot box repudiation by his own party— the first GOP presidential candidate to be so spurned in history— rather than an "urban" revolt. As Chart 19 shows, the cities were the place of the *least* anti-Goldwater revolt. What dragged the Goldwater vote down to levels previously untouched by Republican candidates in the Northeast was a 20 per cent to 30 per cent Democratic trend in the most pedigreed of Yankee counties and the richest silk-stocking districts. Chart 20 shows the 1964 Goldwater vote by states.

In 1968, a book was published—Milton Viorst's *Fall From*

CHART 20

Northeastern Presidential Voting, 1964-68

Share of the Total Presidential Vote

State	1964		1968		
	Goldwater	Johnson	Nixon	Humphrey	Wallace
Maine	31%	69%	43%	55%	2%
Vermont	34	66	53	44	3
New Hampshire	36	64	52	44	4
Massachusetts	23	76	33	64	4
Rhode Island	19	81	31	65	4
Connecticut	32	68	44	50	6
New York	31	69	45	50	5
Pennsylvania	35	65	43	48	8
New Jersey	34	66	46	45	9
Delaware	39	61	45	42	13
Maryland	35	65	42	43	15

Grace—which intelligently analyzed the Grand Old Party's Yankee genesis and longtime identification. Mr. Viorst, however, carried his theory too far by seeing fit to analyze the Goldwater movement as the ultimate extension of Yankee puritanism.* In actuality, the Goldwater movement was nothing of the sort: it was a Southern-, Western- and Irish-backed impetus which lost all but one of the dozens of New York and New England Yankee counties loyal enough to remain two-to-one Republican throughout the Depression. Far from being a consummation of Yankee puritanism, the Goldwater candidacy represented a *breach* with Yankee Republican tradition and a commitment to anti-establishmentarianism rooted in altogether non-Yankee voting streams. And although the Republican Party suffered a bad national defeat in 1964, the new ground broken aligned the GOP with a rising popular impetus, not a declining establishmentarian one. Much of the same breakthrough had occurred in the election of 1928, and pundits of that time showed no more awareness of the upheaval—given the obvious national defeat of the Democrats—than did the prognosticators of 1964.

In structuring the 1960-64 change in Northeastern partisan presidential preference, Chart 44 illustrates how heavily Irish, German and Italian Catholic precincts in the New York area often gave Barry Goldwater a higher vote share than they had given to Richard Nixon. Some normally Democratic Irish election districts actually gave Goldwater a majority of their vote. On a statewide basis, Goldwater ran considerably behind the 1936 GOP presidential showing in the Northeastern states, but the contrast between different voting streams was enormous. Negro precincts where Landon had won a third of the vote went fifty-to-one Democratic; small Yankee towns which had been three-to-one Republican in 1936 went two-to-one Democratic in 1964; traditionally Democratic rural townships in Maryland, Delaware and southern Pennsylvania showed little change between 1936 and 1964; and Catholic urban precincts which had been four-to-one for Roosevelt gave Barry Goldwater a narrow edge.

As a result of Goldwater's abysmal vote in rural counties and establishmentarian districts (urban and suburban), Northeastern Republican strength declined to a point where the Northeast was again the most Democratic section of the country, and by a wider

---

*Milton Viorst, *Fall From Grace* (New York, 1968).

margin than in 1960. The 1964 election constituted a Rubicon for the Republican Party; and its crossing marked off an era. The Grand Old Party was no longer the party of the Yankee Establishment. Traditionalist New England, where Hoover had won a razor-thin majority of the vote in 1932, gave the 1964 GOP nominee only 27 per cent support.

Such was Goldwater's unpopularity in the Northeast that Republican congressmen fell in the 1964 elections like wheat before a scythe. With the loss of sixteen Northeastern congressmen, GOP regional strength in the House of Representatives sunk to an all-time low. Upstate New York and New England elected only seventeen Republicans to the Eighty-Ninth Congress, considerably fewer than the two dozen elected in Depression-trough 1936.

Citing the simultaneous triumphs of several liberal Republicans in Northeastern states and districts which had rebuffed Barry Goldwater by huge majorities, the liberal Establishment offered the 1964 election returns as vivid proof that conservative Republicanism had no future, especially in the Northeast. And in the wake of the 1964 debacle, Northeastern Republicanism accelerated its liberal trend. While the Southern and Heartland GOP forces controlling the party position in Congress opposed the liberal programs of Lyndon Johnson's Great Society, a considerable minority of Northeastern Republicans in Congress joined with the Democrats.

But this liberal stance of Northeastern Republicans proved insufficient to remold the party image or stem the tide of regional re-alignment. The 1966 congressional elections brought a Republican resurgence, but in the Northeast, the GOP recaptured only four of the sixteen seats lost in 1964. Even this figure is deceptive: only one of the thirteen districts lost in the Yankee Northeast was won back; all three districts lost in southern Pennsylvania and southern New Jersey were recovered and two new ones won in Delaware and Maryland. The poles of partisanship were reversing. Much of the traditionally Republican Northeast was enmeshed in a liberal and Democratic trend; and the limited Republican trend centered in areas of Catholic and rural non-Yankee Democratic tradition. If the 1966 off-year races saw the Democrats achieve an unprecedented sweep of Maine's congressional districts, the GOP scored a few Northeastern records too: Republican congressmen won overpowering victories in the Southern-leaning Eastern Shore of Maryland (1st Maryland C.D.) and the leading national Italo-Irish bailiwick (24th New York C.D.).

True, liberal Republicans occupied the governorships of Rhode Island, Massachusetts, New York and Pennsylvania, and other Northeasterners captained the thin ranks of party liberals in the U.S. Senate, but despite the 1966 victories of some of these men—Rockefeller, Case, Brooke and Volpe—the more telling statistics were ones indicating slippage at the congressional level (where national party image has more effect and personalities less). Northeastern Republicanism was waning as the party grew increasingly Southern and Western. New York's Governor Nelson Rockefeller sought to capture the 1968 presidential nomination and stem this tide, but his inability to command much support outside the Northeast proved fatal. By 1968, the New Deal liberalism so bitterly fought by the Northeastern Establishment of the Nineteen-Thirties had become the new establishment, and the Northeast was once again fighting a rearguard action.

In 1968, Hubert Humphrey won majorities in Maine, Massachusetts, Rhode Island and New York, as well as pluralities in Connecticut, Pennsylvania and Maryland. A majority of voters in Vermont and New Hampshire backed Nixon; only a plurality gave him victory in New Jersey and Delaware. As in both 1960 and 1964, the Northeast was the most Democratic part of the nation, and in similarly repetitive fashion, New England was the most Democratic part of the Northeast. Back in 1932, New England had furnished four of the six states which clung to Herbert Hoover; in 1968, New England produced three of the six statewide majorities for the candidate of the departing Democratic Party.

In no other section of the nation did George Wallace do so poorly as in the Northeast; and here also New England took the lead, giving the former Alabama governor only 4 per cent of its votes. Within the Northeast, Wallace support was parochially concentrated among two voting streams. As Chart 21 shows, Wallace's vote was strongest in the non-Yankee Northeast and weakest in northern New England. This reflects the location of the principal bloc of Wallace backers—Southern-oriented conservatives. Besides Southern-leaning Maryland, Delaware and lower New Jersey, urban Catholic precincts also gave Wallace fair support in northern New Jersey, Philadelphia, New York City, Connecticut and Boston.

In his second presidential race, Richard Nixon received about the same share of the *two-party* vote as he had received in 1960, but there were changes within the region which confirmed the shifting GOP power base. Basically, Nixon gained ground in the non-

CHART 21

The Wallace Vote in the Northeast, 1968

A. *Wallace Share of the Total Presidential Vote by States*

Maine—2%	Connecticut—6%
Vermont—3%	Pennsylvania—8%
New Hampshire—4%	New Jersey—9%
Massachusetts—4%	Delaware—13%
Rhode Island—4%	Maryland—15%
New York—5%	

B. *A Geographic Spectrum of Wallace Support*

County	Wallace Share of Total Vote for President	County	Wallace Share of Total Vote for President
Wicomico, Maryland (Salisbury)	24%	Richmond, New York (Staten Island)	9%
Prince Georges, Maryland (D.C. suburbs)	19%	Suffolk, New York (NYC suburbs)	8%
Kent, Delaware (Dover)	19%	New Haven, Conn. (New Haven)	8%
Franklin, Penna. (Chambersburg)	13%	Lackawanna, Penna. (Scranton)	4%
Cape May, New Jersey (Wildwood)	13%	Albany, New York (Albany)	4%
Allegheny, Penna. (Pittsburgh)	11%	Suffolk, Mass. (Boston)	5%
Erie, New York (Buffalo)	7%	Nantucket, Mass. (Nantucket)	3%
Philadelphia, Penna. (Phila. City)	8%	Orange, Vermont (Rural)	3%
Passaic, New Jersey (Paterson)	10%	Hancock, Maine (Bar Harbor)	2%

C. *An Ethnic Spectrum of Wallace Support*

Chesapeake Bay Rural Protestant (Wicomico County, Maryland)—24%

Greater New York City Catholic-Italo-Irish (Richmond)—9%

New England Yankee (Hancock County, Maine)—2%

Urban Negro (Central Harlem)—0%

CHART 22

*1960-68 Changes in Nixon's Share of the Major-Party Vote in Selected Representative Cities, Towns and Assembly Districts of New York State**

Republican Gains

French-Canadian
(Clinton County)—
plus 9%

Upstate Italian
(Oneida County-Utica)—
plus 6%

Urban Irish
(Yonkers)—
plus 4%

New York City Middle-Class
Catholic (Staten Island)—
plus 6%

Middle-Class Suburban
(Oyster Bay)—plus 4%
(Smithtown)—plus 8%

Low-Middle-Income Jewish
(East Flatbush; 41st
Assembly District of
Brooklyn)**—plus 3%

Republican Losses

Silk-Stocking Urban
(66th Assembly District
of Manhattan, Park and
Fifth Avenues)**—
minus 18%

Silk-Stocking Suburban
(Scarsdale)—minus 19%

Upper-Middle-Class Jewish
(Riverdale; 84th Assembly
District of the Bronx)**—
minus 15%

Urban Negro
(72nd Assembly District
of Manhattan; Central
Harlem)**—minus 15%

Upstate Rural Protestant
(Otsego County)—
minus 6%

*The major-party vote includes that cast for the Republican and Democrat-Liberal candidates.
**Because New York State assembly district lines were redrawn between 1960 and 1968, a strict comparison of vote trends by assembly district is impossible. The above-listed assembly districts were not greatly changed, however.

Yankee Northeast (Maryland, Delaware, New Jersey and southern Pennsylvania), as well as in Catholic areas from Connecticut south; while the Democrats picked up in New England's Yankee districts, silk-stocking areas throughout the Northeast and Negro precincts. Chart 22 illustrates the 1960-68 movement of key voting streams in New York State. Quite simply, the Republican Party was gaining among those Northeastern sociocultural groups—rural non-Yankees and Catholics—which were compatible with its rising Southern and Western support base, even as it lost among incompatible groups. As regards Northeastern Catholics, only those in and around New York City actually gave Nixon a majority of their votes, but it should be noted that New York City's Catholics—the Irish in particular—have usually been a good advance indication of developing alignment and behavior among their co-religionists.

Given the two decades of growth which had occurred since World War II, suburban votes bulked large in the Northeast in 1968. Suburbia divided along cultural and ethnic lines, however. Most of Boston's suburbs voted Democratic. Around New York City, Jewish suburbs backed Humphrey while Christian areas favored Nixon. Montgomery County, Maryland, a Washington, D.C., suburb and the county with the highest *per capita* income in the nation, supported the Democratic nominee, while suburban Baltimore went for Nixon. Ethnic, cultural and social patterns exercised a greater influence than income levels. Richard Nixon ran well in ordinary suburbs, but the strongholds of the affluent intelligentsia backed Hubert Humphrey.

As America moved into a new political era in 1968, the Northeast once again assumed its position of 1800, 1828, 1896 and 1932 as the national stronghold of the old order, which this time was an institutionalized liberalism.

A. Northeastern Sociopolitical Voting Streams

Inasmuch as Megalopolitan growth is unifying Northeastern culture and politics while the decline of Civil War tradition erodes obsolescent rural partisanship, local ballot conflict is becoming more sociological than sectional. In 1948, rural Yankee Vermont was twice as Republican as Maryland's rural Eastern Shore; however, by 1964 there was little difference. The trend is towards a politics of social and economic voting streams.

At the close of the New Deal era, Northeastern liberal and Democratic strength was essentially rooted in three voting streams: the silk-stocking Establishment, Negroes and Jews. The Yankee outliers of the Establishment, albeit still Republican, were caught up in something of a liberal and Democratic trend. Paradoxically, this grouping was similar to that which had supported the *conservative* establishment of the Nineteen-Twenties.

On the other hand, the voting streams evincing a popular conservatism during the late Nineteen-Sixties were those same groups—the urban Italo-Irish, rural non-Yankees, new suburbanites, Appalachians and milltowners—whose fidelities of the Roosevelt era had underpinned New Deal majorities. To a meaningful degree, the two major parties were shifting roles and support bases. Given this intriguing *volte-face,* the changing partisan structure of Northeastern politics can best be analyzed by tracing the behavior of these principal voting streams.

1. The Establishment

Throughout American history, the Northeast has been the seat of a number of establishments—of a number of nationally dominant economic and political interest groups. An establishment is necessarily "conservative" in that it defends a status quo or a powerful impetus. However, that status quo or impetus may reflect the success of *any* interest group, liberal or conservative.* Today's Establishment is liberal: New Deal liberalism institutionalized. There is considerable confusion over this, especially among those who came of voting age before the Nineteen-Sixties.** They will continue to be a majority of the electorate for many years, and they grew up thinking of the national Establishment as conservative. Until the Nineteen-Sixties, the Establishment *was* basically conservative—the perpetuation of exhausted Coolidge-Mellon-Hoover politics—but in recent years, a new, *liberal* Establishment has replaced it.

A full political cycle has passed since a conservative Establishment harassed the new administration of Franklin D. Roosevelt. Who can doubt that today's Establishment—the great metropolitan newspapers, the Episcopal and other churches, the Supreme Court, Beacon Hill and Manhattan's fashionable East Side—to some extent reflects the institutionalization of a successful New Deal, just as the

---

*In his essay *The American Establishment,* Richard H. Rovere has observed, "It is characteristic of most writers and thinkers on the subject to define the Establishment in such a way as to keep themselves outside it and even victimized by it. Werner Von Fromm has suggested that they all tend toward a mild paranoia, and what little clinical evidence there is tends to support him." Rovere, *The American Establishment* (New York, 1962) p. 5. But as Rovere, Digby Baltzell and Stephen Birmingham have demonstrated, "The Establishment" is a useful and reasonably legitimate term even if it is not a precise entity.

**The college generation which came of age in the Nineteen-Sixties understands full well that a collection of vested liberal interests constitutes much of the contemporary Establishment.

Roosevelt-baiting press lords, industrialists and Supreme Court justices of the Nineteen-Thirties represented a weakening conservative Establishment rooted in the post-Civil War reign of industrial laissez faire and political Republicanism? A new Establishment—the media, universities, conglomerate corporations, research and development corporations—has achieved much of the power of the industrial and financial establishment dethroned politically by the New Deal. This new Establishment thrives on a government vastly more powerful than that deplored by the business titans of the Nineteen-Thirties.

This did not come about overnight. In the first place, the old Establishment did not yield power gracefully. When Franklin D. Roosevelt first ran for President in 1932, he received considerable upper-class support, although he was badly beaten in residential seats of Northeastern affluence like Park Avenue and Beacon Hill. But if 1932 saw Roosevelt talking about a balanced budget while receiving one third of his campaign war chest from bankers, things were quite different in 1936, by which time the policies of the New Deal had made the President's name a hated one in old-guard circles. However, the Establishment could not spitefully refrain from intercourse with the federal government; industry and finance require access to power. The trickle of commuters between Washington and Wall Street began to increase, especially with the coming of World War II. Franklin Roosevelt's pro-British policies were popular among establishmentarians, many of whom were Anglophiles to some degree, and some businessmen went to Washington to help with the war effort. Generally speaking, the controversial president was stronger among Establishment voters in 1940 and 1944 than he had been in 1936.

Although Harry Truman, who succeeded Roosevelt, was not viewed as a "traitor to his class" as the Hyde Park patrician had been (Truman was a former county judge from Missouri who talked about Wall Street "bloodsuckers"), the establishmentarian bailiwicks of the Northeast staunchly opposed him in 1948, preferring New York's Republican Governor Thomas E. Dewey. But even then—and still more during the Nineteen-Fifties—the Establishment showed a perceptible shift from McKinley-Root-Mellon conservative Republicanism towards institutionalization of New Deal liberalism. Consider New York's fashionable East Side: it went almost two-to-one for Eisenhower in 1952 and 1956, but in the latter year, for the first time since the Depression, middle-class Catholic suburban and urban residential districts surpassed the silk-stocking precincts in Republican enthusiasm. Many of the fashionable East Siders preferred urbane Princetonian Adlai Stevenson to the bourgeois retired army general.

This was not simply a reflection of the changing face of the silk-stocking districts, where brownstones once housing a single rich family were being replaced by high-rise buildings full of young professionals. Residential demolition and construction told only part of the tale; the rest lay in the success of the New Deal—the 5,000-dollar-a-month middle-aged affluence and influence of many of the leading blueprinters and braintrusters of the New Deal, backstopped by the rising clique of Roosevelt-era entrants into the publishing houses, universities, government agencies and the arts. Furthermore, not only were many businessmen realizing that the activities of government can mesh with private enterprise, but an increasing number of private sector employees were technicians and specialists more akin to government planners than to the small entrepreneur of Horatio Alger legend and old-line Republican sympathy. Even big labor, its hierarchies enobled and bureaucracies expanded by the New Deal, took its place in the power elite.

As the Establishment began to turn liberal, a similar trend colored silk-stocking politics. On Manhattan's East Side, the Union League Club, citadel of the old Republican oligarchy, grew politically passe. Chic establishmentarians gathered in the Lexington (Reform) Democratic Club, led by Mrs. Marietta Tree, daughter of an Episcopal headmaster and wife of an English ex-Member of Parliament.* Farther downtown, where Tammany had once plotted

*The establishmentarian caste of "Reform" Democratic liberalism can readily be seen in the make-up of the Lexington Club. In his book *The Amateur Democrat* (Chicago, 1962), James Q. Wilson discusses the Club: "In 1960, there were 36 men and women nominated for office in the Lexington Democratic Club, the oldest of the reform organizations. Of the 34 who had graduated from college, 19 had attended the desirable schools of the Ivy League. The majority (20) had completed law school and were practicing law in New York City (mostly with firms in and around Wall Street). Most of the rest were in public relations, advertising, the theater, college teaching, radio and television and so forth. Of the five who were in other businesses, most were associated with investment houses. . . . When another reform club, the Riverside Democrats, was organized in 1957, all eight of its officers were college graduates and seven had done graduate work in prestigious eastern universities such as Harvard, Yale, Columbia and Princeton." Within Manhattan, "Reform" ultra-liberalism controls the Democratic Party in the richest districts; old-line organizations rule only in the poorer districts.

the overthrow of crusty conservatism, young Jewish and Anglo-Saxon Greenwich Village professionals sharpened liberal hatchets for the scalp of sleek Tammany sachem Carmine DeSapio and his old-world *paisans* of the Tamawa Club. The same currents swayed the GOP. Unhappy with conservative Republican Representative Frederic Coudert, the East Side silk-stocking district edged toward the Democrats during the Nineteen-Fifties until Coudert finally retired in 1958, giving way to liberal Republican John V. Lindsay.

John F. Kennedy did not carry the silk-stocking GOP strongholds in 1960, but he fared relatively well. After his election, he helped to consummate the intercourse of Democratic liberalism and the increasingly bipartisan Establishment. Scarcely a Norris, Wheeler or John L. Lewis came to be seen. Liberalism became the creature of Georgetown, Hyannisport and Brattle Street—a long way from Muscle Shoals on anybody's map; its captains were McNamara, Rusk, Dillon and Bundy of Ford Motor Company, the Carnegie Foundation, Dillon, Read and Company, and Harvard. There was no WPA culture or hot dogs for visiting royalty on the New Frontier: the Harvard Chief Executive and his Vassar First Lady brought Casals and *haute cuisine* to the White House. Then too, the Establishment was developing an awareness that many of the activities of the federal government, from Food For Peace through urban renewal, were lucrative and potentially more so. Big government began to evoke fewer and fewer complaints from the Establishment, and in the meantime, blue-collar and middle-income taxpayers were growing increasingly restive and conservative, with the result that conservatism, the one-time credo of the Establishment, grew steadily more populist.

Until the Nineteen-Sixties, most of the Establishment was still Republican, though in a liberal and internationalist way quite unlike the dominant Republicanism of the Heartland. But when the GOP nominated Barry Goldwater for President in 1964, in response to the rising conservative voice of the South and the West, the Northeastern Establishment balked. The Arizona Senator was the declared enemy. After the Goldwater nomination had been unsuccessfully opposed by establishmentarian Republicans Rockefeller, Scranton and Lodge, the Establishment carried its apprehension to the general election. From Bar Harbor to Beacon Hill, Block Island, Beekman Place and Bryn Mawr, the GOP vote plummeted between twenty and thirty percentage points to hitherto unfathomed depths.

In giving Lyndon Johnson 60 per cent to 75 per cent of the vote, the Establishment showed unprecedented Democratic support.

Of course, the anti-Goldwater vote did not in itself bespeak an irreparable Establishment breach with the Republican Party. For one thing, Some Northeastern Republicans of liberal and Establishment bent—Congressmen John V. Lindsay and Ogden Reid, for example—had refused to support Goldwater and won sweeping victories in their constituencies. The Establishment was prepared to forgive the Republican Party its aberration; and establishmentarian liberal Republicans were quick to label the party's 1964 venture as just that—an aberration.

CHART 23

The Goldwater Decline in the Silk-Stocking Northeast

	Republican Share of the Total Vote for President	
	1960	1964
Scarsdale, New York	64%	35%
Pound Ridge, New York	73	43
9th Assembly District of Manhattan (Park-Fifth Avenues)	57	28
5th Ward of Boston (Beacon Hill-Back Bay)	55	30

In the wake of the 1964 elections, the Northeastern Republican Establishment turned even more liberal. Effecting an alliance with New York's Liberal Party, Congressman John Lindsay won the 1965 New York City mayoralty election; meanwhile, the Republican governors of the Northeast promulgated urban-oriented liberal policies and the Northeastern liberal Republican bloc in the Senate —Senators Javits (N.Y.), Case (N.J.) and Scott (Penna.) in the lead—furnished vital support for the urban liberalism of the Great Society.*

Virtually all of New York City's fashionable suburbs, as well as

---

*There was nothing notable about Lindsay's victory insofar as voting trends are concerned; he simply added the Liberal Party's ballots to a typical Republican share of the vote. He did not win a majority, just a plurality. Had the prior Republican mayoralty nominee, New York State Attorney General Louis Lefkowitz, commanded the Liberal Party's support, he too would have won election with a plurality in a multi-party contest.

chic midtown Manhattan—all districts that had opposed the New Deal—elected Great Society liberals to Congress in 1964. And whereas a generation earlier no progressive would have labeled himself "the Banker's Senator," New York's Jacob Javits, generally accounted the most liberal Republican on Capitol Hill, proudly did so. To complete the triangle, many prominent business leaders (the New York *Times* hailed them as "big business progressives") urged Congress to support Lyndon Johnson's 1965-67 Great Society social programs (the War Against Poverty, Model Cities, Rent Supplements and related endeavors). No longer just the credo of the downtrodden, liberalism was becoming a vested interest. This was truer in 1967 than it had been in 1964; the Goldwater upheaval accelerated the forces at work.

One point must be made clear: the concept of an emerging Liberal Establishment does not simply imply the increasing liberalism of the old-line financial and industrial establishment. Granted that some of the old-line conservatives were turning liberal, much of the old financial, commercial and industrial establishment remained conservative and Republican. But the influence of this group was being displaced by a new collectivity of research, scientific, consulting, internationalist and social interests which, benefiting from the expenditures and activities of big government, propagated an ideology which promoted big government. Most sugar brokers, bulk press manufacturers, fuel distributors and insurance executives still backed the GOP; it was the research directors, associate professors, social workers, educational consultants, urbanologists, development planners, journalists, brotherhood executives, foundation staffers, communications specialists, culture vendors, pornography merchants, poverty theorists and so forth who keynoted the silk-stocking liberal and Democratic trend. No other vocations have waxed so prosperous—and multiplied so Parkinsonially—during the New Deal era as the propagators of environmentalism (as beneficiaries of resultant social remedial spending) and architects of the Permissive Society. Their increasingly dominant position in Megalopolitan silk-stocking neighborhoods, affluence and opinion-molding has changed fashion and establishmentarian outlook; but it has also created a milieu in which the contrast between hypocritical humanism and socioeconomic reality has engendered youthful alienation and anarchy.

The Negro cause is a very useful adjunct of the Liberal Establishment. Not only do Negroes overwhelmingly support institutions of liberal government—including the Democratic Party—but the Negro revolution and the "urban crisis" provide much of the impetus for vast government urban planning, educational, welfare, social research and housing expenditures. And however limited the benefit of such outlays in Negro neighborhoods, they are as essential to the prosperity of key vocational segments of the Liberal Establishment as defense spending is to the Southern California military-industrial complex.

As Chart 24 clearly illustrates, the Establishment voting areas of Metropolitan New York City have given much greater support to liberal than to conservative candidates. Indeed, liberalism has become sufficiently in vogue that silk-stocking liberals occasionally seem more concerned with the establishmentarianism of their politics than its contents. One such is the afore-mentioned Marietta Tree, conservative Republican during the New Deal era, Reform Democrat during the transition period of the Nineteen-Fifties and contemporary elder stateswoman of *salon* liberalism. The bias of her liberalism can be perceived in her haughty description of her family (the Peabodys of Massachusetts) as:

> The people who built and administered the schools, universities, boys' clubs and hospitals. They were the sinews of society. They gave generously of themselves for the public good and prudently lived on the income of their incomes. They valued educated women as well as educated men; daily exercise; big breakfasts; President Eliot; beautiful views; portraits by Sargent; waltzing; Harvard; travel; England; comradeship between the sexes; Patou dresses for "swell" occasions; long correspondence with family and friends; J. P. Morgan; mahogany and red plush; and, most of all, they believed that if you tried hard enough, you could make the world a better place. And you *must* try.*

*Stephen Birmingham, *The Right People: A Portrait of the American Social Establishment* (Boston, 1968), p. 340. The Ripon Society, a Harvard-based group of young Republican liberals, evinced a kindred pre-occupation in their June, 1968 *Forum* in describing their group necktie: "A British firm is preparing the design using the crest of Ripon, England, a lovely cathedral town from which Ripon, Wisconsin, the birthplace of the Republican Party, took its name."

CHART 24

The Liberalism of the Northeastern Establishment

AS SHOWN BY SILK-STOCKING AND PROFESSIONAL DISTRICT VOTING PATTERN IN NEW YORK, 1960-66

	Conservative (GOP share of major party vote for Pres., 1964; Goldwater)	Moderate Conservative (GOP share of major party vote for Pres., 1960; Nixon)	Moderate Liberal (GOP share of major party vote for Governor; Rockefeller) 1962	Moderate Liberal ... 1966	Liberal (GOP share of major party vote for Senator, 1962; Javits)	Liberal (GOP share of major party vote for Mayor, 1965; Lindsay)*
ASSEMBLY DISTRICT						
*New York City***						
5th Manhattan AD (West Side Jewish)	17%	32%	44%	51%	61%	66%
8th Manhattan AD (East Side)	32	52	64	64	70	75
9th Manhattan AD (East Side)	28	57	69	69	77	78
SILK-STOCKING SUBURBS						
Scarsdale (Moderately Jewish)	35	64	80	78	84	—
Bedford	42	69	73	65***	74	—
Pound Ridge	43	73	77	77	80	—

*Lindsay vote includes Liberal Party vote

Further evidence of the growing establishmentarian impulse of liberalism came in the 1968 pre-convention and post-convention presidential campaigns of both parties. Whereas the elections of the Nineteen-Twenties and even of 1932 had produced very little support for the Democrats in expensive boarding schools like St. Paul's—only 18 per cent of St. Paul's students backed F.D.R. in the Depression year of 1932!*—students from the fashionable private schools of the Northeast volunteered in droves to assist in the 1968 primary campaigns of liberal Democratic Senators Robert F. Kennedy and Eugene J. McCarthy. And contrary to the anti-Establishment image he presented, Senator McCarthy's New York area support was concentrated not in poor precincts but in the most fashionable neighborhoods (Manhattan's East Side) and suburbs (Great Neck, Scarsdale, Wilton and Westport).** Although less Establishment interest focused on the Republican candidates, Nelson Rockefeller was greatly preferred to the more conservative Richard Nixon. A cross-section of Northeastern Establishment Republicanism's key men—New Jersey's Senator Case, Pennsylvania's Governor Shafer and Senator Scott, New Yorkers Javits and Lindsay, Rhode Island's Governor Chafee, Massachusetts Senator Brooke—gave a decisive and fatal coloration to Rockefeller's bid for the nomination.

Even against Hubert Humphrey, who was certainly not the choice of the affluent intelligentsia for the 1968 Democratic presidential nomination, GOP nominee Richard Nixon did poorly in the home precincts of the Establishment, running well behind his 1960 levels. Chart 25 shows Nixon's slippage in key silk-stocking areas.

During the early part of the 1968 campaign, Hubert Humphrey's popularity was down sharply in the richer reaches of establishmentarian liberalism, where resentment at the Democratic convention treatment of silk-stocking favorite Eugene McCarthy ran deep. However, as Humphrey courted McCarthyites and Nixon maintained a basically conservative stance, the contest became one between insurgent conservatism and established liberalism, and Humphrey ultimately ran a very strong race in most seats of affluent

*Lipset, *Political Man* (New York, 1963), p. 313.
**These areas were not only the strongest for McCarthy in the local Democratic conventions (Connecticut) and primaries (New York), but they epitomized the typical residential addresses of the people who volunteered to help McCarthy or telephoned their support of his candidacy.

CHART 25

The 1960-68 Silk-Stocking Democratic Trend

District	Republican Share of the Total Vote for President	
	1960	1968
8th Assembly District* of Manhattan (East Side)	52%	38%
9th Assembly District* of Manhattan (Park, Fifth Avenues)	57	39
5th Ward of Boston (Beacon Hill)	55	38
Scarsdale, New York	64	45

*Assembly districts redrawn in 1966, boundaries slightly different

liberalism. Support for Wallace was predictably negligible—one to two per cent.

On New York's East Side, not only did Hubert Humphrey win easily over Richard Nixon, but for the first time in thirty years, the chic "silk-stocking" congressional district sent a Democrat to the House of Representatives, and two Republican-held seats in the state legislature were lost to young liberal Democratic scions of prominent families.

The silk-stocking election returns were full of little-discussed import. For the first time since the founding of the Republican Party in 1854, a Republican President had been elected *over the opposition* of the principal residential citadels of Megalopolitan money, media and fashion, having built victory on the support of constituencies to whom the Northeastern Establishment is an alien, although enigmatic interest group. A continuing Democratic trend in the Northeastern Establishment seems assured.

In closing, it should be noted that while the Liberal Establishment is principally a creature of the Northeast, it has more than a few outposts—to say nothing of individual adherents—in the Heartland and West. Cleveland, Detroit and San Francisco, together with lesser cities like Berkeley, Portland, Minneapolis, Madison and Ann

Arbor, tend to reflect liberal establishmentarian trends. And even in anti-establishmentarian Los Angeles and Chicago, there are sections—Beverly Hills, Lake Shore Drive and the University of Chicago area—of distinct Liberal Establishment cast.

2. The Yankees

From the first days of the Republic, Yankee America has been a major sociopolitical force, invariably captaining one of the nation's principal political parties. Only a few periods of transition have seen Yankee loyalties betwixt and between. The Federalist party of Hamilton, Adams and Washington was the earliest instrumentality of Yankee interests; later the Whigs enjoyed strong support among the mercantile aristocracy of New England and the Yankee-settled regions to the west. Prior to the Civil War, Yankeedom forged a new party, and during the following century, Yankee America persisted in its adherence to the Republican Party. Now Yankee loyalties are changing once again.

Different sections of the United States have promulgated varying definitions of "Yankee." New Englanders often limit the species to natives of the six states with Anglo-Saxon antecedents, while Southerners use the term (frequently with the prefix "damn") to refer to all inhabitants of states north of the Mason-Dixon line. As with so many things, the truth lies in between. Not all Northerners are Yankees and there are many Yankees outside New England.

From their original lands in the New England colonies of New Hampshire, Massachusetts, Rhode Island and Connecticut, America's Yankees have spread far afield. In the years between the American Revolution and the Civil War, New England Yankees— an Anglo-Saxon aggregation of Congregationalists, Methodists, Quakers and other Protestants—poured west through Vermont, upstate New York, northern New Jersey, northern Pennsylvania and the old Northwest (the present day Great Lakes). Some stayed and some moved on. Many such Yankee settlements show the clear imprint of their origins even today. Beyond the Mississippi, eastern Kansas was partly settled by anti-slavery New Englanders; others went by ship and the Oregon Trail to the Northern Pacific Coast. No region is so emphatically Yankee Republican (especially to New Deal-era schoolboys) as Down East Maine, Cape Cod and the Green Mountains of Vermont. Yet Yankee influence is also strong in New York's Finger Lakes, Genesee Valley and Adirondack re-

MAP 7

The Yankee Environment

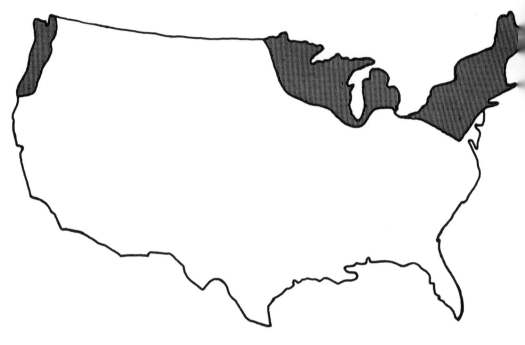

The shaded region is that generally delineated by agricultural geographers as the dairy cattle and hay section of the United States. The great majority of emigrants from New England, seeking a similar land and clime, stayed within this region. Not only did local agriculture resemble that of New England, but there were pine forests, lakes and coastlines—the socio-scenery so dear to New Englanders.

gions, Pennsylvania's upper Susquehanna Valley and Lake Erie coast, Ohio's onetime Western Reserve (of Connecticut), the Lawrence-Topeka stretch of Kansas, Michigan timber and dairy-land, Oregon's Willamette Valley (Portland-Salem), California's Redwood Coast and Walla Walla, Washington. Ripon, Wisconsin, where the Republican Party was formed in 1854, is another old Yankee settlement.

Many of these areas have evinced considerable sociopolitical kinship to New England—in local government, in education, in matters of government and morality like abolition and prohibition, and in the ups and downs of partisan political allegiance and preference. Granted that Yankee political behavior can be most easily isolated and identified in New England, it is also quite important elsewhere in the nation.*

The common Southern reference to all Northerners as "Yankees" is a backhanded tribute to the part that the Yankee segment of the North played in precipitating and carrying out the Civil War. From Maine to Minnesota, Yankees sparked the anti-slavery and free-soil impetus; finally, in 1854, dissident Democrats, Whigs and Know-Nothings (nativists) joined together under Yankee auspices to form the new Republican Party. As the political instrumentality of Yankeedom, the young party sunk its roots in New England and Yankee-settled areas, faring less auspiciously beyond this cultural pale. The first Republican presidential candidate, John C. Fremont, carried every Yankee county in the nation but not many others. Nor was Lincoln's 1860 victory much of an improvement on Fremont's 1856 effort; Lincoln won a minority victory because his opposition split three ways.

The slave-owning South took great umbrage at Lincoln's election, not just because of Yankee predilections for abolitionism—abolitionists did not dominate the Republican Party in 1860—but because of the longstanding sectional rivalry between the South and Yankeedom. In many ways, the Civil War triggered by Lincoln's election represented a clash of cultures—the individualistic, non-moralist South against the ultra-moralist, community-action-minded

*The Yankees who moved west took their politics, religion and culture with them. When they set up new towns, they did so in New England fashion and named them for existing Yankee communities. Connecticut emigrants, for example, named more than a dozen cities after Hartford—New Hartford, Connecticut; New Hartford, New York; Hartfords in Vermont, Maine and New York; Hartfords in New Jersey and Ohio; Hartford City, Indiana; Hartfords in Michigan, Illinois, Wisconsin, Iowa and Kansas; New Hartfords in Iowa, Missouri and Minnesota; Hartfords in South Dakota and Washington. They also took their prejudices and tastes with them. As Stewart Holbrook has written in his book *Yankee Exodus* (New York, 1950): "If you wanted to know exactly where the Yankee had gone, you could walk into the offices of Cross Company, bakers of Montpelier and St. Johnsbury, Vermont, and see on the books which western stores in Minnesota, Iowa, California and Oregon had been clubbed by transplanted New Englanders into ordering Montpelier or St. Johnsbury crackers. None but a Yankee wanted them. It was much the same with Mrs. Gorton's dried codfish from Massachusetts and Portland Star Matches from Maine." The Yankees who left New England (and subsequent Yankee departure points) remained members of the psychological Greater New England community. Their politics likewise generally followed the lead of New England.

Yankee North—and also a clash of regional economies, with Yankee industry and commerce opposing Southern agriculture.* While many Yankee abolitionists glorified the Civil War as a moral crusade, it was also a profitable one, and even such friendly observers as Stewart Holbrook and Chard Powers Smith have noted the Yankee propensity for mixing up morality and commercial success. The Yankee impulse is one of couching a profitable venture in moralist terminology—and the Negro cause has long been a favorite corollary of Yankee socioeconomic anti-Southernism.**

The Civil War was a great Yankee victory. King Cotton proved to be no king at all, summoning no European vassals to the aid of the beleaguered Confederacy. And with the return of peace—on Yankee terms—a new industrial and financial aristocracy, captained largely by Yankees, took the nation's helm. Politically, Yankeedom led the effort to prevent a re-emergence of Southern power by using federal troops to maintain Negro-Scalawag-Carpetbagger Republican governments in power throughout the Southern states. This "Reconstruction" only came to an end in 1876.

Only a very small minority of the country's Yankees were part of this oligarchy, yet most of them gave it firm political support. The Yankee-sprung Republican Party was the party of Caleb Hoskins, Vermont farmer, and Asa Gardner, Maine lobsterman, as well as that of Nelson Aldrich and John D. Rockefeller. Sociologically, Yankees saw the GOP as theirs—the instrumentality of their caste and culture—while the Democratic Party was the alien creature of

---

*To make this point, it is not necessary to embrace the much-debated theory of an America divided between Southern Cavaliers and Northern Puritans. Suffice it to say that economic thrust of Yankeedom—manufacturing, shipping, finance and small-scale farming—conflicted with the impetus of the plantation slaveocracy. Even though the large plantations of the South were not so socioculturally dominant as legend has made them, most of the South (excluding mountaineers) shared a general concern with the way of life maintained by slavery and Southern national political hegemony. Yankeedom, in turn, sought political control of the United States to advance its own economic interests. The pre-Civil War period was one of stalemate. Sooner or later, Yankee-based industry or Dixie-based plantation agriculture must have triumphed.

**Yankee abolitionism and opposition to the expansion of slavery coincided with the economic interests of New England. As for Yankee attitudes towards Negroes per se, throughout the entire Yankee territory from Ohio to California, Negroes were not allowed to vote; the Yankee-backed Kansas constitution prohibited free Negroes from even entering the state. The Negro cause has been useful to the Yankee Establishment because it generally diverges from the interests of Yankeedom's traditional Irish and Southern foes.

Catholics and Carolinians (or "Rum, Romanism and Rebellion" as one Yankee preacher put it).

Between 1860 and 1896, the majorities by which the GOP carried New England, Michigan, Ohio, Wisconsin, Iowa, Minnesota and Oregon (and intermittently, New York, Indiana and Illinois) were forged by lopsided Yankee support. Chart 7 shows the Republican Party's dependence on these Yankee states. After 1896, when fear of Bryan's economics—and of employer wrath—drove workers into the Republican Party, GOP presidential majorities in the Northeast rose sharply. However, Yankee solidarity remained the essential ballot-box underpinning and prevailing ideological force.

During this Republican heyday, Yankee politics were conservative. The orthodoxy of Northeastern Republicanism stood in marked contrast to the dissident progressivism of Western Republicans (who railed against Wall Street and the Yankee oligarchy). Chart 26 illustrates the loyalty with which the arch-Yankee counties of the Northeast supported such pillars of conservative Establishment Republicanism as Warren Harding, Calvin Coolidge and Herbert Hoover.

The economic crash of 1929 did not severely dislocate the Republicanism of Yankeedom. Yankee New England, upstate New York and rural Michigan all gave vote majorities to Herbert Hoover in 1932 and Alfred Landon in 1936. However, urban and Catholic voting kept Landon from winning any states except heavily Yankee Maine and Vermont. Fought at the height of New Deal popularity, the 1936 election shed clear light on the ballot-box bedrock of the Republican Party. The areas Landon carried—from New England-settled eastern Kansas to Maine—along with a few other Yankee-settled areas in Iowa and Oregon, elected almost all of the handful of Republicans sent to the House of Representatives in 1936. Three generations after the Civil War, the sociological core of the Republican Party was still solidly Yankee.

Throughout most of the nation, the Republicans raised their presidential vote share between 1936 and 1940, but Yankee precincts were an exception. Especially in New England, Yankee culture was vehemently Anglophile, so that archetype Yankee bailiwicks in rural Vermont, Beacon Hill and Down East Maine evidenced a distinct Democratic trend in support of Franklin D. Roosevelt's controversial policy of all aid short of war to Hitler-

CHART 26

Presidential Voting in the Yankee Northeast, 1920-68*

Republican Percentage of the Total Vote for President

County	1920	1924	1928	1932	1936	1940	1944	1948	1952	1956	1960	1964	1968
Maine													
Hancock	72%	77%	82%	64%	72%	66%	69%	78%	83%	87%	78%	46%	63%
Lincoln	74	77	79	64	73	68	70	81	84	86	76	44	59
New Hampshire													
Carroll	65	65	77	70	66	66	68	76	83	85	80	55	72
Vermont													
Orange	82	86	85	70	69	64	68	74	85	84	76	46	67
Lamoille	79	83	85	69	73	69	74	77	84	84	77	41	68
Massachusetts													
Barnstaple	84	86	77	70	69	69	70	75	81	83	63	43	58
Dukes	87	87	76	69	63	62	61	70	76	83	61	32	50
New York													
Essex	78	74	66	64	68	68	68	70	76	82	65	35	62
Yates	76	78	79	71	74	76	76	74	81	83	74	42	69
Pennsylvania													
Tioga	83	81	87	75	69	72	76	77	79	78	73	49	67

*These counties were selected on the basis of their behavior in the 1928 election which, by dint of Al Smith's candidacy, sharply delineated county-by-county ethnic and religious patterns. The five counties of upper New England, most Republican in their states in 1928, are almost wholly Yankee. The New York and Pennsylvania counties are less homogeneous, but they were the most Republican of the Yankee-settled counties in the two states. The two Massachusetts counties are less purely Yankee, having larger Catholic minorities. Essex County, ____ ____ ____ substantial French Catholic minority.

threatened Great Britain (see Chart 12).* After the war, these and
other Yankees returned to the GOP—the New England Yankee
GOP trend between 1940 and 1948 was just about the sharpest in
the nation (along with that of Jewish voters affected by World
War II). By 1948, Republican strength in the Yankee Northeast
was back at the high levels of the Nineteen-Twenties. The party
presidential candidate, New York Governor Thomas E. Dewey, was
an ex-Michigander of Yankee stock, and whatever his prim and
establishmentarian image cost him in the Farm Belt and the Catholic cities, he did very well in Yankee districts. Little improvement
was possible: in 1952, Eisenhower registered generally miniscule
advances. (Chart 26 probably overstates the 1948-52 Republican
gain in the Northeast's prime Yankee counties. Because these counties have small Catholic minorities, they reflected the strong Catholic pro-Eisenhower trend. Perusal of township returns in upper New
England and even rural Connecticut provides better proof of the
negligible Yankee trend between 1948 and 1952.)

With the election of General Eisenhower, Yankeedom returned
to power. From Massachusetts came Christian Herter, Henry Cabot
Lodge and Sinclair Weeks; from New Hampshire, Sherman Adams;
from New York, John Foster Dulles, Herbert Brownell and William
P. Rogers. Lawyers and bankers with summer houses in Bar Harbor,
Cohasset, Fisher's Island and the Berkshires assumed the under-
secretaryships and kindred positions from which Franklin D. Roosevelt had displaced their fathers. But paradoxically, and for the first
time, the Yankee wing of the GOP was no longer the bastion of
conservatism, opposing Western progressivism as in the Nineteen-
Twenties. Not only had England's fight against Nazism turned
Northeastern Republicanism toward a more internationalist view-
point, but the growing populist conservatism of the South and West
—already coming to dominate the national GOP—was stimulating
Yankee liberalism. Early in the Eisenhower era, the campaign
against Senator Joseph McCarthy, symbol of Southern, Western,
German and Irish popular conservatism, was led by such Yankees
as Boston lawyer Joseph Welch, New Hampshire Senator Charles
Tobey, Maine Senator Margaret Chase Smith, Vermont Senator
Ralph Flanders and his colleague, Senator George Aiken. These

---

*The northern roof of New England adjacent to Quebec also showed a pro-
Roosevelt trend but French-Canadians rather than Yankees were principally
responsible.

and other Yankees gave important support to foreign aid proposals and civil liberties bills opposed by most Southern, Western, German and Irish Republicans.

Despite Yankee power within the Eisenhower Administration, Republican strength was beginning to weaken in Yankee bailiwicks. Although the President won most small Yankee towns by three- and four-to-one majorities in 1956, his percentages sometimes slipped below those of 1952—and other Republicans were less successful than the popular President. Edmund Muskie, elected Maine's first Democratic governor in two decades in 1954, easily retained office in 1956, and Vermont chose a Democratic congressman in 1958, its first since the formation of the Republican Party.

In 1960, New England, once the most Republican section of the nation, turned in the highest Democratic vote share. True, most of this rested on Catholic rather than Yankee voting—the successful Democratic Presidential candidate was Irish Catholic John F. Kennedy—but even Yankee counties trended towards the Democrats, as Chart 26 illustrates. Meanwhile, the number of Republican congressmen from upstate New York and New England dropped below the Depression levels of the Nineteen-Thirties. Vermont elected a Democratic governor in 1962; New Hampshire both a Democratic governor and a United States Senator. All of this bespoke a considerable decline of Yankee conservatism and Republicanism, nor was it mere chance that these Democratic breakthroughs in Yankeedom coincided with kindred GOP breaches in the old Confederacy.

Thus the ground was broken for the upheaval of 1964. Caught in an adverse intra-party tide and political re-alignment, Northeastern Republicanism lacked the power to select a liberal and internationalist presidential nominee; the party convention chose Arizona Senator Barry Goldwater, a conservative allied with the Deep South. (Goldwater had even mused aloud that the Northeast ought to be set adrift from the rest of the nation.) Most Yankee Republicans did little or nothing to help the Goldwater candidacy, and the Democratic current of 1954-62 became a torrent. All of the leading Yankee counties listed in Chart 26 had backed Alf Landon in the Democratic presidential landslide of 1936, but only one gave a majority to Barry Goldwater. Several counties where the GOP vote had not once dipped below 60 per cent in presidential races since 1920 gave Goldwater only 30 per cent support! So abandoned,

Goldwater won just 34 per cent of the vote in Vermont and 31 per cent in Maine, the only two states Landon had carried in his ill-fated candidacy. For the first time, the Yankees abandoned the party of their forefathers, and it was this trend, not some mythical urban revolt, which devastated the Goldwater candidacy from Portland, Maine to Portland, Oregon.*

Sharp and harsh as it was, such a break may have been necessary to the GOP. So long as party fortunes remained linked to a Yankee base—one losing its national importance—the Republicans could not forge a new Southern, Western and Catholic alliance.** The 1964 election tore the Republican Party lose from its Yankee roots and the 1966 elections confirmed the separation. Whereas no section of the United States had lost more Republican congressmen in 1964 than the Yankee Northeast (13 seats), the 47-seat gain in the House of Representatives scored by the resurgent GOP in 1966 included a net gain of only *two* seats in that area.*** As a result of the 1966 elections, Maine, New Hampshire and Vermont all had Democratic governors, and for the first time, Maine chose an all-Democratic House delegation—two Harvard men. The politics of Yankeedom were in strong flux.

During the Ninetieth Congress, the voting records of GOP congressmen from rural and small city Yankee districts trended emphatically leftward. Whereas the liberal contingent had been a minority even among Northeastern Republicans in previous House sessions, it now became a majority. From the rural Great Lakes to New England, Republican congressmen from Yankee districts began to oppose the Western and Southern majorities of their party with increasing frequency on issues like rent subsidies, model cities, anti-poverty funds, school busing and open housing. Granted that Yankees have a historic penchant for government social planning and moral proselytizing, only a few years before, most of these same representatives had voted against such measures; their reversals were principally a recognition of the nature of the intra-GOP strug-

---

*From the Atlantic to the Pacific, the sharpest Democratic 1960-64 presidential vote gains came in rural Yankee counties and kindred silk-stocking precincts. In Oregon, Kansas, Iowa and Ohio, rural Yankee counties turned in Goldwater declines only a little less severe than those of upper New England.

**Yankee political strength is not what it used to be. Maine, New Hampshire and Vermont now have five congressmen; a century ago they had fifteen.

***The Yankee Northeast includes New England, New York (outside New York City), northern New Jersey and northern Pennsylvania.

gle for control of the emerging political cycle: the Northeastern Republican cause was linked to a liberal impetus.* With few exceptions, these Yankee-area congressmen supported the 1968 GOP presidential nomination drive of New York Governor Nelson Rockefeller.**

Neither the 1964 Goldwater rout nor the ensuing Yankee liberal and Democratic trend placed the Republican Party in a minority status among Yankee voters. However, by turning away from the century-old stewardship of Yankeedom, the GOP lost the imprimatur by which it had won staggering Yankee majorities as a matter of course, and 1968 Republican presidential strength in the Yankee Northeast reflected this loss. Richard Nixon won a majority of Yankee votes, but a smaller one than he had received in 1960, and smaller than any other post-1920 GOP presidential candidate except Barry Goldwater. Maine, long one of the most Republican states in the nation, cast a majority of its votes against a nationally successful Republican nominee for the first time in history. Part of the Maine trend was attributable to the Democratic vice-presidential bid of the state's popular junior Senator, Edmund Muskie, but Yankee towns and counties across New England—no other part of the nation was more Democratic in 1968—showed similar though lesser trends. Likewise, no part of the United States gave George Wallace so little support (4 per cent) as New England, with many Yankee townships giving the Alabama ex-governor 1 per cent or less. Chart 26 shows the 1960-68 decline in Nixon's vote levels across a representative spectrum of Yankee counties, and Map 8 illustrates the movement of a group of Massachusetts Yankee towns.

The 1968 election saw Yankee counties of New England and kindred areas from Oregon's Willamette Valley to Ohio's Western Reserve return to the Republican fold, but with less solidarity and enthusiasm than they had shown prior to 1964. During the second Nixon candidacy, the GOP was no longer the Yankee party it once had been, and the lopsided partisan traditions and majorities of the Republicans' Yankee era were a thing of the past. Having entered

---

*Despite the strong tradition of aiding and patronizing Negroes which exists in upper echelons of the Yankee Establishment, most GOP congressmen representing rural Yankee districts shunned urban subsidy legislation until it became a matter of sectional and party factional interest.

**From the Pacific Northwest to eastern Kansas, Minnesota, Lake Erie and the Northeast, Rockefeller support was parochially concentrated in Yankee (and Scandinavian) districts.

CHART 27

The Yankee Metamorphosis

Congressional Districts In Which
the Republican Representative
Demonstrated Growing Support Of
Great Society Legislation In The
90th Congress As Compared With
the 89th Congress

Vermont (At-Large)
Gloucester-Marblehead, Massachusetts
Cape Cod, Massachusetts
Endicott-Johnson City-Binghamton-Elmira-Ithaca, New York
Genesee Valley, New York
Southern Tier-Lake Erie, New York
Northern Tier-Scranton, Pennsylvania
Western Reserve, Ohio (three districts)
Northern Tier-Rockford, Illinois
Saginaw, Michigan
Muskegon-Lake Michigan Shore, Michigan
Royal Oak, Michigan
Northfield-Southeast, Minnesota
Minneapolis Suburbs, Minnesota
Topeka-Northeast, Kansas
Willamette Valley, Oregon

Comparable behavior was shown by Republican Congressmen elected from similar areas (especially in Michigan) recaptured from the Democrats in 1966. Most of these districts—and most of their congressmen—supported New York Governor Nelson Rockefeller's 1968 quest for the GOP presidential nomination.

into communion with the populist conservatism of the South, West and New York Irish, the GOP found its support among Yankees— historically hostile to the politics of this new Republican coalition —ebbing accordingly. Although a majority of Yankees voted Republican in 1968, their states—New England, New York, Michigan, Minnesota and the coastal Pacific Northwest—are shaping up as the ideological and partisan base of the new Democratic liberal minority.

As a new Republican majority emerges in the Heartland and

MAP 8

The 1960-68 Republican Decline in Yankee Massachusetts

Township	Republican Share of the Total Vote for President		
	1960	1964	1968
1. Egremont	77%	50%	66%
2. Northfield	72	44	65
3. Harvard	74	50	62
4. Rockport	68	37	54
5. Marblehead	67	38	51
6. Duxbury	76	48	65
7. Yarmouth	68	47	61
8. Nantucket	64	33	56

Outer South, Yankee GOP fidelities should continue to weaken. But while lopsided four- and three-to-one Republican ratios in rural Yankee counties have been replaced by closer contests, so that GOP statewide futures are clouding from Passamaquoddy Bay to Lake Superior, the erosion of purely tradition-based loyalties in such areas is unlikely to strip away enough Republicanism to create local Yankee Democratic majorities. The basic socioeconomic character-istics of the rural Yankee Northeast suggest that after the flux of obsolescent Civil War loyalties, a predominance of the rural Yankee electorate should prefer Heartland Republicanism to big city-biased Democratic policies. Fashionable Megalopolitan liberalism—the credo of an urban-oriented communications, planning and educa-tional elite—does not exercise the same rural Yankee appeal that Protestant hegemony and Calvinist commercialism did in the days of "Rum, Romanism and Rebellion."

Divided rather than united, their states losing population and electoral votes to the South and West, Yankees—no longer in con-trol of the party they dominated for a century—are a fading force in American politics.

3. The Negroes

Until the late Nineteen-Thirties, Negroes were an insignificant political force in the Northeast. Most still lived in the South, where they were disenfranchised. Those that lived in the North, where they could vote, were psychological captives of the party of Abraham Lincoln. The Depression changed all this. Many Southern Negroes fled the local agricultural doldrums for the cities of the Great Lakes and Northeast, where they added numerical strength to the general Depression-prompted Northern Negro trend away from the party of Lincoln's memory and towards the party of Franklin D. Roosevelt's more tangible welfare, economic and labor programs. Chart 28 illustrates the chronology of Northern urban Negro population growth.

In 1944, Adam Clayton Powell won the Harlem congressional seat in New York City to become the Northeast's first Negro con-gressman. But although Negro numbers were growing, their strength was not such as to exert much policy influence or threaten white party leadership; they were increasingly useful auxiliaries of the New Deal coalition, and white Democratic organizations were glad to have such loyal Election Day adherents.

This situation prevailed well into the Nineteen-Fifties. Beyond FEPC and fair housing laws, not much legislation was drawn with the Negro vote principally in mind. Inside the Democratic Party, Negroes occupied a few conspicuous positions (who could expect non-Negroes to represent Harlem in Albany or Washington?) but

Northeastern Negro Demographic and Political Trends

CHART 28

Northeastern Negro Population Growth, 1940-65

Negro Percentage of City Population

City	1940	1950	1960	1965
Boston	3%	5%	9%	11%
Buffalo	3	6	13	18
New York	6	9	14	16
Jersey City	4	7	13	17
Newark	11	17	34	40
Philadelphia	13	14	26	29
Baltimore	19	24	35	41
Washington	28	38	54	63

CHART 29

Declining Negro Presidential Republicanism, 1956-64

REPUBLICAN SHARE OF NEGRO TWO-PARTY PRESIDENTIAL VOTE*

City	1956	1960	1964	City	1956	1960	1964
Boston	48%	33%	5%	Philadelphia	26%	26%	15%
New York	35	27	8	Baltimore	55	28	7
Pittsburgh	27	19	5				

*Data taken from Republican National Committee 1964 Election Analysis. Wards and precincts cited were heavily Negro, but white "stay-behinds" exaggerate Negro Republicanism.

smaller concentrations of Negroes were frequently the objects of gerrymanders which split up a potential electorate while buoying Democratic strength in adjacent white districts. In the main, the Democratic Party used Negroes rather than vice versa; but the conservatism of the GOP in economic matters discouraged Negroes, even though the Republicans were at least as liberal as the Catholic Democratic machines on civil rights issues. Republican Senator

Irving Ives, who had earlier sponsored New York's FEPC law, won a mere 11 per cent of the vote in South Harlem's assembly district in his 1954 gubernatorial bid; and Eisenhower climbed from 15 per cent in 1952 to 26 per cent in 1956. There were a few exceptions to Negro Democratic preference, such as in Southern-flavored Maryland, where Governor (later Baltimore Mayor) Theodore McKeldin won heavy Negro support on the GOP ticket.

Seeking re-election in the wake of the 1954 Supreme Court school desegregation decision, President Eisenhower ran strongly—for a Republican—by averaging one-third of the (sparse) vote in Northeastern urban Negro districts. Thereafter, the Republican share of the vote declined as Northeastern Negroes grew more numerous—immigration from the South was proceeding apace—and gained the wherewithal to carve a niche for themselves in the Democratic Party and mount the party ladder as other ethnic groups had done before them. By the beginning of the Nineteen-Sixties, New York City Negroes held a dozen judgeships and the borough presidency (county administration) of Manhattan. Elsewhere, although they

Negro Voting Trends in New York City, 1960-68

CHART 30

Negro Presidential Voting Trends, 1960-68

Assembly District*	Republican Share of the Total Vote for President		
	1960	1964	1968
14th Manhattan (South Harlem)	19%	5%	11%
11th Manhattan (Central Harlem)	22	4	7
6th Brooklyn (Bedford-Stuyvesant)	31	11	10
6th Bronx (Crotona Park)	20	8	9

*Because assembly district lines were redrawn between 1964 and 1968, comparisons of 1968 with 1960 and 1964 figures are not exact.

courted Negro voters, white Democratic organizations were less yielding of jobs and power.

Between 1956 and 1960, the GOP share of the Negro presidential vote declined somewhat, although not as much as the party share of the Catholic vote. (The latter decreased in response to the Kennedy candidacy.) Chart 29 sketches this diminution of Negro Republican presidential support; the 1956-64 downtrend paralleled the rise of Southern influence within the party. Finally, Barry Goldwater matched his unprecedented Republican landslide in Mississippi with an equally unprecedented—and practically non-existent—share of the Negro vote in the urban Northeast and the rest of the nation. Hardly any Negroes voted Republican in 1964.

But if conservative Republicans did not fare well in Negro districts, neither did liberal Republicans. For all their advocacy of programs aimed at the Negro vote, liberal Establishment Republicans like Nelson Rockefeller, Jacob Javits and John Lindsay proved unable to induce sizeable numbers of Negroes to vote for them. Chart 31 shows the minimal Republican backing won by both Rockefeller and Javits in the leading Negro assembly districts of New York City. Not only were Negroes gaining an important stake in the Democratic Party, but their Democratic proclivities were further reinforced by the increasing Republicanism of their tradi-

CHART 31

Negro Support for New York Liberal Republicans, 1966-68

Assembly District	Republican Share of the Total Vote	
	Rockefeller, 1966	Javits, 1968*
70th Manhattan (South Harlem)	26%	17%
72nd Manhattan (Central Harlem)	31	18
55th Brooklyn (Bedford-Stuyvesant)	30	19
78th Bronx (Crotona Park)	25	18

*This does not include the small vote won by Senator Javits as the nominee of the Liberal Party.

tional Irish and Southern foes. It is also worth pointing out that Negro turnout on Election Day is light; in New York City, Negro assembly districts have typically cast less than half the number of ballots cast in Italian, Irish and Jewish districts (see Chart 32).*

CHART 32

Comparative Negro-White Vote Turnout, 1966-68*

	Total Vote Cast	
	1966 (000's)	1968 (000's)
Negro—70th AD (South Harlem)	21	20
72nd AD (Central Harlem)	21	20
55th AD (Bedford-Stuyvesant)	18	16
78th AD (Crotona Park)	22	20
White—66th AD (Park, Fifth Avenues)	47	54
58th AD (Staten Island)	46	54

*The Assembly Districts listed have substantially equal populations based on the 1960 census.

Notwithstanding these statistics, Northeastern liberal Republicans made a major effort to rally Negroes behind Rockefeller's 1968 bid for the GOP presidential nomination. This effort failed; few Negroes chose to operate in the Republican context.

No other voting bloc was so loyally Democratic in 1968 as the black community. From Boston to Washington, D.C., Negroes consistently turned in better than ten-to-one Humphrey majorities. Their turnout and impact, however, was inhibited by low registration (Washington, D.C.'s Negro enrollment was down 15 per cent from 1964; New York, Newark and Philadelphia also showed significant declines). Negro solidarity obviously gave Hubert Humphrey's candidacy a numerical boost, but at the same time, Democratic Party identification with the Negro revolution cost Humphrey dearly among Northern Catholics and Southerners. Chart 30 shows the

*Thus, in the eleven Negro districts comprising most of New York City's Negro vote, Nelson Rockefeller won only 45,000 more votes in his 1966 gubernatorial race than Barry Goldwater had won in the 1964 presidential race.

overwhelming majorities given to the Democratic presidential nominee in the leading Negro assembly districts of New York City. Solidly Negro wards and districts elsewhere in the nation gave Humphrey comparable backing.

Negro power within the Democratic Party is mounting rapidly. In longtime Democratic strongholds of the urban North and rural South, Negro voting strength is establishing an important and sometimes dominant influence. An unprecedented number of Negroes served as delegates to the 1968 Democratic National Convention; and shortly thereafter three more Negroes were elected to Congress, bringing the national total of Negroes in the House of Representatives to nine (all Democrats). Furthermore, below the Mason-Dixon line, Negroes cast a clear *majority* of the votes garnered by the national Democratic presidential nominee, Hubert Humphrey; Southern whites are leaving the national Democratic Party just as definitely as Negroes across the country are embracing it. Given (1) the increasing Republicanism of the Southern, Western and New York Irish entente with which Negroes have always been uncomfortable, and (2) the Democratic impetus among groups —silk-stocking liberals, Yankees and the intelligentsia—whose political and economic interests are more compatible with Negro goals, the political future of Negroes is likely to be nearly unanimously Democratic, an allegiance which in turn will ingrain the Republicanism of conservative groups.

Although Negroes account for most of the Northeast's non-white population, New York City also has substantial numbers of Puerto Ricans, Chinese and Japanese, albeit they are not very important beyond the metropolitan area. None of these groups is as Democratic as the Negroes, nor are they as dependent on governmental welfare and civil rights efforts. In New York City, a Puerto Rican backlash against Negroes showed itself in 1968, both in community violence and tensions and at the polls on Election Day. Richard Nixon averaged 20 per cent to 25 per cent of the vote in the Puerto Rican precincts of East Harlem compared with his 5 per cent levels in the nearby solidly Negro election districts of central Harlem. Over the last ten years, the Negroes and Puerto Ricans of New York City have generally voted in much the same fashion for statewide and national offices, but they are increasingly uneasy allies. As for the city's prosperous Chinese and Japanese population, they tend to be conservative and Republican. Chinatown, located in lower Manhattan, is the strongest Republican enclave in the area. Many other orientals—both Chinese and Japanese—live along Manhattan's Upper West Side, where once again they are more generally Republican than most of their neighbors. In 1966, the GOP candidate for the State Assembly from lower Manhattan was a Chinese named Hong, and in 1968, Upper West Side Republicans ran Japanese Moonray Kojima for the Assembly. Nixon carried New York's Chinatown, just as he won the much larger Chinatown in San Francisco. Racial politics in the Northeast is more complex than a simple polarization of whites and non-whites.

This varying two-party context of Hispanic American and Oriental political behavior makes the intensity of Negro one-party commitment unique among American minorities. In a similar Nineteenth Century vortex of particularized animosity from other segments of society, the Irish also chose to band together and seek advancement through cohesive (one-party) group action. Negro Democratic regularity, re-inforced by increasing municipal power, party primary and patronage success, is coming to match that of yesteryear's Irish. Perhaps Negroes will have similar success in using such solidarity as a tool of socioeconomic advance. And at the same time, the Republican Party will be obliged to take care lest the unavailability of substantial Negro vote support engender a dangerous apathy regarding problems in which the nation as a whole also has an interest.

4. The Jews

Two thirds of the United States' six million Jews live in the Northeastern Megalopolis, half of them in greater New York City. Jews constitute an important voting bloc in New York, Massachusetts, Pennsylvania and Maryland, but their relative importance is greatest in New York State, where about one-fifth of the electorate is Jewish (one-third in New York City, about one-fourth in suburban Nassau and Westchester counties). New York is the seat of American Jewish cultural and political influence.

In 1880, there were only about 80,000 Jews in New York City. Most of them were of German extraction—and many were Republican. But between 1896 and 1914, two million Jews—principally Eastern European—came to the United States, and a good number of them stayed where they first came ashore. By the outbreak of World War I, over a quarter of New York City's population was

Jewish. Politically, New York Jews were fragmented among the Republican, Democratic and Socialist parties. In Boston, where the Democratic Party was purely Irish, the Jews were strongly Republican. Elsewhere, the pattern was mixed.

From 1896 through 1920, New York's Jewish voters more often than not gave majorities to Republican presidential candidates.* In the peak year of 1920, New York Jews, like so many other ethnic groups, went for Republican presidential nominee Warren Harding, and New York City elected six Jews to Congress—five Republicans and a Socialist. The 1896-1920 Jewish pattern was closely linked to caste and class within the Jewish community. Only in a few areas were the Jews solidly Democratic. Generally speaking, they disliked Tammany's Irish flavor enough to search out other political vehicles. As indicated, well-established German Jews were Republican to the point where Meier Steinbrink and Samuel Koenig were the Republican county chairmen in Brooklyn and Manhattan. The newly arrived Eastern European Jews, on the other hand, took a different view. Not a few of them were sympathizers of the Russian Revolution of 1917, and they viewed the party of the Anglo-Saxon Establishment as dimly as they viewed the party of the Gaelic brogue; from this Eastern European group came much of the strength of New York's Socialist Party.

Most Irish politicians had no more use for the Jews than the Jews had for them. New York Governor Alfred E. Smith was a prominent exception. He relied on a number of Jewish advisers and worked hard to bring Manhattan Jews into the Democratic fold.** When Smith recaptured the governor's mansion in 1922, revenging his defeat in the 1920 GOP sweep, three new Jewish Democratic congressmen were elected from New York City, and four of the five Jewish Republicans chosen in 1920 were defeated. The three Jewish congressmen—Sol Bloom, Louis Dickstein and Emmanuel Celler—all became well known and enjoyed long careers in the House of Representatives. The future of Jewish politics was becoming Democratic.

This did not happen all at once. In 1924, for example, Democratic presidential nominee John W. Davis had so little appeal on

*The 1912 and 1916 elections, where the Democratic nominee was Woodrow Wilson, were an exception.
**His reliance on social worker Belle Moskowitz and Judge Joseph Proskauer led to a song: "Moskie and Proskie are the brains of City Hall." Connable and Silberfarb, *Tigers of Tammany* (New York, 1967), page 266.

the sidewalks of New York that approximately half of the city's Jewish voters backed Republican Calvin Coolidge or Progressive Robert LaFollette. And even in 1928, when Al Smith carried New York City's Jewish districts against Herbert Hoover, the Democratic triumph was not overwhelming and many of the Happy Warrior's Jewish supporters retained their Republican registration. Chart 33 shows the alignment of Jewish partisanship during the period between 1920 and the depression election of 1932.

CHART 33

*Jewish Presidential Voting in New York County (Manhattan), 1920-32**

	1920	1924	1928	1932
Republican	43%	27%	28%	18%
Democratic	19	51	72	82
Socialist or				
Progressive	38	22	—	—

The 1928 and 1932 figures exclude the Socialist vote.

*The figures above come from sanitation districts with a better than 90 per cent Jewish population. Burner, *The Politics of Provincialism* (New York, 1968), page 239.

The 10 per cent to 15 per cent vote New York City Jews gave to Socialist presidential candidate Norman Thomas in 1932 detracted from their initial support of Franklin Roosevelt, but the President increased his Jewish backing in 1936 after the New Deal had evidenced its commitment to social and welfare legislation. Notwithstanding their staunch support of Roosevelt, many New York City Jews did not want to vote for him on the voting machine line of the much-distrusted (Irish Tammany) Democratic Party. As a result, a number of Jewish labor leaders formed a new party— the American Labor Party—which began by polling 274,000 votes (mostly Jewish) for the President in 1936. On the local level, New York City Jews vented their displeasure with Irish Tammany by voting for Fusion mayoralty candidate LaGuardia (who was half Jewish).

As the shadow of Hitler spread over the late Nineteen-Thirties, Jewish liberal commitment to the domestic programs of the New

Deal and the anti-fascist interventionism of Roosevelt's foreign policies grew ever more complete. Such Jewish attitudes prevailed up and down the economic spectrum. Unlike Gentile voters, Jews showed little more Republicanism at the top of the economic ladder than at the bottom. Even Jewish suburbanites gave F.D.R. whopping majorities, although their support fell considerably short of the 90 per cent Gallup has estimated that the *national* Jewish electorate accorded Roosevelt in 1940 and 1944.

By no means all of these Jews were willing to vote for Franklin D. Roosevelt on the Democratic line of Tammany Hall. Chart 34 shows how the percentage of the New York State vote cast for

CHART 34

Radical Voting in New York State During the New Deal Era, 1932-44

A. The Decline of the Socialist Party and the Rise of the Anti-Tammany New Deal Left Parties

	Total Presidential Votes Received in New York State			
	1932	1936	1940	1944
Socialist Party	177,397	86,897	18,950	10,553
Liberal and American Labor Parties	———	274,924	417,418	825,640

B. The Magnitude of Radical Voting

	1932	1936	1940	1944
Total Percent of New York State Presidential Vote Cast for Left Minor Parties*	5%	7%	7%	13%
Percent of New York State Presidential Vote Cast for Roosevelt on Left Minor Party Lines**	0	5	6	13

*Socialist, Communist, Liberal, American Labor Party and Socialist Labor.
**Liberal and American Labor.

Roosevelt on a non-Democratic ballot line—mostly by New York City's large and anti-Tammany Jewish population—grew steadily first as radicals were won over to the New Deal (abandoning the Communist and Socialist tickets) and then as ethnic considerations influenced Jewish preferences.

As World War II mobilized many Socialist and Communist voters of 1936 behind Roosevelt's re-election attempts, while also heightening Jewish distaste for the isolationist, often illiberal and sometimes anti-Semitic Irish machine Democrats, the Jewish tendency to vote for F.D.R. on a left-liberal third-party line reached an important level. In 1944, when 13 per cent of the statewide vote was cast for F.D.R. on two minor-party lines, a near-majority of New York City's Jewish population may have been so disposed! The two left-liberal splinter parties were quite different. The American Labor Party, founded before the 1936 election, had, by 1944, become riddled by Communists and fellow-travellers. As a result of this transformation, a second minor party—the Liberal Party—was pulled together as an anti-Communist alternative to the ALP. Both the ALP and the Liberal Party endorsed Roosevelt; his leftist acceptance was well-nigh complete by 1944.

Despite the rapid emergence of a Russian-American Cold War in the wake of World War II, backing for the pro-Soviet American Labor Party did not dry up. On the contrary, the radical left wing of the New Deal coalition refused to accept Cold War policies, and in 1948, the New York City-based American Labor Party formed the nucleus of national support for the Progressive Party presidential candidacy of Henry Wallace (whose ultraliberalism had denied him vice-presidential renomination with Roosevelt in 1944). The Progressives touted a foreign policy not too remote from that propounded by the Communist *Daily Worker* and they couched their oratory in the typical peace and brotherhood phraseology of the Left.

Wallace won a half-million votes in New York State—just about half of his national total—and most of these votes came from New York City Jews. Several heavily Jewish *assembly* districts gave him more than one-fifth of the vote; many wholly Jewish *election* districts gave him one-third or more of their ballots; and a few election districts—two in the Bronx were a utopian cooperative housing project where Lenin's picture long had graced the lobby—actually gave him a majority. By and large, Wallace repeated the 1944 support pattern of the American Labor Party, and although most of these voters were Jewish, another large bloc consisted of Italians from the East Harlem bailiwick of ALP Congressman Vito Marcantonio.

Jewish support for Wallace had several wellsprings. In the first place, many Jews were highly susceptible to the vehement anti-fascist and brotherhood themes of the Progressives. Some Jews had pro-Russian attitudes—reaching back to the wartime alliance or beyond it to the Russian Revolution—which had not yet succumbed to the Cold War. And even though the Third Reich had fallen, the ethnic trauma of its rise (and practices thereafter) had left Jews with a pronounced sense of group apprehension and cohesion. Harry Truman, whose roots were in isolationist country and who hobnobbed with many Irish Democratic politicians (prominent among them the Bronx's Ed Flynn), lacked Franklin D. Roosevelt's great appeal to the Jewish electorate, and he compounded their disaffection in 1948 by taking what some Jews considered to be an equivocal and lukewarm position towards the new State of Israel. All of these factors interacted to split Roosevelt's solid Jewish support between Wallace and Truman. Little gain accrued to the Republicans who, nationally at least, were even more conservative and isolationist than the Democrats.

The minimal trend towards Eisenhower in 1952 confirmed the degree of Jewish liberal commitment which had been forged by World War II and the New Deal. Democratic nominee Adlai Stevenson epitomized the learning, internationalism and social liberalism which appealed so much to a Jewish community unable quite to forget the concentration camps, pogroms and Cossacks of Europe. General Eisenhower, on the other hand, represented military tradition and the social conservatism of the Anglo-Saxon middle class, a less attractive combination to Jews, even in the man who had led America's armies against Hitler.

Such Jewish Republican trending as occurred in 1952 took place largely among Jews whose ethnic outlook had been weakened by frequent exposure to non-Jewish values; such persons were inclined to vote on *more* of a class than purely ethnic basis.* Most

---

*Within solidly Jewish districts of New York City and Boston, researchers found that the Democratic vote varied little between income groups; it varied between the sexes (men were more Republican) and along other cleavages of *exposure to non-Jewish values* (working women were more Republican than housewives).

Jewish Republicanism thus evidenced itself in the suburbs, albeit even suburban Jews gave Adlai Stevenson a majority of their vote.

In 1956, while most Northeastern voting streams were giving Eisenhower a larger vote than in 1952, the Jews moved the other way. Much of this was a reaction to the Eisenhower Administration's pro-Egyptian handling of the mid-October, 1956, Suez crisis. Always ready to suspect the GOP of hostility to Jewish interests, some Jews read exactly this attitude into the Administration's diplomatic moves to halt the (successful) Franco-British-Israeli invasion of the Suez Canal area. As Chart 35 shows, the President's Jewish losses were minor, but they ran counter to the considerable gains he scored elsewhere in the urban Northeast.

Given the downtrend of 1956, little Jewish support remained to be lost in 1960, and as things finally worked out, Richard Nixon actually exceeded Eisenhower's vote levels in two of the leading old-line Jewish strongholds of Boston and New York.* For the allegedly most part, however, Nixon dipped a few points below Eisenhower in strongly Jewish districts. Like Adlai Stevenson, 1960 Democratic nominee John Kennedy was an urbane, Ivy League liberal and internationalist, and he was popular among Jewish voters despite their image of his father (Ambassador Joseph P. Kennedy) as a pre-war conservative Irish isolationist. Stevenson remained the first choice of most Jewish liberals, but they gave overwhelming support—roughly 80 per cent—to Kennedy. Paradoxically, it was Jewish votes that provided the margin of victory in New York State —and in the Electoral College—for the nation's first Catholic President.

Four years after New York's Jewish voters helped to put the first Catholic in the White House, they declined to support a man who would have been the first President of Jewish ancestry—Barry Goldwater. The Arizona Senator won about 10 per cent of the Jewish vote in New York City and perhaps a few percentage points

---

Once the exposure to non-Jewish values was there, Jews were more likely to vote like other persons in their income brackets; thus the Republicanism of some suburban Jews. Lawrence H. Fuchs, "American Jews and the Presidential Vote" *American Ethnic Politics* (New York, 1968), pp. 63-68.

*As Chart 35 shows, Nixon ran 1 per cent ahead of Eisenhower in deep Jewish Brooklyn and in Boston's 14th Ward (Mattapan). Both areas are old-line, substantially Orthodox and strongly Zionist. Eisenhower's 1956 percentages were depressed by reaction to his Suez policies; Nixon may have profited from a certain amount of anti-Catholicism and antagonism towards John Kennedy's Irish background.

CHART 35

Jewish Presidential Voting in the Northeast, 1952-68

	Republican Share of the Total Vote for President				
Assembly District or Ward*	1952	1956	1960	1964	1968
New York City					
3rd Bronx (Grand Concourse)	27%	27%	22%	19%	22%
4th Manhattan (Lower East Side)	22	28	23	17	23
15th Brooklyn (Brownsville)	13	12	13	8	16
18th Brooklyn (East Flatbush)	31	27	23	18	31
19th Brooklyn (Boro Park)	31	34	27	23	32
Boston					
Ward 14 (Mattapan)	20	20	21	7	14

NOTE: The districts cited above are heavily Jewish lower-middle and middle-income urban residential neighborhoods. Assembly district figures have been used in preference to precinct-level statistics because of the subjectivity involved in choosing the latter, however several of these assembly districts have undergone population change in the last decade, becoming more Negro and Puerto Rican and less Jewish. Redistricting has also affected year-to-year comparison.

* The New York City assembly districts have been identified by their 1954–64 listings. Prior to 1954, the assembly districts had different boundaries, albeit those listed above were substantially similar. The New York legislature, redistricted itself again in 1965 and 1966, and the assembly districts for which 1968 figures have been given are the 61st (Manhattan), 76th (Bronx), 40th, 41st and 48th (Brooklyn).

more in suburbia. In poor Jewish city districts, Goldwater's vote share did not dip much below Nixon's, but in suburbia, the Republican loss was considerable. Barry Goldwater won less than half of the usual GOP share—about one-third—of the suburban Jewish vote. Goldwater's civil rights, social welfare and foreign policy positions, as well as his general aura of association with the Right, did not appeal to the Jewish community. This was true not only in New York but up and down the Megalopolis.

During the Nineteen-Sixties, an increasing number of urban Jews moved to suburbia; others left old Jewish neighborhoods for semi-suburban city sections. This trend weakened Jewish Democratic loyalties, and liberal Republicans like Nelson Rockefeller, John Lindsay, Jacob Javits, William Scranton, Clifford Case and Edward Brooke ran well in Jewish districts of the Megalopolis. And while the suburban and silk-stocking Jewish electorate generally withheld support from non-liberal Republicans, conservative GOP opportunities were also beginning to take shape in crime-menaced Jewish low-middle-income urban districts. As the 1968 election hove into view, more than a few liberals were decrying the urban Jewish electorate's increasingly conservative response to the Negro revolution.

Preliminary evidence of this Jewish trend had already occurred in another and more parochial contest—New York City's 1966 referendum on whether or not to abolish the newly created (and non-white oriented) Police Civilian Review Board. In a contest which saw the city's most prominent liberal politicians equate opposition to the Board with fascism, poor and middle-class Jewish districts, plagued by the rising crime rate, voted with the Catholic districts in support of the police and opposed the liberal urban coalition of Harlem and Park Avenue. Chart 36 sketches the vote pattern.

By 1968, the Republicans seemed on the verge of scoring heavy gains among Jewish voters. In New York City, the large Jewish community was particularly incensed over the treatment accorded to anti-Humphrey delegates to the Democratic national convention; several New York delegates, including a few who were obviously Jewish, were manhandled by convention authorities or police officers as network television transmitted the spectacle to the nation. To many Jews, the Democratic national convention raised the specter of Nazi Germany, and even though the Chicago confrontation gave Jews new hesitation on the subject of "law and order," resentment against Hubert Humphrey and the way in which he had been nominated was so strong that the post-Democratic convention Gallup poll gave Richard Nixon 41 per cent of the nation's Jewish vote.

But this did not last. As memories of Chicago faded, Humphrey began to recover, and this process speeded up as he edged away from the Johnson Administration's position on Vietnam. Ultimately, the contest became one of Establishment liberalism against the populist conservatism of Southerners, Westerners and New York

CHART 36

The 1966 Police Civilian Review Board Vote in New York City

Assembly District	Area	% Support for Review Board
Negro		
55th Brooklyn	Bedford-Stuyvesant	73%
78th Bronx	Morrisania	74
70th Manhattan	South Harlem	77
Silk-Stocking		
66th Manhattan	Park and Fifth Avenues	62
Jewish		
40th Brooklyn	Brownsville	36
73rd Manhattan	Washington Heights	36
76th Bronx	Grand Concourse	35
Catholic		
80th Bronx	Parkchester, Throgs Neck	20
50th Brooklyn	Bay Ridge	16
58th Richmond	Staten Island South	15
30th Queens	Elmhurst, Maspeth	15

Irish—and most Jews swung to Humphrey, however minimal their enthusiasm. In New York City, the 1968 presidential election spotlighted a cleavage within the Jewish community similar to that which had occurred in the 1966 Civilian Review Board voting. Because of the heterogeneity and size of its Jewish population, New York is really the only city in the United States with a sizeable belt of low-income and low-middle-income Jewish neighborhoods. These were the Jews who had voted against the Civilian Review Board, and it was in these neighborhoods—Brownsville, Crown Heights, Bensonhurst, Boro Park, Washington Heights, Flatbush and the Lower East Side—that Richard Nixon maintained, or, as in most cases, improved his 1960 support levels. On the other hand, in the upper-middle-income and silk-stocking Jewish districts where the Board had carried the day—areas of the East Side, Forest Hills and Riverdale, for example—Nixon slipped far below his 1960 strength. Inasmuch as most New York City Jews are middle-income or better, Nixon's losses outweighed his gains, and in the suburbs, his slippage was particularly acute.

The 1968 election marked a distinct watershed in the pattern of Republican voting among New York City Jews. Heretofore, GOP support had been highest among upper-income, suburban Jews and lowest among poor urban Jews; but in 1968, Nixon appears to have done better among the low- and low-middle-income Jews of Manhattan's Lower East Side than among their affluent co-religionists of the fashionable East Side. In other words, the poorer Jews, although still overwhelmingly Democratic, showed a low-keyed trend towards the populist conservatism engulfing similarly situated Catholics, while the upper-middle-income Jews, many of whom were engaged in professions bound up with establishment liberalism, paralleled the silk-stocking trend. And regarding the latter, not only had an ongoing Jewish population influx helped reshape the outlook of greater New York's silk-stocking precincts, but Jews constituted such a large part of the electorate of places like midtown Manhattan, Scarsdale, Pound Ridge and Great Neck that their trend was a major factor in determining the political behavior of the affluent intelligentsia.

Between 1960 and 1968, the Nixon vote slipped five to twenty percentages points in the strongly Jewish suburbs of New York City. This reflected Jewish population increases and Jewish trending, but it has frequently been misread as the behavior of surburbia *per se.* And around Boston, where Jewish Republicanism had hitherto been stronger than elsewhere because of distaste for the Irish cast of the local Democratic Party, the 1960-68 Nixon falloff reached 23 per cent in the preponderantly Jewish suburb of Brookline. The Jewish sections of northeast Philadelphia, as well as nearby ethnically kindred suburbia, likewise gave the GOP presidential candidate a smaller slice of the vote than he had received in 1960. Jewish shifting away from Nixon reached from one end of the Megalopolis to the other, even though its major impact came in New York.

In the future, most of the Northeastern Jewish community can be expected to give heavy support to Establishment liberalism. Few other groups can match the collective Jewish involvement in social work, education, organized labor and related endeavors profiting from the political impetus of liberal government. Whatever small strides the GOP may make in low-middle-income New York City neighborhoods filled with Jewish postal workers, storeowners and taxi drivers, the overall thrust of Jewish ballot behavior is clearly liberal, and there is little reason to expect Northeastern Jews to give

MAP 9

Northeastern Ethnic and Settlement Patterns, 1790

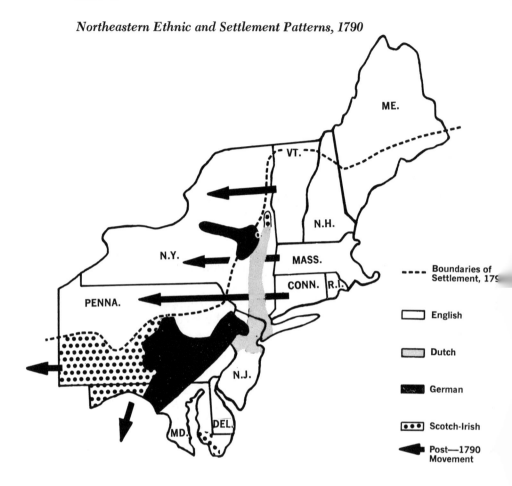

From their first European settlement in the Northeast (New Amsterdam), the Dutch spread up the Hudson and into New Jersey. In 1664, the English took over the Dutch territory.

Before that time, the English had settled in Plymouth and Massachusetts Bay during the Sixteen-Twenties; colonization of Rhode Island, Connecticut, New Hampshire and lower Maine began soon after. Another stream of English settled in Maryland in 1634, and in Delaware and lower New Jersey soon after. Philadelphia, laid out in 1682, was settled by William Penn and his English Quakers. The Puritans of New England were very different from the Catholics and cavaliers (Anglicans) of Chesapeake Bay.

The Middle Atlantic provinces—New York, New Jersey and Pennsylvania —not only separated the two mainstreams of Anglo-Saxon settlement (New England and Virginia-Maryland tidewater) but they received the bulk of non-substantial support to a Republican coalition with a Southern-Western-New York Irish base.

5. The Non-Yankee Northeast

Besides the Yankee sections of the Northeast where Republican traditions are crumbling, there are other areas, traditionally Democratic and often Southern-oriented, where the GOP is gaining. This disparity relates back to varying Civil War reactions—and wartime political partisanship—rooted in different ethnic settlement, agricultural and socioeconomic patterns. A sizeable group of rural Northeasterners did not like Yankees, their Civil War or their Republican Party. And inasmuch as the Civil War was the fire from which arose much of the American party system of the next century, an analysis of the non-Yankee Northeast is obliged to begin with early colonial settlement patterns.

At the time of the signing of the United States Constitution, New England Yankeedom—almost entirely of English stock and largely Congregationalist (the Puritan-established church of several states) by religion—stood apart from nearby states to the west of New England, New York still showed many signs of its original Dutch settlers, especially the corridor of Dutch population reaching from New York City up the Hudson past Albany. Beyond the Dutch lived a small group of Palatine Germans, concentrated in the Schoharie Valley. New York also had Irish and Scottish elements, as well as quasi-feudal Anglican landholders (the DeLanceys and Livingstons) and Dutch patroons (the Schuylers, Van Cortlandts and Van Renssalaers). Other considerable numbers of Dutch lived in nearby northern New Jersey.

Even more than New York, Pennsylvania had a citizenry of di-

Anglo-Saxon immigrants. Germans first came to Schoharie, New York in 1713. However, their concentration soon switched to Pennsylvania. At about the same time, leasehold difficulties on the Ulster Plantations triggered an outpouring of Scotch-Irish who likewise emigrated, mainly to Pennsylvania. Both groups spread south and west down the Appalachian valleys.

The dotted line shows the extent of settlement in 1790. Thereafter, Yankee New England pushed west into upstate New York, northern Pennsylvania and lakeshore Ohio, while the Pennsylvania and Maryland Germans and Scotch-Irish moved south down the Appalachian valleys and west towards Pittsburgh and Ohio.

verse origin. As a result of successive waves of immigration, population spread across the state in ethnic layers. In the southeast, around Philadelphia, English and Welsh origins prevailed (a number of the English were Quakers, descendents of original settlers); next came Germans of varied Protestant sects who established themselves in the rich farming country north and west of Philadelphia; and after them came the Scotch-Irish who dominated the Cumberland and other Appalachian valleys. In 1790, one third of Pennsylvania's population was German and another third was Scotch-Irish. Nor was this unimportant. As New England began to expand westward during the Seventeen-Seventies and Eighties, ethnic and provincial emnities were such that pitched battles were actually fought between Yankees and non-Yankees, Pennsylvanians and New Yorkers.*

Despite an influx of Scotch-Irish and Germans into western Maryland from neighboring Pennsylvania, the predominant character of Maryland continued to be defined by the tidewater area around Chesapeake Bay where most of the state's population lived. Like Delaware Bay (lower New Jersey, Delaware and the southeastern corner of Pennsylvania), Chesapeake Bay was almost entirely English-settled. Otherwise the area bore less resemblance to Anglo-Saxon New England than to the Dutch, German and Scotch-Irish-tinged Middle Atlantic states. Lying below the Mason-Dixon line, Delaware, southern New Jersey and Maryland (especially the Eastern Shore of Chesapeake Bay) were—and still are—rich agricultural flatlands blessed with a 185-day growing season. Maryland and Delaware, finding slavery feasible, allowed it, even though they were not so well suited to the institution as states farther south. Agricultural productivity, together with abundant fish and waterfowl, made the Delaware and Chesapeake Bay areas a land of easy

---

*The area around what is now Wilkes-Barre, Pennsylvania witnessed three "Pennymite" wars. Immigrants from Connecticut, which state projected her boundaries west to encompass territory also claimed by Pennsylvania, took up residence and spurned Pennsylvania jurisdiction. Open conflict took place between armed forces of Connecticut men and Pennsylvanians three times beween 1770 and 1784. While the New Englanders were not dislodged, Pennsylvania sovereignty was eventually acknowledged. The populations of New York and New England were long separated by the Taconic and Berkshire mountains, but beginning in the Seventeen-Seventies, they clashed over the territory which was eventually to become the State of Vermont. The Green Mountain Boys, as the farmers of Vermont called themselves, defied the authority of both New Hampshire and New York, but they were particularly suspicious of New York with its patroons and Dutch, German and Scotch tenantry.

MAP 10

Scotch-Irish Pennsylvania

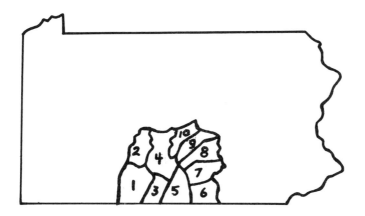

The counties of principal settlement are listed below along with towns evidencing the heritage of Northern Ireland and the western coast of Scotland and Northern England.

1. *Bedford County*
   Coleraine
   Londonderry

2. *Blair County*
   Blair
   Tyrone

3. *Fulton County*
   Ayr
   Belfast
   Dublin

4. *Huntington County*
   Barree
   Dublin

5. *Franklin*
   Antrim
   Hamilton
   Letterkenny
   Lurgan

6. *Adams County*
   Abbotstown
   Cumberland
   Hamilton
   Straban
   Highland

7. *Cumberland County*
   Carlisle

8. *Perry County*
   Duncannon
   Toboyne
   Tyrone

9. *Juniata County*
   East Waterford
   Fermanagh

10. *Mifflin County*
    Armagh
    Derry

living—in marked contrast to the rocks and rills of New England farmlands.*

As the Founding Fathers were drawing up the Constitution, Yankee New England was moving west, into the western New York and northern Pennsylvania lands cleared of Indians during the Revolution (isolating the upstate New York Dutch and Germans in the process); and the Scotch-Irish and Germans of Pennsylvania were moving south down the Appalachian highways and west into the Ohio Valley. It was not long before Northeastern settlement patterns had more or less stabilized; the frontier shifted to the Ohio Valley and Great Lakes and Northeastern sociopolitical alignments began to take shape. Map 9 illustrates the pattern and post-Revolutionary thrust of Northeastern settlement patterns. Rural Maryland and Delaware were definitely not Yankee; most of New Jersey and Pennsylvania were not; and by the early Nineteenth Century, the German-Dutch corridor stood out from the Yankee mass of upstate New York.

Although the political cleavage of the first half of the Nineteenth Century was not so much between Yankee and non-Yankee as between ethnic and economic rival groups, it is accurate to say that Yankees were wont to be Federalists and (later) Whigs, while the Germans, Dutch and Scotch-Irish gave enthusiastic support to the Jeffersonian and Jacksonian Democrats. Democratic Presidents Jackson and Polk were Scotch-Irish; Martin Van Buren was a Dutchman from New York's Hudson Valley; and James Buchanan, whose fate it was to preside over the disintegration of the Union, was a Scotch-Irish Pennsylvanian who came from German farming country.

For the most part, the Germans, Dutch and Scotch-Irish had little to do with—and did not hail—the formation of the Republican Party in 1854; nor did the tidewater Whigs of Maryland, Delaware and lower New Jersey who had frequently made cause with Yankee

---

*The contrast was vivid. New England's dour Puritans, unable to till a bountiful life from their stony fields, organized their lives, religion, politics and commerce to a degree unknown in the South. Puritans and dissenters even before they embarked for the new world, their asceticism matched their culinary style. The boiled codfish and "boiled dinners" of New England stood in marked contrast to the rich oyster stuffings and sherried terrapin of Chesapeake Bay. Along the hazy inlets of the Chesapeake, especially the Eastern Shore, cavaliers, farmers and fishermen—Catholics, Episcopalians, Methodists, but never Congregationalists—saw no good moral or local reason for adopting the highly organized life of New England, and they disliked Yankees, their strong governments and their omnipresent "causes."

New England on economic issues not involving slavery. The non-Yankee Northeast gave very little support to the Republican Party's first presidential bid in 1856. Chesapeake Bay voted for the conservative and nativist American (Know-Nothing) Party; the Scotch-Irish and German counties went handily Democratic; New York's Dutch (and increasingly Irish) Hudson River counties backed the Democratic presidential nominee; and the Delaware Bay area likewise opposed the new Republican movement. Of all these groups, the Scotch-Irish were the most Republican. Many Scotch-Irish were active in the anti-slavery underground railroads of southern Pennsylvania and others—among them Simon Cameron, soon to be governor—were about to join the new party.

Lincoln's election—a minority victory—witnessed little change in the patterns of 1856. Maryland and Delaware gave the GOP candidate minimal support and southern New Jersey went heavily against him. Nor did Lincoln carry New York's Hudson Valley. The only non-Yankee state in the Northeast to back Lincoln was Pennsylvania, where the Republican candidate fashioned his majority out of Yankee and some Scotch-Irish support over the ballot opposition of the state's large German minority.

Quite naturally, these partisan attitudes closely paralleled local feelings regarding the Civil War, the worth of which was questioned by much of the non-Yankee Northeast. As slave states, Maryland and Delaware even toyed with the idea of secession. Maryland voted to stay in the Union only after the Assembly moved from tidewater Annapolis, a strong pro-slavery center, to Frederick, where recalcitrant legislators could be overawed by federal troops. Martial law had to be imposed on Baltimore, and the Potomac tidewater counties—Prince Georges, Charles and St. Marys—were considered "occupied enemy territory" from the beginning of the war.* In Delaware, Major General Henry Du Pont, commanding officer of the state militia, headed off rising secession sentiments by wiring north for federal troops.

Disaffection in Pennsylvania and New Jersey was less widespread, and neither state threatened secession. However, Confederate agents actively encouraged the unrest of Pennsylvania Germans by reminding them of their cultural treatment at the hands of English-speaking Pennsylvanians. (The Pennsylvania Germans' frequent demands

---

*Gutheim, The Potomac (New York, 1954), p. 315.

for German-language schools and the keeping of official records in both German and English had always been denied.) The agents promised them that they would be given preferred status if they brought Pennsylvania into the Confederacy. The Pennsylvania German press usually referred to the war as the "Brothers' War," labeling it useless and contrary to German interests. Even Philadelphia had considerable Southern sentiment; an avowedly Confederate newspaper was published under the name "Palmetto Flag," and the city's social clubs contained so many Southern sympathizers that Unionists formed new clubs. The leading zealots organized the Union League club, the prototype of similarly named organizations which became the postwar bastions of industrial Republicanism. All during the war, suspicions of Confederate-inspired uprisings gnawed at Pennsylvania authorities. Finally, in 1864, Major General Darius Couch and a body of more than one thousand troups marched into Columbia County to storm an alleged fortress (complete with Confederate cannon smuggled in from Canada!) high above Fishing Creek near the Susquehanna. First a number of local Democrats were rounded up and sent to jail at Fort Mifflin; then the federal troops advanced. But there was no fortress: the Fishing Creek Confederacy did not exist. All that could be said of Columbia County, and of Pike County farther east in the Poconos, was that local hills were a haven for draft dodgers.

New Jersey, the only Northeastern state above the Mason-Dixon line which refused to support Lincoln, mixed war-doubting Dutch —"Bergen County Dutch"—and Southern-leaning outlooks. Cape May resorts drew their clientele from Washington, Richmond and Baltimore as well as Philadelphia; and Princeton attracted a large number of Southern students. The northern reaches of New Jersey looked to New York City; not so the rest of the state. In his book, *The Delaware,* Harry Emerson Wildes describes the factors which influenced the Delaware Bay area:

> Perhaps the key to the confusion lay in the geographic fact that Pennsylvania, Southern Jersey and Delaware lay on the borderline between North and South. Plantation farming in southeastern Pennsylvania bred a character not too unlike that of the leisured South; people of the Delaware had never been close friends with the "eastern states" nor with New York, but had close ties, socially and economically, with those who were now formal enemies. Delawareans and Jerseymen could not be

moved by northern propaganda that the South was vicious, corrupt and treacherous. Yet folk in Jersey, Delaware and Pennsylvania were no friends of slavery, and they loved the Union. It was extremely difficult to make a final choice, and ofttimes families split badly in deciding, but the weight of popular opinion lay finally on the northern side.*

Division also prevailed in New York State; not just in New York City, where the Irish were anti-Yankee, anti-Negro and quite pro-Southern, but along the Dutch-settled Hudson Valley and in German-populated Schoharie. During the war, the Hudson Valley and Schoharie remained Democratic, opposing Lincoln and casting gubernatorial ballots for Horatio Seymour. (Elected governor in 1862, Seymour was called a Copperhead by Republicans for his dubious view of the Civil War.)**

Understandably, the Civil War was a crucible of postwar politics as well as wartime dissent. Later partisanship jogged along in the ruts of wartime opinion. In the years between 1868 and 1896, Delaware, Maryland and New Jersey each supported only one GOP presidential nominee, and although Pennsylvania was loyally Republican by dint of machines in the industrial cities, much of the Susquehanna Valley and Pennsylvania German Country voted Democratic.*** From Schenectady to Yonkers, New York's Hudson Valley usually gave Democratic presidential nominees a majority, and, teaming up with New York City, often put New York State's electoral votes into the Democratic column. One non-Yankee area which strongly supported the Civil War—the Pittsburgh-centered Black Country of western Pennsylvania—voted Republican under the guidance of local party machines backed by powerful iron, coal and steel interests.****

Northeastern rural Democratic traditions shrank back somewhat

---

*Wildes, *The Delaware* (New York, 1940), p. 305.
**Mitchell, *Horatio Seymour* (Cambridge, 1938). The maps facing pp. 256, 382 and 474 show the concentration of Democratic voting strength in the Hudson Valley.
***Two German counties—Lancaster and Lebanon—were Republican. Both were rich farm counties; they were also the seats of Pennsylvania's Amish and other "plain" sects. Whig before the Civil War while other German counties were Democratic, Lancaster and Lebanon voted Republican thereafter.
****Greene County, in the extreme southwest of Pennsylvania, once a part of Virginia and originally settled from that state, was the laeding Democratic county in the western part of the state.

MAP 11

Rural Democratic Strength in the Non-Yankee Northeast, 1916

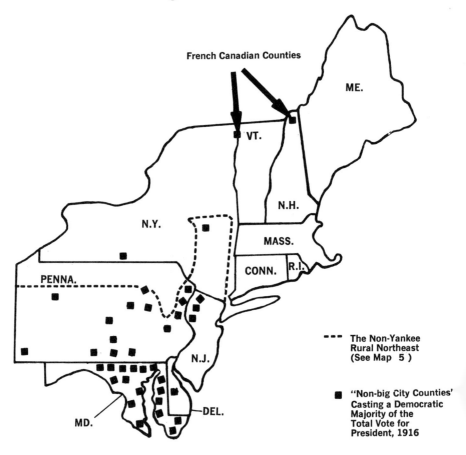

French Canadian Counties

ME.

VT.

N.H.

N.Y.

MASS.

PENNA.

CONN.   R.I.

- - - The Non-Yankee
Rural Northeast
(See Map 5)

N.J.

■ "Non-big City Counties'
Casting a Democratic
Majority of the
Total Vote for
President, 1916

DEL.

MD.

from William Jennings Bryan in 1896; his Wheat Belt and free silver radicalism offended the rich, rolling German farm counties and the bayside bailiwicks of the Delaware and Chesapeake. But Bryanism did not work any substantial re-alignment, and in 1916, although Wilson lost all of the Northeast states save New Hampshire and Maryland, he carried a substantial number of rural counties in the non-Yankee Northeast, as shown in Map 11. Meanwhile, not one rural Yankee county backed the scholarly president.

Eventually, the rise of the immigrant cities and the increasing coloration that they lent to the Democratic party of the Nineteen-

CHART 37

Presidential Voting in the Non-Yankee Northeast, 1916-68

Democratic Share of the Total Vote for President

County	1916	1920	1924	1928	1932	1936	1940	1944	1948	1952	1956	1960	1964	1968
New York														
Schoharie	57%	39%	35%	29%	45%	37%	36%	39%	37%	28%	27%	36%	63%	36%
Greene*	51	34	32	31	48	42	39	35	31	26	21	35	56	31
New Jersey														
Sussex	57	40	35	25	46	46	42	37	33	25	19	31	55	28
Pennsylvania														
Pike	63	39	34	30	52	51	41	34	30	27	23	30	51	29
Columbia	68	51	48	27	54	59	57	51	50	42	40	38	61	38
York	66	40	38	20	51	60	57	54	49	47	45	41	63	36
Greene	57	56	54	43	65	65	60	59	62	59	57	56	75	58
Maryland														
Frederick	52	44	45	37	59	53	52	43	42	35	35	43	61	31
Wicomico	58	54	54	41	64	53	60	53	51	39	36	46	54	29
Delaware														
Kent	53	52	50	41	57	56	53	53	49	49	47	50	59	36

*Greene County also includes a substantial Irish population.

Twenties began substantially to erode rural Democratic tradition. The first areas to crack were New Jersey's Delaware Valley and the Schoharie and Hudson valleys of New York. As the Democratic parties of both states came under full-fledged control by urban Catholics—led by Al Smith in New York and Jersey City's Frank Hague in the Garden State—the German Protestant rural areas began to shift to the Republicans. Schoharie County, New York, site of the original German Palatine settlement of 1713 and never before Republican in a presidential race, broke ranks in 1920 and remained Republican thereafter. Other New York counties, as well as Sussex and Warren counties in New Jersey, also historically Democratic, shifted to the GOP column in 1920. Of course, the movement was not confined to New York and New Jersey—rural Pennsylvania, Maryland and Delaware also trended Republican—but elsewhere the Democratic Party remained more attuned to rural and non-Catholic support. In New York and New Jersey, however, the rural re-alignment to the GOP was not to be undone.

Chart 37 illustrates the non-Yankee Republican trend of the Nineteen-Twenties. In 1928, when the nomination of Alfred E. Smith signaled the triumph within the Democratic Party of factions which were anathema to the countryside, the trot broke into a gallop and counties with well-nigh unbroken Democratic voting records went two- and three-to-one Republican. The trend was by no means wholly anti-Catholic; a broader spectrum of sociological objections —distaste for Tammany, Smith's flagrant violations of Prohibition and his raucous accent—was at work. Still, as seen in Chart 37, religion was clearly the major force behind the massive trends of counties like York and Columbia, Pennsylvania.*

Despite the mortal blow national Republicanism suffered in the Depression, party strength did not retreat uniformly across the non-Yankee Northeast. In hotbeds of anti-Catholicism like York and Columbia counties, the 1932 GOP vote share slipped about 30 per cent below religion-inflated 1928 levels (although remaining above 1916 levels), but counties like Schoharie, New York and Sussex, New Jersey, both reliably Democratic until 1920, remained Re-

---

*Anti-Catholic voting was particularly strong in southern and central Pennsylvania because of the deep-seated anti-Catholicism of the Scotch-Irish Presbyterians, the Lutherans, and the Reformed and German Protestants. Both the Germans and the Scotch-Irish had emigrated to America at a time when and from places where religious feeling ran high on each side.

publican in 1932 notwithstanding Hoover's hard times. A changing Democratic Party was leaving these counties behind.

As Chart 37 shows, most of the rural non-Yankee Northeast did not respond favorably to the urban, labor and ethnic minority group bias of the New Deal; Roosevelt's 1936 vote levels dipped well below those of 1932 (except in Pennsylvania). The President's slippage continued in 1940, although no ethnic factors gave the trend artificial size. Four years later, the Republicans gained again, and then again in 1948, although there were a few aberrations each year. Just as the urban, New Deal revolution solidified the Democratic hold on Northern cities, eradicating Civil War vestiges and machine holds, it shifted some rural Democratic areas into the Republican camp. (The principal hold-out area, despite its slow trend to the GOP, was Maryland's conservative Democratic and Southern-leaning Eastern Shore.)

There was, however, one major exception to the trend—a pro-New Deal movement by the western Pennsylvania Black Country. Not only the Catholics but the Appalachian whites of the steel towns, coal centers and railroad yards broke away from Republican machines to support the WPA and the multitude of other essential New Deal Democratic programs. Map 12 shows the Pennsylvania-Maryland-West Virginia-Ohio Appalachian industrial area drawn to the New Deal. In 1936, southwest Pennsylvania was far and away the most Democratic part of the state—Roosevelt swept the area by two-to-one majorities even though it had been strongly Republican during the Nineteen-Twenties. The Black Country is not really akin to the stereotyped rural non-Yankee Northeast of the Schoharie, Eastern Shore or Pennsylvania Dutch country; but neither is it a Catholic concentration set down among rural Yankees, and its Appalachian strain is an important element of non-Yankee Northeastern politics.

General Eisenhower was popular across the entire non-Yankee Northeast, albeit he did not win the core areas of the Pennsylvania Black Country in either 1952 or 1956. In the rural non-Yankee Northeast, he amassed support levels unprecedented except in the anti-Catholic outpouring of 1928. Only in the anti-Catholic reaches of rural Pennsylvania did Eisenhower fall well short of Hoover levels; and by no coincidence, it was only in these same areas that Richard Nixon, running in 1960 against Catholic John Kennedy,

MAP 12

The Appalachian Industrial Area

Bituminous Coal-Producing Areas

Cities

1. Cleveland, Ohio
2. Youngstown, Ohio*
3. Erie, Pennsylvania
4. Steubenville, Ohio
5. Wheeling, West Virginia*
6. Pittsburgh, Pennsylvania*
7. Morgantown, West Virginia
8. Cumberland, Maryland
9. Altoona, Pennsylvania
10. Johnstown, Pennsylvania*

*Steel-Producing Centers

gained over Eisenhower.* By the end of the Eisenhower years, there was not too much difference—on the presidential level—between the Republicanism of the rural Yankee and non-Yankee Northeast.

As the Nineteen-Sixties began, the rural Democratic bias of counties like Schoharie (New York), Sussex and Warren (New Jersey) and Pike (Pennsylvania) was a thing of the past, but Democratic tradition and local ballot dominance still persisted in Pennsylvania Dutch country and especially below the Mason-Dixon line in Maryland and Delaware. Whatever Richard Nixon's presidential majorities on the Delmarva peninsula, the area remained satisfied with Democratic state leadership epitomized by the old-line and rural-based administrations of Governor Tawes (Maryland) and Governors Carvel and Terry (Delaware). In these two states, the Democratic Party had not yet repudiated its old semi-Southern tra-

---

*Throughout the entire non-Yankee Northeast, Kennedy slid below Stevenson levels in only fifteen counties, all of them in rural Pennsylvania. Except for Appalachian Greene County, all of these counties were German and/or Scotch-Irish.

ditions. However, such a change was soon to begin as a result of the Negro socioeconomic revolution and the U.S. Supreme Court's "One Man, One Vote" decisions which transferred political power to the cities, destroying the rural support base of old-line Democratic machines.

In Maryland and Delaware, the civil rights revolution of the Nineteen-Sixties bore down heavily on local segregation patterns. Acting on behalf of African diplomats refused service on travels between New York and Washington, the federal government applied pressure to desegregate roadside facilities along the main highways. Resentments accumulated among white Marylanders until May, 1964, when Alabama Governor George C. Wallace almost won the state's Democratic presidential primary. (Only unanimous Negro opposition denied him victory.) Map 13 shows how Wallace's strength was negligible in western Appalachian Maryland, middling in the rolling foothills, heavy on all shores of Chesapeake Bay and fierce in the Southern-oriented Cambridge-Salisbury area of the Eastern Shore.

Much of the Chesapeake and Delaware Bay area experienced difficulty in the process of eradicating racial discrimination. Cambridge, Maryland, in the heart of the Eastern Shore, was troubled by racial friction from 1962 to 1964; finally, actual rioting broke out—one of the first of the mid-Sixties riots later to become so commonplace. However, notwithstanding these problems and the resentment evidenced by George Wallace's primary success, the Democratic Party not only avoided further losses but carried the Chesapeake and Delaware Bay areas in the 1964 presidential election.

Against a nominee other than Barry Goldwater, this might not have been possible. However, the Arizona Senator was fatally caricatured as an extremist. Only one county in the non-Yankee Northeast—Dorchester County, scene of the Cambridge, Maryland riots —gave Goldwater a better share of the vote than it had given to Nixon in 1960. Elsewhere, the Democrats gained—strongly in rural Pennsylvania, New Jersey and New York (where behavior was coming to resemble that of Yankee areas), moderately in the western Pennsylvania Black Country and to a somewhat lesser extent in Delaware and Maryland's Eastern Shore. Generally speaking, Goldwater pushed the GOP vote back to mid-depression levels, but here historic fidelities were not shattered as they were in the case of his

MAP 13

The Location of Support for George Wallace in Maryland, 1964-68

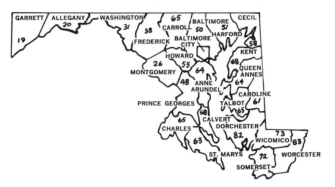

Percentage of Democratic Presidential Primary Vote Cast for
George C. Wallace, May, 1964 (By County)

Percentage of Total Vote for President Cast for
George C. Wallace, November, 1968 (By County)

Yankee losses. Whereas in 1936, the arch-Yankee counties of New
England had produced Republican support twenty-five percentage
points higher than that of the non-Yankee Northeast, the spread
narrowed to virtually nothing in 1964. For the first time, a GOP
presidential candidate fared much better on the Eastern Shore of
Maryland than in Yankee Vermont. Throughout the Northeast, the
civil rights revolution was overcoming Civil War political traditions.

But if Barry Goldwater's 1964 support in the non-Yankee Northeast was meaningful only in *relative* rather than *absolute* terms, the
absolute trend was confirmed by the 1966 elections. Reacting
against the social programs and philosophy of the Great Society,
the non-Yankee Northeast elected a number of new Republican

congressmen. In New England, New York, northern New Jersey and northern Pennsylvania, the GOP made a net gain of just two congressmen, recouping only a few of the dozen seats lost in the Goldwater landslide, but in southern Pennsylvania, southern New Jersey, Delaware and Maryland, the party recovered all three seats lost in 1964 and won two others.* Representative Rogers C. B. Morton, later to be Richard Nixon's 1968 pre-convention campaign manager, achieved an unprecedented 71 per cent re-election triumph in Maryland's Chesapeake Bay district even as Maine elected its first all-Democratic House delegation since the creation of the Republican Party.

As Civil War voting tradition ebbed between 1966 and 1968, the division of the Northeast into Yankee and non-Yankee segments became increasingly appropriate as a portrait of change, not just between the parties but within them—and especially within the ascending GOP. During the Ninetieth Congress, many Yankee Republicans in Congress showed a trend towards support of Great Society measures like open housing, rent subsidies and the War Against Poverty; not so the new Republican congressmen from Delaware, southern New Jersey and southern Pennsylvania. And in a like vein, the non-Yankee Northeast gave considerable Republican convention support to Richard Nixon while Yankeedom—save for the middle-level party stalwarts of upper New England—on balance preferred Nelson Rockefeller.

In 1968, rural non-Yankees broke against the Democrats more sharply than any other Northeastern voting stream save the New York Irish. Maryland, Delaware, southern New Jersey and south-central Pennsylvania differed with Yankeedom over government policies towards the Negro socioeconomic revolution just as they had held different opinions on the Civil War a century earlier. In contrast to its gains in the Yankee Northeast between 1960 and 1968, the Democratic Party suffered a loss of five to twenty-five percentage points in the non-Yankee Northeast (excluding Pennsylvania's Black Country) as conservatives lined up behind Richard Nixon and George Wallace. In 1968, Maryland and Delaware were the two worst Democratic states in the Northeast—even Vermont, New Hampshire and especially Maine gave Humphrey a higher

---

*Two southern New Jersey seats were regained, as was the York-Gettysburg district of Pennsylvania. The GOP also captured the At-Large Delaware seat and a newly created Maryland suburban district.

MAP 14

The Geography of 1968 Wallace Strength in the Northeast

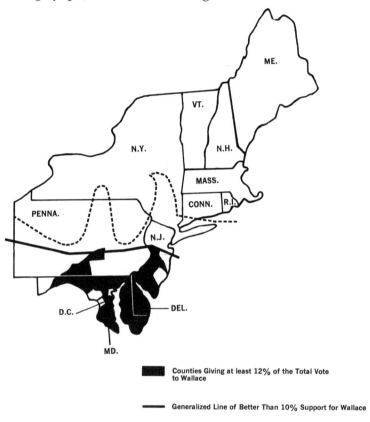

Counties Giving at least 12% of the Total Vote to Wallace

Generalized Line of Better Than 10% Support for Wallace

Generalized Line of Better Than 7% Support for Wallace

share of the total vote—and New Jersey was not far behind. As a result of Wallace inroads and straight GOP gains, Nixon's share of the two-party (Republican-Democratic) vote rose considerably over 1960 levels in formerly Democratic strongholds like Pennsylvania Dutch York County and the Eastern Shore of Maryland. (See Chart 37.) As for Wallace's support, Map 14 shows how it was concentrated near and below the Mason-Dixon line; only in Maryland, Delaware, southern New Jersey and a handful of south-central Pennsylvania counties did the American Independent candidate pull better than 12 per cent of the total vote.

By and large, Wallace support in the Northeast correlated with rural or Southern-oriented Democratic tradition rather than with blue-collar unionism. The highest Wallace votes in the non-Yankee Northeast thus came from conservative Democrats, the great majority of whom had been trending Republican and would have voted for Richard Nixon in a two-party contest, as had been indicated by the considerable GOP gains in the prior off-year elections. In all likelihood, the Wallace candidacy stimulated the erosion of Democratic voting habits among Maryland, Delaware and southern New Jersey conservatives, and this erosion, together with accelerating Democratic identification with Yankees and Negroes, should speed Republican gains.

But if traditionally Democratic rural and non-industrial areas of the Northeast moved away from the Democrats, the Black Country did not. Western Pennsylvania, as well as kindred Appalachian mining, steel and railroad centers in West Virginia, extreme western Maryland and eastern Ohio gave Hubert Humphrey a higher share of the major-party vote than John F. Kennedy had won in 1960. Lack of a religious issue played a part; late in the campaign, the Democrats trumpeted alleged Republican opposition to Social Security, Medicare, full employment, union-backed labor legislation and Appalachian aid programs, all vital concerns in the Black Country, and succeeded in scaring many voters; and what is more, George Wallace cut into the usual Republican vote while failing to divert anything like the predicted number of blue-collar Democrats. Solid majorities in the Black Country helped Humphrey to carry Pennsylvania.

Chart 38 shows how the Wallace strength in western Pennsylvania came from potentially Republican sources. Instead of reaching his best western Pennsylvania levels in the blue-collar precincts of Pittsburgh, Braddock or McKeesport, the former Alabama governor scored his best percentages in conservative lower-middle- and middle-class areas. The only two Allegheny County (Pittsburgh) townships to back Wallace were Kilbuck and Indiana; their GOP preference in other contests is shown below.

Except for the Black Country, the non-Yankee Northeast has clearly moved out of the Democratic orbit. In most of rural Delaware and Maryland, Hubert Humphrey's 1968 share of the total presidential vote was the lowest recorded for a Democrat since the Civil War, and in Pennsylvania Dutch country (Adams, York, Lebanon and Lancaster counties) and the Scotch-Irish citadels (Fulton, Perry, Franklin and Cumberland counties), only the re-

CHART 38

*The Republican Leanings of Wallace Strength in
    Western Pennsylvania, 1968**

Share of the Total Vote, 1968

	President			Senator	
Township	Wallace	Nixon	Humphrey	Schweiker (R)	Clark (D)
Kilbuck	52%	33%	15%	73%	27%
Indiana	56	21	23	57	43

ligious landslide of 1928 produced a smaller Democratic slice of the total vote for president. Along Maryland's Eastern Shore, a majority of the (few) votes cast for Humphrey came from local Negroes. Of course, George Wallace was responsible for much of the Democratic decline, but although he swung some conservative Democrats away from their party for the first time, he principally injured Richard Nixon by diverting non-Yankee traditional Democrats who had been trending Republican. If non-Yankee Northeastern movement towards a Southern- and Western-dominated GOP continues, as appears likely, then Wallace's third-party effort may be remembered as a way-station—even as far north as central Pennsylvania—for Democratic traditionalists following party realignment into the Republican Party. Under such a regime, the non-Yankee states of Maryland, Delaware, New Jersey and Pennsylvania would become the most likely Republican presidential campaign election targets in the Northeast.

6. The Catholics

    The emerging Democratic and liberal coalition of Negroes and silk-stocking voters is engendering an important conservative (and increasingly Republican) counter trend among working-class and lower-middle-class Catholics. This is yesteryear's Al Smith electorate, anti-establishmentarian today (albeit less obviously) as it was upon disembarkation a century ago.

    The first and foremost group of Catholic immigrants to arrive in the United States was the Irish; next in chronology and importance were the Germans. Both streams of migration increased sharply in

*Statistics revised by Pennsylvania Board of Elections substantially changed figures, but were received too late for inclusion.

CHART 39

Immigration to the United States, 1820-1910

Number of Immigrants Coming to the United States By Decade

Immigrant Group	1820-30	1830-40	1840-50	1850-60	1860-70	1870-80	1880-90	1890-1900	1900-10
Total European	98,817	495,688	1,597,501	2,452,660	2,065,270	2,272,262	4,737,046	3,558,978	8,136,016
			The Irish-German Era						
Irish	50,724	207,381	780,719	914,119	435,778	436,871	655,482	388,416	339,065
German	6,761	152,454	434,626	951,667	787,468	718,182	1,452,970	505,152	341,498
								The Eastern European and Italian Era	
Italian	409	2,253	1,870	9,231	11,725	55,759	307,309	651,893	2,045,877
Russian*	75	277	551	457	2,512	39,284	213,282	505,290	1,597,306
Austro-Hungarian (includes Polish)*	NR	NR	NR	NR	7,800	72,969	353,719	592,707	2,145,266

NR—Not Reported

*Includes a substantial number of Jews.

Note—During the years of preponderantly Irish and German immigration, many of the remaining immigrants were British and Scandinavian. Northern European immigration was strongly dominant until 1890.

the late Eighteen-Forties after Ireland's appalling potato famine and the suppression of the 1848 revolutions in Europe. Before long, Catholics were numerous enough throughout much of the Protestant Northeast to excite harsh nativist feelings which gave excuse for violence, birth to the Know-Nothing party and coloration to the generally anti-Catholic Whigs. Chart 39 structures the mid-century impact of Irish and German immigration; these two groups dominated the arrival lists until the Eighteen-Eighties.

Although quite a few Catholics went to Pennsylvania, lower New Jersey, Delaware and Maryland—Philadelphia had anti-Irish riots and Baltimore absorbed enough Germans to support many a brewery—most came ashore at New York City or points north. Once in America, the Irish took to politics like ducks to water, utilizing their unique familiarity (among immigrant groups) with Anglo-Saxon language, customs and political institutions. Almost to a man, they became Democrats, taking up cudgels first against the pro-British Federalists and later against the bourgeois and frequently anti-Catholic Whigs. Local politics offered the Irish a chance to continue the rivalries of the old country—on more advantageous terms. Most German Catholics found themselves on the same side as the Irish. By the Civil War, the Irish were a major political influence in New York City, trans-Hudson New Jersey, Albany and Boston.*

When the Civil War came, the Irish were not too enthusiastic. For one thing, the Washington representatives of the devoutly Democratic New York Irish had worked in close partisan harness with Southern congressmen. And unlike other Northern Democrats of more establishmentarian caste, the Irish did not seek to vanquish the South in order to end slavery and extend the sphere of existing Northern culture and influence westward. On the contrary, the

*In these cities, where the Irish lived in large numbers, they stamped an unmistakable imprint on local politics. New York's Tammany Hall, the archetypal Irish political institution, was founded by William Mooney, an Irish Catholic upholsterer in 1789. To a large degree, the Irish reproduced the climate of political morality which they had known in British-ruled Ireland. Daniel Moynihan has described how the Irish not only repeated the British practice of selling titles, jobs and elections, but recreated the central role which the saloonkeeper had occupied in old-country political life, and—in Tammany's clubhouse system of extreme (Assembly district) parochialism and required submission to a slow, conformist advance through a hierarchy of prestige—more or less duplicated the basic social system of an Irish village. Glazer and Moynihan, *Beyond the Melting Pot* (Cambridge, 1963), pp. 223-228. Colorfully named gangs—the Dead Rabbits, for example—were another seemingly inevitable fact of Celtic politics from Nineteenth-Century New York to the Kansas City, Missouri of Pendergast-Truman days.

typical Irishman feared Negroes as cheap labor competitors, Yankees as bigoted, self-serving moralists and industrialists as enemies of the working class. A few of New York City's leading Democrats were openly pro-Southern and anti-Lincoln; there was even talk of secession.*

The most striking evidence of Irish unrest occurred in New York City in 1863. Infuriated by military conscription which the rich could avoid by paying $300 for a substitute, thousands of New York Irish rioted in the streets, attacking both Negroes and such Establishmentarian institutions as Brooks Brothers clothing store and the offices of the *Herald Tribune.* Similar sociological instinct drew the mob toward the Wall Street financial district, but the authorities were able to turn them back. In the end, the death toll was considerable. Local Democratic politicians were not too firm with the rioters, but the Protestant Republican Establishment seethed with indignation. There was no redress of socioeconomic grievance; the Establishment labeled the rioters as carrion and cartoonist Thomas Nast—he is credited with originating the Republican elephant—drew the Irish as gorillas.

Elsewhere in the Northeast there was less trouble, although troops were needed (or requested) to put down Irish-stirred insurrections in Albany, Newark and the Pennsylvania anthracite country. New York's Irish, it should be added, carried their doubts about the Civil War just so far. Regiment upon regiment of them fought in Union blue—one regiment under Tammany Sachem Colonel William Kennedy. But very few of the Irish embraced the overall war with the ideological fervor of the Yankee Republicans, and New York City voted strongly against Lincoln in 1864 as it had in 1860.

The caste and class overtones of the Civil War further ingrained the Democratic bias of the largely lower-class Irish and Germans. And when the war was over and Reconstruction at an end, New York City's Irish Democratic politicians fell back into their old pattern of cooperation with the South in Washington and Tammany spoilsmanship at home. By the last quarter of the Nineteenth Cen-

*Fernando Wood, New York City's flamboyant mayor at the beginning of the Civil War, went so far as to say "It would seem that a dissolution of the Federal Union is inevitable. . . . It cannot be preserved by coercion or held together by force. . . . With our aggrieved brethren of the Slave States we have friendly relations and a common sympathy. . . . Why should not New York City, instead of supporting by her contributions in revenue two-thirds of the expenses of the United States, become also equally independent?" Connable and Silberfarb, *Tigers of Tammany* (New York, 1967), p. 134.

tury, Tammany was practically an Irish institution under sachems like "Mister" Murphy and "Honest John" Kelly; most key places in the organization were held by Irishmen. The same was true of the Democratic Party in Boston. Having been denied office by the Yankees in bygone days, the Irish reciprocated when their municipal day arrived in the Eighteen-Eighties.

At the turn of the century, the Irish controlled New York City (Irish-run Brooklyn had become a part of the city in 1898), Boston, Albany, Jersey City and some lesser cities, and they dominated the Democratic state parties of New York and New England. By and large, Irish immigration sought out the Northern climes which had also beckoned Yankeedom. And this contrast between the vocal working-class Catholic minority and the Calvinistic Anglo-Saxon majority, inevitable combatants, gave Northeastern politics its basic cleavage. In the more southerly states of Delaware and Maryland, together with much of Pennsylvania and lower New Jersey, Irish numbers were smaller, and the 1896-1932 era of Republican hegemony found many of them mute adherents of GOP machines (Philadelphia, Scranton, Pittsburgh, Camden and Wilmington) scattered through a closely divided countryside. If Irish politics derived strength from numbers, cohesion came from proximity to the Yankee enemy.

But not all of the cities of New York and New England were run by Irish Democrats, not even many that were predominantly Catholic. In the last quarter of the Nineteenth Century, the industrial prosperity of Yankeeland drew many non-Irish Catholics to the mills and factories; many of these last-wave immigrants came from Southern and Eastern Europe, others from the rural poverty of neighboring Quebec.* Whereas the German Catholics had been—and remained—mostly allies of the Irish (in New York City), the Italians, Poles and French Canadians who began to pour into Yankeeland in the late Nineteenth Century disliked the exclusionary brogue of the Democratic Party. Along with the Portuguese of coastal Massachusetts, all of these blocs were thus induced to give considerable

*Maps 15 through 18 show the location of the Irish, Italian, Polish, Slavic and French Canadian populations of the Northeast. In New England, the Catholics are concentrated in the major cities and in the factory towns, except for the French Canadians, considerable numbers of whom are dispersed along the United States-Quebec border. The New York City area harbors the great (Italo-Irish) concentration of the Middle Atlantic states. In Pennsylvania, the coal mines and steel towns are the focal point of the state's Catholic population, which includes the nation's largest Czech-Polish-Hungarian-Slav bloc.

The Catholic Northeast

MAP 15

*Major and Minor Irish Concentrations**

MAP 16

Major and Minor Italian Concentrations

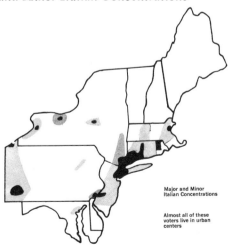

*Older Irish immigration no longer identifiable from Census data.

MAP 17

Major and Minor Slavic, Czech and Polish Concentrations

Major and Minor Slavic,
Czech and Polish
Concentrations

These voters are mostly
located in mining and
industrial centers.

MAP 18

Major and Minor French Canadian Concentrations

Major and Minor French
Canadian Concentrations

Especially along the
Canadian frontiers, many of
these voters are rural as
well as urban. The population
along the border, while
heavily French, is not
numerous.

support to the Yankee Republicans. In a few cities—Rochester is an example—even the Irish adhered to the local Republican machine, and throughout New England, there were small towns and cities where Yankee industrialists and mill-owners controlled their employees' ballots. The Republican predilections of all of these working-class Catholics were reinforced by the Democratic campaign of 1896; William Jennings Bryan's aggressive agrarianism and evangelical Protestantism did not please them, and they were likewise scared by employer threats that Bryan's election would force the closing of the mills.* The Grand Old Party had a clever and implicitly threatening slogan—McKinley's "full dinner pail"—and profited considerably from it.

Well before the turn of the century, Yankees no longer cast a majority of the vote in Massachusetts and Rhode Island—the result of heavy Catholic immigration and the Yankee Exodus—but strategic appeals to the non-Irish ethnic groups kept both states unfailingly in the GOP presidential column.** In New York, the numerous Italian and Jewish arrivals of the Eighteen-Nineties and thereafter gave as much support to the Republicans as to the Democrats. To unite the ethnic groups and dethrone the Yankees, the Irish needed a cause greater than their own fortunes—and they rarely had one.

Until the Nineteen-Twenties, neither of the two major parties had a decisive rural or urban bias on a *national* basis. True, the Irish cities gave the Democrats a large urban toehold, but other major cities—Philadelphia in particular—were Republican; and although the rural Yankee Northeast was solidly Republican, non-Yankee sections of the rural Northeast (and, of course, the South) were traditionally Democratic. Still, although either party could, in theory at least, have embraced a national urban orientation, the Democrats enjoyed a clear institutional and sociological headstart. Despite the basic conservatism of the Northeastern Irish Democratic hierarchies, the Irish were underdogs; they were Catholic; and they understood the essential problems of the urban working class much better than did the Yankee and Protestant GOP oligarchy. By its very establishmentarian nature, the Republican Party could not become the vehicle of anti-establishmentarian Catholic political self-assertion, while the Irish Democratic machines, albeit rarely in the

*The Irish alone among the Catholic blocs generally stuck by Bryan in 1896.
**The Republicans did not offer the newly arrived ethnic groups much by way of jobs; they used economic leverage and power and played on anti-Irish feeling.

vanguard of progressivism, were often obliged by the socioeconomic status of their flocks to further a necessary amount of social and economic reform.

The forging of an urban progressive majority was not easy. Many of the Irish politicians were actors, scoundrels and rogues who enjoyed their clubhouses, saloons, volunteer fire companies, police parades and municipal contract graft; only a few who were more perspicacious gave careful leadership to the fight for badly needed legislation.* Under the prodding of Alfred E. Smith, New York's Tammany Hall, although unpopular with intellectuals and the liberally inclined (Republican or Socialist) majority of Jews, did sponsor some important reform measures.

World War I and its after-effects also put a crimp in the emerging ethnic and reform coalition. To many Catholics, not least the Irish and German pillars of the Democratic Party, Woodrow Wilson's foreign policies were extremely unpopular. Germans understandably resented Democratic-sponsored United States participation in the war with the *Vaterland*—all the more so after the Peace of Versailles dismembered Germany and showed the cynicism of Allied aims. Many Irish voters were infuriated by United States intervention of 1917 in support of a Great Britain which had just put down Ireland's Easter Rebellion (1915), and Anglophile Woodrow Wilson proceeded further to antagonize Erin's sons by countenancing British refusal to discuss Irish independence at the peace conference. Even Italo-Americans took umbrage at the war—and at the failure of Italy to receive the Adriatic port of Fiume. One can exaggerate the importance of the purely territorial aspects of the peace conference as a factor in ethnic ballot unrest; it may be truer to say that ill-fated United States participation in European war and diplomacy caused a general stress and identity crisis among hyphenated Americans and evoked a "return to normalcy" support of Republican presidential nominee Warren Harding.

At any rate, the ethnic anti-Democratic vote of 1920 was quite emphatic. Enough Irish voters deserted the party ticket to put Boston

*Two New Yorkers who epitomized the worst Irish rascal style of the early Twentieth Century were First Deputy City Clerk James J. McCormick, who ultimately accumulated $385,000 in gratuities from couples he married, and Brooklyn Registrar (later Sheriff) James "Peter-to-Paul" McQuade, who banked $520,000 in six years, all money allegedly borrowed here and there to support relatives—"the thirty-four starving McQuades." Boston and Jersey City had many like them, and all in all, the Irish political opportunists far outnumbered those Celtic officials and legislators actually concerned with economic and social reform.

in the Republican column; Jersey City and Albany likewise broke ranks; and only one Irish assembly district in New York City (Manhattan's "Gas House") supported Democratic presidential candidate Cox. The Italian, German and Jewish trend was also important. Chart 40 shows the Irish, Italian and German voting patterns of the Nineteen-Twenties in New York City.

CHART 40

Irish, Italian and German Presidential Voting in Manhattan, 1920-32

Share of the Total Vote Cast for President*

	Republican	Democratic	Third-Party	
1920				
Irish	50%	47%	3%	
Italian	50	47	3	} Socialist
German	61	28	11	
1924				
Irish	25	63	12	
Italian	44	48	8	} Progressive
German	37	46	17	
1928				
Irish	18	82		
Italian	23	77		
German	27	73		
1932				
Irish	19	81		
Italian	21	79		
German	20	80		

*The figures represent the vote cast by sanitation districts better than 70 per cent populated by the ethnic group in question; they are taken from Burner, *The Politics of Provincialism* (New York, 1967), pp. 234-236.

This Republican strength did not last. For example, thirteen New York Republican congressmen, by-products of the 1920 landslide, lost their seats in 1922. But whatever the recovery of local Democrats, the national Democratic Party did not take up the positions needed to appeal to the Catholic vote. New York Governor Al Smith, re-elected in 1922 after defeat in 1920, sought the Democratic presidential nomination in 1924, only to fall slightly short of victory. Torn between the rising Catholic power of the cities and the old-line Protestant South and West (ebbing Bryanism), the Democratic party compromised, and in the process refused by a majority of one vote at the 1924 convention to condemn the Ku Klux Klan. As a compromise Democratic presidential candidate, Wall Street corporation lawyer John W. Davis ignited no passions on the sidewalks of New York or anywhere else in the Catholic Northeast, so that even laconic, coldfish, typical Yankee Calvin Coolidge was able to garner a plurality of the vote in many urban Catholic districts.*

As Chart 39 shows, so many Southern and Eastern European immigrants came to the United States in the period between 1890 and World War I that the national Northern European Protestant majority finally moved to cut off immigration in the early Nineteen-Twenties. However, by that time the demographic die had been cast, and the Italians, Jews and Slavs of the Northeast began to come of political age, although their loyalties awaited full commitment.

In 1928, the urban Catholic wing won control of the Democratic Party by achieving the presidential nomination of Governor Smith. But the Governor did more than stamp the Democratic Party with the image sought by urban, immigrant America; he flaunted his origins and beliefs with a parochialism that smacked of a lack of concern for rural Protestant America. He consumed his highballs in practically open mockery of the Prohibition laws; he was unnecessarily willing to reaffirm his ties to the nationally suspect Tammany Hall; he paid little attention to speech patterns which grated on rural ears; and he participated in certain Catholic religious ceremonies—ones he was not obliged to—in such fashion as to heighten church-state separation fears.** Smith's image offended the countryside, prompting an unprecedented GOP rural landslide, even as it occasioned a vast gain for the Democratic Party in the Northern Catholic cities. In the long run, Democrats lined

---

*Many Catholic voters split away from the Democrats to back the third-party Progressive candidacy of Senator Robert LaFollette. The Wisconsin Senator's candidacy was strongest in the Farm Belt, Rocky Mountains and Pacific. However, he also showed some strength in the working-class East.

**Years later, Smith himself recognized how parochial he had allowed himself to appear. His actions are discussed at length in Burner, *The Politics of Provincialism* (New York, 1968), pp. 180-216.

up on the side of the urban revolution—a decisive breakthrough which outlived the year's transient (largely religious-based) losses.

Quite naturally, Smith scored his sharpest gains over John W. Davis in New York and in New England, more particularly in the urban Catholic centers. In Boston, Fall River, New Bedford, Springfield and New York City, the Democratic presidential vote share climbed more than 25 per cent over 1924. Chart 10 lists the Democratic improvement by states and Chart 40 shows the gains Smith made among the Irish, Italian and German blocs in New York City.

As it happened, Smith won such heavy Catholic support in 1928 that Franklin D. Roosevelt was not always able to match it in 1932, despite the advent of the Depression. Heavily French Catholic Clinton County, New York, gave Hoover 1 per cent greater support in 1932; Hoover's vote climbed 6 per cent in Elk County, Pennsylvania (a mining section with the state's highest ratio of Catholics); and F.D.R.'s 1932 support in Boston fell six thousand votes short of that won by Al Smith. Granted that Smith's 1928 candidacy had drawn Catholic urban blocs towards the Democratic Party, the 1932 vote suggests that much Catholic support for Smith was purely religious, and that without the Depression, a non-Catholic like Roosevelt might have slipped considerably below the levels reached by the Happy Warrior.

In retrospect, the urban Catholic commitment to the Democrats in 1928 was tentative; the Depression transferred the religion-achieved levels of 1928 to a non-Catholic in 1932; and in most cases, the New Deal policies of 1933-36 confirmed or ingrained these sociopolitical loyalties. A few Republican machines bucked the tide in 1928 and 1932, but by 1936 urban Catholic support for the Democratic Party was solid.

To the Irish, the New Deal brought a large treasure-trove of power and patronage. In the Northeast, a very large proportion of Democratic county chairmen and party officials were Irish; they had been faithful throughout the lean years and now they gathered in spoils accordingly. But in another sense, the enlargement of the Democratic Party into a national majority and a force for social change promised to undo urban Irish hegemony. Under the auspices of the New Deal, no small part of which was anathema to the socially conservative Irish Democratic hierarchy, Poles, Italians, Jews and intellectuals began to come increasingly to the fore in the Democratic Party, originating and implementing new programs and policies for which Roosevelt and the Depression had fashioned a majority. Comfortable in their old role as the leaders of an institutionalized, parochially powerful and only occasionally progressive opposition to the conservative Yankee Establishment, the entrenched Irish Democratic machines were not suited to innovative social programming and leadership.* As the New Deal took hold and became an ongoing cause, non-Irish ethnic groups looked for ways of supporting Roosevelt *without* supporting the local Irish Democratic Party. Nowhere was this feeling stronger than among New York City's Jewish-run labor unions—and this liberal dissidence quickly took shape in the form of the (New York) American Labor Party.

Except among the Irish and the kindred Germans, Roosevelt increased his Catholic support between 1932 and 1936. Even as New Deal economic and labor reforms solidified upper-class toryism, they fully convinced the Catholic working-class and white-collar voters of the Northeast that the Democratic Party had their best interests at heart. Throughout the Northeast, urban and industrial counties which had been closely fought in 1932 (often with little change over 1928) went handily for Roosevelt in 1936.**

Roosevelt's minor 1936 German and Irish losses were not attributable to Republican gains but to the isolationist inroads of Congressman William Lemke, the presidential candidate of the right-wing Union Party. World War II was slipping into focus by November, 1936: Hitler had already moved into the Rhineland. Civil War was raging in Spain, pitting Franco and the army—with moral support from the Catholic Church and military aid from the Nazis and Fascists—against the Spanish leftists, whose support came from the Communist-led International Brigade and Lincoln Brigade—and from the Soviet Union. Isolationists generally felt that Soviet Russia was as much or more of a threat to America

*Many Irish machine adherents saw politics as a game and as a vehicle of (Irish) group status and power. Social change—the displacement of *their* interests as well as those of the conservative Establishment—was not their goal. Nor did they like some elements of New Deal wlfare legislation. WPA projects, with their familiar patronage and navvy gang overtones, were acceptable, but government-provided social services undermined the position of the political clubhouse as the guardian and benefactor of grateful needy voters. *Established* Irish Democratic machines were often at odds with the forces unleashed by the New Deal.

**The sharpest Democratic gains came in industrial Pennsylvania where New Deal socioeconomic legislation and the 1934 downfall of the state GOP machine created a good climate for party pickup over the slim, machine-gathered Hoover triumph of 1932.

than was Nazi Germany, and they were also disposed to support Franco's side in Spain. American Catholics were particularly likely to give approval to Franco, praising the Church-backed insurgent cause and overlooking its alliance with Nazis and Fascists. They saw Spain as a bulwark against atheistic communism. Liberals and leftists invariably favored the Soviet-backed Spanish Loyalists. Political analyst Samuel Lubell has written how voter attitudes towards the Spanish Civil War delineated mainstreams in American and especially Democratic politics, the conservative side thereafter frequently breaking away in presidential elections as a result of disagreement with liberal internationalist Democratic foreign policies.*

Although the 1936 Lemke candidacy was not very important in the Northeast (its focal point was the Midwest), it achieved some importance in Irish and German Catholic areas. Union Party ballots were most numerous in Massachusetts, reaching 15 per cent to 25 per cent of the total in Irish wards of Boston, Lowell, Lawrence and Cambridge; elsewhere in New England, Lemke did fairly well in Irish precincts of Providence, Rhode Island, and Manchester, New Hampshire. Doubtless the German and Irish assembly districts of New York City would have given some comfort to the North Dakota isolationist, but the Union Party was not on the New York ballot.

Besides the populist isolationism Lemke brought to the surface in working-class Irish districts, another form of Irish discontent was taking shape in areas of cohesive and longtime group power— middle-class and upper-class distaste for the New Deal, its philosophy of government and its sociological impact on Democratic Party leadership. Such discontent was keenest in New York City, where Irish power had flowered first and most fully.** After opposing Roosevelt at the 1932 Democratic convention, Tammany failed to mend the breach. In turn, Roosevelt gave overt support to New York's anti-Tammany "Fusion" Mayor Fiorello LaGuardia, elected to office in 1933 and kept there in later years by a coalition of Italian, Jewish, Negro and silk-stocking voters. Few Irish Demo-

*Samuel Lubell, *Revolt of the Moderates* (New York, 1956).
**But while *established* Irish machines and their flocks often resented New Deal upheaval, things were different in cities of Pennsylvania, upstate New York and New England where the Roosevelt Revolution turned Irish-led Democratic *minorities* into *majorities*. In such localities, the Irish were second to none in their applause for the New Deal.

crats had joined Al Smith in bolting to support the Republican presidential nominee in 1936. But as 1940 approached, anti-Roosevelt sentiment grew because of (a) the third-term issue; (b) Roosevelt's pro-British foreign policy impetus; (c) the Roosevelt-approved formation in New York of the American Labor Party—designed to give liberals (mostly Jewish) a chance to back the New Deal without supporting the Tammany party; and (d) the President's 1938 attempt to purge Irish conservatives from the party.

Despite the multiple Irish grievances, the principal factor in the 1940 election—Irish, Jewish, Yankee, French and Italian trends all pivoted on this one issue—was Hitler's war and Franklin D. Roosevelt's plans with regard to it. Pre-war Irish opinion was so strongly opposed to United States intervention in another pro-British war that Roosevelt felt obliged to reassure a Boston audience that their sons would not be sent to fight overseas—a campaign pledge he probably did not expect to honor. As for the Italians, the President had alienated many of them by labeling Mussolini's last-minute 1940 attack on Hitler-prostrated France a "stab in the back." Perhaps it was, but Italo-Americans were sensitive to such analogies. Chart 12, which shows the ethnic pattern of 1940 trends, also conveys their particular intensity in Catholic areas of greater New York.

Historically, the trend-setting Catholic precincts have been those of New York City, the first and longtime citadel of Irish politics. In this vortex of Catholic conflict with the Protestant Establishment and other non-Catholic ethnic groups, Irish voting patterns have generally forecast the cyclical direction of Catholic politics. This was true in the Jacksonian prelude of the Eighteen-Twenties and in the Al Smith struggle of the Nineteen-Twenties—even if Gaelic wishes did not control the ensuing eras. The remote milltowns, where there is a directional lag in social conflict, also lag politically. Even in 1940, only eight years after the commencement of the New Deal cycle, the fact that the sharpest Republican trend in the East came in the Catholic Democratic bastions of New York City hinted at the next direction of Catholic politics.

Obviously, much of the Irish, German and Italian trend of 1940 stemmed from the ethnic stress of the war in Europe and related Rooseveltian foreign policy. But the 1940 vote was not the transient Republicanism of 1920—a short-lived adherence totally dissipated by 1928. While some of the wartime anti-Roosevelt voters would return to the Democratic Party in peacetime, many others were to

remain alienated by the liberal internationalism which had plunged one generation of Americans into two wars and imposed a considerable strain on the psyches (although not the loyalty) of several major ethnic groups. In this way, an important new source of Republican votes took general shape as part of the membership of the groups experiencing their second wartime trauma began to forge pervasive isolationist and anti-Establishment attitudes akin to those enunciated by the increasingly dominant Midwestern wing of the Republican Party. Samuel Lubell has described this phenomenon as the "politics of revenge"—a desire to justify retrospectively in patriotic terms foreign policy beliefs originally rooted in ethnic stress.*
This behavioral stream persisted long after peace returned to Europe.

Despite the Catholic isolationist Republican surge of 1939-45, Franklin D. Roosevelt retained a solid majority of the Northeastern Catholic vote, perhaps 60 per cent in New York and 70 per cent in New England. This degree of Catholic support, however, would not have sufficed to overcome Protestant GOP strength in New York in 1940 or 1944; Roosevelt's Empire State majorities depended on lopsided Jewish support.

The end of the war and the death of President Roosevelt removed the immediate sources of the disaffection of many Catholics from the Democratic Party. And perhaps more to the point, the new Democratic President, Harry S. Truman, did not grate on isolationist or anti-establishmentarian nerves. Truman indicted Russia as America's principal enemy. Furthermore, he had not preferred Russia to Germany during the pre-Pearl Harbor era, and he pursued a generally anti-Soviet foreign policy.** A onetime county judge, National Guard captain and unsuccessful haberdasher, he hobnobbed with Irish politicians, flailed Wall Street, tolerated a considerable amount of cronyism and graft, and was, in sum, quite acceptable to many of the Democrats who had opposed the patrician, Anglophile and condescending Franklin Delano Roosevelt.

Running in 1948 for election to the White House in his own right, Truman did very well among Northeastern Catholics. In Massachu-

---

*Lubell, *The Revolt of the Moderates* (New York, 1956), pp. 52-74.
**In 1941, Truman had said: "If we see that Germany is winning, we ought to help Russia, and if Russia is winning we ought to help Germany and that way let them kill as many as possible, although I don't want to see Hitler victorious under any circumstances." Adler, *The Isolationist Impulse* (New York, 1961), p. 285.

setts, where a birth control referendum brought out a whopping Catholic vote, Truman approached Roosevelt's 1936 highs, winning more votes in arch-Catholic Boston than Roosevelt ever did. But Boston's satisfaction with the Democratic party was not matched by the Catholic areas of New York City, where minority group influence (there was practically none in Boston), gave the party a socially liberal cast and whetted foreign policy conflicts and memories. Even though Truman gained stature among Catholics as a result of his unpopularity with the leftist- and Jewish-dominated American Labor Party, he failed to carry Italo-Irish Staten Island and (then) Irish-German Queens, the two most Catholic counties of New York City. Chart 41 shows how most of the Queens and

CHART 41

New York Catholic Presidential Voting Trends, 1936-48

	Republican Share of the Total Vote for President			
	1936	1940	1944	1948
New York City				
Queens (German-Irish)	33%	53%	55%	51%
Richmond (Irish-Italian)	33	50	57	54
Nearby New Jersey				
Passaic (Italian)	40	48	50	46
Hudson (Irish-Italian)	22	34	38	37
Upstate New York				
Oneida (Utica-Rome; Italian)	51	52	50	48
Albany (Irish)	42	43	46	43

Staten Island voters who trended Republican in 1940 remained with the GOP in 1948. Upstate New York Catholics were less responsive to wartime or social conflict trends; the Jewish-Catholic conflict in New York City and environs had a unique effect in sharpening the policy animosities which were driving politically conservative Catholics into the Republican Party.

Before long, Truman lost the vigorous anti-Communist image he had enjoyed in 1948. Names like Harry Dexter White and Alger Hiss began to figure prominently in public conversation; evidence of Communist subversion of the government and foreign policy of the United States began to mount. Republican orators launched an attack on World War II policies, especially F.D.R.'s Yalta agreement with Stalin, as Communist-influenced, and this general approach evoked an enthusiastic response among Irish, Germans and Italians (many of them convinced since 1936, for one reason or another, that the Soviet Union, not Germany or Italy, was America's principal enemy, and that United States policies were unduly "soft" on communism). Finally, in June, 1950, North Korean troops crossed the 38th parallel and the cold war turned hot.

Although the isolationist contingent of Irish, Italians and Germans supported the anti-Communist struggle in Korea, many of them also saw the struggle as evidence of exactly the Communist threat they had postulated a decade earlier; this resurrected their resentment of Rooseveltian foreign policies and engendered a feeling that the Korean "police action" could have been avoided. Frustration grew, and with it Democratic vulnerability. Into this sociopolitical gap rode a young United States Senator from Wisconsin, a man with roots among rural German Catholics and the physiognomy of the Black Irish—Joseph McCarthy.

The Junior Senator from Wisconsin suggested that America's difficulties lay in conspiracy, subversion and betrayal by the Establishment. From his first statement in Wheeling, West Virginia, in May, 1950—he claimed to have in his hand a list of a specific number of Communists in the U.S. State Department—he probed ever deeper towards the jugular vein of anti-Establishment politics. Not only did he blame World War II policy mistakes on Communist subversion, but he blamed the Protestant Establishment for both treason and old school tie tolerance of it. He was by no means entirely wrong on either point, and the prospering new middle classes enjoyed hearing privilege and education correlated with treason or lack of patriotism.

As the Korean War lost popularity and bogged down, and the Administration seemingly refused to take the same firm line against the Soviet Union that had been taken against Hitler and Mussolini —Truman's dismissal of MacArthur fueled this fire—McCarthy's plausibility and political importance grew. A powerful figure in the 1950 congressional elections, he threatened to be even more pivotal in the 1952 presidential race. In the Irish and German Catholic communities whose Democratic trend had given Truman essential support in 1948, Senator McCarthy was little less than a hero. The typical Irish plumbing contractor and his work crew shared hearty amusement over McCarthy's yanking of the English moustache of Secretary of State Dean Acheson (Groton, Harvard *et al.*); the nation's largely Irish Catholic hierarchy also responded favorably to McCarthy.

The twin issues of Korea and Communist subversion keynoted the 1952 Republican presidential campaign in the Northeast, as the GOP successfully sought to capitalize on the ethnic thrust of McCarthyism.* Although General Dwight Eisenhower was the candidate of the Northeastern Republican Establishment, he did not repudiate McCarthy and indeed emphasized some of the same themes McCarthy stressed that year. Throughout the Northeast, Eisenhower's sharpest gains came in Catholic precincts, and Catholic votes provided the margin of victory in all of the Northeastern states which had backed Truman in 1948. Because of his strong showing among Catholics, Eisenhower swept the entire Northeast.

Not that foreign policy was the only impetus of the 1952 Catholic GOP trend; World War II prosperity had brought many Irish, Italians and Germans up the ladder to middle-class status. Like other middle-class voters, they were tired of Truman inflation, price controls and scandals; they were looking for a chance to enjoy their recently achieved affluence. From Boston to Washington, D.C., mile after mile of subdivisions were luring the new ethnic middle class into suburbia (where circumstances lent added focus to these bourgeois political considerations). It would have been difficult for some of these voters to support a Republican like Ohio's Senator Taft, symbol of the remote and austere Protestant Establishment, but Dwight Eisenhower was a war hero and a fatherly figure in the *Saturday Evening Post* vein—many New Deal voters gave him their first GOP presidential ballots.

Eisenhower's first term in office was generally applauded by Northeastern Catholics. The Korean War was brought to a halt six months after the retired general's inauguration, and prosperity increased, crippling the Democratic bogeyman that a Republican

---

*Not all Republicans rode the same impetus: liberal and internationalist Senator Henry Cabot Lodge was defeated in Massachusetts by John F. Kennedy, son of the isolationist wartime United States Ambassador to England, Joseph P. Kennedy. Some pro-Taft and pro-McCarthy Republicans backed Kennedy.

administration would bring on a depression. Perhaps the only fly in the ointment was resentment over the treatment—censure and Coventry—the Eisenhower Administration accorded Senator McCarthy, but the Wisconsin Senator's irresponsibility in his last years undermined his public support.

As a result of this record, Eisenhower won even stronger Catholic backing in 1956 than in 1952. Chart 42 shows his gains in a cross

CHART 42

Northeastern Urban Catholic Presidential Voting Behavior, 1948-60

	Republican Share of the Total Vote for President			
County*	1948	1952	1956**	1960
Androscoggin, Maine (Lewiston, Auburn)	39%	51%	56%	36%
Bristol, Mass. (Fall River, New Bedford)	37	51	58	33
Suffolk, Mass. (Boston)	27	40	46	25
Providence, R.I. (Providence)	38	48	56	33
Oneida, New York (Utica, Rome)	48	61	70	48
Albany, New York (Albany, Cohoes)	43	52	57	40
Richmond, New York (Staten Island)	54	66	77	57
Hudson, New Jersey (Jersey City)	37	47	62	39
Middlesex, New Jersey (Perth Amboy)	43	50	61	42
Lackawanna, Penna. (Scranton)	41	49	54	38

*Exact religious data is impossible to come by, but most of these counties are more than 50 per cent Catholic.

**Given the high Republicanism of the Protestant vote in New England and the area around Scranton, Pennsylvania, Eisenhower's 46 per cent to 58 per cent vote figures in Androscoggin, Bristol, Suffolk, Providence and Lackawanna counties probably indicate 35 per cent to 50 per cent Catholic support. Nixon probably won 20 per cent to 25 per cent of the Catholic vote in these counties.

section of predominantly Catholic Northeastern counties while Chart 43 structures the Republican support level in the most heavily Catholic New York City assembly districts. It is no exaggeration to say that Catholics brought about the overwhelming share of the 1948-56 increment in Northeastern GOP presidential strength. In the eleven Northeastern states, Eisenhower's 1952 showing exceeded Dewey's by 9 per cent, and in 1956, the President added another 5 per cent, reaching near landslide levels. And within these states, Yankee areas gave Eisenhower only a few percentage points more than they had given Dewey, but the difference in bellwether Catholic precincts was 15 per cent to 25 per cent.

While Eisenhower gained heavily throughout the Catholic Northeast, his actual 1956 Catholic vote shares were by no means constant throughout the region. In upper New England, where the Republican-Democratic conflict was Protestant-Catholic, mill owner-mill worker, Eisenhower may have won 30 per cent to 40 per cent of the Catholic vote. Whether along the dun-colored industrial canyon of the Merrimack or in remote factory towns, the typical local Catholic worker (unlike his restive colleagues in New York City) thought of the Democratic Party as *his* party and a vehicle of *his* ethnic group and class interests—and he was loathe to vote for the Republicans.* Catholic support for Eisenhower climbed highest in the greater New York City where the Democratic Party was coming under silk-stocking and minority group influence. Chart 43 illustrates the huge Republican vote in the strongly middle-class Catholic assembly districts in Bay Ridge (Brooklyn), Staten Island, the North Bronx and Queens. Similar outpourings occurred in nearby New Jersey and Connecticut. These are the blue-collar, clerical and middle-managerial neighborhoods at the end of the subway lines; they are a kind of sociopolitical "outback," to borrow an apt Australian term. In 1956, the middle-class Catholics of these semi-suburban pales appear to have endorsed Eisenhower by three-to-one majorities, and for the first time their leading assembly districts racked up higher GOP presidential percentages than the Manhattan silk-stocking bastions. Nor was this vote just Eisenhower's; Republican congressional percentages also soared in the

---

*Even as Eisenhower was achieving a high level of popularity among the Irish, Polish and French Canadian working-class Catholics of Maine, Democratic Governor Edmund Muskie won about 85 per cent to 90 per cent of their votes in the September, 1956 gubernatorial election. Industrial cities like Waterville, York, Lewiston and Biddeford turned in huge Democratic majorities.

CHART 43

Catholic Political Volatility in New York City, 1954-60

Assembly District*	GOP % of Total Vote for Governor, 1954	GOP % of Total Vote for President, 1956	GOP % of Total Vote for President, 1960
13th Queens** (German-Irish)	66%	80%	64%
9th Brooklyn (Scandinavian-Irish-Italian)	60	80	60
2nd Richmond (Italian-Irish)	52	78	58
9th Queens** (German-Irish)	64	76	56
1st Richmond (Italian-Irish)	51	75	55
3rd Queens** (German-Irish)	55	74	59
12th Brooklyn (Italian-Irish)	50	73	53
10th Bronx (Italian-Irish)	49	70	49
20th Brooklyn (German-Irish)	43	70	45
3rd Brooklyn (Italian-Irish)	49	67	47
8th Brooklyn (Italian-Irish)	40	66	42

*Assembly Districts are listed in the order of their support of President Eisenhower in 1956; all of the top Republican districts were heavily Catholic. These were Eisenhower's top thirteen Assembly Districts.

**Queens Germans, being more strongly Republican than the Irish or Italians, showed somewhat less volatility. The sociological makeup of the 9th Queens was changing by 1960—it was becoming more Jewish.

Note: the two East Side Manhattan silk-stocking Assembly Districts (the 8th and 9th) were not among Eisenhower's best, giving him 61 per cent and 63 per cent support. In these districts, where the Catholic vote is much less important, Eisenhower made small (6 per cent to 12 per cent) gains over the 1954 gubernatorial candidate, and Nixon's losses were relatively diminished in 1960.

middle-class Catholic reaches of New York, New Jersey and Connecticut.

A new Catholic political direction was writ large in the 1956 elections, and the Democratic Party—dependent on Catholic adherence—took apprehensive note. Even before Eisenhower's massive 1956 re-election, Democratic strategists concerned about the party's Catholic appeal had drawn up a memorandum urging the choice of a Catholic vice-presidential nominee. Surveying the statistics of 1956, Democratic politicians gave the memorandum new attention. But notwithstanding the actual percentages and Democratic gains achieved by Al Smith in 1928, especially in the Northeast, false legends had sprung up around the Happy Warrior's defeat which made many Democratic leaders uneasy about the prospect of nominating a Catholic.

As 1960 approached, however, a Catholic—young Massachusetts Senator John F. Kennedy—took the lead for and ultimately won the Democratic presidential nomination. Far from exemplifying the social characteristics typical of the turn-of-the-century Catholic immigrant, Kennedy—Harvard graduate, author, naval hero and millionaire—symbolized the consummation of the immigrant quest; and instead of flaunting his ties to Catholicism, he took pains to show that they exercised no sway over his decision-making process. The Kennedy nomination was eminently politic because Protestant America would have carped at a sociological reincarnation of Al Smith, and pro-Eisenhower Catholics (many of them middle-class and conservative) would have balked at a candidate who linked Catholicism to immigrant and lower-class behavior patterns.

Several political scientists and sociologists—Peter Viereck, Richard Hofstadter and Seymour Lipset—have described how conservatism exerts a special appeal on socially mobile individuals who are loosening ethnic group ties and rising in economic status.* In 1956, middle-class Catholics gave extremely heavy support to Eisenhower Republicanism, and their return to the party fold in 1960 was crucial to Democratic victory hopes. One can see how John F. Kennedy would have appealed to these normally conservative voters as a personification of Catholic political and social coming of age in America.

*See Viereck, *The Unadjusted Man* (New York: Capricorn Edition, 1962), and articles by Hofstadter and Lipset in *The Radical Right* (Garden City: Anchor Edition, 1964).

The Kennedy candidacy, or some other like it, was almost inevitable in the evolutionary maneuvering of American politics. By 1960, as the New Deal cycle was entering its last decade, two major groups of the old coalition—the South and the Catholic North—were trending Republican. (The old progressive West had moved even farther.) A Southern Democratic nominee was unlikely; a Catholic nominee offered a chance to arrest somewhat artificially and roll back a major column of the GOP advance. But at the same time, no Catholic president could halt the trend that was turning Catholics Republican, while such an administration, by shattering the myth that no Catholic could be elected, would ease the social cohesion tending to keep Catholics together in the Democratic Party. Inasmuch as most Catholics were Democrats, and almost all of their leverage occurred within that party, the first Catholic president obviously had to come from Democratic ranks. Nevertheless, as we have just seen, his election would serve the long-range Catholic trend to the GOP. Such was the meaning—dimly perceived at the time—of what was happening in 1960.

As had been predicted, Kennedy peeled away Eisenhower's massive Catholic vote increment (over 1948), and with these 20 per cent to 25 per cent gains among Catholics, the Democratic nominee swept Massachusetts, Rhode Island, Connecticut, New York, New Jersey, Pennsylvania, Maryland and Delaware into the Democratic column; the last six states for the first time since 1944. The Democratic trends of the several states correlated with the size of their Catholic populations, and within each state county patterns showed similar linkage (see Charts 16-18). Just as Eisenhower's 1948-56 increment was largely Catholic, so was Nixon's 1956-60 decline.

To an extraordinary degree, Kennedy recouped exactly those voters, mostly Catholics, whom Eisenhower had attracted to the GOP. Chart 43 lists Eisenhower's top thirteen assembly districts in New York City, all heavily Catholic. These were the very districts where Eisenhower had run *farthest ahead* of other Republicans (1948 presidential candidate Dewey and 1954 GOP gubernatorial candidate Ives). They were also the districts where Kennedy led the Democrats to the strongest comeback, with the result that Richard Nixon's vote retreated to the inauspicious Ives levels.* Most of

---

*Legislative reapportionment (1954) complicates comparison of 1956 voting with pre-1954 patterns.

the 1948-60 political volatility of the Northeast was Catholic; the Protestant and Jewish electorates shifted very little in comparison.*

Some observers were wont to minimize the religious (pro-Catholic) factor in the 1960 election by observing that the suburban Democratic trend was practically as strong as that of the cities—and so it was—but there too for religious reasons. Whereas in 1928 greater New York City's Catholic trend had been confined to the city proper, by 1960 large numbers of Catholic urbanites had moved to the suburbs, so that the latter contained much of the 1960 Catholic trend.

In 1960, as in previous years since the evolution of the New Deal philosophy, Italian and Irish Catholics, whatever their bickering within the Democratic Party, demonstrated quite similar voting patterns. Both groups were socially conservative; their intra-party disputes hinged on power and not ideology. Generally speaking, they have moved together in national elections, although local elections have been something else again.

Despite his large and religion-correlating vote pickup over Stevenson in New York City, John F. Kennedy did not win an overwhelming majority of the local Catholic vote. His 20 per cent gain boosted Democratic Catholic levels to only about 60 per cent. And the large Catholic middle class of New York City seems to have given Nixon a clear majority.** In *Beyond the Melting Pot,* Daniel Patrick Moynihan has told how Alfred E. Smith, Jr. backed Nixon; how the grandson of The McCooey rang doorbells for the Republican ticket in Greenwich, Connecticut; and of the fact that only the votes of Jewish students in the School of Pharmacy saved Irish and Jesuit Fordham University from going on record straw-pollwise as opposed to the election of the first Catholic president of the United States.***

John F. Kennedy's achievement among New York City area Catholics lay not in lopsided success—he did not achieve it—but in turning Stevenson's disaster into victory. Outside the sociological cockpit of greater New York, Nixon's Catholic strength was much

---

*Jewish volatility occurred largely in 1948.

**As Chart 43 shows, most of the leading Catholic middle-class Assembly Districts either voted for Nixon or gave him heavy minority support kept under 50 per cent by the 4-to-1 Democratic voting of local Jews and Negroes (usually 10 per cent to 25 per cent of the electorate even in the top Catholic Assembly districts).

***Glazer and Moynihan, *Beyond the Melting Pot* (Cambridge, 1963), p. 272.

less—about 20 per cent in New England, for example. Massive Catholic support enabled Kennedy to carry Massachusetts, Rhode Island and Connecticut, but he lost Maine, Vermont and New Hampshire where the Yankee vote predominates.

As for sheer political power, expressed in terms of people and their positions, 1961 was something of an Irish Catholic heyday. At no time before or since have Irish politicians been arrayed in so many high national offices (President, Speaker of the House, Senate Majority leader and others), but the sociological ascent which had kept the Irish in the forefront of the working-class party was already dispersing Irish residential blocs, partisan loyalties and intra-Democratic Party influence. Nowhere did Irish local displacement throb more poignantly than in New York City, seat of yesteryear's glory. True, Irish leaders controlled the Democratic county organizations in several boroughs, but by 1961 they had lost Tammany, the New York City mayoralty and control of the state Democratic Party. There were many Irish at the top of the ladder in national Democratic politics, most of them men who got their start in another and more Irish Democratic era, but the bottom rungs of the party were becoming less hospitable and less attractive to wearers of the green. Nor were the Irish successful in turning their increasingly Republican voting pattern into leadership within the GOP; they were fended off by the Protestant Establishment, Jews and Italians.

Within both parties, the Irish trend was strongly conservative, and in 1961, dissident Irish Republicans and a few like-minded Democrats founded the New York State Conservative Party. The party was not organized as an Irish political vehicle, but from the first it had a decidedly Gaelic coloration. And in confirmation of its Irish thrust, as well as the radical wellsprings of neo-conservatism, the Conservative Party's principal founders were almost all connected with families which had been active in the Irish Republican Brotherhood during the Ninetween-Twenties.*

John Kennedy's religion warmed Catholic hearts, and he himself especially pleased the Irish by his 1963 return to the land of his fathers, but all in all, the socioeconomic thrust of the early Nineteen-Sixties was not conducive to easing the Catholic trend to conservatism. The civil rights revolution began to move into high gear, and across much of the Northeast the economic and geographic

*J. Daniel Mahoney, *Actions Speak Louder* (New Rochelle: Arlington House, 1968), p. 28.

frontiers of the restless black ghetto impinged on Catholic trade unions and neighborhoods; rising taxes for escalating welfare bore down on small home-owners; soaring crime rates jeopardized blue-collar and middle-class lives; new sociological concepts hamstrung the police and undermined the neighborhood school; and new hiring policies and political realities disrupted the Catholic political clubhouses and municipal bureaucracies. More than any other Northeastern religious group, Catholics tended to inhabit the socio-economic "combat zone," confronting the Democratic Party with the cruel dilemma of aborting its ideological thrust or alienating the loyalties of its largest bloc of longtime supporters.

Signs of "backlash" emerged up and down the Megalopolis. By a record vote, Boston elected the neighborhood school advocate, Louise Day Hicks, as School Board Chairman in 1961; New York's Conservative Party drew a surprisingly large vote in 1962; Phila-delphia's Irish and Italian enthusiastically backed conservative GOP mayoralty candidate James McDermott in the 1963 election; and Baltimore's blue-collar Catholic wards endorsed segregationist Alabama Governor George C. Wallace in Maryland's 1964 Demo-cratic presidential primary. As a result of these trends, especially Wallace's near majority in Maryland, observers predicted a major backlash in the 1964 presidential election.

But when November's votes were counted, the backlash was exceedingly weak. Boston and Baltimore wards that had gone heavily for Louise Day Hicks and George Wallace went six- and eight-to-one against Barry Goldwater. Whatever the appeal of the 1964 GOP nominee's civil rights stance, it was outweighed by the unpopularity of his position on labor legislation, aspects of the Social Security system and economic issues in general (none of which handicapped free-spending populist Democrats like Mrs. Hicks and Governor Wallace). As a result of his unpopular positions on issues of economic importance to the blue-collar and lower-middle-class electorates, to say nothing of the image given him as a foreign policy deviate, Senator Goldwater was able to tap only a small amount of the vast Catholic discontent with Democratic social policies.

Most of the Catholic Northeast gave Goldwater about the same degree of support which it had given to Richard Nixon in 1960. From Boston to Baltimore, arch-Catholic wards showed little 1960-64 change in their GOP presidential vote shares (see Chart 19), although in core precincts within these wards—neighborhoods where delicatessens stocked Guinness, oatmeal and soda-bread (or mozarella, pasta and olive oil)—Goldwater often topped Nixon levels. Chart 44 illustrates the pattern in some ethnic strongholds of the Bronx, New York.

CHART 44

Italo-Irish Presidential Voting Trends in The Bronx, New York, 1960-64

	Republican Share of Total Vote for President	
Assembly District	1960	1964
10th Bronx	49%	45%
Italo-Irish EDs,* Throgs Neck	—60%	—65%
Italian EDs, Pelham Bay	—56%	—56%
9th Bronx	29%	25%
Irish EDs, Bedford Park	—44%	—42%
8th Bronx	30%	27%
Irish EDs, Fordham	—46%	—48%
7th Bronx	26%	20%
Italian EDs, 187th St.-Little Italy	—40%	—44%

*Election Districts (Precincts)

In strongly Catholic areas of New England—Irish South Boston is a good example—the fact that Goldwater held or bettered Nixon strength was of minimal importance. The vote shares in question were 10 per cent to 20 per cent, hardly the stuff of which electoral success is made. But Goldwater's success in Catholic areas of New York City was something else again. There is good reason to suggest that Goldwater won a majority of the middle-class Catholic vote and perhaps 40 per cent of the city's total Catholic vote.* And it is no coincidence that Catholic and middle-class Staten Island was Goldwater's best county in all of New York State—the *same Staten*

*Barry Goldwater won 27 per cent of the vote in New York City. Among Jews, Negroes and Puerto Ricans, who cast about half of the city vote, his level of support was roughly 10 per cent. With 10 per cent strength among the minority-group half of the electorate (giving him 5 per cent of the *total* vote), he must have won 44 per cent of the votes of the other half of the city (white Christian) to amass, in sum, 27 per cent of the city's ballots. In outlying middle-class sections of Queens, Staten Island, Bay Ridge and the North Bronx, many Catholic neighborhoods gave solid majorities to the Arizona Senator.

Island that in 1936 had been more Democratic than any of the state's counties outside New York City! Sociopolitical upheaval in New York was turning Catholic voters into the vanguard of conservatism.

Very few observers commented on Goldwater's degree of support among New York Catholics, albeit the statistics were camouflaged in the ethnic heterogeneity of the city's much gerrymandered assembly districts. But the phenomenon deserved attention. By dint of a position in the sociological vortex of political establishmentarianism, Catholic New York is an early and accurate litmus of Northeastern Catholic politics. New York Irish support of Tammany Hall helped mold the Jeffersonian coalition to which the then small Catholic population rallied; the Gotham Catholics of Andrew Jackson's day helped forge his new majority to which inflowing Catholics adhered; and the Al Smith revolution, born in New York's Irish "Gas House" assembly district, brought Catholic America into the future New Deal coalition even before the Depression. In all of these upheavals, Catholic New York took up its position with a Southern and Western alliance. Even in defeat, the embryonic reemergence of this alliance was a major message of the 1964 election.

Far from reversing after Goldwater's defeat, the Catholic conservative trend accelerated. In New York City, silk-stocking Republican Congressman John V. Lindsay, who had disavowed Goldwater in 1964, ran for mayor in 1965 and was elected as a result of Liberal Party support. But political commentator and journalist William F. Buckley Jr. opposed him for the Conservative Party, polling 25 per cent to 30 per cent of the vote in the leading Catholic Assembly districts. Some observers dismissed the 1965 Conservative vote as a Buckley-linked fluke, but the 1966 gubernatorial results—a large vote was cast by Catholics whose turnout was swollen by a desire to vote against the Police Civilian Review Board on referendum—confirmed the conservative impetus.

Other areas manifested a similar trend. Baltimore's Catholic working-class wards helped segregationist Democrat George Mahoney to win the party's 1966 Maryland gubernatorial primary, and they went on to give him overwhelming backing in the November general election. Irish and Italian Philadelphia wards gave GOP candidates a considerably higher level of support in 1966 than they had in 1964. And in the wake of the bloody race riots that spread across northern New Jersey (Newark in particular) during the summer of 1967, a heavy Italo-Irish trend helped transform a two-to-one Democratic legislature into a three-to-one Republican body. The off-year election of 1967 also saw Boston's large Catholic population, especially the Irish, give a ballot majority to School Board Chairman Louise Day Hicks in her barely unsuccessful mayoralty bid. (Had her non-racial policies been somewhat more plausible, she might well have won.)

However widespread the conservative trend in Catholic politics, it found different outlets in Baltimore and Boston as compared with metropolitan New York. Still largely under Catholic control, the Democratic parties of Baltimore and Boston—or at least a major faction of them—represented Catholic blue-collar beliefs while the local Republican parties or leadership cliques stood for silk-stocking liberal inclination towards a Negro alliance. A different situation prevailed in metropolitan New York, where minority-group influence and more advanced re-alignment had carried a large number of Catholics into the ranks of the Republican electorate, with the result that the conservative tide helped accelerate Catholic change-over rather than manifesting itself principally within the Democratic Party. George Mahoney and Louise Day Hicks kept Catholic conservatism within the Democratic orbit in Baltimore and Boston, whereas in the Middle Atlantic states, Catholics trended Republican.

Good evidence of the little-appreciated post-Goldwater metamorphosis of the New York State Republican Party came in February, 1968, when the New York State Senate approved legislation to provide state dollar aid to (mostly Catholic) parochial schools. Only a handful of Democrats voted for the bill—most Democratic state senators were Jews and Negroes; there were not many Catholic Democrats representing Democratic New York City where the Irish had once ruled supreme.* Where had all the Irish gone? To the suburbs and the Republican Party, as one alphabetical section of the list of pro-parochial school GOP senators (Conklin, Curran, Day, Donovan, Dunne, Flynn) proved quite vividly. The silk-stocking liberals in opposition could well have observed that "Rum, Romanism and Rebellion" was changing parties.

Competing against Protestant Hubert Humphrey in 1968, Richard Nixon fared better among Northeastern Catholics than he had

---

*In 1968, only two Irish Democratic state senators were elected in New York City and suburbs, whereas the same area elected thirteen Jewish Democrats and three Negro Democrats to the State Senate.

in 1960, although once again there was a regional difference in Catholic voting behavior. In upper New England, from Democratic vice-presidential nominee Edmund Muskie's home state of Maine to Rhode Island, Nixon proved unable to win even one quarter of the Catholic vote. With Protestants lined up on the Republican side, although less solidly than in the past, and with few minority groups to sway the local Democratic parties, the latter retained the allegiance of most Catholics. And although the Democrats made inroads among Yankees, it was the Catholic vote that furnished the numerical foundations of Hubert Humphrey's 1968 New England victories. (Much the same Catholic-Protestant cleavage prevailed in western New York and Pennsylvania.) Furthermore, these areas where Humphrey ran well among Catholics also lacked the impetus to produce a sizeable Catholic vote for George Wallace. The former Alabama governor did poorly among the Catholics of New England, even (to a lesser extent) those of belligerently Irish South Boston.

Only within psychological range of greater New York City did Nixon's Catholic trend take shape. Blue-collar areas of Connecticut's suburban Fairfield County produced 1960-68 gains in the Nixon share of the two-party vote even as the silk-stocking suburbs showed a Democratic advance. A considerable Italian trend enabled Nixon to better his 1960 positions in such ethnic centers as New Haven and Bridgeport, Connecticut; Utica, New York; and Paterson, Camden and Newark, New Jersey. Oneida County (Utica) and Passaic County (Passaic and Paterson), both of which had backed Kennedy in 1960, switched to Nixon. Likewise, Irish strides enabled the GOP candidate to surpass his 1960 two-party vote shares in the Celtic strongholds of Yonkers and Jersey City. Along New York State's Quebec frontier, Nixon recaptured two counties —Franklin and Clinton, both heavily French Canadian—where Catholics had broken ranks in 1960 to support their co-religionist John F. Kennedy. And in New Jersey's blue-collar Middlesex County, the large Hungarian and Czech population trended sharply to Nixon. The only major Catholic group in Connecticut, New York and New Jersey *not* to show a 1960-68 shift to Nixon was the Polish contingent, and much of their Democratic loyalty stemmed from the Polish ancestry of Democratic vice-presidential candidate Muskie.

George Wallace also ran fairly well among the Catholics of the three-state area, particularly in locales where racial violence had broken out in 1967 or 1968. The third-party contender won 10 per cent of the vote in Bridgeport, Connecticut, and more in the New Jersey cities which had been badly hit by the riots in the summer of 1967. Wallace appears to have won 10 per cent to 15 per cent of the Italian vote in New Jersey. Most of the pro-Wallace Italians had voted Republican in the 1967 legislative elections; probably they would have done so again, had Wallace's name not been on the ballot. One interesting sidelight: in a contest between Negro Black Power advocates and White Power Italians for a seat on the Newark City Council, victory in the citywide race went to pro-Wallace vigilante leader and karate expert Anthony Imperiale.

Taking into consideration both the Nixon and Wallace votes, there is no doubt that the Catholic electorate of Connecticut, New Jersey and upstate New York (excluding Buffalo) executed a sharp

CHART 45

The 1960-68 Catholic Trend to Nixon in New York, New Jersey and Connecticut

	Nixon Share of the Two-Party Vote for President	
County or City	1960	1968
Substantially Italian*		
New Haven County, Connecticut	42%	45%
Bridgeport, Connecticut	36	42
Richmond County, New York	56	62
Oneida County (Utica), New York	48	54
Passaic County (Passaic and Paterson), New Jersey	45	52
Substantially Irish*		
Yonkers, New York	51	55
Hudson County (Jersey City), New Jersey	39	42
Substantially French Canadian		
Clinton County, New York	45	53
Franklin County, New York	49	55

*In all of these cities and counties, the local Irish and Italian populations are only a minority, although a powerful one, and their trends, as evidenced here, have been diluted by the behavior of other voting streams.

1960-68 movement away from the Democrats. This Catholic shift played a major part in Richard Nixon's New Jersey victory and in the Democrats' failure to match the combined Nixon-Wallace total in Connecticut.

But the most emphatic evidence of the Catholic trend to Nixon came in New York City itself, where large numbers of Catholics who had backed J.F.K. in 1960 changed to Nixon. The result was that *all* of Nixon's top eighteen New York City assembly districts in 1968 were largely Catholic in makeup. Whereas in 1960, New York City's German, Irish and Italian Catholics had favored John F. Kennedy by an approximately five-to-four ratio, in 1968 they appear to have preferred Nixon over Humphrey and Wallace by a ratio of at least five-to-three-to-one. This trend took place despite the heavy Catholic exodus to the suburbs between 1960 and 1968 which removed many middle-income Republicans. Of all the Catholic groups, none matched the Irish in Republican impetus. For the first time, the New York Grand Council of Irish Societies endorsed a Republican presidential nominee; and one of the very few New York City show-business personalities to endorse Nixon was Brooklyn-born and Irish Jackie Gleason, whose program is one of the most Celtic-flavored on television.

Chart 46 lists Nixon's eighteen top assembly districts in New York City. All of them were predominantly Catholic, although some in Brooklyn and the Bronx had sizeable (and trend-offsetting) Negro or Jewish minorities. Almost every Irish, Italian or German election district in New York City, however buried in other-minded environs, produced a Nixon (or Nixon-Wallace) majority. Richard Nixon ran better among the Irish firemen and bus drivers of Inwood —or the Italians of Little Italy—than among the sophisticates of the new residential tracts of Manhattan's East Side.

Nixon was not the only conservative to do well among New York City Catholics; George Wallace captured 7 per cent to 10 per cent of the total vote in the leading Catholic assembly districts and he reached 15 per cent in some lower-middle-class Irish election districts. Perhaps three quarters of the 122,000 votes Wallace won in New York City came from Catholics, especially Italian and Irish policemen, firemen, bus drivers and sanitation workers. By and large, Nixon support and Wallace support occurred among the same groups and in the same predominantly Catholic districts—conservative Republican or Conservative Party trend areas, for the most

CHART 46

The 18 Top Nixon Assembly Districts in New York City, 1968

Assembly District (Neighborhood)	Percentage of the Total Vote for President*		
	Nixon	Humphrey	Wallace
49th Brooklyn (Bay Ridge)	61%	32%	7%
50th Brooklyn (Bay Ridge)	60	33	7
58th Richmond (Staten Island)	58	33	9
30th Queens (Elmhurst, Ridgewood)	56	34	10
20th Queens (Cambria, Hollis)	56	36	8
28th Queens (Woodhaven)	55	36	9
59th Richmond (Staten Island)	53	38	9
80th Bronx (Parkchester, Throgs Neck)	50	41	9
34th Queens (Sunnyside, Maspeth)	50	41	9
29th Queens (South Ozone Park)	49	42	9
22nd Queens (Douglaston)	51	44	5
85th Bronx (Morris Park, Pelham Bay)	49	45	6
32nd Queens (Steinway, Woodside)	48	45	7
33rd Queens (Astoria, Long Island City)	47	45	8
53rd Brooklyn (Gowanus)	44	47	9
86th Bronx (Baychester)	45	48	7
38th Brooklyn (East New York)	44	48	8
35th Brooklyn (Greenpoint)	41	50	9
Citywide (68 AD's)	34	61	5

*Based on figures reported by the *New York Times,* November 8, 1968.

Note: All of these districts are predominantly Catholic; the other districts which, despite substantial numbers of Jews and Protestants, could be called predominantly Catholic—Brooklyn's Park Slope and the Bronx's Fordham-Kingsbridge—would follow almost immediately on an extended list. These heavily Catholic districts were also the best Wallace districts; only one other assembly district gave him over 6 per cent of the vote. Not one of the East Side Manhattan assembly districts was among the eighteen best Nixon supporters.

part—and the overwhelming majority of Wallaceites would have chosen Nixon in a two-party contest with Hubert Humphrey. Had Nixon been able to run under the banner of New York's Conservative Party as well as that of the state GOP (top New York Republicans blocked such endorsement), he would have garnered much of the Wallace vote in the city and its (New York State) environs.

As a result of the 1968 presidential and legislative voting trends in New York City and its suburbs, the local Republican Party moved towards an increasingly Catholic image and constituency. Not only was Nixon's city electorate about 75 per cent white Catholic—with the exception of white Protestants, he ran poorly among other groups—but Catholic districts elected twelve of the city's thirteen Republican state assemblymen. Most of these were Republican-Conservatives; their abbreviated designation "R.-C." conveyed the religion of their constituents as well as their own politics. Two of the new Republican state legislators elected in 1968 in lower-middle-class Italian and Irish districts were not even Republicans of more than immediate convenience: Queens neighborhood school advocate Rosemary Gunning was a Conservative, and Brooklyn property-tax-revolt agitator Vito Battista was a past mayoralty candidate of the United Taxpayers Party (a very minor party of minimal significance). Because of the lingering establishmentarian aura of the New York GOP, Battista and Mrs. Gunning needed the backing of a popular conservative third party to win election, but their success indicates the extent to which such politics are gaining control of New York City Republicanism.

As in the past, the Catholic political upheaval in New York City is being led by the Irish. Although the city's Italians are almost as conservative, they were a wave behind the Irish in leadership and power within the Democratic Party, and they do not yet suffer the Irish degree of alienation. (Even in 1969, there were fourteen Italians among New York City's Democratic assemblymen but only three Irishmen.) The Irish-led Conservative Party, which polled 1.1 million votes in its 1968 New York U.S. Senate effort, is the principal fulcrum of changing Catholic loyalties;* the city's small cadre of conservative intellectuals—*National Review et al.*—is substantially Irish;** and Richard Nixon, himself a black Irishman whose

*The three principal movers of the Conservative Party are its state chairman, J. Daniel Mahoney; his brother-in-law, Kieran O'Dougherty; and Fordham Law School professor Charles Rice. When the Conservative Party mounted its first major campaign in the 1965 New York City mayoralty race, all three of its citywide candidates were Irish Catholics.

**William F. Buckley, Jr. is the most eminent of the Irish conservative intellectuals. With the assistance of several members of his family, he also puts out *National Review*.

family came from the counties of Cork and Kildare, was elected to the presidency in a campaign substantially planned by New York Irish conservatives.*

Given the considerable 1960-68 Nixon trend among Catholics in and around New York City, together with the sizeable majorities given Nixon and other conservative candidates, there can be no doubt that the New York City Catholics—the Irish in particular— are joining the new Southern and Western conservative Republican coalition in its struggle with liberal Northeastern Democrats. As Yankees and upper-middle-class liberals turn Democratic, Catholic Republicanism ought to spread outward from New York City. In the first place, state and national Republican parties will become more populist in ideology and Catholic in makeup, thus gaining in appeal to Scranton miners and Boston bartenders; and secondly, the Democratic Party will increasingly become the party of just those groups—silk-stocking voters, Yankees, Negroes and Jews— against whom Northeastern Catholics have traditionally aligned themselves.

7. Suburbia

At one extreme, suburbia resembles prosperous urban blue-collar precincts; at the other, silk-stocking strongholds. The suburbia of crabgrass and commuter fame falls more or less in the middle. Back in the Nineteen-Twenties, suburbs were few in number, limited in importance and silk-stocking in character. Since that time, suburbia has multiplied twentyfold and its socioeconomic character has been revolutionized by a middle-class and increasingly non-Anglo-Saxon exodus from the cities. No longer the upper-middle-class group described by F. Scott Fitzgerald and later by John O'Hara, most of today's suburbanites live and vote more in the fashion of their friends and cousins still residing in The Bronx or Jamaica Plain.

During the Nineteen-Twenties, suburbia was solidly Republican, although not too powerful. New York City's two principal suburban counties, Nassau and Westchester, cast only one-eighth of the vote of the parent city itself. Along with the similar affluent outliers of Philadelphia and Boston, suburban New York stuck by Hoover and

*The Nixon family hailed from Cork; the Milhous family came from Kildare. Nixon's 1968 national campaign manager was John Mitchell; his deputy campaign manager was Peter Flanigan. A large number of his domestic and foreign policy research and idea men were Irish.

Landon in the presidential elections of the Nineteen-Thirties and elected an unbroken roster of anti-New Deal Republicans to Congress. Chart 47 illustrates the presidential voting behavior of the leading New York and Pennsylvania suburban counties.

CHART 47

Suburban Presidential Voting, 1920-48

Republican Per Cent of the Total Vote for President

County	1920	1924	1928	1932	1936	1940	1944	1948
Westchester, N.Y.	68%	64%	56%	51%	51%	62%	62%	61%
Nassau, N.Y.	76	71	63	55	55	66	67	70
Montgomery, Pa.	70	76	76	64	53	60	62	67

Suburban growth lagged during the Nineteen-Thirties; the economic conditions of the decade prompted a migration to rather than from the big cities. From World War I until the end of World War II, the percentage of the total New York statewide vote cast by New York City continued to rise; only thereafter did the real suburban boom begin and the relative position of Gotham weaken (see Chart 13).

The first few years of post-war suburban growth were well-heeled years; the war-accumulated upper-middle-class housing demand was satisfied. But by 1949 and 1950 the great middle-income trek was underway, and names like Levittown entered the urbanologist's lexicon to characterize the phenomenon. As a result of this growth, suburban political power swelled. In New York, the three suburban counties increased the size of their vote by more than 40 per cent between 1948 and 1952 (a greater gain than they had ever shown before or would show again).

While a heavy majority of the new suburbanites joined older residents in backing Dwight Eisenhower in 1952, their numbers nevertheless tended to dilute Republican suburban strength. Chart 48 shows how the fastest-growing New York suburban county (Nassau) evidenced almost no Republican gain between 1948 and 1952. There were considerable Republican sentiments among the new middle class, but these voters were not nearly so Republican as the older suburbanites.

CHART 48

The Political Impetus of the Great New York Suburban Boom, 1948-52

County	% Vote Growth 1948-52	1952 GOP Vote %	% Increase in GOP Vote Share 1948-52
Nassau	65%	69.8%	0.3%
Suffolk	44	74.5	4.7
Westchester	21	67.3	6.2

During the Nineteen-Fifties, suburbia did not burgeon at the record rate of 1948-52; nevertheless it continued to expand rapidly. Around Boston and New York, one half of the persons moving to lawn-mower country were Catholics, and in New York perhaps another quarter were Jews. By the end of the decade, these displaced Democrats threatened the hegemony of entrenched town and county Republican officialdoms throughout most of suburban New York. Irish and Italian voters formed the bulwark of suburban Democratic strength (and the Irish generally officered the suburban Democratic Party organizations). Although an orthodox liberal Democratic presidential or gubernatorial candidate might offend them, many of the new middle-class Irish and Italian suburbanites preferred the *local* Catholic-run Democratic Party to still-ensconced old-line Anglo-Saxon Republicanism. The great Republican hero of the suburban new middle class was Dwight Eisenhower. In 1956, he further increased his suburban vote share over the already high levels of 1952. Not only was Eisenhower popular in his own right, but Adlai Stevenson, his Democratic opponent, was an alien being to upwardly mobile suburban Catholics. Locally, however, the Catholic new middle class was more likely to take sociocultural umbrage at an old-line Protestant Republican village trustee. For this reason, the years between 1958 and 1964 saw a large number of suburban offices and patronage fall to the Democrats.

One graphic illustration of both the growth of suburbia and the emigration of city Democrats can be fashioned in a chart of the relative vote cast by Manhattan (the central city core of New York) and archetypal middle-class suburban Nassau County. Furthermore, no set of statistics better gives the lie to the allegation that the political future of America pivots on the central city.

CHART 49

Manhattan-Nassau County Total Votes* Cast for President, 1920-68

	1920	1924	1928	1932	1936	1940	1944
Manhattan	464	463	521	565	711	774	773
Nassau	43	65	113	144	172	217	238

	1948	1952	1956	1960	1964	1968
Manhattan	738	765	678	635	626	519
Nassau	265	438	539	588	632	639

*In Thousands

As a result of the large Catholic exodus to the suburbs, New York's suburban counties contained a more heavily Catholic population in 1960 than such minority group-populated boroughs of New York City as Brooklyn, the Bronx and Manhattan. Thus, even though Richard Nixon carried all of the suburban counties in 1960, the religion-linked 1956-60 Democratic trend was stronger in suburbia than in the city's urban core. Nixon fell only 10 per cent below Eisenhower's 1956 levels in Manhattan, Brooklyn and the Bronx (largely as a result of fall-off in Catholic neighborhoods), but he slid 14 per cent to 18 per cent in the three major suburban counties. Indeed, many substantially Catholic middle-class suburban tracts turned in Democratic gains of 20 per cent to 25 per cent— comparable to those of the city's middle-class Catholic assembly districts. The pro-Kennedy trend reached into *all* Catholic precincts, urban, suburban and rural, with equal attraction.*

But although the great exodus to suburbia was filling up station-wagonland with longtime urban Democrats and dethroning old-line and typically unresponsive Republican local administrations, it was not, in the ultimate context of the Nineteen-Sixties, a liberal movement. On the contrary, much of the suburban exodus was prompted by the changing demography of the cities—Southern Negroes were moving to the Northeast in large numbers—and thus when the politics of the Nineteen-Sixties began to pivot more and more on the

*As indicated, the New York county showing the sharpest pro-Kennedy trend was Clinton, a rural and small-city (Plattsburgh) county along the United States-Quebec border. Clinton County is the most heavily Catholic in the state.

Negro socioeconomic revolution, the newer reaches of suburbia proved highly unresponsive. To many new suburbanites, their relocation represented a conscious effort to drop a crabgrass curtain between themselves and the increasingly Negro central cities. The Census Bureau is less than accurate in referring to suburban population growth as urbanization; psychologically, the suburban boom is an anti-urban phenomenon—an attempt to escape crime, slums and slumdwellers.

Of course, not all segments of suburbia shared these sentiments. Some of the most frequently caricatured (yet atypical) reaches of New York commuter country—Scarsdale, Great Neck and so forth —were rich silk-stocking bailiwicks fully participating in the establishmentarian liberal trend.* Generally speaking, these areas were extremely affluent and little inhabited by ordinary middle-class refugees from the socioeconomic threat of changing urban neighborhoods. They are as unlike Levittown as Park Avenue is unlike, say, Hollis or Flatbush.

Barry Goldwater's 1964 presidential candidacy evoked a mixed response from suburbia. On the surface, the suburbs broke with the politics of a lifetime as Goldwater lost every suburban county in the Northeast: Norfolk, Massachusetts; Fairfield, Connecticut; Westchester, Nassau and Suffolk, New York; Bergen, Morris and Union, New Jersey; Montgomery, Bucks and Delaware, Pennsylvania; and Montgomery and Baltimore, Maryland. Within these counties, however, striking behavioral differences emerged. While all of suburbia was generally leery of the portrait painted of Goldwater's foreign and military policies, there was a considerable difference of opinion regarding his social policies; and his decline (in comparison with Nixon's 1960 strength) was anything but uniform across suburbia's socioeconomic spectrum. In New York's three suburban counties, Goldwater dropped 15 per cent to 19 per cent below 1960 levels; however, the decline ranged from 30 per cent in the richest silk-stocking suburbs to less than 10 per cent in Catholic middle-class bailiwicks. In Westchester County, the only suburb which combined a heavy Republican bias with a small anti-Goldwater trend was rich *and* Catholic Pelham; it was the only town in the county Goldwater carried. Suburbia is a composite of the trends

---

*For many years, Scarsdale was a caricature of conservative suburbia—the Scarsdale matron jokes, for example. Now it is a caricature of liberal suburbia. The common denominator is Scarsdale's continuing wealth and fashion.

already analyzed—silk-stocking, Yankee, non-Yankee, Catholic, Jewish and Negro—and so was the "suburban" Democratic trend of 1964.

But notwithstanding Johnson's 1964 victory and Democratic claims of a new middle-class majority following, suburbia and Great Society social programs were essentially incompatible. Suburbia did not take kindly to rent subsidies, school racial balance schemes, growing Negro immigration or rising welfare costs. A few silk-stocking suburbs joined in experimental racial balance or pupil-exchange schemes—actual integration was obviously no threat at all to such rich communities—but the great majority of middle-class suburbanites opposed racial or welfare innovations. In general, suburbia voted Republican in the 1966 elections, although the Democrats managed to retain most of the silk-stocking congressional seats which they had gained in 1964.

Conservative currents flowed more strongly in 1967 in the wake of the summer's racial violence. From one end of New Jersey to the other, Republican candidates unhorsed suburban state legislators, while in New York, the Conservative Party won heavy enough support to deny election to liberal Republicans and oblige the local GOP to become more ideologically responsive.*

Despite the seeming suburban orientation of Richard Nixon's 1968 presidential appeal to the "forgotten man," suburbia did not respond with one approving voice; instead, the cleavage of 1964 recurred. Middle-class suburbia showed a heavy conservative shift in comparison with both 1960 and 1964, but silk-stocking suburbia (and Jewish suburbs of all income levels) gave the Republican nominee a much smaller vote share than he had won in 1960.

The sharpest 1960-68 Nixon suburban decline occurred in the fashionable bedrooms of Boston (Wellesley, Newton, Brookline and Lexington), along Philadelphia's rich Main Line (Montgomery County) and in the best-established suburbs of New York (Scarsdale and Pound Ridge in Westchester County; Westbury, Great Neck and Roslyn in Nassau County). Chart 50 sketches Nixon's 1960-68 slide in silk-stocking suburbia, comparing it with the gains scored by Nixon in anonymous middle-class suburbs.

---

*New York's suburban GOP organizations are also becoming more responsive from an *ethnic* point of view. Italians and Irish are playing an increasing role. The Nassau, Suffolk and Westchester delegations in the state legislature contain the plenitude of Irish and Italians necessary to harness the support of these groups.

CHART 50

Suburban Voting Trends in the New York Metropolitan Area, 1952-68

Town	Republican Share of the Major-Party Vote for President				
	1952	1956	1960	1964	1968
Upper & Upper-Middle Class Suburbs					
Wilton, Conn.	77%	79%	73%	47%	66%
Scarsdale, N.Y.*	78	72	63	35	45
Pound Ridge, N.Y.*	80	76	73	44	57
Upper-Middle Class Largely Catholic Suburbs					
Pelham, N.Y.*	84	86	73	59	71
Middle-Class Suburbs (Substantially Catholic)					
Orangetown, N.Y.**	68	75	58	41	60
Babylon, N.Y.***	71	76	55	43	62
Smithtown, N.Y.***	72	77	57	45	65
Oyster Bay, N.Y.****	72	73	53	42	57
Yorktown, N.Y.*	70	72	60	42	60

*Westchester County; **Rockland County; ***Suffolk County; ****Nassau County

Legend and misinformation rather than fact produced a substantial post-1968 election impression that suburbia had moved towards the Democrats. Relatively few suburbs either in the Northeast or the nation as a whole evidenced a Democratic trend, and those that did were given undue importance. After all, places like those listed above are some of the best known suburbs in the country; twenty years ago, when two-thirds of today's suburbanites still lived elsewhere, these were the archetypal homes of *The Man In The Grey Flannel Suit;* but now, with growing numbers of tweedy foundation executives, research directors, publishers and educators taking up residence—while low-middle-income groups flood into a very different breed of suburb—towns like Wellesley, Bryn Mawr and Scarsdale have become completely atypical. In comparison with the new subdivisions populated by salesmen, electricians, and supermarket managers, silk-stocking suburbia casts ever fewer votes, and its 1960-68 Democratic trend was no indicator of the general party slump in Northeastern suburbia (sketched in Chart 51). Neither was the movement of Jewish suburban tracts.

Of course, the substantial 1960-68 Democratic vote slippage in Northeastern middle-class suburbia was not always matched by equal—or even any—Republican gains. George Wallace diverted many conservative votes, reducing the lead that the middle-class suburban conservative trend would otherwise have given Nixon over Humphrey. Throughout suburbia, the Wallace vote tended to be strongest in middle-income areas shifting towards Nixon and weakest in silk-stocking towns trending towards Humphrey. In Scarsdale, New York, the Alabaman captured only one per cent of the vote, but in Suffolk County, the fastest growing suburban area in the state and simultaneously the bastion of the New York Conservative Party, Wallace captured 30,000 votes (8 per cent of the total), almost all of them at Nixon's expense. Clearly, middle-income and low-middle-income suburban conservatives of the type who backed Wallace would have chosen the Republican nominee in a two-party contest. The *conservative* majority over Democrat Hubert Humphrey was much higher than the comparable edge over John Kennedy in 1960, although this was partly disguised by the fact that the Wallace-Nixon split in the conservative total enabled Humphrey to run close enough to Nixon in some areas to cause talk about a "suburban" Democratic trend.

Contemporary suburban demography is very much on the conservative side. Across the nation, suburban growth is centered in middle-class locales—the suburbs of the South and Southwest—which gave Nixon and Wallace vast leads over Humphrey.* Each year, the environs of Los Angeles, San Diego, Houston, Dallas and many Southern cities add 10 per cent to 20 per cent to their populations, whereas the leading silk-stocking suburban counties around New York and Philadelphia—storied Westchester and Main Line

---

*One of the fastest-growing suburban areas in the nation, while not yet a part of the Megalopolis, appears likely soon to extend Megalopolitan boundaries southward. Greater Richmond, Virginia, is expanding very rapidly, as are the northern Virginia suburbs of Washington, D.C. Before long, the Megalopolis should extend south to Richmond. Since 1960, the suburban Richmond counties of Henrico and Chesterfield have doubled their vote, and there is considerable meaning in the fact that these fastest-growing of all suburban counties from Virginia to Massachusetts were also the *least* pro-Humphrey. Henrico and Chesterfield are Republican presidential bastions; Nixon won heavy majorities and Democratic candidate Humphrey captured only 15 per cent of the total vote in the two counties.

CHART 51

Northeastern Suburban Growth and Voting Trends, 1960-68

Suburban County (Ranked by Democratic Loss)	Democratic Share of Total Vote Cast for President		Percentage Increase in the Total Vote, 1960-68
	1960	1968	
Prince Georges, Maryland (D.C. Suburbs)	58%	40%	60%
Baltimore, Maryland (Baltimore Suburbs)	50	37	10
Middlesex, New Jersey (New York-Newark Blue-Collar Suburbs)	58	46	13
Delaware, Pennsylvania (Philadelphia Suburbs)	48	40	−1
Suffolk, New York (New York Suburbs)	41	33	33
Burlington, New Jersey (Camden-Philadelphia Suburbs)	48	42	21
Bucks, Pennsylvania (Philadelphia Suburbs)	46	41	8
Fairfield, Connecticut (New York Suburbs)	47	43	6
Montgomery, Maryland (D.C. Suburbs)	51	48	37
Bergen, New Jersey (New York Suburbs)	41	39	8
Nassau, New York (New York Suburbs)	45	44	9
Montgomery, Pennsylvania (Philadelphia Suburbs)	39	40	−1
Westchester, New York (New York Suburbs)	43	44	0

Note: Prince Georges, Baltimore, Middlesex, Suffolk and Burlington counties are the prime examples of fast-growing middle- and low-middle-income suburbia. The only other fast-growing suburban county, Maryland's rich Montgomery County, is a bedroom for Washington's civil servants, and is thus a rather specialized product of the escalation of federal employment. The two particularly silk-stocking counties are New York's Westchester and Pennsylvania's Montgomery (Main Line Philadelphia). The two Montgomerys, Bergen, Nassau and Westchester counties include most of the Megalopolis' suburban Jewish population. Boston's suburban periphery is divided among a number of counties.

Montgomery County—are showing little or no growth. Even within the Northeast, there is considerable suburban growth, but it is coming in low-middle and middle-income tracts in counties far beyond the parent city, while the close-in, old-line suburban counties are gripped by unchanging, manicured (and unsubdivisible) estate sections and decaying urbanized areas increasingly attractive to Negroes. Chart 51 shows how the major increase in Northeastern suburban voting power is occurring in new middle-income conservative-trending areas, while the relative population and influence of silk-stocking suburbia declines.

A new suburbia is being built across America by many millions of blue-collar and middle-level white-collar families in their twenties and thirties. This is the new young America on the move, and from Southern California to Richmond, Virginia to Long Island's Suffolk County, the movement is conservative. As Chart 13 shows by using New York as an example, the old, liberal cities are casting an ever-lower percentage of the vote in their states and nation. The power is shifting to this new suburbia; some call it the "white noose" around the increasingly Negro cities. Attempts to magnify the importance of the liberal Democratic trend among silk-stocking voters, whether young urban professionals or upper-middle-income suburbanites, constitute statistical myopia. A generation after Al Smith and Franklin Roosevelt, the burgeoning middle-class suburbs are the logical extension of the new popular conservatism of the South, the West and the Catholic sidewalks of New York.

B. The Northeastern Future

Whereas in 1932 the New Deal era had begun with the Northeast —and New England especially—as the most Republican section of the nation, the end of the Democratic cycle in 1968 saw the Northeast—and once again New England in the lead—giving nationally unequaled support to Democratic liberalism.

But the Northeast is not a regional monolith. Even while New England was moving one way, Chesapeake Bay was moving another. Maryland, by far the best Northeastern state for the Democrats of 1932, trailed only neighboring Delaware in the littleness of its 1968 support for party nominee Hubert Humphrey. In sum, the Democrats are gaining in the old states of post-Civil War Republican ascend-

CHART 52

The Relationship of the Northeast and the South in the Republican Party During the Entire New Deal Cycle

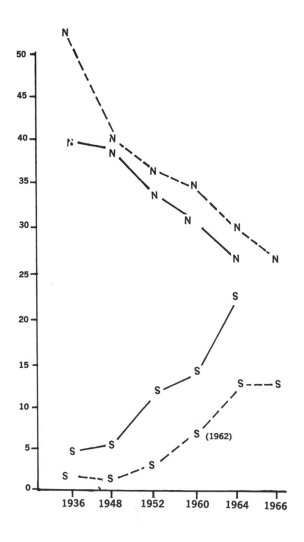

——— N ———   PERCENTAGE OF TOTAL REPUBLICAN PRESIDENTIAL VOTE CAST
            BY 11 NORTHEASTERN STATES.
— — N — —   PERCENTAGE OF TOTAL REPUBLICAN HOUSE OF REPRESENTA-
            TIVES MEMBERSHIP ELECTED BY 11 NORTHEASTERN STATES.
——— S ———   PERCENTAGE OF TOTAL REPUBLICAN PRESIDENTIAL VOTE CAST
            BY 11 SOUTHERN STATES.
— — S — —   PERCENTAGE OF TOTAL REPUBLICAN HOUSE OF REPRESENTA-
            TIVES MEMBERSHIP ELECTED BY 11 SOUTHERN STATES.

ancy, while the Republicans are turning the tables on their opponents in the non-Yankee bailiwicks of post-Civil War Democratic tradition.

This turnabout, which bodes poorly for the GOP in New England —even Vermont and New Hampshire are no longer safe—augurs well for Republican presidential chances in Maryland, Delaware and New Jersey, the three Northeastern states that spurned party candidates in almost all of the races between 1860 and 1892. George Wallace scored his best Northeastern percentages in these three states, and this electorate is one in motion between the parties. Because of similar, although reduced, influences, Pennsylvania should also be a presidential battleground of the upcoming cycle. On the basis of history, these are the Northeastern states to which the Republicans can look for support of a political movement rooted in the South and West.

The Republican future is also greatly aided by demographic trends not only internally reshaping the Northeast, but diminishing the region's national influence. Chart 142 shows how the voting power of the big Northeastern cities diminishes as population shifts to suburbia, local and distant.

As Chart 52 illustrates, the Northeast and the South have maintained a changing position with regard to one another and the Republican Party throughout the entire New Deal cycle. From the peak years of the New Deal, the power of the Northeast within the Republican Party has been declining as the influence of the South has been rising. This upheaval was more or less consummated by the Goldwater nomination and defeat; in some ways, the 1968 election was merely a ratification, although it was the *sine qua non,* powerwise, of the basic geopolitical trend spotlighted and accelerated in 1964. The Republican Party is no longer the party of the Northeast—and an increasing part of its Northeastern strength is rooted in voting streams like the urban Catholics and rural non-Yankees who have historically been allies (often a local minority) of the political vehicle of the South and West.

To understand the position of the Northeast in national politics, it is also useful to consider the position of the South as a historic political foe of the Northeast; the two never seem to be going in the same partisan or ideological direction.

III. THE SOUTH

$$\text{⊏⊐⊏⊐ ⊏⊐⊏⊐ ⊏⊐⊏⊐ ⊏⊐⊏⊐ ⊏⊐⊏⊐ ⊏⊐⊏⊐ ⊏⊐⊏⊐}$$

TOGETHER WITH THE HEARTLAND, THE SOUTH IS SHAPING UP AS the pillar of a national conservative party. Granted that the South and Heartland have long worked together in Congress, they have not done so in the same partisan harness. However, the extraordinary 1968 debacle of the Democratic Party—a collapse never before experienced by the Democrats throughout the *entire* region— bespoke a sharp acceleration of the Republican trend in Dixie. At the same time, liberal fragments of the South—Miami, Tampa, Gulf Coast and Mexican Texas, elements of French Louisiana and Black Belt areas dominated by Negro electorates—disassociated themselves from the emerging national conservative grouping (just as most had sent liberal representatives to the last congresses of the Great Society).

The South is a many-faced political entity. In Texas and Arkansas, it turns Western; in Virginia and Kentucky, it turns Northern. Nor can it be easily bounded. There are Southern areas in Northern states (Maryland's Eastern Shore) and in Western states (New Mexico's "Little Texas"), as well as across the Border (the "Little Dixies" of Kentucky, Missouri and Oklahoma). Perhaps the best way to approach the South is to define it as the eleven states of the old Confederacy, and then divide it into two distinct geopolitical sections—the Deep South and the Outer South (see Map 19).

MAP 19

The Dual South

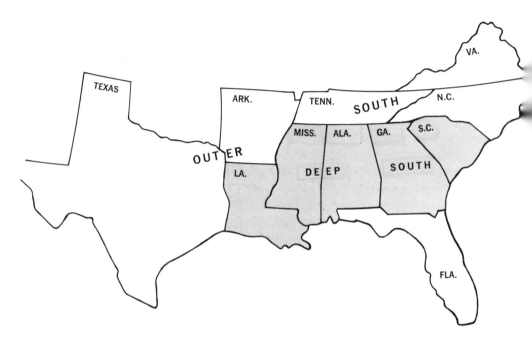

In terms of social and cultural patterns, the Deep South sweeps from "Southside" Virginia through the lowlands of eastern North Carolina and South Carolina across Georgia, Alabama, Mississippi and Louisiana and into East Texas. But in terms of the states predominantly Deep Southern in politics, the subregion is as follows: South Carolina, Georgia, Alabama, Mississippi and Louisiana. These are the states with the largest Negro populations and the most acutely Negrophobe politics. This is the South of stereotyped tradition of watermelons, pickaninnies, mint juleps and plantations, —but also of Black Panther militancy, murdered civil rights workers, George Wallace and the Ku Klux Klan.

More than a century ago, it was the Deep South—along with Florida and Texas, two states then essentially Deep South in character—that led the South out of the Union upon the election of Abraham Lincoln as President. Beyond the Deep South, there was much less enthusiasm for secession. The four northernmost Confederate states—Virginia, North Carolina, Tennessee and Arkansas—were the last to secede. Virginia, North Carolina and Tennessee include large Appalachian highland areas, while Arkansas includes a substantial part of the Ozarks. By and large, the mountains opposed the cause of the lowland slaveowners, and many mountaineers fought their Civil War in Northern blue. Since then, the Ozark-Appalachian states just enumerated, along with Texas and Florida, have constituted a kind of Southern periphery, where changing socioeconomic patterns have submerged ante-bellum Deep South hegemony. In the half-century since 1920, these six states have differed considerably from the race-preoccupied politics of the Deep South. With considerable justification, the six can be considered as the "Outer South."

CHART 53

The Southern Seats of Democratic Power, 1880-1932

The Leading Democratic States (Number of Times Supporting Democratic Party Presidential Nominee in the Fourteen Elections Between 1880 and 1932)

Mississippi—14	Texas—13	Missouri—9
Alabama—14	North Carolina—13	Nevada—7
Louisiana—14	Florida—13	Maryland—7
Georgia—14	Virginia—13	New Jersey—6
South Carolina—14	Tennessee—12	West Virginia—6
Arkansas—14	Kentucky—11	(Oklahoma—5*)

*Oklahoma was not admitted to the Union until 1907; Southern-leaning Arizona and New Mexico did not enter until 1912.

Note: Election results in the South between 1868 and 1876 were distorted by Reconstruction.

As Chart 53 shows, the Southern states were the geopolitical heartland of the Democratic Party for almost a century after the Civil War. Indeed, the party was something of a Southern institution. Democratic fidelity, most intense in the Deep South, weakened in the Outer South and then eroded to a marginal point in the Border. From the Civil War until the New Deal, only a few allies—a varied skein of Westerners, Irish and German Catholics, and Pennsylvania

Southern Settlement Patterns

Extent of Settlement in 1860

As the map shows, Virginia, North Carolina, Tennessee and Ozark Arkansas, as well as the Border states of Kentucky and Missouri, represent one mainstream of Southern settlement while the Deep South—South Carolina, Georgia, Alabama, Mississippi, Louisiana and the early populated sections of Texas and Florida—represent another. In 1860, West Texas and southern Florida were barely settled; their rapid growth of a later era overwhelmed the initial Deep South settlement patterns of the two states.

The chart below shows the distribution of Virginian, North Carolinian and South Carolinian-Georgian emigrants in 1850:

Emigrants From Original Southern States by Regions of Residence as Shown by the 1850 Census

Original State	Old Northwest (Ohio, Indiana and Illinois)	Border (Kentucky, Mo. and Tenn.)	Deep South (Ala., Miss., Fla., Ark., La. and Texas)
Virginia	156,000	142,000	38,000
North Carolina	52,000	108,000	103,000
South Carolina/Georgia	12,000	80,000	280,000

Dutch—reliably embroidered on this fundamentally rural pattern of regional strength.

Actually, there is more to the cohesion of the Cotton states—or the Ozark-Appalachian group—than mere similar topography, although topography is an important underlying factor. Middle and eastern Tennessee and upland Arkansas were largely settled from the Piedmont, the valleys and highlands of Virginia and North Carolina; Alabama, Mississippi and Louisiana, as well as nothern Florida and east Texas, were principally settled from Georgia, South Carolina and the lowland eastern part of North Carolina. As a result there are two major streams of population origin in the white South, one Outer Southern and relatively moderate and the other archetypal Deep Southern (see Map 20).

The distinction between the Deep South and the Outer South is real and basic. Chart 54 shows how this split has characterized the Southern politics of the last half-century.

For two generations after the Civil War, Southern politics showed the cleavage between mountain Republicanism and the predominant and generally lowland-oriented Democratic Party. The now booming west of Texas and south of Florida were of only minor political importance. Creole Louisiana provided a variation on the basic theme, but in essence, regional politics followed a very simple pattern—a refighting of the Civil War. Many Deep South counties—after the Negro disenfranchisement measures of the Eighteen-Nineties, only whites voted—cast ten-, twenty-, and thirty-to-one Democratic majorities, while the most partisan Republican mountain counties turned in four-, five-, and six-to-one majorities on the other side. And the Piedmont, being in between the mountains and Black Belt politically as well as culturally and altitudinally, normally voted two-, three-, or four-to-one Democratic.

But this post-Civil War alignment did not take shape immediately after Appomattox. For ten years, at least part of Dixie lay under the heel of Northern troops and political (Republican) Reconstruction. And even after the federal troops left, it was some years before Negroes were generally disenfranchised and Southern politics took on a nearly lily-white color.

During the Eighteen-Eighties and Nineties, Southern highland Republicans briefly made cause with lowland poor whites—and in some states, even with Negroes—in a Populist-GOP alliance. By this strategy, the Republicans won some local successes, even capturing the North Carolina governorship for two years. However,

CHART 54

The Two Political Faces of Dixie, 1928-66

State	Negro Population, 1960	1928 States Voting for Hoover over Smith	1948 States Voting for Dixiecrats	1952 States Voting for Eisenhower	1960 States Voting for Nixon	1960 States with Independent Elector Candidates	1960 States Electing Republicans to Congress	1964 States Voting for Goldwater	1966 States Electing New Republican Congressmen*
Outer South									
Virginia	22%	X		X	X		X		X
Tennessee	16	X		X	X		X		X
N. Carolina	26	X					X		X
Florida	22	X		X	X		X		X
Texas	13	X		X			X		X
Arkansas	22								X
Deep South									
Georgia	31							X	
Alabama	32		X			X		X	
Louisiana	33		X			X		X	
S. Carolina	39		X					X	
Mississippi	45		X			X		X	

*States where at least one new Republican congressman was elected and no old districts were lost

Bourbon Democrats triumphed and then enacted poll taxes to disenfranchise Republican or Populist-leaning poor whites and Negroes alike. Chart 55 shows the chronology of disenfranchisement in South Carolina, where more than half the population was Negro. Some of the remnants of the broken Populist parties lined up with the Republicans against the conservative Democratic commercial and plantation establishment, but notwithstanding these accretions, GOP strength proved inadequate to win a single statewide election in the South during the quarter century between 1896 and 1920.

CHART 55

South Carolina Presidential Voting, 1876-1928

Total Vote Cast for President (Thousands)

1876	1880	1884	1888	1892	1896	1900
182.8	160.4	91.6	79.6	68.1	68.9	50.9

1904	1908	1912	1916	1920	1924	1928
55.1	66.4	51.3	63.5	66.4	50.8	68.6

Between 1896 (when Negro disenfranchisement was effectively completed) and 1920, Southern Republican strength depended on the mountaineer vote. In Virginia, North Carolina and Tennessee, that vote was adequate to give the GOP one third or more of the statewide total. Mountain support in Arkansas, Alabama and Georgia was usually not enough to give the Republicans more than 20 per cent of the statewide vote. Texas had some cattle country and German refugee Republican strength, but the wholly Deep South states—Mississippi, South Carolina and Louisiana—were practically devoid of Republican adherents.

In 1920, the Republicans breached the hitherto "Solid South" by winning the electoral votes of Tennessee. The principal impetus behind GOP gains in the South in 1920 was a great outpouring of mountaineers desirous of voting for Harding's promised "Return to Normalcy" (isolationism). A similar trend in the Ozarks buoyed Republican totals in Arkansas and Missouri. Interestingly enough, French Louisiana also turned on the Democrats, possibly because of Wilson's vocal differences with French Premier Clemenceau. By

1924, the isolationist ardor of the mountaineers had cooled during four years of peace and Prohibition-engendered "moonshine" prosperity. Most of Creole Louisiana also returned to the Democratic column, although a few French parishes supported Coolidge. At the same time, the Southern economic boom of the Twenties helped the GOP to make considerable strides in hitherto overwhelmingly Democratic Southern cities.

Then in 1928, the Republicans split the "Solid South" like a melon.

Chart 56 illustrates how much predominantly Negro and predominantly white counties differed in their response to Catholicism and the 1928 election. In state after state, the predominantly white counties were those switching to Hoover (187 of the 266 Southern counties with white majorities backed the Republican nominee), and it was the Black Belt counties—184 out of 191 with non-voting Negro majorities—which stuck by the Democratic Party. Moreover, not only did the hitherto twenty-to-one Democratic Black Belts keep

CHART 56

Black Belt Loyalty in the 1928 Election

State	Number of Counties More Than Half Negro, 1930	Number With Al Smith Majority	Number of Counties Less Than 5% Negro, 1930	Number With Al Smith Majority
Alabama	18	18	6	1
Arkansas	9	9	29	21*
Florida	4	4	1	0
Georgia	48	46	11	3
Louisiana	16	16	0	0
Mississippi	35	35	0	0
North Carolina	9	9	14	1
South Carolina	25	25	0	0
Tennessee	2	2	37	11
Texas	4	4	150	37
Virginia	21	16	18	5
Total	191	184	266	79

*Democratic vice-presidential candidate came from Arkansas

faith with Smith, but local voters turned out in record numbers and showed little or no pro-Hoover trend. Running against Catholic Al Smith, Hoover carried five Southern states—Virginia, Tennessee, North Carolina, Florida and Texas—through a combination of these trends: increasing middle-class Republicanism in the Piedmont (North Carolina and Virginia); growing economic Republicanism in the new resort and plains cities (Florida and Texas); heavy anti-Catholic voting in the Gulf Coast pineywoods (Florida); Baptist anti-Catholicism in the West Texas and Tennessee "Bible Belts"; and hereditary Republican voting by transplanted Northerners in the urban areas of Florida and Texas. Thus, while anti-Catholicism was important, it was by no means the only factor at work for Hoover. The urban Republican trend of the Nineteen-Twenties was strong enough so that even in 1932 Hoover was able to do better in some Southern cities—Richmond, Dallas and Charlotte—than had the GOP prior to the Nineteen-Twenties.

Even while the Outer South was venting its tradition-breaking, anti-Smith and (more genuine) economic Republicanism, the Deep South was sticking by the Democratic faith and giving Smith a record vote. In Mississippi, Georgia and Louisiana, Smith won more votes than any previous Democratic presidential nominee. Except for its pineywoods and upcountry fringe, the Deep South was too preoccupied with Negrophobia and loyalty to the one-party system as an instrument of white supremacy to worry about anti-Catholicism. The late eminent authority on Southern politics, Professor V. O. Key, Jr., has analyzed and documented this phenomenon, which will be more thoroughly explored in the subsequent pages describing the Deep South. Suffice it to say that in 1928, while white counties throughout the South broke Democratic ranks to support Hoover, the Black Belt remained loyal. (It must be remembered that nearly all Black Belt votes were cast by whites. Negroes were effectively kept from voting.)

As Chart 57 shows, the Catholic and anti-Catholic overtones of the 1928 election had little effect in the two Southern subregions of fierce traditional partisan bent—the antagonistic Republican mountains and the Democratic Black Belts. The hearts of both subregions voted as usual: bitterly Republican and bitterly Democratic by better than ten-to-one majorities. It was only outside of the Deep South—in the cities, along the Gulf Coast, in the Piedmont and foothills, on the Texas plains, in tropical Florida, along the North

CHART 57

Relative Republican Trends of Selected Southern County Groupings, 1924-28

Section (Counties)	GOP Share of Two-Party Vote for President, 1924	GOP Share of Two-Party Vote for President, 1928
Anti-Catholic Voting		
Florida-Mississippi Gulf Coast Pineywoods (Okaloosa, Santa Rosa; Fla.)	24%	74%
West Texas Baptist Bible Belt (Cottle, King)	17%	52%
Tennessee Valley Bible Belt (Morgan, Madison; Ala.)	17%	53%
Traditional GOP Strength		
Ozark Arkansas (Newton, Searcy)	64%	70%
North Carolina-Tennessee Appalachian Highlands (Sevier, Tenn.; Avery, N.C.)	87%	91%
Virginia-North Carolina German Piedmont (Shenandoah, Va.; Cabarrus, N.C.)	46%	61%
New South		
Urban Boom-Resort Areas (Palm Beach, Fla.; Dallas, Texas)	44%	62%
Outer South Cities (Norfolk, Va.; Atlanta, Ga.; Charlotte, N.C.)	28%	54%
Old Deep South		
Mississippi Delta Black Belt (Sunflower, Leflore)	7%	4%
South Carolina Tidewater Black Belt (Colleton, Dorchester)	2%	3%
Pro-Catholic Voting		
French Creole Louisiana (Catholic) (Terrebonne, La Fourche)	46%	13%

Carolina "Outer Banks" and in the few traditionally Democratic mountain counties—that Democratic traditions gave way to anti-Catholic Republicanism.

A few years later, embryonic Southern Republicanism proved to be one of the first casualties of the Great Depression. Southerners gave Franklin D. Roosevelt extremely heavy support in 1932, and they welcomed the Democratic Party's return to power. The local courthouse faithful queued for patronage, and Southern Democrats of great seniority took over congressional leadership posts in Washington. By 1938, however, the labor and urban bias of the New Deal had alienated many Southern conservatives, and their doubts were reinforced as Roosevelt tried to purge leading conservatives in that year's Democratic primaries. In half of the Southern states, Roosevelt's huge Southern percentages of 1932 shrank a bit in 1936. And in 1940, the decline was more uniform. After the United States entered World War II, mountaineer isolationism prompted a renewed GOP trend in the highlands, and in 1944, the Southern Republican vote climbed back to 1924 levels, setting the stage for another Dixie flirtation with the two-party system.

After World War II, the desegregation impetus gathered momentum in the United States to the disquiet of the Deep South (in 1944, the Supreme Court had ruled that the white Democratic primary—mainstay of Southern one-party politics—was unconstitutional). Finally, in 1948, after failing to halt the civil rights trend at the Democratic national convention, the Deep South decided to bolt the Democratic Party and field a third-party candidate of its own. To that end, "Dixiecrats," representing the states of Mississippi, South Carolina, Louisiana, Alabama and Georgia met in Birmingham and nominated South Carolina Governor J. Strom Thurmond for President and Mississippi Governor Fielding Wright for Vice President. A few Arkansas, North Carolina, Virginia and Tennessee politicians showed some interest in the Dixiecrat movement, but for the most part, it drew on the Deep South.

As the Deep South sowed, so it reaped—a parochial Deep South harvest. Thurmond and Wright carried only Mississippi, South Carolina, Louisiana and Alabama. For obvious reasons, the Dixiecrats did well where Al Smith had run strongly in 1928. Besides conservative (often urban) middle- and upper-class economics, the Dixiecrat movement represented much of the same white supremacist impetus which had kept the Deep South loyal even to a

Catholic Democrat (back in the days when the Democratic Party was still loyal to the Deep South). There is a very clear county-level correlation between Smith loyalty in 1928 and Dixiecrat rebelliousness in 1948. The worst Dixiecrat states were the five which Hoover had carried—Virginia, North Carolina, Florida, Texas and Tennessee. The best Dixiecrat states—Mississippi, Louisiana and South Carolina—were the banner Smith states. Chart 58 shows the distinct relationship between the 1928 and 1948 patterns.

CHART 58

Relationship Between Dixiecrat Support Levels in 1948 and Democratic Loyalty in 1928

State	Democratic Share of the Total Vote for President, 1928	Dixiecrat Share of the Total Vote for President, 1948
Mississippi	82%	87%
South Carolina	91	71
Louisiana	76	49
Alabama*	51	(*)
Georgia	57	20
Arkansas**	61	16
Tennessee	46	13
Florida***	42	16
Virginia	46	11
Texas	48	10
North Carolina	45	9

Alabama: Abnormally Republican in 1928 because Alabama Senator Heflin bolted to support Hoover. No contest in 1948 because Alabama Dixiecrats pre-empted the Democratic line on the ballot.
**Arkansas:* Abnormally Democratic in 1928 because Arkansas Senator Robinson was Democratic vice-presidential nominee.
***Florida:* Abnormally Republican in 1928 because of heavy concentration of Gulf Coast voters who opposed Smith in 1928 (but gave fair support to Dixiecrats in 1948).

Notwithstanding the failure of the Dixiecrat strategy to throw the 1948 election into the House of Representatives (Thurmond won only 39 electoral votes), Deep South animosity towards the national

Democratic Party persisted. In 1952, a sizeable vote was cast in the three die-hard Dixiecrat states—49 per cent in South Carolina, 47 per cent in Louisiana and 40 per cent in Mississippi—for the Republican candidate, General Eisenhower. This support centered in the cities and Black Belt areas of all three states and correlated with the Thurmond and Smith votes. The Deep South, whatever its feelings towards the national Democratic Party, still refused to support Republican candidates by voting for them on the Republican line. Most of the Mississippi and South Carolina Eisenhower vote came from slates of independent electors.

In the Deep South, the bulk of the Eisenhower vote was cast in the cities, where the list of the General's victories and near victories reads like a gazetteer of the Confederacy—Charleston, Savannah, Mobile, Montgomery, Jackson, Natchez, Vicksburg and New Orleans. Except for a minority of vehemently Dixiecrat Black Belt counties, the rural Deep South did not show the same enthusiasm for the Republican candidate. All in all, Eisenhower did astonishingly well—for a Republican—in South Carolina, Louisiana and Mississippi, but he did less well in Alabama (35 per cent) and Georgia (30 per cent). Within the Deep South, 1952 Eisenhower support occurred where Dixiecrat rebelliousness had breached Democratic traditions in 1948.

On a regional basis, however, Eisenhower's victories came where Hoover's had—in the Outer South. Although Eisenhower failed to

CHART 59

Southern Urban Republicanism, 1952

State	GOP Plurality in State	GOP Gain Over 1948 In Urban Counties
Florida[1]	99,086	169,400
Tennessee[2]	2,437	120,600
Texas[3]	132,750	271,800
Virginia[4]	80,360	72,710

1. Counties including Miami, Jacksonville, Tampa and St. Petersburg.
2. Counties including Nashville, Memphis and Chattanooga.
3. Counties including San Antonio, Dallas, Houston and Fort Worth.
4. All Virginia Independent Cities (including Richmond, Norfolk, Roanoke and others).

win North Carolina, he did carry Florida, Texas, Virginia and Tennessee. Eisenhower tapped the same Outer South Republican socioeconomic trend (since resurrected by postwar prosperity), which briefly bloomed in 1928, only to be cut short by the Depression. Throughout the South, Eisenhower's vote soared in the same cities where Hoover had made major breakthroughs in 1928. It was substantially as a result of urban vote gains that Eisenhower won Texas, Florida, Virginia and Tennessee.

Although important, urbanism was not the only key to Eisenhower's Southern gains. In the first place, the underlying base of GOP victory in the Outer South was traditional—the mountaineers of Virginia, Tennessee and Arkansas, and the Northerners and Westerners of Florida and Texas. Secondly, there was a very strong correlation between 1952 Republican gains and 1948 Dixiecrat strength, which accounted for part of Eisenhower's urban pickup—the Dixiecrats had been strong in cities like Memphis, Richmond and Jacksonville—as well as some of the rural increase. In the Outer South, as in the Deep South, the 1952 trend of 1948 Dixiecrats was strongly Republican. Chart 60 illustrates the correlation between 1948 Dixiecrat strength in Tennessee and the Eisenhower gains by which the GOP carried the state in 1952. But while Eisenhower generally picked up 1948 Dixiecrat supporters, it is worth noting that such voters were not necessarily Black Belt residents, at least not in the Outer South states of Virginia and North Carolina.*

The Eisenhower vote patterns in the Deep South and Outer South were basically different. In the Outer South, the GOP built on its traditional electorate, adding urban and Dixiecrat votes, while the Democrats held most Black Belt counties (many were non-Dixiecratic and conditioned by years of opposition to mountain, ranchland or emigrant Northern Republicanism). But in the Deep South, where no traditional Republican support existed, the GOP gained "instant" support from many Dixiecrat Black Belt counties.

In his 1956 re-election bid, President Eisenhower gained in the Outer South but slipped somewhat in the Deep South, largely as a result of the Supreme Court's 1954 school desegregation decision. Within the Deep South, Eisenhower's gains came in the cities and in

---

*In Virginia and North Carolina, conservative Democratic organizations had their roots in the Piedmont; and Tidewater Virginia and Black Belt North Carolina, far from being prime Dixiecrat territory, had records of *liberal* insurgency within the Democratic Party.

CHART 60

*The Correlation Between 1948 Dixiecrat Strength and 1944-52
Republican Gains in Tennessee*

The 7 Highest Dixiecrat Counties, 1948		*The 7 Highest 1944-52 Republican-Gain Counties*	
County	Dixiecrat % of Total Presidential Vote	County	1944-52 Increase in GOP Share of the Total Presidential Vote
Fayette	86%	Fayette	36%
Haywood	44%	Shelby	29%
Hardeman	42%	Madison	22%
Shelby	41%	Obion	22%
Maury	33%	Haywood	20%
Lake	33%	Coffee	20%
Madison	29%	Maury	20%

*The 5 Worst Dixiecrat
Counties, 1948*

County	Dixiecrat % of Total Presidential Vote	1944-52 Increase in GOP Share of the Total Presidential Vote
Morgan	0.5%	9.6%
Monroe	1.2%	4.9%
Scott	1.2%	3.2%
Pickett	1.5%	1.2%
Union	1.8%	2.1%

Note: As regards Tennessee, one can only conclude that the leading force behind
Eisenhower's narrow victory was the addition of West and Middle Tennessee Dixiecrat strength to the traditionally Republican ballots of Appalachian East Tennessee.

Creole Louisiana. To the surprise of most observers, Louisiana became the first Deep South state since Reconstruction to choose a
Republican slate of presidential electors. Whereas the belligerently
Dixiecrat northern section of Louisiana had turned Republican in
1952, most of the French Catholic bayou parishes had remained

Democratic. Thus, when the Creoles switched to Eisenhower in 1956, Louisiana joined Texas, Tennessee, Virginia and Florida in the Republican column. (North Carolina barely remained Democratic.)

As the 1960 election approached, pitting a Protestant Republican against a Catholic Democrat in repetition of the 1928 confrontation, many people wondered how the South would respond. Given existing presidential GOP strength in the South, a strong anti-Catholic tide would have swept the region into the Republican column. As things turned out, however, there was very little anti-Catholic voting in the South, although pro-Catholic voting elsewhere won crucial Northern electoral votes and probably the election for Democrat John F. Kennedy.

In Chart 57, several groups of counties were cited as showing rampant anti-Catholic bias in 1928. This was not the case in 1960. The only notable Southern anti-Catholic voting occurred in the Oklahoma-West Texas and Tennessee Valley Baptist "Bible Belts," and even that was on a smaller scale than in 1928. Chart 61 shows the 1956-60 vote change of the counties which had demonstrated

CHART 61

Southern Religious Voting in the 1960 Presidential Election

Section (Counties)	GOP Share of Two-Party Vote for President, 1956	GOP Share of Two-Party Vote for President, 1960
Florida-Mississippi Gulf Coast Pineywoods (Okaloosa, Santa Rosa; Fla.)	32%	36%
West Texas Baptist Bible Belt (Cottle, King)	22%	26%
Tennessee Valley Bible Belt (Morgan, Colbert; Ala.)	24%	32%
French Creole Louisiana (*Catholic*) (Terrebonne, La Fourche)	63%	22%
Mexican Texas (*Catholic*) (Webb, Duval)	32%	16%

religious voting behavior in 1928. The heavy pro-Catholic voting of the French Catholic Louisiana parishes (counties) was complemented by similar voting in Mexican areas of Texas. (Few Mexicans had voted in 1928.)

After the last votes were tallied, Nixon had held Tennessee, Virginia and Florida. The latter two states turned in legitimate GOP victories, but it was anti-Catholic voting that carried the day in Tennessee, where Nixon won a bigger share of the vote than Eisenhower. Notwithstanding Baptist "Bible Belt" behavior, Texas went Democratic for the first time since 1948 because of the presence of Texas Senator Lyndon Johnson on the ballot as the Democratic vice-presidential nominee and the unprecedented size of the Mexican vote. As expected, a heavy pro-Catholic Democratic shift in French Louisiana returned that state to the Democratic column.

Nixon's Virginia, North Carolina, Texas and Florida totals were also reduced by a decline in the GOP vote in the cities where Eisenhower had done so well. (See Chart 75.) Apart from the anti-Catholic "Bible Belts," only the Deep South and the Black Belt counties of the Outer South showed a Republican trend between 1956 and 1960. Most of the Piedmont sections of North Carolina and Virginia moved slightly toward the Democrats, while the mountain districts remained about where they had been in 1956.

As a result of Nixon's ability to win Florida, Virginia and Tennessee—the three states chalked up their third successive GOP presidential victory—while running a close race in Texas, Arkansas, North Carolina and South Carolina, observers generally agreed that two-party presidential politics had become a reality across much of the South. Even in the Deep South, Nixon brought the GOP vote to record heights, although he did not win any statewide majorities. These were not religious-based gains; the Deep South had other preoccupations. In large measure, Nixon's strides were attributable to growing Southern suspicion of the social and civil rights policies of the national Democratic Party.

To accelerate Republican penetration of the old Confederacy, the Republican National Committee put new emphasis on its existing "Operation Dixie." In the next few years, the GOP cause met with considerable Southern success. Texas elected its first Republican United States Senator since Reconstruction, John Tower, in a 1961 special election to fill the vacant seat of Vice President Lyndon Johnson. Then in the 1962 congressional elections, the GOP won four new House seats—one each in North Carolina, Florida, Tennessee and Texas. Alabama almost elected a Republican United States Senator.

Not content with forging evolutionary gains in the Outer South, GOP conservatives set up the "Southern Strategy," which helped achieve the 1964 nomination of Barry Goldwater. Simply put, the idea was to join the South and West in a conservative coalition. What would have happened had the GOP been able to nominate a more moderate conservative will never be known. Instead, the party chose Barry Goldwater, and his platform—quite conservative to begin with—was quickly propagandized as barely disguised racism in the Deep South vein. This image gained so much credence that Goldwater swung the Deep South into the Republican column but sacrificed the rest of the nation, including the Outer South. In essence, Goldwater won where Thurmond had won in 1948, largely for the same reasons. Like Thurmond, Goldwater captured Mississippi, South Carolina, Alabama and Louisiana, and added Georgia —the next-best Dixiecrat state—to the list.

As part of the Goldwater landslide in the Deep South, the Republicans won five new congressional districts in Alabama, one in Mississippi, and one in Georgia. Early in 1965, pro-Goldwater South Carolina Democratic Congressman Albert Watson turned Republican. But at the same time that these Deep South advances were being made, the GOP lost two Congressional seats in Texas and opportunities elsewhere in the Outer South.

Florida, Virginia and Tennessee were among the Southern states carried by Lyndon Johnson, marking the first time since 1944 that any of the three states had given a majority of their vote to a Democratic presidential candidate. Much of the GOP vote decline can be attributed to a strong Democratic trend in the cities, occasioned by white and Negro voting alike.

In contrast to their Northern compatriots, many Southern Negroes had voted Republican in 1956 and 1960. But Goldwater failed to keep this support. And in Florida, the worst 1960-64 GOP decline came in staunchly Republican Pinellas County (St. Petersburg), heavily populated by retired persons whose voting reflected their fears of Barry Goldwater's widely alleged opposition to Social Security. Chart 75 illustrates the 1964 GOP difficulties in Pinellas and other normally Republican Southern urban areas. It was not just minority group trending that undercut Goldwater in Texas, Florida, North Carolina, Virginia and Tennessee; the Arizona Senator also suffered from the apprehensions of a sizeable group of basically conservative Republicans.

As the smoke of battle cleared, there could be no doubt that "revolutionary" Republicanism had failed throughout much of the South which it was supposed to take by storm. Most GOP politicians recognized that the Deep South could not be sought on its own terms, and that the Republican Party must first achieve an evolutionary pre-eminence in the Outer South.

Shortly after Goldwater's defeat, the extremely liberal Eighty-Ninth Congress passed (and the President, of course, signed) the Voting Rights Act of 1965. This legislation struck down the literacy tests of Southern (although not Northern) states on the ground that such requirements were rooted in discrimination; moreover, one of the bill's key provisions specified circumstances under which federal registrars could go into Southern counties and actively register Negroes as qualified voters. Before long, the federal registrars were enrolling Negroes throughout the Black Belt, and by November, 1966, large numbers of Negroes were registered to vote in Deep South states where, since the turn of the century, only a few Negroes had been permitted to vote.

Their peculiar 1964 identification with the Deep South having gone by the boards as of 1966, the GOP lost four of the Alabama, Mississippi and Georgia House seats picked up in the Goldwater landslide.* At the same time, however, they gained in the Outer South, electing a United States Senator in Tennessee for the first time since Reconstruction, and with similar lack of precedent capturing the statehouses of Florida and Arkansas. In contrast to the loss of Deep South House seats, two new ones were won in Piedmont Georgia (Atlanta), one in Piedmont North Carolina, one in the western Virginia mountains, one in suburban Florida, one in Memphis, one in Ozark Arkansas and two in Texas. Gains of this magnitude bespoke more than an upsurge; they were a sign of breakthrough.

Another upheaval was also taking shape—a sharp conservative trend among hitherto populist Southern poor whites. In part, this

*The loss might not have been so great had three of the incumbents not decided to seek other offices instead of re-election.

was a result of the implementation of the Voting Rights Act. Displeased by federal intervention on behalf of Negroes, poor whites registered to vote in greatly increased numbers, offsetting enlarged Negro enrollment in many states. For many years, the poor whites of the Deep South had shunned the conservatism of States Rights, Dixiecrat and Republican candidates, but by 1966 they were becoming disillusioned with the stance of the national Democratic Party. Trading on this alienation, conservatives Lurleen Wallace and Lester Maddox swept the poor white sections of Alabama and Georgia in the two states' Democratic gubernatorial primaries, winning areas that had previously supported relatively liberal candidates. Quite simply, as liberalism metamorphosed from an economic populist stance—supporting farm, highway, health, education and pension expenditures against conservative budget-cutting—into a credo of social engineering, it lost the support of poor whites. Equally important was conservatism's adoption of some economic populism to augment its opposition to Negro-oriented social innovation. The Negro socioeconomic revolution gave conservatism a degree of access to Southern poor white support which it had not enjoyed since the somewhat comparable Reconstruction era.

On the level of presidential politics, this frustration with the civil rights revolution and the national Democratic Party served to generate yet another of the South's ill-fated third-party efforts—the 1968 American Independent Party candidacy of former Alabama Governor George C. Wallace. Blending populism and some legitimate complaints about American society with an unspoken opposition to further government assistance for Negroes, Wallace mobilized the most widespread Southern poltical rebellion in a century. Compared to Thurmond, Wallace was much the stronger candidate. Moreover, he won his victories under a full-fledged third-party banner (except in Alabama, where he usurped the Democratic Party line as Thurmond had). And whereas the 1948 Dixiecrat had been a candidate of little more than the Deep South Black Belts, Wallace was also the choice of the upcountry, pineywoods and bayous. Together, Wallace and Nixon swept at least four-fifths of the white Southern electorate. Unlike Thurmond, who left white Democratic loyalties untouched throughout much of the South, Wallace left few intact.

In 1968, Nixon focused the Republican trend in the mountains,

Piedmont and white middle-class urban and suburban areas of the Outer South, while Wallace marshaled the anger of most white voters in the Deep South and Outer South Black Belts. Notwithstanding their transient Goldwater Republicanism of 1964, most Deep Southern whites preferred to support Wallace rather than Nixon. The GOP nominee won a respectable Deep South vote only in the cities.* As a result of the two-pronged attack of Nixon and Wallace, Hubert Humphrey was annihilated below the Mason-Dixon line. Taking the eleven ex-Confederate states together, it is doubtful whether Humphrey won as much as 20 per cent of the white vote. His support was principally concentrated in Negro and Latin precincts, although he won substantial white backing in Jewish sections of Miami and Atlanta, Gulf Coast Texas, unionized mining counties in western Virginia and some brass-collar Democratic rural counties in central Texas. On a statewide basis, Nixon carried Florida, Tennessee, Virginia, North Carolina and South Carolina; Wallace captured Louisiana, Alabama, Mississippi, Georgia and Arkansas. In Texas, the most liberal of the Southern states, the Nixon-Wallace split in the white conservative vote allowed Humphrey to put together a thin plurality.

Chart 62 lists the Nixon, Wallace and Humphrey vote shares in the eleven states of the old Confederacy. Charts 63 and 74 illustrate the decline and fall of the Democratic Party in the Deep South and Outer South over the last thirty-six years. Never before has a Democratic presidential candidate been reduced to Hubert Humphrey's ruinous 1968 straits in both the Deep South *and* the Outer South. The election statistics of 1968 signaled the end of an era.

Because the political history of the South divides so strikingly into two mainstreams, so must the telling of it. The first subchapter which follows discusses the Deep South, seat of regional political tradition, and the second progresses to the Outer South, where non-Southern influences have invariably been strongest. Last comes an assessment of the future of Southern politics.

*Nixon's only good showings in the Deep South came in the cities and suburbs. In South Carolina, he swept the Charleston, Greenville and Columbia areas. Suburban Atlanta went strongly for Nixon, and the Republican candidate also did well in Savannah and Augusta. Urban Louisiana turned in a respectable Nixon vote, and in heavily pro-Wallace Alabama and Mississippi, the bulk of the Nixon votes were cast in the cities. But although the GOP nominee carried the opinion-maker precincts of the urban Deep South, Wallace won huge white majorities in the small towns and countryside.

CHART 62

Southern Presidential Voting Patterns, 1960-68

State	1960 (GOP Outer Southern Strategy) Nixon Share of Major Party Vote for President	1964 (GOP Deep Southern Strategy) Goldwater Share of Major Party Vote for President	1968 (GOP Outer Southern Strategy) Share of Total Vote for President		
			Nixon	Wallace	Humphrey
Virginia	53%	43%	43%	24%	33%
North Carolina	48	44	40	31	29
Tennessee	54	45	38	34	28
Florida	52	49	41	29	31
Texas	49	37	40	19	41
Arkansas	46	44	31	39	30
South Carolina	49	59	38	32	30
Georgia	37	54	30	43	27
Louisiana	36	57	24	48	28
Alabama	42	70	14	66	19
Mississippi	40	87	14	64	23

MAP 21

The South—A Geopolitical Division

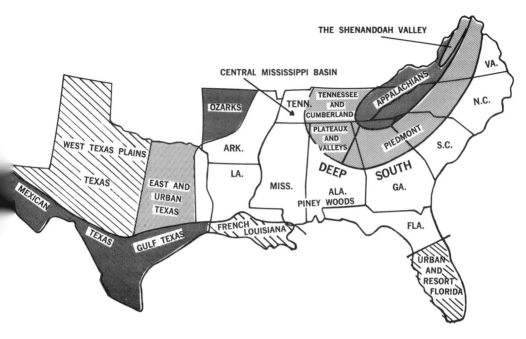

A. The Deep South

Based on local criteria of culture, geography, agriculture, large Negro populations and well-nigh unanimously Democratic voting from 1876 to 1948, the Deep South extends into at least a small section of every Southern state. From a statewide political stand-point, however, only South Carolina, Georgia, Alabama, Mississippi and Louisiana are sufficiently dominated by counties of a lowland, substantially Negro cast to be called Deep Southern states.

Just as archetypal Deep Southern characteristics extend far be-yond the core states of the Confederacy, it is likewise true that many non-Deep Southern sections exist in South Carolina, Georgia, Alabama, Mississippi and Louisiana. First of all, the Appalachian highlands brush South Carolina and extend over small portions of Alabama and Georgia. Secondly, a belt of poor and predominantly white Piedmont or clay hill counties reaches from northeastern

Mississippi to South Carolina. Thirdly, a stretch of coastal piney-woods—where there are few Negroes and scarcely any plantations—runs from southern Georgia to Gulf Coast Mississippi. Lastly, the bayou country and Mississippi River delta of southern Louisiana are populated by French Catholics who constitute a political behavioral stream quite distinct from the Cotton States' Anglo-Saxondom. Map 21 shows the geopolitical regions of the South.

In the Outer South, other sections balance or outweigh Deep Southern influence, but in the five Cotton States, the attitudes and conflicts of the Black Belts are dominant. Indeed, the Black Belts—the old plantation lowland slave counties—are the source of most Deep South stereotypes, and statewide predominance of such influence is the hallmark of the core Deep South. In states where Black Belt counties and Negro populations constitute only a small statewide minority—Texas and North Carolina, especially—local white voters have not shared the racial fixations characterizing Black Belt electorates in heavily Negro states such as Mississippi or South Carolina. (Both states were about half Negro as late as the outbreak of World War II.)

From the end of Reconstruction until 1948, the Deep South Black Belts, where only whites could vote, were the nation's leading Democratic Party bastions. Because the South was the homeland of the Democratic Party and the Black Belts were the ultimate South, Black Belt counties typically gave Democratic presidential nominees 90 per cent to 100 per cent support. Beginning in 1948, however, the white voters of the Black Belts shifted partisan gears and sought to lead the Deep South out of the Democratic Party. Upcountry, pineywoods and bayou voters felt less hostility towards the New Deal and Fair Deal economic and racial policies which agitated the Black Belts, and for another decade, they kept the Deep South in the Democratic presidential column.

Ultimately, Deep South politics changed to reflect the civil rights revolution of the Nineteen-Sixties. In 1964, the pineywoods, bayous and even substantial parts of the upcountry left the Democratic Party. Shortly thereafter, the Democratic national administration, having become totally estranged from its onetime Southern stronghold and oriented instead towards the urban Northeast, enacted federal voting rights legislation and enrolled large numbers of Deep Southern Negroes as qualified voters. And in 1968, this new Negro voting power turned the same Black Belts which had been the Dixiecrat, Republican or States' Rights bastions of 1948-64 into

CHART 63

Deep South Presidential Voting, 1932-68

Democratic Share of the Total Vote for President

State	1932	1936	1940	1944	1948*	1952	1956	1960	1964	1968**
Louisiana	93%	89%	86%	81%	33%	53%	40%	50%	43%	28%
Mississippi	96	97	96	94	10	60	58	36	13	23
Alabama	85	86	85	81	—	65	57	57	30	19
Georgia	92	87	85	82	61	70	66	63	46	27
South Carolina	98	99	96	88	24	51	45	51	41	30

*Democratic percentage of the Republican-Democrat-Dixiecrat vote.
**Democratic percentage of the Republican-Democrat-American Independent vote.

the *best* national Democratic counties in the Deep South. However, although most Negroes voted for Humphrey, they no longer constituted a majority in many Deep South counties—local Negro populations had been depleted by emigration—and could not play a very decisive role. Meanwhile, virtually all white Deep Southerners, from the bayous to the upcountry, abandoned the Democrats. Hubert Humphrey won a mere 5 per cent to 10 per cent of their 1968 presidential vote.

When the New Deal political cycle began, in 1932, Franklin D. Roosevelt won 92 per cent of the total presidential vote in the five Deep South states. No other section of the nation ever approached this level of enthusiasm. The cycle ended 36 years later, when Hubert Humphrey touched bottom—26 per cent—in the same five states. Most of this Democratic backing was Negro. Few corollaries of the Negro sociopolitical revolution have a greater national significance than the 1932-68 about-face of the Deep South. Chart 63 shows the erosion of Democratic presidential support during the New Deal cycle.

A detailed explanation of Deep Southern politics is best launched with an analysis of the Black Belt, the seat of white conservatism for most of the 1932-68 cycle but now the center of Deep South Negro support for the national Democratic Party. Logic then leads us to the upcountry and pineywoods areas, where long standing rivalry with Black Belt conservatism has given way to cooperation against newly registered Negroes. Louisiana's atypical French population also merits a short commentary. Generally speaking, the political patterns of the Deep South are a product of these behavioral streams.

1. The Black Belt

From "Southside" Virginia to east Texas, the Deep South centers on a rich farming area which, by dint of its suitability for plantation agriculture, was the seat of ante-bellum slavery in the United States. Even today, many of these counties have predominantly Negro populations, although local agriculture no longer requires vast numbers of field hands and the lure of Northern employment and welfare payments has prompted a considerable migration. Map 22 shows the present distribution and concentration of Southern Negroes. Most of them still live in the Deep South "Black Belts"—so named for their dark rich soil rather than large Negro populations (although the two coincide).

MAP 22

Southern Negro Concentrations

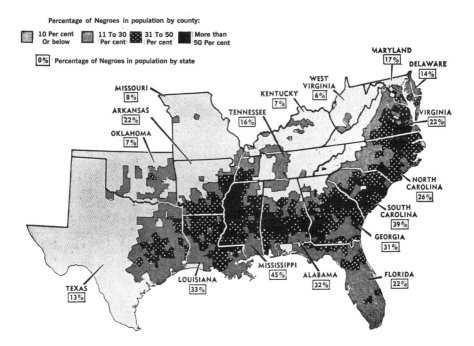

Percentage of Negroes in population by county:

- 10 Per cent Or below
- 11 To 30 Per cent
- 31 To 50 Per cent
- More than 50 Per cent

0% | Percentage of Negroes in population by state

MARYLAND 17%
DELAWARE 14%
WEST VIRGINIA 6%
MISSOURI 8%
KENTUCKY 7%
ARKANSAS 22%
TENNESSEE 16%
VIRGINIA 22%
OKLAHOMA 7%
NORTH CAROLINA 26%
SOUTH CAROLINA 39%
GEORGIA 31%
MISSISSIPPI 45%
ALABAMA 32%
FLORIDA 22%
LOUISIANA 33%
TEXAS 13%

From the early Nineteenth Century, slavery and later white supremacy have been the principal concerns of Black Belt politics. In 1860 and 1861, the Dixie Black Belts sparked the cry for secession from the Union in order to protect the institution of slavery, which Lincoln's election was thought to jeopardize. For ten years after the Peace of Appomattox concluded the Civil War, many of these counties were occupied by Northern troops and administered by Negro Republicans and white "scalawag" local courthouse cliques kept in power by federal bayonets. As these federal military governments departed from Southern soil, the white minorities of the Deep South Black Belts set to work to re-establish local white political supremacy. More often than not, force was required and it was readily forthcoming: many a Negro and white "scalawag" was terrorized by the hooded white riders of the Ku Klux Klan. After Northern military support was withdrawn, Negro political activity diminished, although it did not immediately cease.

White political Negrophobia in the post-bellum South was pre-

CHART 64

The Political Behavior of the Black Belt, 1924-68

Democratic Share of the Total Vote for President

State (County)	1924	1928	1932	1948	1952	1956**	1960***	1964	1968
					Deep South				
Alabama									
Dallas	92%	73%	97%	*	45%	40%	44%	11%	32%
Wilcox	98	79	98	*	58	53	67	8	36
Georgia									
Lee	86	86	98	46%	66	86	68	19	29
Burke	83	73	95	24	55	63	53	29	34
Louisiana									
Claiborne	96	86	98	16	35	21	13	11	26
Tensas	94	79	96	23	50	32	20	10	32
Mississippi									
Sunflower	96	97	98	5	51	51	30	6	32
Holmes	93	94	97	3	52	41	25	3	52
South Carolina									
Edgefield	100	100	100	2	31	26	37	25	31
Clarendon	97	99	98	7	32	25	44	22	45

Crittenden	89	84	98	25	61	44	52	50	32
St. Francis	66	69	93	47	58	50	54	52	36
Florida									
Gadsden	85	76	95	51	60	63	54	47	36
Madison	91	74	88	52	57	67	64	43	29
North Carolina									
Bertie	92	84	98	96	90	88	87	78	45
Halifax	90	85	95	87	80	77	79	65	32
Tennessee									
Fayette	93	90	96	13	53	33	32	47	40
Haywood	96	92	95	49	72	73	56	49	30
Texas									
San Jacinto	84	63	98	66	68	57	71	83	54
Waller	85	57	93	50	46	39	49	68	49
Virginia									
Brunswick	90	79	96	49	60	43	66	42	38
Dinwiddie	83	74	90	64	59	49	64	51	30

*National Democratic candidate Truman was not on the Alabama ballot; the Democrat place was given to Dixiecrat Thurmond. Elsewhere, *both* candidates appeared.

**Independent or States Rights elector tickets appeared on the ballot in Alabama, Arkansas, Louisiana, Mississippi, South Carolina, Tennessee and Virginia (generally with only minimal to moderate impact).

***Six of Alabama's eleven Democratic electors ran unpledged; in effect they constituted a partial States Rights ticket. A minor third party ticket ran in both Tennessee and Texas, while major Independent or States Rights elector tickets appeared on the ballot in Louisiana and Mississippi.

Note: The counties cited are among the most heavily Negro in each state. Large-scale Negro voting did not begin until varying dates in the Nineteen-Sixties. Negroes cast most of the 1968 Democratic ballots.

mised on fear of Negro voting power, particularly in those Black Belt counties where illiterate ex-slaves outnumbered their former masters by ratios of six- and eight-to-one. On a statewide basis, Negroes constituted a majority of the post-Civil War populations of Mississippi, Louisiana and South Carolina and more than 40 per cent of the populations of Alabama and Georgia.

As soon as Black Belt whites were free to do so, they used physical and economic pressure to keep Negroes from voting, and thus re-established white political power. Later on, after the populist era of the Eighteen-Nineties had scared the Southern Establishment, further disabilities, such as literacy tests and poll taxes, were heaped on Negroes and poor whites alike. Chart 55 illustrates how the total presidential vote cast in South Carolina declined from 182,800 in 1876 to 50,900 in 1900.

During the Twentieth Century, another Southern political institution came to the fore—the "white primary." Because the Democratic Party was a "private" institution, Negroes had no legal right to participate in its processes (until the Supreme Court decided otherwise in 1944). After victory in a white Democratic primary, the general election was a mere formality to most Southern candidates. Given white apprehension of Negro political activity, the Democratic Party served the South not just as a political party but as a racial and cultural institution. For this reason, the Democratic loyalties of the Deep South were immovable so long as the national Democratic Party did nothing to trespass on Southern sensibilities. Chart 64 illustrates the intense pre-1948 Democratic commitment of Black Belt counties throughout the South.

Because of the importance of the Democratic Party as a fulcrum of white supremacy, the Deep South remained staunchly Democratic in 1928 despite the unpopular Catholicism of party presidential nominee Al Smith. The genesis of this loyalty is clear. As illustrated earlier in Chart 56, Smith won almost all of the South's Black Belt counties, but he lost most of the predominantly white counties. In the Black Belt counties, commitment to the Democratic Party as an instrument of white supremacy was firm enough so that anti-Catholicism made only the most minimal inroads. For example, Democratic loyalties were so strong in the heart of Mississippi's "Delta" that the GOP share of the presidential vote in two of the most heavily Negro counties (Leflore and Sunflower) declined from 7 per cent in 1924 to only 4 per cent in 1928. Outside the Black

Belt, where white loyalties to the Democratic Party were weaker, voters were readier to vent their anti-Catholicism by supporting the Republican presidential nominee. Similarly, Black Belt white supremacist Democratic loyalties were weaker in Outer South Black Belts—those in Virginia, Florida and Texas—than in Mississippi and South Carolina because Outer South Black Belt whites were comforted by statewide white majorities.

At first, the Depression slightly increased the already overwhelming Black Belt Democratic pluralities. Leflore and Sunflower counties in Mississippi gave Roosevelt 99 per cent of their vote in 1936, 3 per cent more than they had given Smith. But by 1938, Southern conservatives were becoming disillusioned with the later phases of the New Deal. Nevertheless, the Democratic Party had not yet trespassed on Southern racial practices, so the basic loyalty of the Deep South persisted.

During World War II, the cause of civil rights gathered momentum and the 1948 Democratic national platform included civil rights measures which the Deep South found intolerable. The two principal Negrophobe states—Mississippi and South Carolina—spearheaded a movement to form a third party. Aberration was strongest in 1948, just where loyalty had been staunchest in 1928 and for precisely the same reasons. The Mississippi and South Carolina rebels drew support from Black Belt counties across the South, but no other Black Belt counties enjoy the statewide power of those in Mississippi and South Carolina, although the Alabama, Georgia and Louisiana Black Belts have significant influence. The Dixiecrats convened in Birmingham, Alabama, to nominate a third party presidential ticket in the hope of throwing the election into the House of Representatives by winning enough electoral votes to hold the balance of power. Mirroring the parochialism of their power base, they nominated South Carolina Governor J. Strom Thurmond for President and Mississippi Governor Fielding Wright for Vice President.

Thurmond's general election support in the South closely corresponded to the pre-election enthusiasm expressed for a Dixiecrat bolt; that is to say, he ran well only in the Deep South, carrying the states of South Carolina, Mississippi, Alabama and Louisiana. Except for limited strength in some prosperous urban precincts and certain Black Belt areas of the Outer South, the Dixiecrats did very poorly in North Carolina, Texas, Virginia, Florida, Georgia,

Arkansas and Tennessee, confirming the hostility that the Democratic parties of those states had earlier expressed to a Southern third-party strategy. These seven states gave the Dixiecrats only 9 per cent to 20 per cent of their statewide vote. Needless to say, the "balance of power" strategy failed. The Thurmond electoral votes (39) did not affect the outcome of the 1948 presidential election. Truman won without them.

Even in the Deep South, local sentiments did not unanimously favor the Dixiecrats. A number of Piedmont (South Carolina), Tennessee Plateau (Mississippi and Alabama) and French Creole (Louisiana) counties supported the national Democratic Party. Thurmond might not have carried Alabama except for the fact that the state Democratic Party threw President Truman off the ballot and put the Dixiecrat candidate next to the Democratic rooster.

The split which marked Deep South voting in 1948 essentially pitted the white professional and business classes of the Black Belts and cities against the poorer voters of the overwhelmingly white counties of the foothills and coastal bayou and pineywoods peripheries of the region. In the poor white counties, there was no preoccupation with white absolutism such as characterized the Black Belts, nor was there any interest in furthering the anti-New Deal economic policies of the Black Belt and urban Deep South oligarchies. More often than not, the poor white counties supported New Deal and Fair Deal economic and welfare policies.

Rooted in areas like Delta Mississippi and Black Belt Alabama, which had been strongholds of Whig conservatism in the pre-Civil War Southern two-party context, the Dixiecrat movement represented socioeconomic conservatism more than raw Negrophobia. Until the Nineteen-Sixties, poll taxes and literacy tests, by excluding Negroes from the political process and discouraging many poor whites, saw to it that the voters of the Black Belt and urban Deep South were a prosperous and privileged minority to whom conservatism and white supremacy were culturally instinctive. Traditionally leery of the GOP, they marshalled as Dixiecrats to curb and remake the national Democratic Party.

Outside the Black Belts and middle-class urban areas, many poor whites did not share this socioeconomic commitment to a system which excluded them. Negroes were not much of a numerical threat in the foothill and pineywoods counties, while Black Belt conservatism was a longtime, proven enemy. The plantation and commercial classes generally opposed the economic, welfare and public works programs craved by the poor white counties. Within the historic one-party framework of the Deep South, the poor white counties usually opposed the Democratic primary candidacies of Black Belt conservatives, but in 1948, the antagonism took on a new shape, as the Black Belts bolted to the Dixiecrats while the poor white counties remained Democratic or produced less emphatic Dixiecrat successes.

This poor white-Black Belt opposition has shed useful light on the dynamics of Deep South voting. In 1948, even as the great majority of South Carolina and Mississippi counties were chalking up Dixiecrat landslides, a number of upcountry counties dissented. Back in 1928, these counties had shown a different tendency to ignore Democratic tradition and bolt to Hoover, in response to Al Smith's Catholicism. But there is rationality in this seeming disparity. Whereas the upcountry had a sufficiently minimal Negro preoccupation to respond to either anti-Catholicism or the economic appeal of the Fair Deal, the Black Belt has always been wrapped up in the politics, sociology and economics of race, favoring the Democratic Party for many years and spurning it only when it abandoned Dixie for civil rights.

In 1952, Eisenhower combined enlarged GOP Outer South strength with a Dixiecrat impetus in the Deep South. However, he won statewide victories only in the Outer South. As for the Black Belts, those of the Outer South and Deep South performed differently, just as in 1948.

Although Eisenhower did well in the Deep South Black Belts where Dixiecrat dissidence was rampant, he made lesser strides in the Black Belts of the Outer South, where Dixiecrat sentiments were weak and statewide two-party contests were a long-established reality. In the Black Belts of Virginia, North Carolina, Georgia, Tennessee and Arkansas, 1952 Democratic voting was fortified by meaningful and longstanding traditions of opposition to highland Republicanism. To Black Belt Democrats of these states, Republicans were not wholly remote Northerners of similar economic ideology, but partisan mountain and Piedmont neighbors of sufficient number to cast one third of the statewide vote in general elections. Given this state of affairs, most Black Belt voters shunned Republicanism. Nonetheless, the GOP did win Virginia and Tennessee.

Only in the Deep South, where white Republican tradition was non-existent, did the Black Belts shift to the GOP in 1952. Dixiecrat "instant" Republicanism in these states, resting on *ad hoc* strength, could be proffered or withheld at local whim. Chart 64 compares the behavior of the Deep South and Outer South Black Belts. In the four Dixiecrat states, Eisenhower won 50 per cent to 65 per cent of the vote in the conservative Black Belt core areas; but the Black Belts of the Outer South remained Democratic. In Mississippi and South Carolina, most of the Eisenhower vote was cast for independent electors, but in Alabama and Louisiana, Eisenhower gathered his Black Belt support on the GOP line—an extraordinary breach of tradition.

In talking about 1952 Republican trends in the Deep South Black Belts, a major qualification is necessary. Only the rabidly Dixiecrat cores of the Black Belts actually switched to the GOP. The lesser Black Belts, along with the pineywoods and upcountry, remained Democratic. In Mississippi, for example, although the prosperous Delta counties turned to Eisenhower, the northeastern hills gave him little support. Chart 65 shows how the poorest Dixiecrat counties

CHART 65

Comparative 1948-64 Presidential Voting in the Deep South Upcountry and the Black Belts

State (County)	Democratic Share of the Major Party Presidential Vote				
	1948*	1952	1956	1960	1964
Mississippi					
Itawamba (Upcountry)	37%	80%	87%	63%	35%
Leflore (Black Belt)	5	43	49	26	6
Alabama					
Limestone (Upcountry)	—**	87	87	81	56
Dallas (Black Belt)	—**	45	40	44	11
South Carolina					
Anderson (Upcountry)	64	78	77	78	58
Dorchester (Black Belt)	5	27	27	40	24

*Democratic share of Republican-Democratic-Dixiecrat vote.
**No Democratic candidate on ballot.

produced the least Eisenhower backing. Thurmond's worst Deep South state—Georgia—was also Eisenhower's.

Despite Eisenhower's great Black Belt gains, his most numerically significant Deep South strength occurred in the cities, especially those where the Dixiecrats had been strong. In cities like Charleston, Savannah, Augusta, Mobile, Montgomery, Shreveport and Jackson, Eisenhower amassed high support levels, much higher than he won in the surrounding countryside. All of these cities had a large and generally voteless Negro lower class, and most white urban voters were lower-middle-class to upper-class conservatives far more sympathetic than the average country voter with the philosophy and economics of Northern Republicanism. Whereas in the countryside only the Black Belt core areas turned Republican in 1952, the Deep South cities were less reticent. Had it been their decision to make, the states of the Deep South would have voted for Eisenhower.

By 1956, Black Belt Republicanism had flagged somewhat as a result of the Supreme Court school desegregation decision handed down in 1954, for which the South blamed the new Republican Chief Justice, Earl Warren. In all four of the states which had supported the Dixiecrats in 1948, States Rights electors were on the ballot in 1956. For the most part, they drew support which had gone to Eisenhower in 1952. In the Outer South Black Belts also, the GOP vote declined in 1956—except in Arkansas and Texas, where Black Belt Negroes were beginning to vote. (The substantial Southern Negro vote Eisenhower won in 1956 was generally amassed in the cities rather than in the Black Belts, where few Negroes voted.) One Deep South state voted Republican in 1956—Louisiana, where Black Belt Dixiecrat-Republicanism was swollen by a pro-Eisenhower French turnout.

Eisenhower's 1956 decline in the Deep South Black Belts did not extend to the Deep South cities. He carried Mobile, Montgomery, Birmingham, Savannah, Augusta, New Orleans, Shreveport and Baton Rouge with a larger vote than he had won in 1952. Furthermore, if States Rights electors had not been on the ballot in Mississippi and South Carolina, Eisenhower would have swept Charleston, Columbia, Jackson, Meridian and Biloxi as he did in 1952. The urban Deep South was strongly pro-Eisenhower and much readier to vote Republican than the rural Deep South (with the exception of a few Dixiecrat bastions).

At the close of the Eisenhower Administration, the principal

Black Belts of the Deep South—those in Mississippi, South Carolina, Alabama, and Louisiana—were neither Republican nor Democratic. For the most part, they looked to States Rights electors, hoping against hope to exert anti-civil rights leverage on the two major parties. The lesser Black Belts and other predominantly white counties of the Deep South, being poorer and less disposed to arch-Dixiecrat "instant" Republicanism, were heavily Democratic and little concerned with the independent elector schemes which were always afoot. Likewise, the Black Belts of the Outer South were still heavily Democratic in the late Nineteen-Fifties. Most of the growing Republican (as opposed to States Rights) strength in the Deep South was concentrated in the cities, where industry and commerce were breeding sentiments akin to those of middle-class Republicanism elsewhere in the nation.

This pattern persisted in 1960. Nixon won most of the major Deep South cities (Charleston, Augusta, Savannah, Birmingham, Montgomery and Shreveport) but none of their states. Still discontented with both parties, the Mississippi and Louisiana Black Belts cast a majority of their votes for slates of independent electors, gaining success only in die-hard Mississippi. The arch-Dixiecrat South Carolina Black Belt voted Republican, while the Alabama Black Belt divided between the GOP and Democratic electors (some of whom were pledged to vote for Virginia's Senator Byrd). In Georgia and the Outer South, the Black Belt counties voted Democratic. The GOP gained in the Florida and Tennessee Black Belts, but lost ground in those of Arkansas and Texas—where Negro voting was on the rise.

Throughout the Deep South, Negro disenfranchisement was still widespread in 1960, particularly in the Alabama-Mississippi Black Belts, where the nation's greatest Negro concentrations occur. Nevertheless, Negro votes turned out to be crucial in South Carolina, providing the support whereby Kennedy overcame the small white majority cast for Nixon. Kennedy won South Carolina by ten thousand votes because of his considerable majority among the state's seventy-five thousand Negro voters. Negro voting also occurred on a considerable scale in Georgia and Louisiana, but in the other Deep South states it was minimal. Chart 66 shows the extent of 1960 Negro disenfranchisement in the heart of the central Alabama (Selma area) Black Belt, which is the most heavily Negro group of counties in the United States.

CHART 66

Negro Disenfranchisement in the Alabama Black Belt, 1960

County	White Population	Negro Population	Registered White Voters	Registered Negro Voters
Macon	4,777	25,784	3,016	1,100
Lowndes	3,214	14,804	2,306	0
Wilcox	4,912	18,564	3,183	0

Although a considerable number of Negroes voted in the South in the presidential elections between 1952 and 1960, few of their votes were cast in the rural Deep South. Beyond the Dixiecrat Black Belts, however, local voting registrars were more permissive. Negroes voted in considerable numbers in the Piedmont and in cities throughout the Outer South, furnishing a meaningful part of Eisenhower's 1956 strength in Texas, Florida, Virginia, Tennessee and North Carolina.

Across much of the Outer South, Black Belt voters—they were still mostly white, but larger number of Negroes were beginning to vote—cast their usual Democratic ballots in 1960. As in 1952, only the Deep South Black Belts, where Negroes were voteless and existing Republicanism negligible, opted for the GOP or States Rights tickets. In the Outer South, large statewide white majorities permitted the Black Belts to assume a more relaxed posture, while traditional antagonism towards a local GOP kept Democratic loyalties burning. Actually, the Democratic majorities of the Outer South Black Belts were important to John F. Kennedy. Had the Democratic presidential nominee lost his 1960 Black Belt majorities in North Carolina, Texas and Arkansas, he would have lost those states, and neither he nor Nixon would have obtained a majority in the Electoral College.

Black Belt victory hopes were a major factor in the GOP's 1964 "Southern Strategy." But the party found that when it acted like the Dixiecrats, it fell into the Dixiecrat pattern. The Deep South Black Belts exalted Barry Goldwater and those of the Outer South for the most part opposed him. Goldwater won only the 1948 Dixiecrat states, plus Georgia (and his home state, Arizona). The rest of the South backed Johnson. To the Deep South, the election was a

CHART 67

Estimated Negro Voter Registration in 11 Southern States in 1956 and 1964

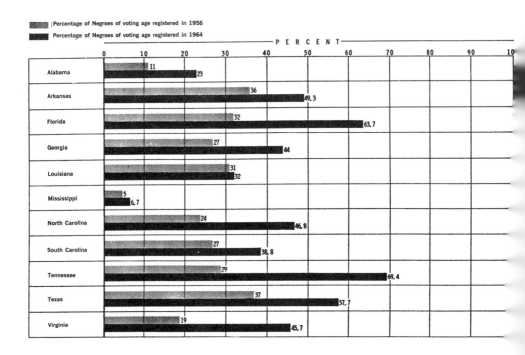

final battle against Negro voting rights. Whatever the future might bring, 1964 found only 44 per cent of Georgia's eligible Negroes registered, 39 per cent of South Carolina's, 32 per cent of Louisiana's, 23 per cent of Alabama's, and a mere 7 per cent of those in die-hard Mississippi. Nevertheless, to the extent that Negroes were able to vote, they went virtually unanimously for Johnson, offsetting part of the white pro-Goldwater vote. Chart 68 shows how Deep South GOP strength correlated with Negro population *and* disenfranchisement, the latter being greatest in Mississippi and Alabama.

Throughout the Black Belts of the Deep South, Barry Goldwater won the same heavy white vote—and it was nearly unanimous— that had been accorded to the Dixiecrats and pre-1948 Democratic nominees. However, Negro registration in Georgia and South Caro-

CHART 68

Racial Aspects of the Goldwater Vote in the Deep South, 1964

State	1960 Census Negro Population (%)	1964 Percentage of Eligible Negroes Registered to Vote	1964 Goldwater Percentage of the Two-Party Presidential Vote
Mississippi	45%	7%	87%
Alabama	32	23	70
Louisiana	33	32	57
South Carolina	39	39	59
Georgia	31	44	54

lina had risen to a point where Negroes were able to give Lyndon Johnson one-fifth to two-fifths of the vote in many of those states' Black Belt counties. Chart 69 illustrates Barry Goldwater's strength in some Deep South counties where Negroes were not allowed to vote in 1964.

Not all Deep South whites were as enthusiastic about Goldwater as the Black Belt voters. Chart 65 shows how Goldwater's best counties in Mississippi and Alabama were the pro-Dixiecrat and pro-Eisenhower counties, while his worst counties adhered to the anti-Dixiecrat pattern laid down in 1948. But in all five Deep South states, conservatives predominated over upcountry whites and Negroes and gave statewide majorities to Barry Goldwater.

In the wake of the 1964 elections, many observers sought to tag Goldwater support as a rural phenomenon repudiated by the modern urban South, but this was simply not the case. Between 1960 and 1964, the Republican presidential vote declined in the cities and most non-Black Belt counties throughout the Outer South, but rose in both cities *and* rural counties across the Deep South. Regionalism —the cleavage between the Deep South and the Outer South— rather than urbanism was the principal denominator of the 1964 presidential voting pattern in Dixie. Although he lost normally Republican Outer South cities like Dallas, Charlotte and Richmond, Goldwater scored record-level Republican votes in most Deep South urban counties, i.e., those including Danville, Virginia; Rocky

CHART 69

White Republicanism in the Deep South Black Belts, 1964

County	Negro Percentage of Total Population (1960)	Percentage of Negroes Registered to Vote (1964)	Goldwater Percentage of Two-Party Vote for President
Alabama			
Dallas	51%	2%	89%
Lowndes	71	0	83
Wilcox	70	0	92
Georgia			
Lee	56	2	81
Miller	24	1	86
Terrell	57	2	78
Louisiana			
Claiborne	44	2	89
Tensas	61	2	89
Mississippi			
Holmes	65	0	97
Claiborne	70	1	93
Jefferson	68	0	95
South Carolina			
Clarendon	60	7	78

Mount and Wilmington, North Carolina; Charleston, South Carolina; Jacksonville, Pensacola and Tallahassee, Florida; Athens, Thomaston and Macon, Georgia (Savannah and Augusta, although strongly pro-Goldwater, had done even better by Eisenhower in 1956); Birmingham, Mobile and Montgomery, Alabama; Jackson, Biloxi, Meridian, Vicksburg and Natchez, Mississippi; Baton Rouge and Shreveport, Louisiana; and Pine Bluff and Texarkana, Arkansas. Within the Black Belt reaches sketched in Map 22, Goldwater amassed record strength, but elsewhere in the South, he slipped below Eisenhower-Nixon levels (see Charts 75 and 77).

Beyond the Deep South and kindred areas like northern Florida, the Memphis area and Southside Virginia, Goldwater did not carry many Black Belt counties; first as a result of considerable Negro voting, secondly because local white politics were considerably less Negrophobe than in the Deep South. Nevertheless, as Chart 64 shows, Goldwater did score considerable gains over prior Eisenhower and Nixon levels, upsetting Democratic traditions in Outer South areas historically at odds with same-state mountain or urban-suburban Republicanism.

Whatever Barry Goldwater's Black Belt success—and even that would soon be countered by federally sponsored registration of Black Belt Negro voters—his candidacy was a failure in the context of the entire South. After an agonizing reappraisal, the GOP abandoned its flirtation with the Black Belt psychology and returned to its longtime Outer South strategy. And in 1966, the off-year congressional election results showed a GOP support pattern much changed from that of 1964.

One side effect of the Goldwater landslide in the Deep South had been the election of seven new Republican congressmen in the Deep South—the first since Reconstruction. Five of them came from Alabama, one from Georgia and one from Mississippi. The solitary Republican from Mississippi could have been given several colleagues had the GOP chosen to contest more than one district; Goldwater's local landslide was all-powerful. A few months after the 1964 election, the Republicans picked up an eighth Deep South constituency when Goldwater Democrat Albert Watson resigned his South Carolina seat and won easy re-election as a Republican.

Four of these House seats were lost in 1966. The meaning of this can be exaggerated because three of the four lost seats were vacated by their incumbents to make (unsuccessful) bids for statewide office. Nevertheless, these losses, occurring as they did in a year of great Republican gains—the only other GOP loss came in Maine—indicated that Deep South voters, given a choice between conservative Democrats and conservative Republicans, were once again disposed to pick the Democrats. After all, the Democratic parties of the Deep South were offering the electorate undoubted conservatives like Mrs. George C. Wallace and Lester Maddox, the successful 1966 candidates for the governorships of Alabama and Georgia. Within the Deep South, Republican support held up best in the cities. The countryside returned to the (conservative) Democratic fold.

This was eminently logical. As a result of its 1964 chastening, the Republican Party had once again assumed a stance much too mild to attract voters—or hold Goldwater levels—in the rural Deep South. Moreover, the white Deep South was angrier than ever. After the enactment of the 1965 Voting Rights Act, federal registrars had come into rural Black Belts from South Carolina to Louisiana, enrolling Negroes in counties where none had voted for years. Negroes no longer constituted a majority of the population in any Southern state, but they still predominated in a minority of Black Belt counties. Large-scale Negro voting thus threatened the whole social and political structure of the Black Belt, and local whites took umbrage accordingly. Exactly these threats had rallied the Deep South behind Goldwater in 1964, and post-Voting Rights Act upheavals often produced the fiercest white reactions in just those counties where Goldwater had run strongest.

Shunning a Republican Party that was no longer pursuing the 1964 Goldwater theme, the white Deep South looked instead to the arch-conservative local leadership of the Democratic Party. Many Deep Southerners began to rally around former Alabama Governor George C. Wallace, who, in a state where chief executives cannot succeed themselves, preserved power by having his wife elected governor in 1966. Wallace had already sought the Democratic nomination in 1964, later forswearing an independent candidacy when Barry Goldwater won the GOP nod. But as 1968 approached, there was no likelihood that either party would nominate a candidate able to pre-empt Wallace's impetus. The Deep South was definitely headed for another third-party fling.

Amidst increasing signs of Negro political strength in the Deep South—occasional successes in county legislative, school board and sheriff's races—George Wallace began mobilizing his presidential support in Alabama and Mississippi, the two top Goldwater states of 1964. Wallace's candidacy got a boost in 1967 when Goldwater Democrat John Bell Williams swept Mississippi's Democratic gubernatorial primary. The Williams victory showed the power of white as opposed to black bloc voting even in the nation's most heavily Negro state. Besides provoking a new outpouring of white registrants, Negro enrollment had united Black Belt and upcountry white voters. In Mississippi, as in the 1966 Alabama and Georgia Democratic primaries, many poor whites paid little attention to questions of economic progressivism and voted against the candidate who they thought was favored by the Negro bloc.

Until 1968, the Wallace movement was regarded by many as a

Black Belt phenomenon unlikely to score any success beyond Alabama or Mississippi, and perhaps Louisiana. Few observers realized the extent to which the Negro socioeconomic revolution was alienating conservatives beyond the Deep South—and even beyond the Outer South. As Wallace stepped up his tour of the United States and received increased publicity, his prospects burgeoned. As of midsummer 1968, Republican strategists felt it realistic to concede the Deep South to Wallace and focus on the Outer South. And by late September, some pessimistic Republicans feared that Wallace would win the entire Deep South plus Tennessee, North Carolina, Florida and Arkansas. The Alabaman enjoyed a strong impetus in the Black Belts (and pineywoods) of these Outer South states.

As the campaign entered its last weeks in an increasingly two-party context, Wallace's strength steadily retreated to its original Deep South crucible. Only Arkansas, Louisiana, Mississippi, Alabama and Georgia remained loyal on Election Day. Even the Deep South state of South Carolina rejected him, partly as a result of the prestige and influence brought to bear by 1948 Dixiecrat presidential nominee Strom Thurmond, now a pro-Nixon Republican United States Senator from the Palmetto State.

Wallace won very high support from Black Belt whites and no support at all from Black Belt Negroes. In the Black Belt counties of the Deep South, racial polarization was practically complete. Negroes voted for Hubert Humphrey, whites for George Wallace. GOP nominee Nixon garnered very little backing in counties where Barry Goldwater had captured 90 per cent to 100 per cent of the vote in 1964. The principal exception to this rule was South Carolina, where Black Belt whites opted for Nixon rather than Wallace.* Georgia, Alabama, Mississippi and Louisiana Black Belt whites all gave substantial majorities to the former Alabama governor. Despite the negligible support which Deep South Black Belt whites gave to the national Democratic Party, Hubert Humphrey amassed higher Black Belt vote shares than Lyndon Johnson had four years earlier. The reason was quite simple—first-time Negro voting. As a result of Negro ballots, the Democratic share of the vote *rose* be-

---

*Some of this must be attributed to the influence of Senator Thurmond; however, South Carolina has been the most Republican of the Cotton States in presidential elections since 1952. Its Dixiecrats have developed Republican presidential voting habits.

tween 1964 and 1968 in the Deep South Black Belt counties (see Chart 64). These gains did not, however, enable the Democrats to carry the Deep South, and as a matter of fact, Humphrey ran *behind* Johnson in every Deep South state except Mississippi. Party losses among poor whites—in the pineywoods, upcountry and bayous—more than offset Democrat gains attributable to Negro backing.

In the Deep South, it was not in the Black Belts that Wallace breached Democratic tradition—Thurmond had done that twenty years earlier—but in the populist pineywoods, upcountry and bayous. These were the sort of counties—all heavily white—where Wallace compiled his best vote. In the Outer South, however, the Black Belts *were* the locale of the major breakdown in Democratic voting habits. Wallace swept the Black Belt counties of Texas, Arkansas, Florida, Tennessee, North Carolina and Virginia, and in so doing he dragged the Democratic vote down to record lows, as Chart 64 illustrates.* Twenty years before, these counties had spurned the Dixiecrat ticket. This time, the white voters of the Outer South Black Belts bolted *en masse,* leaving Hubert Humphrey with few supporters besides Negroes.

These Wallace inroads were particularly important. In 1960 and 1964, Democratic pluralities in the Outer South Black Belts had been crucial components of statewide victory. John F. Kennedy had carried most of Black Belt Texas, Arkansas, Tennessee, Florida, North Carolina and Virginia. Four years later, even Lyndon Johnson captured the majority of Black Belt counties in Texas, Arkansas, Tennessee and North Carolina. Except in Texas, where Latin votes are also important, the Democrats must amass overwhelming white support in Black Belt counties—the bulwark of Outer South Democratic tradition—in order to compile statewide majorities. In 1968, George Wallace ripped these traditions to shreds, forging sizeable Black Belt majorities and pluralities and enabling Richard Nixon's mountain, urban and suburban Republican strength to win Virginia, North Carolina, Tennessee and Florida. Wallace won such heavy support in lowland Arkansas that he beat both Humphrey *and* Nixon. Actually, the anti-Democratic trend among white voters of the Outer South Black Belts was sharper than might appear from the statistics of Chart 64. In 1964, the Democrats carried most of

---

*In most Outer South Black Belts, Wallace ran far ahead of Nixon. The Alabaman's third party, not the GOP, drew most of the aberrant Democrats.

these counties—few Negroes voted—because of white majorities or a substantial minority of white support, but in 1968, the Democratic share of the vote plummeted even though Negro participation increased considerably. The intensity of white disaffection was severe indeed.

The white 1968 trend was such as to obliterate the distinction which had prevailed since 1948—but not before that—between Outer South and Deep South Black Belt white voters. As Chart 64 shows, the Democrats of the Deep South Black Belts never recovered from the Dixiecrat upheaval; and the vehemence of the 1968 revolt among white voters in the Outer South Black Belts suggests that the Wallace movement may be another such upheaval.

All across the Deep South and even through much of the Outer South, Negroes were the only group to rally behind Hubert Humphrey. Thus, 1968 Democratic presidential strength was concentrated in the Black Belts where Negro concentrations are largest. In all of the Deep South states, the top 1968 Democratic counties were unfailingly Black Belt bailiwicks. Map 23 illustrates how 1968 Humphrey support in South Carolina, Georgia, Alabama and Mississippi followed the general contours of the racial core of the Black Belt (as drawn in Map 22). The Democratic nominee actually carried a few predominantly Negro counties in Alabama and a larger batch in Mississippi. Inescapably, the Democratic Party in the Deep South was on its way to becoming the Negro party. Moreover, the Democrats seemed quite willing to accept this re-alignment, meshing as it did with the Democratic Party's increasing Northeastern, Establishment, Yankee and ghetto orientations. (In August, 1968, the Democratic National Convention had evinced a similar re-alignment by unseating the regular Mississippi delegation and half of the regular Georgia delegation and replacing them with largely Negro liberal groups.)

Without large-scale white assistance (which has not been forthcoming), Negro Black Belt populations cannot hope to win statewide elections in the Deep South. Map 22 lists the 1960 Negro percentage of each Southern state's population; since then, the mechanization of plantation agriculture has stimulated a considerable migration of Southern Negroes—especially from the Cotton States—to Northeastern and Great Lakes cities. In 1968, Negroes represented 24 per cent of the registered voters in South Carolina, 18 per cent in Georgia, 17 per cent in Alabama, 30 per cent in Mississippi and

MAP 23

1968 Black Belt Presidential Voting

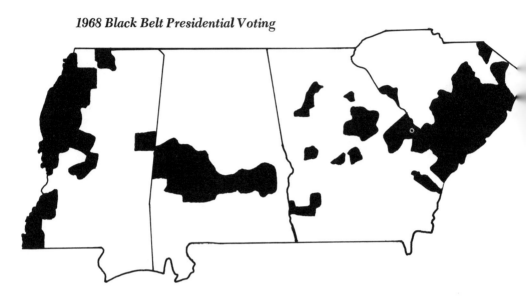

■   1968 Humphrey share of Total Vote over one-third

20 per cent in Louisiana.* These levels are no threat to white political supremacy so long as white voters join together, and the history
of Deep Southern white politics suggests that such cohesion is extremely likely. The fact that Negroes have won offices in a relatively
small number of Black Belt counties, has drawn the white Deep
South electorate—the hitherto somewhat hostile upcountry and
Black Belts—together in statewide contests.

Across the Deep South, the preponderance of white voters endorsed George Wallace in 1968, but the principal exception—substantial and frequently majority support for Richard Nixon in
middle-class urban sections from Charleston to Shreveport—probably points the way to the future of white local presidential politics.
With Negroes as the national Democratic Party's base, Deep South
whites—once third parties no longer seem plausible—should follow
their opinion-molding classes into the Republican Party. Not only
conservatives of Dixiecrat antecedents, but also populist poor
whites, are likely to take such a course.

*The Mississippi figure is imprecise because of inadequate registration data.

2. Dixie Upcountry

Not all of Louisiana, Mississippi, Alabama, Georgia and South Carolina is agriculturally rich, flat, Black Belt Dixiecrat country. A small section of northern Alabama and Georgia belongs to the Appalachian highlands and a much larger area of the Deep South is "upcountry"—the archetypal red hills, clay hills and Piedmont home terrain of the poor white or "peckerwood" Deep South.* Although many Appalachian counties are at least as impoverished, the upcountry operates in a different cultural and political pattern; since Civil War days, it has been institutionally Democratic in the Black Belt manner rather than traditionally Republican like the mountains. For this reason, it was as Democrats rather than Republicans that the dirt farmers of the Mississippi, Alabama, Georgia and South Carolina upcountry became camp followers of populists and demagogues—Democrats all—like "Pitchfork" Ben Tillman, Gene Talmadge, Theodore Bilbo, James K. Vardaman, "Kissin' Jim" Folsom, Tom Watson and J. Thomas Heflin. As delineated in Map 24, the Deep South upcountry is a land of dirt farms, textile mills, relatively few Negroes (see Map 22), multifunctional gas stations, "Yes, We'll Gather At the River" Protestantism, Coca Cola advertisements and a deep-seated Snopesian dislike for both white plantation owners and black field hands. Atlanta, a world apart from its rural environs, is the only major city.**

At the outbreak of the Civil War, most upcountry counties, unlike the mountains, had small but consequential slave populations. The upcountry fought for the Confederacy, not the Union, and forged Democratic rather than Republican wartime loyalties. After the war, all classes of Deep South whites—upcountry and plantation county voters alike—successfully worked to supplant Reconstruction Era Negro (Republican) power with a one-party Democratic system. A few decades later, however, Bourbon-poor white economic animosity flared into the Populist political warfare of the Eighteen-Nineties. In most states, the Bourbons won, and to secure their new position, conservative Southern Democratic state governments enacted poll taxes and literacy tests which disenfranchised not only the

---

*It goes without saying that not all poor whites live in the upcountry, nor are all upcountry whites poor.

**Atlanta, the fast-growing commercial and financial center of the Southeastern United States, is part of the New South, and shares little in culture or politics with surrounding rural Georgia.

MAP 24

The Upcountry Deep South

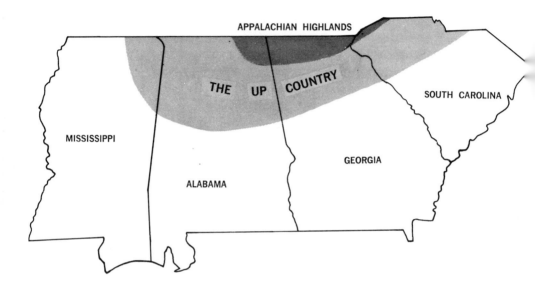

Note: Because substantial Negro populations are found above the fall line,
the political upcountry does not closely follow the boundaries of
physiographic regions.

bulk of those Negroes who still voted but many poor whites as well.
Voters had no meaningful Republican alternative.

From 1896 to 1920, the Republicans won very little support
in the Deep South upcountry (the handful of GOP counties in
Alabama and Georgia were highland areas), but with Prohibition
and Woodrow Wilson's unpopular internationalism drawn into
issue, Republican nominee Warren Harding ran surprisingly well in
the foothills of Alabama and Georgia. Then a much stronger Republican showing came in 1928, when the poor white upcountry
spurned Catholic Democratic presidential nominee Alfred E. Smith
for Protestant Republican Herbert Hoover. In contrast to the racially
preoccupied white voters of the Black Belts, upcountry poor whites
—they were Prohibitionist, revivalist Protestants—felt free to dis-

regard the interrelationship of Negro numbers and loyalty to the one-party system, allowing themselves to vote against the Catholicism of the Democratic candidate. Because of the staunch party regularity of the Black Belts, Smith carried all of the states of the Deep South, but he lost a sizeable number of the hitherto strongly Democratic counties of the upcountry.

The Republican aberrations of 1920 and 1928 did not recur with the advent of the Great Depression. In point of fact, the Deep South upcountry was the one section of the Cotton States which wholeheartedly supported Franklin Roosevelt and the New Deal. During the Nineteen-Thirties, the upcountry invariably backed populists or supporters of New Deal economic reforms in primary contests with Black Belt conservatives. For example, the red hills of northern Louisiana were the seat of the populist Long dynasty (Huey *et al.*); northern Alabama backed liberal economic policies against the Dixiecrat South; the foothill counties of northeastern Mississippi always opposed the candidates of the Delta plantation conservatives; and the millworkers of Piedmont South Carolina stood against the tidewater conservatism of Charleston and the coastal Black Belt. But if economic liberalism—support for wage and hour laws, more schools, hospitals, roads and jobs—predominated in the upcountry, social and religious liberalism did not. Strongholds of economic vested interest like New Orleans, Vicksburg, Natchez, Montgomery, Atlanta, Savannah and Charleston were bastions of tolerance in comparison with the Baptist and sectarian primitivism of the populist upcountry. It is also appropriate to note upcountry insistence on statewide prohibition of liquor sales.*

In 1948, when Dixiecrat Strom Thurmond sought the presidency under the socioeconomic banner of the Black Belts, the upcountry gave him less support than the rest of the Deep South. Upcountry voters did not share Black Belt Negrophobia—at least not to the same degree—and they were much more concerned with the labor, welfare and economic legislation of Harry Truman's Fair Deal. Chart 65 shows how the Dixiecrats won much less support from upcountry Mississippi and South Carolina in 1948 than they won in their urban and Black Belt lairs in both states.

And in 1952, when the Dixiecrat core areas of South Carolina,

*In states like Mississippi and South Carolina, liquor sales referenda would carry the Black Belts and cities but lose the upcountry. The pattern reversed itself for wages and hour legislation.

Georgia, Alabama, Mississippi and Louisiana further defined the scope of their insurgency by voting for Republican presidential nominee Dwight Eisenhower, the upcountry gave heavy majorities to Democrat Adlai Stevenson. They had not greatly shared the protest of 1948, and it was that upheaval among white urban and Black Belt voters that laid most of the foundation of 1952 "instant Republicanism" in the Deep South. Chart 65 illustrates how Eisenhower carried the arch-Dixiecrat counties of Alabama, Mississippi and South Carolina while losing by two-, three-, and four-to-one ratios in the upcountry (and in the politically similar Alabama and Mississippi pineywoods). Little change occurred in upcountry voting when Eisenhower ran for a second term in 1956.

Despite the upcountry's distaste for his Catholicism, John F. Kennedy won Democratic majorities similar to those of Stevenson in the Eisenhower era (see Chart 65). Even in solidly Baptist counties, there was not much anti-Catholic voting—a marked change from the virulence of 1928. Until the national Democratic Party embraced the Negro socioeconomic and civil rights revolution of the Nineteen-Sixties, the Deep South upcountry shunned the economic conservatism of both Republicans and Dixiecrats.

Barry Goldwater did not lead the Republican Party to very substantial upcountry inroads in 1964. Although the civil rights revolution was straining Democratic loyalties all over the South, the poor white hill counties saw Goldwater as a Dixiecrat-style economic conservative whose commitment to New Deal farm, home loan, rural electrification, Social Security and other programs was minimal. Upcountry South Carolina gave Lyndon Johnson a thin edge even though the state as a whole—led by Charleston and the coastal Black Belt—backed Goldwater. Georgia's poor northeastern hill country included the one major bloc of counties in that state to oppose the Arizona Senator, and Alabama's Tennessee Valley and adjacent hill country likewise mounted the state's limited opposition to Goldwater. In Mississippi, Goldwater carried every county, but his worst showings came in the northeastern hills. The upcountry demonstrated quite clearly in 1964 that its economic populism constituted the major source of Democratic and "liberal" strength in the white Deep South. Map 25 portrays the upcountry-Black Belt cleavage in the 1948, 1960 and 1964 Mississippi and South Carolina presidential contests.

But the upcountry's economic progressivism has never extended

MAP 25

Upcountry Democratic Loyalty, 1948-64

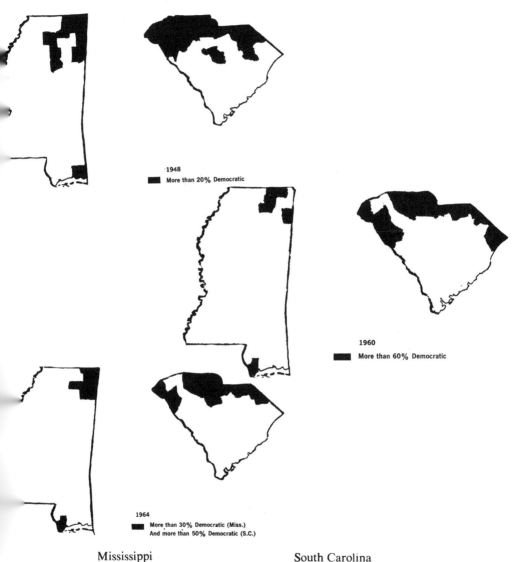

1948
More than 20% Democratic

1960
More than 60% Democratic

1964
More than 30% Democratic (Miss.)
And more than 50% Democratic (S.C.)

Mississippi   South Carolina

to race. Most of yesteryear's populist demagogues found that "nigger-baiting" was one of their most useful devices in the upcountry, where Negroes were feared as job competitors and resented as favored pawns of the plantation system. Thus, when the 1965

Voting Rights Act began to spur heavy Negro registration across the Deep South and the liberal federal establishment embarked on an increasing number of innovative social programs, Southern upcountry white "liberals" trended conservative. Solid proof came in the 1966 Democratic gubernatorial primaries in Alabama and Georgia. Hill country white voters supported populist conservative candidates Lester Maddox and Lurleen Wallace against Negro-endorsed liberals. Then in Mississippi's 1967 Democratic gubernatorial primary, local poor whites likewise rallied to back Goldwater-conservative John Bell Williams against covertly Negro-favored William Winter.

Liberalism lost its support base in the upcountry by shifting its principal concern from populist economics to government participation in social and racial upheaval. And this change likewise turned the hills against the national Democratic Party to which they had generally remained faithful even in difficult presidential years like 1948 and 1964.

Nobody could have better represented this alienation than 1968 third-party presidential candidate George C. Wallace. An ex-Golden Gloves fighter, cotton chopper and truck driver who married a dime store clerk and spent part of the Second World War living in a converted chicken coop in New Mexico, Wallace was the personification of the poor white Deep South. His Dixie crowds roared every time Wallace brandished a New York *Times* clipping which sneered at his wife's dime store job; they cheered his mockery of intellectuals with pointed heads; and in November, 1968, they gave him their votes for the presidency of the United States.

Except in the urban areas and occasional Negro concentrations, Wallace ran far ahead of Nixon and Humphrey. So completely did poor whites abandon the national Democratic Party that Hubert Humphrey typically ran *worst* where John F. Kennedy and Lyndon Johnson had run best. In South Carolina, for example, Kennedy's best 1960 counties were Piedmont Abbeville, Anderson and Cherokee (78 per cent Democratic). Eight years later, Anderson and Cherokee—Humphrey won only 20 per cent of their combined vote —were two of the four worst Democratic counties in the state.* Northeastern Mississippi's hill counties mauled Humphrey, and those in Alabama gave the 1968 Democratic nominee only 4 per cent to 18 per cent of the vote. Almost all of Humphrey's Deep

*Anderson County's trend was not just in Wallace's direction; a Republican was elected mayor of the City of Anderson in 1968.

Southern support came from Negroes, and this identification of Negroes with the national Democratic Party devastated longtime Democratic fidelity in the white Deep South upcountry.

Although the extraordinary populist appeal of George Wallace maximized 1968 Democratic presidential losses in the upcountry, the prospects of future Democratic nominees are not much better, given the Negro and Northeastern establishmentarian impetus of the national party. Upcountry populist politicians could hardly ask for a better target than a national Democratic Party aligned with Harvard, Boston, Manhattan's East Side, Harlem, the New York *Times* and the liberal Supreme Court. The only question is the extent to which third party movements like that of 1968 can delay the upcountry's shift into a nationally dominant Republican Party rooted in the Heartland, West and Outer South.

3. French Louisiana

Long before southern Louisiana was American, it was French. Northern Louisiana, settled by the Anglo-Saxon overflow from Alabama and Mississippi, shows little of the old Creole influence. The latter, however, is pervasive below Baton Rouge and east of Lafayette.* Instead of counties, Louisiana has parishes, some of them colorfully Gallic with names like Plaquemines, LaFourche, Iberville and St. Martin.

Until the Nineteen-Twenties, French Catholics constituted a sufficient part of Louisiana's population to pre-empt one of the state's two United States Senate seats. Today Creole influence is much less. Only one of ten Louisiana senators and congressmen elected in 1968 was a French Catholic, partly because recent economic expansion based on oil, natural gas, sulphur, commerce, shipping and finance has attracted enough new residents to Lake Charles, Shreveport, Baton Rouge and New Orleans to dilute French statewide and local power. In 1968, French Catholics cast 20 per cent to 25 per cent of the Louisiana vote.

Both sections of Louisiana are agricultural areas with large Negro populations, but historically, the languid Creole south of Louisiana has often been at social and political odds with the Protestant,

---

*On a smaller scale, Texas has a French element in the Orange-Beaumont-Port Arthur area adjacent to Louisiana; Mississippi has a substantial French population along the Gulf Coast; and Alabama has a French contingent in and around the old French colonial city of Mobile.

fundamentalist north. Typically, liquor sales, Sunday blue laws or a similar issue has sparked the controversy. In post-Civil War partisanship, the Louisiana French were mostly Democrats, although their fidelity was less than that of other Deep Southerners. The first major GOP breakthrough came in 1920, when the Creole counties trended Republican in protest against Wilsonian foreign policy differences with France, while the Anglo-Saxon north of Louisiana voted Democratic as usual.

The 1920 French revolt was substantial. Harding carried fourteen of the twenty predominantly French parishes. Two—La-Fourche and Assumption—cast better than three-quarters of their vote for the GOP nominee. Even in 1924, eight French parishes gave GOP presidential candidate Coolidge at least 40 per cent support. All of this bespoke a much smaller commitment to the white Democratic one-party system than prevailed in the Anglo-Saxon Black Belts. Most of this transient Republicanism evaporated in 1928 when local Catholics turned out *en masse* to support coreligionist Al Smith. Only a few French parishes gave Republican nominee Hoover even a quarter of the vote. Chart 70 compares the 1920-32 trends of (bayou) LaFourche Parish with those of Anglo-Saxon Winn Parish, home of populist Huey Long.

CHART 70

Ethnic Voting in Louisiana, 1920-32

Parish	Republican Share of the Total Vote for President			
	1920	1924	1928	1932
LaFourche (French)	76%	47%	11%	12%
Winn (Anglo-Saxon)	20	13	32	2

Louisiana remained solidly Democratic throughout the Roosevelt years, although by 1944, the French counties were giving the New Deal better support than the restive Anglo-Saxon counties of the north. In 1948, Louisiana joined Mississippi, Alabama and South Carolina in bolting the Democratic Party to support the Dixiecrat ticket. Surprisingly, the French proved at least as sympathetic to the Dixiecrats as did other Louisiana voters. Both of the top two

Thurmond parishes—Plaquemines and St. Bernard, each better than 90 per cent Dixiecrat—were heavily French (although boss-controlled), and New Orleans, Queen City of French Louisiana, also backed the Dixiecrats.

Dwight D. Eisenhower won 47 per cent of Louisiana's vote in 1952, and most of his impetus came from 1948 Dixiecrats. Fifteen Louisiana parishes voted for Eisenhower; half were northern Anglo-Saxon Dixiecrat fiefs; two of the others were the leading French Dixiecrat parishes, St. Bernard and Plaquemines. The latter, a personal preserve of Dixiecrat baron Leander Perez, gave Eisenhower 93 per cent of its ballots, a level no other county in the nation matched.* Elsewhere in Louisiana, north and south, a large part of the 1948 Dixiecrat strength went back to the Democrats.

Four years later, spurred by a heavy trend in the French parishes located between Lafayette and New Orleans, Louisiana cast 53 per cent of its vote for Eisenhower, becoming the first Deep South state since Reconstruction to back a Republican presidential nominee. Generally speaking, the GOP lost ground in the Deep South between 1952 and 1956 as a result of Dixiecrat reaction to the Supreme Court's 1954 school desegregation decision. The arch-Dixiecrat counties of northern Louisiana's Mississippi flood plain shared this animosity; only the unique French electorate bucked the regional trend and tipped the state into the GOP column.

The 1960 presidential election was a three-sided affair in Louisiana. Democratic candidate John F. Kennedy, profiting greatly from his religious appeal to French Catholic parishes, won an easy victory over Republican Richard Nixon and a ticket of States Rights electors. For the first time since the Nineteen-Twenties, a sharp cleavage emerged between Democratic presidential strength in northern and southern Louisiana. In the northern half of the state, John Kennedy won less than a quarter of the vote, the rest going to Republican and States Rights electors. Below Alexandria, however, Kennedy's share of the vote climbed with the local French population until it reached 70 per cent to 80 per cent in the same parishes between LaFayette and New Orleans where 1952-56 Eisenhower

*Plaquemines Parish stretches one hundred miles from New Orleans to the mouth of the Mississippi River. A demi-swamp, Plaquemines was dependent on wide-spread muskrat trapping for many years. Since the Nineteen-Thirties, however, Plaquemines—Leander Perez especially—has grown rich from the profits of vast local oil and sulfur deposits. Much of Perez' 1948 Dixiecrat sentiment and 1952 Eisenhower favoritism pivoted on the tidelands oil controversy.

gains had been centered. No other counties in the nation showed a
heftier Democratic 1956-60 trend. Few counties, it should be added,
are more Catholic than the core parishes of French Louisiana.
Chart 71 illustrates the intensity of pro-Kennedy trending in some
heavily French parishes, and Map 26 shows 1960 Kennedy support
(and derivatively, the location of Louisiana's French population).

CHART 71

French Presidential Voting in Louisiana, 1956-60

	Democratic Share of the Total Vote for President	
Parish	1956	1960
Assumption	41%	72%
LaFourche	36	76
St. Charles	40	71
St. James	49	82
St. John	47	80

It should be noted that only a part of the French pro-Kennedy
trend was religious in origin. Hardly liberal in the Northern sense,
the French electorate does not share the intensity of northern Louisiana's concern with states rights schemes or candidacies. Many
Eisenhower Democrats simply went back to their party in 1960.
The cleavage of 1960 recurred in 1964 when Barry Goldwater ran
for president. Although the Arizona Senator captured Louisiana in
his sweep of the Deep South, he fared poorly in the French bayou
and Gulf Coast parishes. Unlike the conservative north, some southern Louisiana parishes gave him a mere 25 per cent to 35 per cent of
the vote. However, Leander Perez' perennially conservative French
parish of Plaquemines gave Goldwater solid 86 per cent support.

For different cultural and geographic reasons, French Louisiana
resembled the Deep South upcountry and pineywoods in backing
the Democratic presidential nominees of 1960 and 1964. Like the
rest of the hitherto Democratic white Deep South, the French
parishes then switched to George C. Wallace in 1968. To French
Louisiana, as well as the Georgia and Alabama upcountry, the
national Democratic Party had become the Negro party, and white

MAP 26

Louisiana—The Ethnic Cleavage in 1960 Presidential Voting

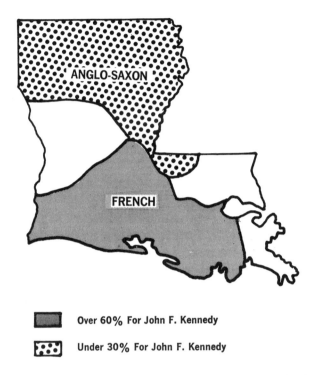

ANGLO-SAXON

FRENCH

■ Over 60% For John F. Kennedy

▦ Under 30% For John F. Kennedy

voters looked elsewhere. Most backed Wallace. Relatively few of Louisiana's Humphrey ballots—28 per cent of the total—were cast by whites. Thus, the Anglo-French cleavage of 1960 and 1964 gave way to a new racial one in 1968. French Louisiana is not as conservative as the Anglo-Saxon north—for one thing, it elects moderates to Congress—but its 1968 voting trends bespoke an inclination to join with the north rather than with local Negroes.

B. The Outer South

In essence, the Outer South is a non-contiguous ring of those Southern states in which the archetypal Black Belts dominant in the Deep South fade into a moderating statewide prevalence of mountains, Piedmont, oil and ranchlands, retirement and technological cities. It divides into two sections: 1) the four most reluctant Confederate states—Arkansas, Virginia, North Carolina and Tennessee—which all include substantial Ozark and Appalachian highland strength; and 2) the New South of Texas and Florida, where the originally settled Deep South-leaning areas have been overwhelmed by post-bellum immigration, based on commerce and technology. All six states have substantial Black Belt areas of traditional Deep South cultural and political bent. However, they also have meaningful elements of local Republicanism, antedating the 1948 Dixiecrat upheavals which engendered overnight GOP strength in the Cotton states. A vivid contrast can be made between the presidential voting history of the Deep South and that of the Outer South. Between 1920 and 1960, only one Deep South state voted for a Republican President (Louisiana in 1956), but the Outer South went Republican as follows:

CHART 72

Outer South Presidential Republicanism, 1920-60

> Tennessee—1920, 1928, 1952, 1956, 1960
> Virginia—1928, 1952, 1956, 1960
> Florida—1928, 1952, 1956, 1960
> Texas—1928, 1952, 1956
> North Carolina—1928

Before the Florida and Texas boom of the Nineteen-Twenties, there were few Southern Republicans beyond the Appalachian and Ozark highlands. Altitude was the primary denominator of the partisan Outer South; most cities behaved in much the same way as their rural environs. But while mountain votes enabled the Republican Party to make a decent showing in Arkansas, Tennessee, North Carolina and Virginia, the highlanders were not numerous enough to win statewide contests, presidential or otherwise. In the years between the Civil War and the New Deal, North Carolina and Virginia were usually governed by Democratic organizations based in the wealthy and moderately conservative Piedmont; Tennessee was controlled by Democratic factions from the Deep South area around Memphis or from moderate Middle Tennessee. Herbert Hoover's 1928 triumphs over Al Smith did not affect state-level

Democratic hegemony. As for Texas and Florida, they were stalwart Southern Democratic states until the boom times of the Nineteen-Twenties spurred rapid urbanization in cities like Houston, Dallas and Miami, bringing commerce and an element of Republicanism.

CHART 73

Non-Historical Denominators of the Outer South

Affluence, Urbanization and Educational Attainment in Virginia, Texas and Florida Relative to the Remaining Southern States

State Data and Rank Among Eleven Southern States (1960)

State	Non-Negro Percent of Total Population	Urban Percent of Total Population	Median Family Income
Texas	88% (1)	75% (1)	$4884(2)
Florida	82% (3)	74% (2)	$4722(3)
Virginia	79% (4)	56% (4)	$4964(1)

State	Median Years of Education Completed	Percent of Population 25 Years of Age or Older Who Have Completed 4 Years of College
Texas	10.4(2)	8.0(2)
Florida	10.9(1)	7.8(3)
Virginia	9.9(3)	8.4(1)

Note: The original Civil War-era "Outer South" pivoted on states including pro-Union Appalachian-Ozark highlands. Twentieth Century economic modernization and population influx then reshaped Texas, Florida and Virginia (where suburbanization centers in the Washington-Richmond corridor).

The Outer South backed Franklin D. Roosevelt with overwhelming majorities in both 1932 and 1936, but as Chart 74 illustrates, the New Deal put the Democratic Party on a slow but steady downtrend. Finally, urban and suburban voters, together with Dixiecrats who had fled the party reservation in 1948, combined with traditional GOP supporters to carry four states of the Outer South for Eisenhower in 1952. Although most observers failed to realize the evolutionary nature of the 1952 Republican victories in the Outer

CHART 74

Outer South Presidential Voting During the New Deal Era, 1932-68

Democratic Share of the Total Vote for President

State	1932	1936	1940	1944	1948*	1952	1956	1960	1964	1968**
Virginia	69%	70%	68%	62%	48%	43%	38%	47%	54%	33%
North Carolina	70	73	74	67	58	54	51	52	56	29
Tennessee	67	69	67	60	49	50	49	46	56	28
Arkansas	86	82	78	70	62	56	53	50	56	30
Florida	75	76	74	70	49	45	43	49	51	31
Texas	88	87	81	71	66	47	44	51	63	41

*1948 figures for each state represent the Democratic share of the Republican, Democratic and Dixiecrat vote total.
**1968 figures for each state represent the Democratic share of the Republican, Democratic and American Independent vote total.

South, Chart 74 makes the process clear. Likewise, Chart 75 shows the developing urban support for the GOP. Without it, Eisenhower could not have shaped Republican majorities in the Outer South.

Far from being simply a personal tribute to Dwight Eisenhower (granted, however, that his personal stature and immense, non-partisan popularity *did* make it easier for many Southerners to vote Republican), the 1952 GOP successes in the Outer South were the logical consummation of an anti-Democratic trend reaching back to 1936. The 1948 Dixiecrat upheaval was an essential prerequisite of Republican success; it shook loose the partisanship of a large number of conservative Democrats whose support proved essential to Eisenhower. Chart 60 shows the 1948 Dixiecrat origins of 1952 GOP gains in Tennessee; the same shift took place elsewhere in the Outer South.

The deep roots of the new Republican position in the Outer South became somewhat more obvious after Richard Nixon held Florida, Virginia and Tennessee in 1960, becoming the first losing GOP presidential candidate to carry a Southern state. But while the 1960 election spotlighted Republican strength in the mountains, ranch counties, suburbs and cities of the Outer South, it also under-scored continuing party weakness in the local Black Belts. From Southside Virginia to delta Arkansas, the Outer South Black Belts, where white voters were completely in the saddle, were the regions where persisting Democratic loyalties menaced or blocked statewide GOP victories along the Dixie periphery. Eagerness to break up these seemingly obsolescent and vulnerable voting habits weighed heavily in the strategy behind the 1964 nomination of Barry Gold-water.

Ultimately, the Arizona Senator did score heavy gains in such areas as Southside Virginia and northern Florida. At the same time, however, the basic Republican electorate of the Outer South— mountaineers, transplanted Northerners, city folk and suburbanites —made known its distaste for Goldwater's Black Belt thrust. As Chart 74 shows, GOP gains among Black Belt Democratic tradi-tionalists were outweighed in every Outer Southern state (especially Texas) by Republican losses among the support groups mentioned above. Goldwater also lost the small Negro vote which Nixon had won in the Outer South four years earlier. Back in 1960, some Negroes had supported Nixon as the candidate of the party *opposed* by local Black Belt whites; Goldwater reversed this earlier pattern.

CHART 75

Urban Presidential Voting in the Outer South, 1948-68

County (City)	1948(*)		Republican Share of the Total Vote for President				1968(**)	
			1952	1956	1960	1964		
Arkansas								
Pulaski (Little Rock)	24%	(23%)	49%	51%	40%***	48%	33%	(33%)
Sebastian (Fort Smith)	33	(9)	56	57	57	56	44	(32)
Florida								
Dade (Miami)	37	(5)	57	55	42	36	37	(15)
Broward (Ft. Lauderdale)	51	(13)	69	72	59	56	55	(16)
Duval (Jacksonville)	26	(26)	48	50	46	51	31	(36)
Pinellas (St. Petersburg)	56	(9)	71	73	64	45	57	(16)
North Carolina								
Mecklenburg (Charlotte)	35	(22)	57	62	55	48	52	(19)
Guilford (Greensboro)	40	(11)	53	60	58	47	47	(23)
Forsyth (Winston-Salem)	41	(10)	52	65	58	49	48	(23)
Buncombe (Asheville)	37	(8)	52	54	55	38	44	(25)
Wake (Raleigh)	20	(7)	39	40	41	42	43	(26)

Tennessee						
Shelby (Memphis)	22 (41)	48	49***	48***	47	32 (33)
Davidson (Nashville)	22 (22)	41	39	46	36	32 (35)
Knox (Knoxville)	54 (5)	62	60	61	50	53 (20)
Hamilton (Chattanooga)	35 (9)	55	53	56	51	34 (38)
Texas						
Dallas (Dallas)	38 (12)	63	65	62	45	51 (15)
Harris (Houston)	35 (17)	58	61	52	40	43 (18)
Tarrant (Fort Worth)	28 (12)	58	60	55	37	43 (15)
Bexar (San Antonio)	40 (6)	56	58	46	33	40 (9)
El Paso (El Paso)	26 (3)	58	55	48	37	45 (8)
*Virginia*****						
Norfolk City	41 (8)	54	54	44	36	36 (23)
Richmond City	41 (12)	60	62***	60	43	39 (13)

(*) Dixiecrat share of the total 1948 presidential vote.
(**) Wallace American Independent Party share of the total 1968 presidential vote.
***Minor third-party vote cast for a conservative or states rights presidential candidate, diluting major-party strength.
****Virginia's cities are independent political entities and their votes are not included in those of surrounding counties which encompass their suburbs. In the case of Richmond, now almost half Negro, its all-white suburbs are larger than the city itself.

All in all, no other section of the country rendered so telling a verdict on the Deep South strategy of 1964.

Thus chastened, the GOP abandoned its revolutionary Deep South scheme and returned to reliance on evolutionary inroads in the Outer South. And paradoxically, the peripheral Southern strategy made even more sense than before. Although Negro support had been lost to the Democrats, all of the other pre-1964 Republican-trending groups returned to the fold, while some Black Belt Goldwater converts also stuck with the GOP. With the help of the civil rights revolution, Civil War traditions were dissolving and a new white majority impulse was taking shape. In 1966, Outer South Republicanism bounced back stronger than ever as Florida and Arkansas elected their first GOP governors since Reconstruction, Texas and Tennessee elected Republicans to full terms in the United States Senate in a similarly unprecedented manner, and a number of congressional districts chose new Republican representatives.

Bearing these gains very much in mind, Richard Nixon's 1968 election blueprint put considerable—and justified—emphasis on the Outer South. Notwithstanding the disruptive candidacy of George Wallace, the GOP nominee won solid victories in Virginia, Tennessee, Florida and North Carolina. George Wallace carried Arkansas, and he diverted enough conservative strength from Nixon to enable Humphrey to eke out a plurality in Texas. Chart 74 shows how the 1968 Democratic share of the total vote plummeted far below the worst previous levels in each of the states of the Outer South. Twenty years before, the local Democratic parties had easily turned back the third party challenge of Strom Thurmond's Dixiecrats, but in 1968, the national Democratic Party practically disintegrated in the face of the twin attacks of Nixon and Wallace.

In Virginia, North Carolina, Tennessee and Arkansas, the majority of the votes cast for Hubert Humphrey came from Negroes. Only in traditionally hotly contested mountain counties—where there were few or no Negroes to arouse Wallace sentiment—did the Democratic candidate garner a decent minority of the white vote. It is safe to say that Nixon and Wallace split 75 per cent to 80 per cent of the white vote, with Wallace winning overwhelming support among Black Belt whites and Nixon taking the lead among the electorate of the mountains, Piedmont, middle-class cities and suburbia. Chart 75 pictures Nixon's important urban strength.

Texas and Florida gave rise to slightly different situations. Besides solid Negro support, Humphrey amassed heavy backing among Latins—Mexican Americans in Texas and Cubans in Florida—and in greater Miami's large Jewish community. In Florida it would appear that at least three quarters of the white voters picked Nixon or Wallace. Texas produced the greatest amount of white support for Humphrey; perhaps one third of the white electorate backed him. Part of this reflected the influence of Lyndon Johnson and John Connally who, apprehensive over the possibilities of re-alignment and/or liberal Democratic scuttling of the state ticket, mobilized the Democratic courthouse cliques of Texas (alone among the Southern states) to work for the national Democratic nominee. The efforts of Johnson and Connally obviously played a crucial part in helping Humphrey to win a narrow victory with 41 per cent of the total vote.

The most useful political segmentation of the Outer South is as follows: 1) the Appalachian and Ozark highlands, long the source of most Outer South Republicanism; 2) the Piedmont (and the Cumberland-Nashville Basin), the partisan middle ground of Virginia, North Carolina and Tennessee; 3) the Outer South Black Belts, longtime bastions of Democratic voting; 4) Urban-Suburban Texas and Florida, the force behind Republican growth in those two states; 5) the Southern Plains, locale of booming oil wells, ranches and conservatism; and 6) the Latin crescent of liberalism, ranging from the Mexican counties of Rio Grande Texas through parts of French Louisiana to the Cuban and Jewish precincts of Miami.

1. The Southern Mountains

Two large north-south mountain groups—the Appalachians and Ozarks—reach into the old Confederacy. The Ozarks extend over a substantial part of Arkansas, as well as sections of the border states of Missouri and Oklahoma. Appalachian highlands sweep across good-sized areas of North Carolina, Virginia and Tennessee, besides crossing Border Kentucky and West Virginia. The tail end of the Appalachian range nudges northern Georgia and Alabama, but neither state is much affected by mountain politics. Map 21 sketches the location of the Southern highlands.

Politically and culturally, the Southern highlands have long been a world apart from the rest of the South. Beginning in the middle of the Eighteenth Century, the Appalachian upcountry attracted a different sort of colonist than the coastal lowlands. English, Germans and, particularly, Scotch-Irish left Appalachian Pennsylvania, Maryland and northern Virginia and flocked down the Great Valley (the Shenandoah) into the western highlands of Virginia and North Carolina. Other Scotch-Irish and English moved west across North Carolina into the highlands. Of all the ethnic strains in the Appalachians, the Scotch-Irish were dominant by far; perhaps memories of the sweeping mountains and valleys of Scotland and northern Ireland made them choose to live in the Appalachians rather than along the coastal plain.*

Even before the American Revolution began in 1775, some hardier pioneers had pushed west into Kentucky and Tennessee. Peace accelerated the growth of both trans-Appalachian territories. After Tennessee and Kentucky became states during the Seventeen-Nineties, many of their frontiersmen pushed further west. Daniel Boone, for example, eventually left Kentucky for Missouri. Because most migrants were prone to look for similar scenery and soil, the Missouri and Arkansas Ozarks were principally settled from the Appalachians, especially the highland areas of Kentucky and Tennessee. To a considerable extent, the Southern highlands are similar among themselves, just as they are quite different from the lowlands. In describing the settlement pattern of the Southern highlands, Professor Frank Owsley's book, *Plain Folk of the Old South,* helps explain the genesis of mountaineer isolationism:

> The rural folk of the upper South dwelling in the limestone valleys and highlands, whose pattern of farm husbandry had been the growing of grain and livestock, did not in migrating erupt into the lower South where climate and soil would force a radical change in farm economy and methods of cultivation. On the contrary, when they migrated, it was usually into the highlands, limestone basins, and valleys of Tennessee, Kentucky, Missouri and northern Arkansas . . . where climate, soil, timber and the grasses indicated that the new country would be hospitable to the familiar old crops.**

---

*In Virginia and the Carolinas, the pre-Revolutionary population of the Tidewater or coastal plain was English, while the mountains and higher reaches of the Piedmont were substantially peopled by Scotch-Irish. See *The American Heritage Pictorial Atlas of United States History* (New York, 1966), p. 87.
**Frank L. Owsley, *Plain Folk of the Old South* (Baton Rouge, 1949), pp. 56-57.

In a nutshell, the Southern mountains are demographically in-bred. Between 1750 and 1825, the Appalachians filled up—largely with clannish Scotch-Irish—and overflowed into the Ozarks. Other sections furnished the highlands with very little sociocultural cross-fertilization, especially after the frontier had come and gone. Remote and inaccessible, the highlands settled into a relatively isolated existence. Some hamlets tucked away in remote valleys or up little known creeks have been only slightly influenced by changing times. As late as the Nineteen-Thirties, there were a few old people in the West Virginia hills who still spoke the German of their pre-Revolutionary War immigrant ancestors. In a similar vein, the Seventeenth Century and Eighteenth Century British speech patterns of a number of highland communities have received considerable analysis. A few mountain areas, notably the tourist-appealing Great Smokies, have grown and changed since World War II (without much effect on partisan political preference), but modernity is not the rule.

Given this isolation, it is not surprising that the politics of the Southern mountains is very much a product of tradition; more specifically, Civil War sentiment and partisanship. Most of the highlands opposed secession, favored the Union and thereafter voted for the Republican Party. For all practical purposes, the mountain counties were devoid of slaves, being suitable only for small farms and livestock rather than the plantation agriculture of the Black Belts. Secondly, the mountain counties were traditional political opponents of the Tidewater and Black Belts, preserving an animosity which dated back to colonial days. After the election of Abraham Lincoln in 1860, the Southern highlands desired neither to secede nor to send their sons to fight in Confederate grey for the interests of the slave-owning lowlands. Of course, there were many variations on this basic theme. Usually, the highest, most inaccessible and Negro-devoid mountain counties—the roof of the Great Smokies, for example—were the most Republican, but sometimes GOP strength peaked at lower altitudes. The German counties of western Virginia and North Carolina backed the Republicans, and they were not so mountainous. Then too, not all mountain counties opposed secession in 1860 or 1861. Settlement ties with the lowlands induced some mountain counties to go against their neighbors. By and large, however, the mountains (and some adjoining plateau and foothill areas) opposed secession, fought for the Union—the Appalachian sections of Tennessee, Virginia, North Carolina and Kentucky put a quarter of a million men in uniform for the North* —and thereafter voted Republican. When the Civil War ended, the Southern highlands, like the rest of Dixie, voted as they had fought. With only minor changes, this pattern persisted from the end of Reconstruction to the Dixiecrat days after World War II. Map 27 shows the correlation between pro-Union opinion in Tennessee and subsequent Republicanism.

MAP 27

The Genesis of Southern Mountain Republicanism

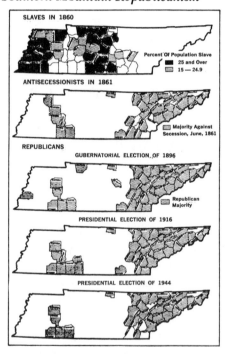

The War and Tennessee Party Lines: Distribution of Republican Popular Strength, 1861-1944

*Even Alabama had its pockets of pro-Union sentiment. Winston County, in northern Alabama, declared itself the "Free State of Winston" rather than volitionally follow Alabama into the Confederacy. An isolated, somewhat mountainous and almost wholly white area, Winston County has voted Republican since the Civil War, often producing the only GOP county majority in the entire state. Several companies of troops from Winston and similar areas fought—as Alabama units—for the Union side during the Civil War.

In Kentucky and Missouri, Border states where the GOP had other than mountaineer strength, the party occasionally won state-wide elections between the Civil War and World War I, but in the old Confederate states, Appalachian and Ozark mountaineers were too badly outnumbered. Between 1900, after Negroes were effectively disenfranchised, and 1916, the GOP averaged 25 per cent to 35 per cent of the vote in Virginia, North Carolina and Tennessee. Party support in Arkansas was something less. Most of the Republican vote came from the mountains, although there were smaller patches in the Piedmont and elsewhere.

In 1920, the mountain vote soared as highlanders throughout the South left their cabins to trek to the polls and vote for Harding, Prohibition and isolationism. Resentment of Woodrow Wilson's internationalism rankled the mountaineers. The 1920 vote was huge, vastly exceeding that which had been cast in 1916. In Tennessee, it was not matched again until World War II. No other state is so swayed by the mountain vote as Tennessee, and the GOP won the state's presidential electors in 1920—the first Republican victory in the Confederacy since Reconstruction—and also elected a governor and five congressmen. Half a dozen mountain and Piedmont districts in North Carolina and even Alabama almost fell to Republican congressional challengers. Chart 76 shows the size of the 1920

CHART 76

Comparative Size of the Mountain Vote, 1916-24

	Total Vote Cast for President		
	1916	1920	1924
Sevier County, Tennessee	3,161	6,412	3,996
Avery County, North Carolina	1,518	2,900	2,560
Newton County, Arkansas	1,225	1,314	944
Winston County, Alabama	1,839	3,344	1,791

Note: These counties are banner Republican areas in their several states.

mountain vote compared with 1916 and 1924 totals in a few selected Southern highland counties. When the mountaineer turnout fell off sharply in 1924, Tennessee voted Democratic in the presidential election.

In 1928, the mountain vote increased in comparison with 1924 but it did not reach 1920 levels. Evidently anti-Catholicism—the chance to vote against Al Smith—did not interest the mountaineers as much as the isolationist cause of 1920. As firmly set in their politics as the Black Belts, the highland GOP counties gave Hoover little more than the usual Republican share of the vote. Chart 77 illustrates the behavior of the leading Ozark and Appalachian counties in the Hoover-Smith contest.

Given their cultural *apartheid* and normally near-subsistence-level standards of living, the highlands were not greatly affected by the Depression, with the exception of coal-mining and urbanized areas. Aside from the labor- and industrial policy-conscious mining counties—largely situated beyond the old Confederacy in eastern Kentucky and West Virginia—most of the high redoubts of Southern mountain Republicanism paid little attention to the New Deal and were among the nation's top GOP counties in 1936. In two of the banner counties—Avery, North Carolina and Sevier, Tennessee—Roosevelt won only 22 per cent and 21 per cent of their ballots respectively; and there were several Kentucky backwaters where FDR never cracked a fifth of the vote! Even the Tennessee Valley Authority, which could have been expected to exert a strong pro-New Deal influence on the areas it so greatly benefitted, produced substantial 1932-40 Democratic gains only in a handful of counties immediately surrounding TVA headquarters in Knoxville. Chart 77 sets forth the persisting Republicanism of the high Ozarks and Appalachians during the New Deal.

World War II brought out Southern mountain isolationism for a second time. In the United States Senate, some of the leading isolationists came from Appalachian and Ozark states. Among them were Rush Holt and Chapman Revercomb of West Virginia, Bennett Champ Clark of Missouri, Kenneth McKellar of Tennessee and Robert Reynolds of North Carolina. Partly in resentment of United States overseas involvement, many mountain counties gave the GOP a higher vote share in 1944 than in any other election between 1928 and 1952. Perhaps the wartime trend had puffed up Republican expectations, but the GOP seriously expected mountain votes to keynote a Southern breakthrough in 1948 (when the Democrats were divided between Dixiecrats and loyalists). As part of a serious attempt to carry Tennessee, the Republicans ran Congressman (and National GOP Chairman) B. Carroll Reece for the United States

CHART 77

The Republican Presidential Vote in the Southern Mountains, 1920-68

	Republican Share of the Total Presidential Vote						
County	1920	1924	1928	1932	1936	1940	1944
Winston, Alabama	69%	61%	76%	50%	53%	55%	63%
Newton, Arkansas	60	61	71	36	53	53	57
Fannin, Georgia	66	60	68	59	55	56	60
Jackson, Kentucky	92	88	97	84	89	89	92
Ozark, Missouri	80	69	83	56	69	78	81
Avery, North Carolina	86	86	89	73	78	71	79
Floyd, Virginia	73	65	77	60	69	67	69
Sevier, Tennessee	94	88	93	77	78	80	87

	Republican Share of the Total Presidential Vote					
	1948	1952	1956	1960	1964	1968(*)
Winston, Alabama	64%	59%	66%	67%	71%	40% (55%)
Newton, Arkansas	50	61	64	68	49	51 (19)
Fannin, Georgia	57	60	64	66	55	58 (21)
Jackson, Kentucky	86	87	88	90	74	84 (8)
Ozark, Missouri	70	78	71	78	59	69 (10)
Avery, North Carolina	75	79	81	80	64	71 (15)
Floyd, Virginia	73	72	71	70	62	64 (15)
Sevier, Tennessee	84	87	87	85	70	75 (14)

*The 1968 Wallace vote is in parentheses.

Note: Most of these counties are the banner Republican counties of their respective states. Geographically, they are mountainous and/or remote.

Senate and "Grand Old Opry" hillbilly singer Roy Acuff for governor. Both lost, however, as the Dixiecrat-Democratic split failed to provide a GOP opening on the statewide level.

In 1952, the highlands turned out a big vote for General Eisenhower, and as in past victory years, landslide mountain majorities were the foundations without which the Republicans could not have carried the normally Democratic states of the Appalachians and Ozarks. This remained true in 1956, when Eisenhower lost Missouri because of farm county slippage, but captured Kentucky and came within a few percentage points of success in both Arkansas and North Carolina. Whatever the urban or Dixiecrat origins of the new margins of statewide GOP success in the Outer South, the ultimate base of Republican strength was highland. Even though the Republican Party was beginning to deal with Black Belt Dixiecrats, the mountains turned in some of their most extraordinary Republican majorities in 1952 and 1956. Richard Nixon maintained and sometimes improved 1952-56 levels when he made his own White House try in 1960, and like Eisenhower, his majorities in Virginia and Tennessee, as well as his near-majorities in Arkansas and North Carolina, were basically rooted in the continuing traditional Republicanism of the Appalachian and Ozark Southern highlands.*

Although Republican tradition in the highlands had proved impervious to the evolutionary 1952-60 GOP collusion with the Dixiecrats, the longtime Republican electorate of the mountains took a much dimmer view of the bluntly Deep South-focused 1964 candidacy of Barry Goldwater. The Arizona Senator lost highland counties which had not voted Democratic since the Civil War. His obvious base in states like Alabama, Mississippi and Louisiana cost him considerable support in counties where local Republican politics were forged out of wartime enmity to the cause of precisely those states.** Chart 77 illustrates the extent to which Goldwater pulled the Republican vote down to record lows in the archetypal counties of Southern highland GOP tradition. More than half of the usually Republican mountain counties backed Goldwater despite their misgivings, but the essential party landslides were not forthcoming. Sixteen Tennessee mountain counties had given Nixon 70 per cent or more of their vote in 1960; only two gave that amount—and barely that amount—to Goldwater.

Senator Goldwater's poor showing almost drowned several GOP Southern mountain congressmen in its undertow. However, once

---

*In some mountain counties, Nixon's 1960 improvement on 1956 Eisenhower levels was a result of local anti-Catholic voting.

**It is sometimes suggested that much of Goldwater's decline in Appalachian East Tennessee resulted from his impolitic observations on the sale of TVA to private power interests. This seems unlikely because his slippage in East Tennessee's big TVA counties was no more than elsewhere, to say nothing of the fact that the 1960-64 GOP slide was much more acute in the unaffected (by TVA) mountains of Kentucky and roughly the same in the distant Ozarks. The sharp Goldwater losses in the Southern highlands were almost certainly a generalized reaction among traditional Republicans to the party's affair with the Cotton states.

the Republican Party reverted to its evolutionary approach to the South, the highlands renewed their prior adherence to party candidates. In 1966, the Ozarks played a major part in electing Arkansas's first Republican governor since Reconstruction, and in their own right they chose a similarly unprecedented GOP congressman. The election of Howard Baker as United States Senator from Tennessee was also much aided by heavy Republican balloting in Appalachian East Tennessee. Across the Appalachians and Ozarks, all of the predominantly highland congressional districts gave Republican incumbents and candidates extremely good support. One reason was isolationist resentment of the seemingly stalemated Vietnamese war; a second was dislike of Great Society civil rights and welfare legislation.* Like the Border, the Southern mountains shrink from the political extremes of both the Deep South and Northern urban liberalism.

Mounting his second try for the presidency in 1968, Richard Nixon swept the Ozark and Appalachian highlands as if the aberration of 1964 had never occurred. While Nixon's share of the total vote was down from 1960 because of Wallace inroads—10 per cent to 20 per cent in the North Carolina, Virginia, Tennessee and Kentucky highlands—normally Democratic strength also shifted to Wallace, enabling Nixon to duplicate previous lopsided mountain Republican-Democratic vote ratios. Mountain Wallace backing considerably exceeded 1948 Dixiecrat support, but the Alabaman's showing in the highlands was much smaller than in other sections of the four states. Predictable as this was, given the anti-Deep South framework in which mountain politics have orbited, it was a boon to the GOP. Chart 77 illustrates the size of Nixon's crucial 1968 Southern highland majorities. Marshaled against a three-candidate split in the traditionally Democratic lowlands, relatively unfragmented Appalachian Republicanism was a key force behind Nixon's capture of the electoral votes of North Carolina, Virginia, Kentucky and Tennessee.

Farther west, Missouri's Ozark Republicans provided Nixon

*Like prior wars, the Vietnamese conflict evoked a particularly negative response in the Southern mountains. A majority of the United States Senators from Arkansas, Tennessee and Kentucky queried the war's worth, and the clearest disengagement sentiments of all were voiced by Republican Congressman Tim Lee Carter of the poor and isolated Kentucky hills: "Let us now, while we are yet strong, bring our men home, every man jack of them. If we must fight, let us fight in defense of our homeland and hemisphere. Our sons' lives are too precious to lose on foreign soil. If they must die, let it be in defense of America."

with a larger majority than he won statewide. Ozark Arkansas, like the small GOP mountain sections of Alabama and Georgia, backed Nixon over Humphrey, although the proximity of the Deep South increased Wallace's strength. And Winston County, Alabama spurned a Republican presidential nominee for the first time since 1932. Only 5 per cent of the county's voters chose Hubert Humphrey, but 55 per cent endorsed former Governor Wallace.

On a local level, 1968 saw the Southern mountains behave as strongly Republican as ever before. Most districts re-elected GOP congressmen with huge and often record majorities. (Two East Tennessee Republicans beat their Democratic opponents by six-to-one edges.) Whatever highland Republican slippage might ultimately flow from the effects of a Deep South changeover to the GOP, the traditional partisanship of the mountains gave no sign of weakness in 1968.

2. The Piedmont

Politically and geographically, the states of North Carolina, Tennessee and, to a lesser extent, Virginia are distinctly segmented: Middle against West, Piedmont against Coastal Plain, Tidewater against Valley, and so forth. In between the traditionally Republican highlands and the historically Democratic lowlands (Tidewater or Black Belt, as the case may be) lie middle zones—Middle Tennessee and the Piedmonts of Virginia and North Carolina. Unlike the upcountry reaches of the Deep South states—populist centers invariably in opposition to the conservatism of Black Belt whites—the North Carolina and Virginia Piedmonts are increasingly middle-class seats of commerce and light industry.

The Piedmont sections of Virginia and North Carolina originally attracted industry because of their proximity to markets, transportation, water power and raw materials. The area is now among the major national producers of textiles, cigarettes, furniture, wood products and chemicals. These are light rather than heavy industries, and their growth has produced a fairly large local class of skilled workers, technicians and white-collar managers. The leading cities of the two states, Charlotte and Richmond, are commercial, insurance, banking and administrative centers. All of the Piedmont cities have grown and prospered since World War II, but Charlotte and Richmond have done especially well, and both are very middle-class in appearance and orientation. The Virginia suburbs of Washington, D.C., also received a large white middle-class population increment during this period.

Except for a few sizeable Negro minorities—50 per cent in Richmond, 20 per cent to 30 per cent in cities like Charlotte, Danville and Greensboro—this new urban Piedmont is overwhelmingly Anglo-Saxon Protestant. Furthermore, while Piedmont cities are gaining importance, by no means all of the area is urbanized or industrialized. North Carolina has an especially large rural population. Substantial tobacco and other cropland spreads across Virginia and North Carolina, and the Shenandoah Valley, where tourist income augments a well developed agricultural economy, is one of the most prosperous rural areas in the nation.

Far from being insurgent centers like the upcountry districts of Alabama, Georgia and South Carolina, the Virginia-North Carolina Piedmont is a fast-growing seat of conservatism and Republicanism. Surging urban and suburban GOP strength in places like Arlington, Fairfax, the Shenandoah Valley, Lynchburg, Richmond and suburbs, Raleigh, Greensboro, High Point and Charlotte has added crucial weight to Republican mountaineer votes and given the GOP the ability to carry North Carolina and Virginia. In Tennessee, the pattern is somewhat different. Middle Tennessee, still heavily rural except for Nashville, is not much more Republican than the West Tennessee cotton counties along the Mississippi River. The GOP carries Tennessee by linking East Tennessee highland votes with those of the former Dixiecrats of Memphis and environs.*

From the close of Reconstruction until the end of the First World War, most of Piedmont North Carolina and Virginia was Demo-

---

*The Memphis area, adjacent to Mississippi, has behaved like a part of the Deep South. Franklin D. Roosevelt won 94 per cent of the vote in populous Shelby County (Memphis) in 1936. And in a Deep South mode unlike Outer South behavior, Shelby County, under the leadership of Boss E. H. Crump, kicked over the party traces in 1948 and went Dixiecrat. In the pre-1948 context of Tennessee's dominant Democratic Party, the Republican leadership and Democratic minorities of East Tennessee had generally supported the Shelby conservatives against the moderate Democrats of Middle Tennessee. Thereafter, when the Dixiecrat movement failed, Shelby trended Republican, joining with East Tennessee to forge GOP majorities in the Volunteer State over the opposition of Middle Tennessee (which, like other Outer South lowlands, remained Democratic). Between 1952 and 1960, GOP presidential candidates won 48 per cent to 49 per cent of the total vote in Shelby County. The Memphis-East Tennessee axis remained the base of successful Tennessee Republicanism in 1968. Of the four GOP congressmen elected, for example, three came from the mountains and one from Memphis. However, Middle Tennessee too began to move away from the Democrats.

cratic, although many counties had strong Republican minorities.*
Mountain and Black Belt traditions met in the Piedmont; local
sentiment had been predominantly Confederate during the Civil
War. Then the Nineteen-Twenties brought an increasing amount of
industry and commerce to the region, and cities like Charlotte and
Richmond began to grow. In 1928, the Piedmonts of both states
supported Republican Herbert Hoover against Democrat Al Smith.
Urbanization and prosperity produced part of the Republican trend;
ethnic, religious and cultural suspicion of Smith accounted for a
good deal more. But whatever its origins, the presidential Republicanism of 1928 was buried by the Depression. Franklin D. Roosevelt swept the North Carolina and Virginia Piedmont in 1932.

As it progressed, the New Deal became steadily less popular in
the conservative middle-class urbanized areas of the Piedmont. And
in 1948, the Democratic Party was undercut by the conservative insurgency of Dixiecrat Strom Thurmond. Scoring higher in middle-
class urban and suburban wards than in most Virginia Tidewater or
North Carolina Black Belt counties, the South Carolina governor
won 22 per cent of the vote in Mecklenburg County, North Carolina (Charlotte), and 12 per cent in Richmond, Virginia. At the
same time, Republican presidential candidate Thomas E. Dewey
substantially increased his party's presidential vote share in these
cities over 1944 levels. There were exceptions—Negro Republicanism was one—but by and large, Dixiecrat and Republican voting
occurred in the same middle-class and upper-middle-class precincts,
and both trends were rooted in the same economic and social conservatism.** The significance of the Dixiecrat vote lay in the fact

---

*A few Piedmont counties regularly voted Republican. These had substantial
German elements in their population. Shenandoah County, and to a lesser extent,
Rockingham and Page counties in Virginia's Shenandoah Valley were settled
during the Eighteenth Century by German Protestants moving down the Great
Valley from Pennsylvania. The town of Strasburg in Shenandoah County was
named for the capital of Germany's province of Alsace. Other Germans continued south into the North Carolina Piedmont (the general area around¹Winston-
Salem). By and large, the Germans disliked the plantation system and lowland
gentry of the Tidewater, opposed secession, disliked the Civil War, and took up
subsequent Republican allegiance. In 1936, Shenandoah County was Virginia's
only non-highland county to back Republican presidential nominee Alf Landon,
and the Kansan also carried several German-influenced Piedmont counties in
North Carolina.

**In his masterful analysis in *The Future of American Politics,* Samuel Lubell has
described how 1948 Dixiecrat and Republican support in the urban Outer
South tended to occur in the same areas—Myers Park in Charlotte, Miami
Shores in Miami, Irving Park in Greensboro, Highland Park in Dallas and

that in Virginia and Tennessee, the combined Dewey-Thurmond vote exceeded Truman's. A movement of Dixiecrat votes into the Republican column would bode ill for the Democrats.

That trend came in 1952. Chart 60 shows how Tennessee's top 1952 Republican presidential gains came in 1948 Dixiecrat strongholds; similar charts could be drawn for Virginia and North Carolina.* Eisenhower did not rally some mythical Southern progressivism; he gathered the middle-class Dixiecrats of 1948 under the same tent with other middle-class conservatives who had gone Republican in the prior election. From Charlotte to Richmond, Eisenhower amassed huge majorities in white middle-class urban and suburban areas. He scored particularly heavy gains in the urbanized sections of Piedmont Virginia and North Carolina (Gastonia, Charlotte, Kannapolis, Winston-Salem, Greensboro, High Point, Danville, Lynchburg, Petersburg and Richmond). Washington, D.C.'s fast-growing Virginia suburbs also went solidly for the GOP nominee. In Tennessee, Eisenhower scored huge gains in the Dixiecrat precincts of white middle-class Memphis and Nashville.

Most of the Virginia, North Carolina and Tennessee cities gave Eisenhower a better vote in 1956 than in 1952, and this was particularly true in Piedmont North Carolina. In all three states, mountaineer votes were the foundations of Republican statewide strength, but large urban majorities—Eisenhower got them—were necessary before the GOP could overcome the tide of Democratic ballots in the lowlands. Chart 75 shows the Eisenhower vote in the cities of the Outer South and Chart 59 points out how the 1948-52 Republican presidential increase in urban areas provided (and often exceeded) the margins of Eisenhower victory in the Outer South.

In 1960, Richard Nixon proved that Eisenhower's welding of the 1948 Republican and Dixiecrat votes was not a transient or personal

---

others. These same sections gave Eisenhower lopsided majorities in 1952, and the GOP nominee's strength often correlated with the combined Republican-Dixiecrat levels of 1948. One point must be underscored just as Lubell underscored it. These areas are *not* in any way poor, uneducated or uncultured, as detractors are often wont to say about locales of Dixiecrat support. On the contrary, the above-mentioned neighborhoods are among the richest and best educated in the South—and in the nation.

*In 1952, Eisenhower's greatest Virginia gains over previous GOP presidential candidates came in Southside Virginia, the principal rural seat of 1948 Dixiecrat strength. Similarly, the sharpest Eisenhower gains in North Carolina came in the Piedmont area between Charlotte and Greensboro, as well as in the Wilmington area; these sections (not the Black Belts) were the center of 1948 Thurmond support in North Carolina.

phenomenon. Nixon held most of Eisenhower's urban backing in Virginia, North Carolina and Tennessee. Only among the fairly numerous Negroes who had supported the popular GOP president did Nixon lose many Eisenhower backers. Chart 78 lists the 1956-64 GOP shares of the Negro vote in some major North Carolina, Virginia and Tennessee cities.

CHART 78

Southern Urban Negro Vote, 1956-64

City	GOP Share of Two-Party Presidential Vote		
	1956	1960	1964
Richmond, Va.	70.4%	36.9%	0.7%
Charlotte, N.C.	38.7	12.1	0.5
Memphis, Tenn.	53.8	30.6	2.2

[Selected Negro Precincts; from Republican National Committee 1964 Election Analysis.]

With the candidacy of Barry Goldwater in 1964, the Republican Party lost the rest of its considerable Eisenhower-era Negro support in the Piedmont. As for white voters, their reaction varied from a considerable anti-Goldwater trend in areas of longstanding GOP strength—western Piedmont North Carolina, Virginia's rich Shenandoah Valley and the District of Columbia's Washington suburbs— to actual Goldwater gains in the fast-growing Richmond suburbs and Southside Virginia cities such as Danville. It makes little sense to talk about an urban, suburban or even Piedmont trend. The anti-Goldwater trends in operation were those of Negroes, independents and (usually mountaineer or transplanted Northern) traditional Republican voters. Most of those switching to Goldwater were conservative Southern Democrats. Because these behavioral streams mixed in the Piedmont, so did the Republican-Democratic ups and downs of 1964. All in all, however, the Goldwater candidacy seems to have provoked more losses than gains in Piedmont North Carolina and Virginia.

Following the Goldwater defeat, the GOP abandoned its short-lived Black Belt orientation. Mountain, urban and suburban Republicans returned to their prior partisanship, although Negroes remained away. Republican candidates scored well in 1966 local and congressional races, showing muscle which augured well for 1968 GOP presidential prospects.

As Nixon strategists had hoped, Piedmont white opposition to the Great Society and the national Democratic Party played a major part in pushing Virginia and North Carolina into the GOP column in 1968. Solid Negro support enabled Hubert Humphrey to eke out a slim plurality of the ballots in Richmond, Virginia, but Nixon thrashed the Democratic nominee by a five-to-one ratio in the city's suburbs (larger than Richmond itself). Mecklenburg County, North Carolina (Charlotte) gave Nixon a nearly two-to-one lead over Humphrey, as did Lynchburg, Virginia. Forsyth (Winston-Salem) and Guilford (Greensboro-High Point) counties, North Carolina, as well as Danville, Virginia, produced three-to-two Nixon edges. The conservative Shenandoah Valley backed Nixon three-to-one. Wallace, of course, ran a strong race up and down the Piedmont. Chart 75 lists the 1968 Nixon and Wallace percentages in the major Virginia, North Carolina and Tennessee urban areas. There was not much left for Hubert Humphrey, and the great bulk of his votes appear to have come from Negroes. Only in the Virginia suburbs of Washington, D.C.—Humphrey garnered about 39 per cent of the vote in the pro-Nixon counties of Arlington and Fairfax —did the Democratic nominee win so much as one third of the white vote.

Chart 75 illustrates how George Wallace's Piedmont totals were well ahead of those scored twenty years earlier by Dixiecrat Strom Thurmond. Perhaps more to the point, Wallace tore lose a different brand of Democratic voter than had swung to the Dixiecrats in 1948. Whereas Thurmond had made his best showings in the upper-middle-class sections of greater Richmond, Charlotte and Greensboro, Wallace scored highest in lower-middle-class and blue-collar areas. As the chart shows, Nixon's 1968 percentages substantially exceeded 1948 GOP presidential support in strong Dixiecrat areas like Memphis and Charlotte. A large number of middle-class Dixiecrats had become firm enough Republicans to stick by Nixon against Wallace; the Alabama candidate made his most successful run among less affluent white Democrats who had backed Truman in 1948 and other party presidential candidates thereafter, until they were soured by the national Democratic Party's increasing identification with the Northeast and the Negro revolution.

As a result of the combined inroads of Richard Nixon and George Wallace, the white electorate of urban Virginia, North Carolina and Tennessee—representatives of the booming and "progressive" South —abandoned Hubert Humphrey in droves. Perhaps the most telling correlation of all was that between heavy urban-suburban growth and the decline of support for the national Democratic Party. The following chart capsules the political impact of the population explosion in Virginia's fastest-growing counties, all suburbs of Washington or Richmond.

CHART 79

Trends in Suburban Virginia (Chesterfield, Henrico, Arlington and Fairfax Counties)

	1924	1936	1948	1960	1968
Total Votes Cast for President (thousands)	8	20	39	146	271
Four-County Share of Total Virginia Vote	4%	6%	9%	19%	21%
Democratic Share of the Total Vote for President	70%	68%	43%	44%	31%

Middle-class white urbanization and suburbanization augur well for the GOP in Piedmont North Carolina and Virginia. As a result of commercial and industrial prosperity, the area is gaining white middle-class conservatives. Negroes constitute a slowly declining share of the local population. Republican prospects are also heightened by the likelihood that much of the 1968 Wallace electorate, alienated by the course of the national Democratic Party, will turn Republican in the same way that many 1948 Dixiecrats took up GOP voting habits in 1952 and thereafter.

Despite a few large Negro concentrations—the city of Richmond in particular—the Virginia and North Carolina Piedmonts are heavily white. Negroes cast perhaps 10 per cent to 15 per cent of the total vote. Together with the Republican highlands, the Piedmont ought to become a reliable component of GOP presidential victory in both of these important Outer South states.

3. The Black Belts

All of the states of the Outer South have substantial lowland areas with Democratic tradition in the Deep Southern mold and—typically—substantial Negro populations. In Virginia, the area in question is Southside Virginia, a heavily Negro bloc of agricultural counties reaching from Norfolk to Danville and Lynchburg. North Carolina's traditionally Democratic stronghold is the state's eastern third—the Tidewater and Coastal Plain. As for Florida, the northern part of the state from Jacksonville down to Gainesville and along the Gulf Coast to Pensacola is the region of longtime Democratic strength. Post-Civil War antagonism to the party of Lincoln produced its best Tennessee Democratic ratios in Memphis and the cotton counties along the Mississippi. And in Arkansas, the Southern party's staunchest support came in the Black Belt cotton counties across the Mississippi River from Memphis and the State of Mississippi's rich Delta section. That part of Texas reaching from the pineywoods of the Louisiana border west almost to Austin encompasses most of the state's Negroes together with the greater part of Texas' most loyally (Southern) Democratic counties. Topographically, these districts range from Black Belts to pineywoods; however, they are similar in having evidenced Democratic loyalties even in the face of strong GOP presidential candidacies like those of Herbert Hoover (1928), Dwight Eisenhower (1952 and 1956) and Richard Nixon (1960). During the century between the beginning of the Civil War and the election of John F. Kennedy as President, these were the Democratic bastions of the Outer South; and theirs were the votes that blocked—or refused to enlarge—Republican victories from Virginia to Texas.

None of the true Black Belts participated in the first Southern breakaway from the Democratic Party—the 1928 bolt prompted by religious objections to Al Smith. Such major GOP gains as occurred took place on the peripheries of the Black Belts; the Democrats suffered sharp 1924-28 declines in overwhelmingly white Outer Banks North Carolina and Florida's Gulf Coast pineywoods, but the white voters of the principal Black Belt counties remained quite loyal to their party.

Twenty years later, after remaining solidly Democratic through the Depression, most of these Black Belts preferred to support Truman rather than chase after the third-party will-o'-the-wisp with the Dixiecrats. There were several reasons for this. First of all,

Negroes were not so numerous on a *statewide* basis as in the Deep South, and Outer Southerners—even Black Belt whites—were less enmeshed in the politics of Negrophobia. Secondly, party loyalties in the Outer South Black Belts were more battle-ingrained by partisan conflict with a very real set of mountain or transplanted Northern Republicans. Lastly, Black Belt politics in a few Outer Southern sections—Tidewater Virginia and Black Belt North Carolina, for example—were actually more *liberal* (in economic policy) than Piedmont-based Democratic Party positions. Thus, the Dixiecrats did not fare particularly well in Black Belt North Carolina, Tidewater Virginia, most of northern Florida and eastern Texas, and much of West Tennessee and eastern Arkansas. Only in the Memphis area, "Porkchop" Florida (between Jacksonville and Gainesville) and Southside Virginia did Thurmond run strongly, and even this support was far below what he garnered in the heart of the Deep South.

Between 1952 and 1960, the Black Belts of the Outer South were always the *worst* Republican sections of their states while the Black Belt cores of the Deep South were often the best.* The Outer South Black Belt exceptions were generally those few areas—Porkchop Florida, Memphis and environs (including Fayette County), and parts of Southside Virginia (especially Prince Edward County)—where there had been civil rights turmoil and/or Thurmond had done unusually well in 1948. By and large, however, the Black Belts had shown little interest in Thurmond and they went on to show little interest in Eisenhower and Nixon.

In 1964, Republican strategists expected the Goldwater candidacy to bring the Outer South Black Belts into the GOP fold, but these hopes were not really fulfilled. Although he ran ahead of Nixon almost everywhere, Goldwater still lost by substantial margins in the Black Belts of Texas, North Carolina and Arkansas. He did better in the Black Belts of Tennessee (Memphis area), Florida and Virginia. One of Goldwater's difficulties lay in the fact that substantial numbers of Negroes were registered to vote in many Outer South Black Belt counties—a corollary of the more relaxed attitudes than prevailed in the Deep South Black Belts—and very few of them backed the Arizona Senator. Chart 64 illustrates Gold-

---

*Only in Texas, where Mexican counties were at the top of the Democratic list, was the Black Belt area not the most Democratic section of the state (at least in general).

water's minimal gains—sometimes they were actual losses in comparison with Eisenhower—in the Outer South Black Belts. While the Goldwater candidacy did help to erode Democratic traditions in these areas, its impact was not in itself too great. Far more important was the change overtaking the Democratic Party.

Unlike the Deep South Black Belts, where Goldwater had scored heavily in 1964 and conservative Democrats then recouped in 1966, the Black Belts of the Outer South followed their Democratic loyalties of 1964 with a pro-Republican 1966 trend. In Texas, most of the Black Belt supported Republican United States Senator John Tower in his re-election bid. The Tidewater and Black Belt of North Carolina gave unprecedented backing to the Republican opponent of Senator Sam Ervin. Arkansas' Black Belt played a major part in the election of Winthrop Rockefeller as the state's first Republican governor since Reconstruction, although many of the votes Rockefeller won came from Negroes. In Florida, the Black Belt and Gulf Coast switched to the GOP and elected Claude Kirk as the first Republican governor in a century. The Black Belts of West Tennessee helped elect the state's first Republican Senator since Reconstruction, Howard Baker. Some of Southside Virginia's trend went to the GOP; some of it occurred in the form of support for the local right-wing Conservative Party. All of these Republican or conservative gains took place despite increasing Negro registration and—typically Democratic—voting.

Although the 1966 elections offered extensive proof that Democratic loyalties were steadily weakening in the Outer South Black Belts, the anti-Democratic trend did not, as it happened, foreshadow large Republican gains in the 1968 presidential election. Throughout most of the Outer South Black Belts, the Democratic share of the vote plummeted between 1964 and 1968—see Chart 64—but the Republican vote share also dipped. The major gainer was third-party candidate George C. Wallace. In all of the six states of the Outer South, Wallace carried a majority of Black Belt counties and invariably scored his highest statewide percentages in such bailiwicks. Simultaneously, these counties were also Hubert Humphrey's best because of the influence of Negro voting behavior. Humphrey appears to have won almost all the Negro votes and very few of the white votes. Beyond the Black Belts, the white Outer South—mountains, plains, Piedmont, suburbs and cities—generally backed Richard Nixon, and as a result of George Wallace's decimation of onetime Democratic Black Belt majorities, the GOP candidate won most of the Outer South states. Nixon's profits came indirectly rather than directly. He himself did not win much by way of support in the Outer South Black Belts except in the strong Dixiecrat areas —"Porkchop" Florida, greater Memphis and Southside Virginia —where post-1948 Republican voting had become somewhat ingrained.

George Wallace's impact in the Black Belt Outer South was without third-party precedent. He tore up traditional Democratic loyalties everywhere, carrying counties where Dixiecrat Strom Thurmond had won only 5 per cent to 10 per cent support. Some evidence indicated that 1968 Wallace support, like 1948 Thurmond voting in the Deep South, represented transitional behavior on the part of Democratic traditionalists turning Republican. In confirmation of the trend of 1966, several two-party contests—the North Carolina gubernatorial race and the United States Senate contest in Florida—saw the traditionally Democratic Wallace electorate break sharply to GOP candidates. Florida, where the Wallace vote broke almost entirely to conservative Republican Senate victor Ed Gurney, is the clearest example. Holmes County, a cracker bastion in northern Florida, was Wallace's best county in the state—the Alabaman captured 88 per cent of the total vote. Gurney also amassed his best statewide percentage—78 per cent—in Holmes.

In North Carolina, Tennessee and Virginia, the collapse of Democratic tradition among lowland whites has created a situation whereby mountain, Piedmont, suburban and urban Republicanism must be heavily favored against national Democratic presidential candidacies. The same should hold true in Arkansas. Republican success also seems indicated in Texas and Florida, although in these two states, the mainsprings of Republican strength lie in fast-growing white middle-class urban and suburban boom areas. The breakdown of Democratic majorities among East Texas and northern Florida white voters ought to bring about the statewide dominion of the new middle-class GOP strongholds. However, the outcome is least certain in Texas, where combined Mexican-Negro strength has a potency lacking elsewhere in the Outer South.

4. The New Urban Florida and Texas

Except for a few mountain cities, most Southern urban centers were overwhelmingly Democratic in the years between the close of

Reconstruction and the First World War. The cities of the South generally pursued much the same politics as their rural environs. Knoxville and other mountain cities were Republican; Black Belt centers from Vicksburg to Charleston were Democratic by ten-to-one majorities.

Some of the cities best known today were largely scrub, swamp or rangeland in 1914. Especially in Florida and Texas, most cities were nothing more than a bare shadow of their contemporary selves. During the subsequent half-century, however, urban growth worked extraordinary plastic surgery on the face of Texas and Florida, re-shaping the politics of both states in the process. Chart 80 illustrates the scope of urban population growth in Texas and Florida.

The great urban boom really began during the Nineteen-Twenties. Beckoned by a swelling real estate bubble in Florida and oil, ranch and agricultural development in Texas, Northerners joined local countryfolk in moving to cities like Miami, Dallas and Houston. These new urban voters did not align themselves with the traditional South. After all, their very locale and orientation defied Southern tradition. Nor were these cities much concerned with the Democratic Party in its role as the one-party mechanism of white supremacy. Unlike the situation which prevailed in the Black Belts, there were few Negroes and they posed no local threat to white political dominance. Besides, some of the new Texas and Florida urbanites were transplanted Northern Republicans, while quite a few of those who were not viewed the Republican Party of the Nineteen-Twenties as the party of business, commerce and un-precedented prosperity. As the urban areas of the two states grew, they also moved towards the GOP, laying part of the foundation for Hoover's 1928 upset victories over Al Smith. Large Republican majorities in counties like Dade (Miami), Dallas (Dallas), Harris (Houston) and Pinellas (St. Petersburg) played an important role in the Republican victory.

The Depression cut short the growing GOP urban threat in the New South. Dallas and Dade counties, for example, voted only 19 per cent and 34 per cent Republican in 1932. Florida and Texas did not vote for a Republican President again until 1952. In the meantime, however, the New Deal Democratic Party slowly but surely alienated the urban middle classes of the New South. The noted political analyst Samuel Lubell has charted the 1936-52 Republican trend of Houston, Texas by economic levels. As Chart

CHART 80

Urban Population Growth in Texas and Florida (1900-60)

City	1900	1910	1920	1930	1950	1960
Florida						
Miami	1,681	5,471	29,571	110,637	249,276	291,688
St. Petersburg	1,575	4,127	14,237	40,425	96,738	181,298
Orlando	2,481	3,894	9,282	27,330	52,367	88,135
W. Palm Beach	564	1,743	8,659	26,610	43,162	56,208
Miami Beach	—	—	—	6,494	46,282	63,145
Fort Lauderdale	—	—	—	8,666	36,328	83,648
Texas						
Dallas	42,638	92,104	158,976	260,475	434,462	679,684
Fort Worth	26,688	73,312	106,482	163,447	278,778	356,258
Houston	44,633	78,800	138,276	292,352	596,163	938,219
Amarillo	1,442	9,957	15,494	43,132	74,246	137,969
Odessa-Midland	—	—	—	8,000	51,208	142,963

CHART 81

Diminishing Democratic Strength in Houston, Texas by Economic Level, 1936-52

Democratic Presidential Vote Share

Average Precinct Home Valuation	1936	1940	1944	1948	1952
Over $30,000	57%	29%	18%	7%	6%
$19-$30,000	71	47	35	29	13
$15-$19,000	81	58	50	25	22
$13-$15,000	79	60	52	23	22
$10-$13,000	86	74	64	33	26
$ 9-$10,000	90	80	68	40	33
$ 8-$ 9,000	93	85	79	61	50
$ 7-$ 8,000	93	88	78	57	49
$ 5-$ 7,000	94	89	84	66	60
Under $5,000	91	89	87	72	60

From: Samuel Lubell, *The Revolt of the Moderates* (New York, 1956), p. 186.

81 shows, the Democrats won at every economic level in 1936, but thereafter the erosion was steady.

In the years during and after World War II, the Texas and Florida booms which had been curtailed by the Depression regained momentum. All over central and southern Florida, new resort and retirement cities and towns sprung up, settled by Northern middle-class pensioners and expatriates. Millions of acres of Everglades, orange groves and coastal flats yielded to the bulldozer. Texas' boom was technological: aerospace, chemicals, electronics, oil and natural gas. "So big" was Texas, particularly in Texan eyes, that it propagandized an oversized image and demonstrated a conspicuous consumption that sometimes made the phrase *nouveau riche* seem inadequate.

The new urban complexes of Texas and Florida, like those of Southern California, bespoke a new urban America. Devoid of Northeastern-type heavy industry, aggressively middle-class rather than stratified along European and Northeastern lines, the new cities of the Sun Belt mushroomed as their Megalopolitan forebears began to stagnate and decay. From the retirement capital of St. Petersburg to the air-conditioned affluence of Dallas, Southern urban populations soared.

Eisenhower's 1952 victories in Texas and Florida were predicated on this urbanization. Chart 59 illustrates how the great Eisenhower groundswell in the metropolitan areas of Florida and Texas produced the necessary statewide GOP majorities in 1952. To some extent, the popular General fused the 1948 Republican and Dixie-crat votes, although he also garnered much new support. Without his large urban majorities, Eisenhower could not have carried Texas or Florida in either 1952 or 1956. Many rural sections of both states, particularly the "cracker" north of Florida, remained strongly Democratic during the Nineteen-Fifties, resting GOP hopes on the cities and suburbs. In 1956, President Eisenhower amassed urban and suburban majorities in Texas and Florida which the GOP has not since been able to equal.

Seeking the presidency for the first time in 1960, Richard Nixon slipped considerably from Eisenhower's high 1956 levels, but he still did well enough in the cities to carry Florida and lose Texas by only fifty thousand votes out of two million. Chart 75 shows Nixon's levels in the major urban boom counties. Urban and suburban support was still the underpinning of Republican victory opportunity, and this could not be expected to change until rural Democratic traditions gave way.

Barry Goldwater sought to erode this rural Democratic strength in 1964, but he met with very little success outside of the Deep South. Moreover, his economic conservatism and Cotton states orientation proved unpopular enough in urban Florida and Texas to deprive him of support prior GOP candidates had needed for statewide victory. From El Paso to Key West, Goldwater's urban backing dropped far below the (essential) levels won by Nixon in 1960. Among the populous counties where Goldwater slipped most emphatically were Dallas, Tarrant (Fort Worth) and Pinellas (St. Petersburg), where the 1964 GOP presidential vote lagged 17 to 19 percentage points behind Nixon's (see Chart 75). The Arizona Senator's only gains over Nixon came in cities like Pensacola, Jacksonville and Tallahassee in northern Florida.

Goldwater did poorly among some of Florida's transplanted Northerners. In Pinellas County, which has one of the nation's highest ratios of retired persons, the 1960-64 GOP slump was readily traceable to local fears regarding Goldwater's alleged opposition to Social Security. The trends of Dallas, Fort Worth and St. Petersburg were the extremes of disaffection, but they suggest the scope of Goldwater's failure. Many middle-class and normally Republican voters in urban Texas and Florida joined Negroes, Jews and Latins in moving away from the GOP in 1964. Like other voting streams of the Outer South, Texas and Florida urbanites shied away from a candidacy seemingly rooted in the Black Belts of Alabama and Mississippi.

Between 1964 and 1966, however, the GOP made an extraordinary comeback. With evolutionary success in the Outer South once more the principal party strategy, the urban and suburban middle classes of Florida and Texas came back to the Republicans. Becoming the first Republican elected to a full term in the United States Senate from Texas since Reconstruction, John Tower swept the Houston, Dallas and Fort Worth metropolitan areas in 1966. Meanwhile, the Houston suburbs elected their first GOP congressman. In Florida, investment banker Claude Kirk won election as Florida's first Republican governor since Reconstruction, garnering large majorities in St. Petersburg, Orlando, Jacksonville, Fort Lauderdale, Palm Beach and all other urban areas except the minority group and labor centers of Miami and Tampa. Fort Lauderdale, like suburban Houston, chose its first Republican congressman. (Together with Cape Kennedy, where a Republican congressman was unopposed for re-election, suburban Houston and Broward County [Fort Lauderdale] are among the fastest growing sections of the two states.) GOP leaders saw the 1966 returns as proof that a Republican presidential candidate could regain or exceed 1960 levels in urban Texas and Florida.

Sure enough, when 1968 came, Richard Nixon amassed considerable leads over Democrat Hubert Humphrey in most of the major urban areas of Florida and Texas. However, the third-party strength put together by George Wallace kept Nixon from equaling his 1960 percentages of the total vote; and in Texas, Wallace diverted enough Nixon urban support potential to enable Hubert Humphrey to carry the state. Chart 75 shows the Wallace and Nixon percentages in urban Texas. Together, the two conservatives beat Humphrey badly, but such a large percentage of Wallace's vote came from a hitherto Republican electorate—people whose votes had been cast for Nixon in his close race of 1960—that the 1968 GOP nominee was unable to amass the white middle-class majorities needed for victory.*

Comparisons of the 1968 votes with those of 1960, when Kennedy narrowly edged Nixon in Texas, show that Wallace reduced the Republican percentages more than the Democratic vote shares in the major urban areas. In Dallas, the Republican percentage was cut eleven percentage points (62 per cent to 51 per cent) while the Democrats lost only four percentage points (38 per cent to 34 per cent) in the creation of Wallace's local 15 per cent showing. Harris County (Houston) gave Wallace 18 per cent of the total vote—12 per cent from 1960 Nixon strength, only 6 per cent from voters who had backed Kennedy in 1960. And in the booming cities of Odessa-Midland—Texas' fastest-growing urbanized area—Wallace ran second to Nixon, diverting right-wing votes from the GOP candidate. Many, but by no means all, of the Wallace voters were blue-collar and lower-middle-class whites. Granted that many of the votes lost were normally Republican, Nixon was able to stave off more severe injury by keeping the Wallace vote low in the upper-middle-class suburbs where the Dixiecrats had once run well (Highland Park in Dallas, for example).

Above and beyond the problem of Wallace inroads—the white Southern middle-class impetus is to the Right, not Left—Nixon's only poor urban Texas showings came in Mexican and Negro areas. These trends were responsible for the poor GOP presidential vote in San Antonio, El Paso and lesser cities in south Texas. On the other side of the railroad tracks, Nixon-Humphrey ratios reached four-, six- and eight-to-one in the white middle-class suburbs of Houston and Dallas. And because such strongholds of the prosperity explosion are assuming an increasingly dominant position in the greater metropolitan areas of Houston, Dallas, Fort Worth and the Plains cities, Nixon did well. Given the increasing share of the Texas vote cast by greater Dallas and Houston as shown in Chart 82, together with the escalating importance of Plains cities like

*Of course, even the Wallace-trimmed leads Nixon took out of Harris, Dallas and Tarrant counties would have suffered for statewide victory had Texas not been politically atypical in several respects. For one thing, no other Outer Southern state had so large a Latin-Negro electorate, and also the efforts of President Johnson and Governor Connally helped keep almost one third of the state's white voters on Humphrey's side. Elsewhere in the Outer South, none of these factors made Wallace's inroads into 1960 Nixon strength in middle-class urban areas so crucial.

CHART 82

Share of the Total Texas Presidential Vote Cast by Dallas and Harris (Houston) Counties

1924	1936	1948	1960	1968
9%	14%	17%	24%	27%

Amarillo, Odessa-Midland, Lubbock and Abilene, to say nothing of the bulk of the Wallace vote that will accrue to future Republican presidential nominees, urban and suburban Republicanism is likely to become the prevailing quadrennial force in Texas politics.

In Florida, the GOP urban-suburban victory was more decisive, and Humphrey was not buoyed by so large a Latin-Negro vote or by any persisting Democratic loyalties among rural whites. Richard Nixon swept Florida, despite his loss of Dade County (Miami), because of his huge pluralities over Hubert Humphrey in the fast-growing suburbanized counties of Brevard, Broward, Orange and Palm Beach (Cocoa Beach, Cape Kennedy, Fort Lauderdale, Orlando and Palm Beach). These counties, Sun Belt strongholds of the new, conservative white middle class, are rapidly seizing control of Florida politics from the hands of both rural northern Florida and the older, more stable city of Miami.* The four counties gave Humphrey only 27 per cent of the vote to Nixon's 52 per cent and Wallace's 21 per cent. Brevard County, seat of the new space-age technocracy clustered around Cape Kennedy, preferred even Wallace to Humphrey. Chart 83 shows how this four-county area is wresting power away from the Miami district.

The new middle-class reaches of Florida are shaping up as the pivot of a conservative Republican domination of the state. In 1968, as in 1966, these counties provided the major impetus for statewide Republican victory. Not only did Nixon carry the state handily, but Congressman Ed Gurney of Orlando-Cape Kennedy won election to the United States Senate. Miami's Democratic majorities—in Humphrey's case it was only a plurality—have been increasingly lost in

---

*Coastal central Florida is not the only part of the state growing at a rapid rate. The northern Florida urban areas of Jacksonville and Pensacola are expanding apace even if the local countryside is not.

CHART 83

The Changing Balance of Power in Urban Florida

	Percentage of the Florida Presidential Vote Cast		
County	1952	1960	1968
Broward, Brevard, Orange and Palm Beach	13%	19%	22%
Dade	22%	21%	16%

the swirl of white middle-class ballots from the new boom counties. Furthermore, the growing predisposition of white rural Florida towards the GOP all but assures party hegemony on the presidential level.

The suburban-urban trends of Florida and Texas are among the best proof in the nation that the overall demographic thrust of the youthful middle class is conservative rather than liberal in political implication. In both of these states, the new white residential stretches are growing with a speed unmatched east of Southern California and Arizona. By comparison, Northeastern suburbia, especially the limited silk-stocking sections of it, is experiencing much less growth. The Sun Belt urban and suburban sections of Texas and Florida are not simply gaining power within the statewide structure of their states; they are also attracting a large and continuing inflow of people, which should steadily increase the *national* influence of the Sun Belt at the expense of the decaying central cities—and their states—of the Northeast.

5. The Southern Plains

Encompassing more than one hundred thousand square miles of wasteland, ranches, wheat and oil lands, yet spanning only a few congressional districts, the West Texas and Oklahoma plains are among the most conservative sections of the nation. Solidly Anglo-Saxon and Protestant (often Baptist), this area was the setting of a considerable amount of the Western history which Hollywood has brought to the screen: Abilene of cattle-drive fame, oil-rich Tulsa, the Canadian, Cimarron and Red River Valleys, Adobe Walls, Palo

Duro and the *Llano Estacado* across which many a cavalry troop chased Comanche raiding parties. The same plains and people reach into New Mexico, causing the eastern part of that state to be known as "Little Texas." Map 21 sketches the plains.

Until the Nineteen-Twenties, the plains area was rural, sparsely populated and traditionally Democratic in politics. The principal exceptions were the Panhandle sections adjoining Republican areas of nearby Kansas and Colorado; the cities of Tulsa and Oklahoma City; and the German-settled area around San Antonio. Although Harding narrowly carried Oklahoma in 1920—the first time that the state had voted Republican since entering the Union in 1907— the principal Republican breakthrough in the Southern plains came in 1928, when Baptist Bible Belt sentiment flared against the Demo- cratic presidential candidacy of Tammany Catholic Al Smith. Not a few plains counties gave Hoover vote shares forty to fifty percent- age points higher than Coolidge had won in 1924, so strong was the feeling involved.

Before long, the Nineteen-Thirties saw much of the Bible Belt turn into a dustbowl and the local electorate flock back to the Democratic standard. Franklin D. Roosevelt won better than 90 per cent of the vote in some counties where Hoover had won heavy majorities in 1928. Generally speaking, Roosevelt maintained a high level of support in the plains although he lost some strength in 1944 to a conservative third-party effort called the "Texas Regulars." The Democratic position weakened further in 1948, and then in 1952 General Eisenhower won many plains counties for the GOP, also amassing sizeable majorities in the urbanized areas of Lubbock, Amarillo, Oklahoma City and Tulsa. With the help of these votes, Eisenhower captured Texas and Oklahoma.

Because of the farm discontent which eroded GOP strength everywhere on the plains in 1956, Eisenhower had less support than in 1952, but he still carried Oklahoma and Texas. Republican strength grew again in 1960, when the Bible Belt once again in- dulged itself in anti-Catholicism, this time at the expense of John F. Kennedy. In the Baptist strongholds of southern Oklahoma, Nixon ran well ahead of Eisenhower, demonstrating an appeal which can only be attributed to religious voting.

Quite apart from the religious voting of 1960, the Southern Plains were shedding the traditions that had underpinned many decades of Democratic preference. In 1964, conservative Republican presi-

CHART 84

Presidential Voting in the Southern Plains, 1960-68

		Share of the Total Vote for President			
State County (City)	Nixon 1960	Goldwater 1964	Nixon 1968	Wallace 1968	Humphrey 1968
Oklahoma					
Garfield (Enid)	69%	55%	62%	13%	25%
Tulsa (Tulsa)	63	56	57	20	23
Oklahoma (Oklahoma City)	61	48	50	18	32
Texas					
Potter (Amarillo)	61	47	49	20	31
Lubbock (Lubbock)	56	44	51	18	31
Ector (Odessa)	54	51	43	36	21
Midland (Midland)	64	58	55	24	21

dential nominee Barry Goldwater ran a comparatively strong race in the plains—his percentages were far above pre-Eisenhower levels— even while he was being badly beaten nationally. Chart 82 shows the behavior of the major plains counties in the 1960-68 presidential races.

Because of the rapid growth of agricultural, oil and commercial centers like Tulsa, Oklahoma City, Amarillo, Lubbock, Odessa and Midland, the political power of the Southern plains is on the rise. Chart 135 shows how these and other Sun Belt cities are among the fastest-growing in the nation. Nor is it coincidence that conservatism is strongest in many of the most booming areas. The drift of middle-class Americans to the South and West is also one of the nation's major political trends. Thirty years ago, the rich oil towns of Odessa and Midland barely existed, but since then, rapid urbanization has created a fiercely conservative two-county metropolitan area of nearly two hundred thousand people.*

Between 1964 and 1968, the conservative trend on the plains moved into high gear. Texas GOP Senator John Tower swept the area in his successful 1966 re-election bid, and two new Republican congressmen were elected in western Oklahoma and the Texas Panhandle. The 1968 presidential election kept the trend in motion. Chart 84 shows Hubert Humphrey winning only 20 per cent to 30 per cent of the total vote in the major Texas and Oklahoma plains cities; the rest of the electorate split between Richard Nixon and George Wallace. Rural returns varied more in the light of traditional loyalties. Only a few counties actually gave George Wallace a plurality of their vote—several in the neighborhood of Odessa-Midland. However, the Alabaman topped 25 per cent of the balloting in a substantial minority of the plains counties. Heavy backing in Oklahoma City and Tulsa, as well as rural western Oklahoma, helped Nixon to an easy victory in that state, but Wallace diversion of potentially Republican plains support was an important cause of Nixon's narrow loss in Texas.

White, Protestant and conservative, the plains of West Texas and Oklahoma have very little in common with a liberal Democratic Party oriented towards Negroes, the Northeastern Megalopolis and the somewhat more proximate Rio Grande Valley Mexican Americans. Rural Democratic tradition survived 1968 Wallace and Nixon

*A description of the Midland phenomenon can be found in Bainbridge, *The Super-Americans* (New York, 1961), pp. 40-51.

erosion better in Texas than elsewhere in the South, largely because of the pro-Humphrey activity of the state Democratic Party. The Plains have already played a major part in pulling Oklahoma into the Republican orbit, and before long, they should play an integral role in mobilizing statewide GOP majorities in Texas.

6. The Latin Crescent

Apart from the growing Negro bloc, the principal source of Southern liberal strength is the Latin Crescent spectrum of ethnic minorities: the Mexicans of the Rio Grande Valley, El Paso, San Antonio (and pockets of other urban areas across Texas); the ethnically heterogeneous maritime and petroleum work force of the Texas and Louisiana Gulf coasts; the French Creoles and Cajuns of New Orleans and southern Louisiana; the Portuguese and Greek fishermen of the Gulf Coast; the Cuban cigar workers of Tampa; the Latin refugees and fortune-hunters of southern Florida; and the Northeastern-born Jewish population of Miami Beach and similar Gold Coast resort areas. Of course, not all of these minorities are Latin, but there are a sufficient ethnic representation and geographic appropriateness to justify the use of the term "Latin Crescent." As drawn in Map 28, the Latin Crescent encompasses most of liberal Texas and Florida and is a leavening without which the two states would be overwhelmingly Anglo-Saxon, Protestant, conservative and (increasingly) Republican.

Although liberals are not strong enough to dominate the politics of either Texas or Florida, Latin Crescent strength is growing. Before World War II, French Louisiana was the only non-Anglo section of any influence. Now Mexican Texas is beginning to come into its own. Not so long ago, however, Mexican votes were bought and sold in Texas like cattle futures. Flagrant sales were everyday occurrences. Perhaps the most interesting took place in 1948, when the state's Democratic United States Senate primary was decided by Mexican votes purchased in one patron-controlled county. For services rendered, George Parr, known as the Duke of Duval, delivered a 4,622 to 40 majority in Duval County to a candidate— "Landslide Lyndon" Johnson, he was nicknamed—who was thus able to carry the state by 87 votes. And in Florida, Latin and Jewish influence was minimal enough in 1948 to be ignored in V. O. Key's definitive book, *Southern Politics,* except for an observation that one statewide candidate of recent vintage had been counted out in the presumably purchasable Latin precincts of Tampa.

MAP 28

The South—The Latin Crescent

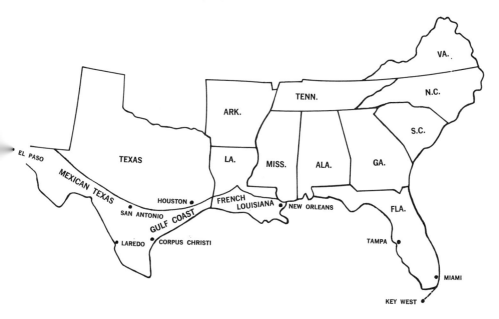

Along Texas' Rio Grande Valley, the Mexican vote began to metamorphose into something more than a salable commodity during the Nineteen-Fifties. Then in 1960, Mexican Americans, mobilized in "Viva Kennedy" clubs, contributed a large bloc of crucial ballots in support of fellow Catholic John Kennedy's successful attempt to win Texas' electoral votes. Subsequently, amidst the civil rights consciousness of the early Nineteen-Sixties, Mexican political awareness continued to mount. Here and there across the heavily Mexican reaches of south Texas, town and local governments came under *Latino* control, and in 1961, Texas' first Mexican American congressman—Henry Gonzalez—was elected after a bitterly fought special election in San Antonio.

As for Florida, the late Nineteen-Forties and early Nineteen-Fifties were boom years, and an increasing number of the migrants flocking into greater Miami were Jews from New York and other Northern cities. The glittering resort city of Miami Beach—the "strip" along which the Miami area's hotels are built—quickly became one of the most heavily Jewish cities in the United States. Revolutions up and down Latin America fed a steady stream of refugees into Miami, a migration which gathered numerical force after Fidel Castro came to power in Cuba in 1959. Tampa already had a sizeable Cuban population at work in the local cigar industry, and now many others, from rich pro-Batista landowners fleeing Castro to unemployed machete hands looking for a new opportunity, poured into the Miami area. While some of the Cuban refugees were right-wing conservatives, most blended socially and economically with the existing low- and low-middle-income Latin population of Miami. During the Nineteen-Fifties and early Nineteen-Sixties, these several demographic changes served to make Miami into an atypical—and atypically liberal—Southern city. Somewhat similar conditions prevailed in Tampa, a growing industrial city where Latin Americans were extremely numerous even though Miami's stalwart Jewish liberal bias was lacking.*

Most of the Mexicans, Cubans and Jews of the Latin Crescent were liberals and Democrats: even Eisenhower had done poorly among them. Miami's Jewish precincts, like those in New York City, gave the Republican President less support in 1956 than in 1952. And when GOP Vice President Nixon sought the presidency in 1960, his Latin and Jewish vote weakened still further. Not surprisingly, 1964 Republican presidential candidate Barry Goldwater fared even worse. Chart 85 shows the shrinkage of GOP presidential adherence in Latin districts.

In 1966, the Latin Crescent became a more obvious cleavage line in Texas and Florida politics. Supported by Latins, Negroes and the Miami-area Jewish community, Miami Mayor Robert King High beat a conservative Democrat in the party gubernatorial primary, and rural conservative Democrats joined Republicans to elect Claude Kirk the state's first Republican governor since Reconstruction. The GOP candidate triumphed everywhere except the Latin, Negro and Jewish precincts. Texas' Senator John Tower, seeking re-election to a full term in the Senate, lost only four congressional districts, among them Laredo and the Rio Grande Valley, the substantially Mexican city of San Antonio, and the Latin-Negro-labor eastern section of Houston. As the white Outer South turned conservative and Republican, the liberalism and Democratic fidelity of the Latin Crescent stood out more and more. In Florida,

---

*Tampa's Cuban population has a liberal past. In 1948, some Cuban blue-collar precincts of Ybor City were the only precincts below the Mason-Dixon line to vote for Progressive presidential candidate Henry Wallace.

the liberal group's ability to command statewide Democratic primaries furthered re-alignment, but the inability of Texas' Mexican-Negro-labor *alianza* to do likewise served as a retarding factor.

Only Negroes proved more Democratic in 1968 Dixie presidential voting than the Mexicans, Latins and Jews of Florida and Texas. Notwithstanding the impetus given to Mexican voting in Texas by the 1965 repeal of the poll tax, Latin balloting did not increase too sharply. It rose in the cities of southern Texas—Brownsville, Harlingen, Corpus Christi and Galveston—but showed no great increase in the overwhelmingly Mexican counties around Laredo. Chart 85 shows Nixon's share of the vote in Texas' five top Mexican American counties. These were Hubert Humphrey's best Texas counties. Allowing for the influence of white votes in largely Mexican counties or precincts, Texas' *Latino* vote—it numbers perhaps 400,000, or 12 per cent of the state electorate—appears to have gone about nine-to-one for Humphrey. Putting these ratios alongside the Democratic nominee's peak strength in Negro precincts and the maritime labor counties along the Gulf of Mexico, the Latin Crescent clearly has become the fulcrum of Texas liberalism and loyalty to the national Democratic Party.

CHART 85

Mexican American Presidential Voting in Texas, 1952-68

County	Republican Share of the Total Vote for President				
	1952	1956	1960	1964	1968
Duval	17%	32%	18%	7%	5%
Jim Hogg	23	31	15	10	14
Starr	17	17	7	14	25
Wells	31	32	15	10	17
Zapata	46	42	28	12	21

Latin and labor votes were powerful enough in Texas to help Humphrey fashion a slim plurality, but they were much less potent in Florida. Despite heavy Latin and Jewish support in Miami, the Democratic nominee could only garner 48 per cent of the total presidential vote in Dade County—and Dade was the only Florida county where he topped the 40 per cent level. Chart 83 shows how the state's growth is no longer centered in Latin-Jewish Miami;

boom times along the coast from Hollywood to Cape Kennedy are turning Florida into an increasingly Anglo-Saxon and middle-class state, diluting the general election influence of Negroes, Latins and Jews. Thus, the ability of the liberal coalition to win Democratic primaries has simply hastened the changeover from Democratic to Republican conservatism. The Latin Crescent is likely to play an increasingly dominant role in Texas and Florida Democratic politics. However, the liberal bloc faces dimmer prospects on the statewide general election level.

C. The Future of Southern Politics

Between the beginning of the New Deal era in 1932 and its end in 1968, the Democratic share of the presidential vote skidded from 90 per cent to 26 per cent in the Deep South and from 77 per cent to 32 per cent in the Outer South. Across the entire nation, only one other political change—the related Negro trend to the Democrats—matches this upheaval in intensity and meaning.

Whereas the 1948 Dixiecrat revolt—the first wave of Southern Democratic deterioration—left about half of the white Southern electorate in the Democratic presidential column, the 1968 Wallace candidacy broke loose all but 10 per cent to 15 per cent, including the upcountry and pineywoods poor whites who had hitherto spurned both Dixiecrats and Republicans. There is a strong precedent for this 1968 estrangement of previously loyal Democrats persisting beyond one election. Back in 1952, for example, a large fraction—perhaps as much as half—of the voters who had backed the Dixiecrats in 1948 cast their first Republican presidential votes for Dwight Eisenhower. From the best suburbs of Dallas to the darkest Black Belts of South Carolina, the Dixiecrat party served many conservatives as a way station between a no longer appealing Democratic Party and the increasingly Southern-concerned GOP. History will doubtless label George Wallace's party a similar way-station for another element of Southern voters. Most of the poor whites whom Wallace broke loose from the Democrats have lined up against newly enfranchised Negroes just as they did in the somewhat comparable Reconstruction Era of a century ago. Now that the *national* Democratic Party is becoming the Negro party throughout most of the South, the alienation of white Wallace voters is likely to persist.

Southern white disaffection from the Democrats has not yet generally translated itself into firm Republicanism. On the basis of the 1968 returns, only the Outer South is definitely moving into the GOP camp. Party strength in the Outer South rests principally on traditional mountain and Piedmont backing, rapid urban and suburban white middle-class growth, and related factors; dependence on the shift of lowland Southern traditionalists into the GOP is only partial. Moreover, this two-party context which exists in the Outer South is likely to impose itself on the Wallace rebels of 1968—to the benefit of the GOP. In the Deep South, however, the majority of the white electorate is suspicious of both major parties, and the Nixon Administration's undoubted enforcement of civil rights and voting rights laws may keep third-party flames flickering.

But third parties are not likely to persist long; they are inevitable casualties of re-alignment. In this particular situation, there are a number of factors which will push the Deep South in the Republican direction. In the first place, Negroes are slowly but surely taking over the apparatus of the Democratic Party in a growing number of Deep Southern Black Belt counties, and this cannot help but push whites into the alternative major party structure—that of the GOP.* Secondly, white psychological dispositions to fight a hopeless rearguard action are shrinking in the face of the inevitable. Thirdly, the national Democratic Party is becoming so alien to the white South as to underscore GOP preferability. Fourth, the opinion-molding upper-middle classes of the urban Deep South are already trending heavily Republican. Fifth, George Wallace's near miss notwithstanding, a new political cycle has begun which should render quite impracticable the Deep South strategy of seeking a balance of power in the Electoral College. Lastly, now that the GOP is mobilizing enough white support to gain the ascendancy in Tennessee, North Carolina and Florida, a social, cultural and political web has been spun around the Deep South. Patterns vary in individual elections, but on a cyclical basis, the party of white Tennessee is going to be the party of white Mississippi. The gathering Republicanism of the Outer South virtually dictates the coming alignment of the Deep South. For national political reasons, the Republican Party cannot go to the Deep South, but for all of the above-mentioned reasons, the Deep South must soon go to the national GOP.

Southern politics, like those of the rest of the nation, cleave along

---

*Maintenance of Negro voting rights is essential to the GOP. Unless Negroes continue to displace white Democratic organizations, the latter may remain viable as spokesmen for Deep Southern conservatism.

distinct ethnic (racial, in this case) lines. Whereas in New York City the Irish are lined up against the Jews, in the South it is principally a division between Negroes and whites. Chart 86 illustrates the Negro voting potential in the South as of 1965. Every year, Negroes constitute a smaller percentage of the population in most Southern states. This is not just because Negroes are being chased out of the South by the mechanization of agriculture or lured away by Northern welfare dollars. Even as Negroes are leaving Dixie, middle-class whites are flooding in, drawn by the climate, expanding commercial opportunities—and perhaps even by the sociopolitical climate. The boom times of Texas and Florida are common knowledge; the rapidly expanding prosperity and population of Richmond, Norfolk, Raleigh, Greensboro, Charlotte, Columbia, Greenville, Charleston, Savannah, Augusta, Atlanta, Huntsville, Birmingham, Mobile, Jackson, Biloxi, New Orleans, Shreveport and Lake Charles

CHART 86

Negro Voting Potential in the South

State	Voting Age White Population[1]	Voting Age Non-white Population	Non-white % of Total
Alabama	1,353,038	481,320	26%
Arkansas	850,643	192,626	18%
Florida	2,617,438	470,306	15%
Georgia	1,797,062	612,910	25%
Louisiana	1,289,216	514,589	29%
Mississippi	748,266	422,256	36%
North Carolina	2,005,955	550,929	22%
South Carolina	895,147	371,104	29%
Tennessee	1,779,018	313,873	15%
Texas	4,884,769	649,412[2]	12%
Virginia	1,812,154	421,051	19%

1. The figures listed here are from the 1960 census as cited in a "Registration and Voting Statistics" report of the U.S. Commission on Civil Rights Information Center dated March 19, 1965.
2. It should be noted that in Texas a large Mexican American community approximately equal in numbers to the non-white community constitutes half of the minorities coalition, which makes up about a quarter of the Texas electorate.

are much less known. Chart 135 shows how these cities are gaining population while the central cities of the Northeast are rapidly losing it. Moreover, the white middle-class influx is making the urban South generally less Negro while the urban North becomes more heavily Negro. For these reasons, Negroes are not likely to exercise a very great direct influence on Southern presidential voting. And where they are most numerous—Mississippi, for example—whites tend to be most firmly united against them. In the foreseeable future, Southern Negro elective success is likely to be confined to the county and state legislative level.

As a result of the influx of immigrants into the new urbanized sections of Dixie, the South's share of the national population is rising. The electoral votes being lost by the Northeast are going to the South as well as the West. Expanding on the pattern of Richard Nixon's 1968 victory, the South, Heartland and California together can constitute an effective *national* political majority.

IV. THE HEARTLAND

᪥᪥ ᪥᪥ ᪥᪥ ᪥᪥ ᪥᪥ ᪥᪥ ᪥᪥ ᪥᪥

MORE THAN A THIRD OF A CENTURY AGO, NEW DEAL LIBERAL-
ism rose to power with the coming of age of urban America and its
lately arrived immigrant millions. Now the era of the big city in
United States politics has come to an end. As 1968 election statistics
vividly document, old cities like New York, Philadelphia, Detroit
and San Francisco are casting steadily fewer votes, as theirs and
other urban populations drain into suburbia. Simultaneously, the
Negro socioeconomic revolution and the related bias of the Democratic Party have displaced the Civil War as the underlying divisors
of American politics. The geography of Richard Nixon's 1968
victory indicates that the great American Heartland—the insular
and interior core of the United States—has abandoned the Civil
War-ingrained loyalties that divided politics along an extension of
the Mason-Dixon line. Because tradition no longer keeps the Arkansas, Kentucky and New Mexico countryside Democratic while the
Dakota, Kansas and Michigan countryside is Republican, the vast
American interior is drawing together as the seat of a conservative
majority. For years, the Northeast has dominated national politics
as Heartland power split along Civil War lines, but now new sociological forces are dividing the Northeast and uniting the Heartland.

As a result of this trend, the Heartland—the land of Methodist
church suppers, mile-high mining camps, county fairs, steamboats

MAP 29

The Heartland

Regions of the Heartland by State
and Electoral Vote Strength

The Border		II. *Great Lakes*		III. *Farm Belt*		IV. *Rocky Mts.*	
West Virginia	7	Michigan	21	Wisconsin	12	Montana	4
Kentucky	9	Ohio	26	Minnesota	10	Wyoming	3
Tennessee	11	Indiana	13	N. Dakota	4	Idaho	4
Missouri	12	Illinois	26	S. Dakota	4	Colorado	6
Arkansas	6		86	Iowa	9	Nevada	3
Oklahoma	8			Nebraska	5	Utah	4
	53			Kansas	7	Arizona	5
					51	N. Mexico	4
							33

and Electoral Vote Total—223

round the bend, cattle drives, waving wheat, Park Forest, Middle-town, German biergartens, Polish polka parties and elm-lined Main Streets, U.S.A.—is shaping up as the mainstay of a new political era. To define the Heartland with more geographic than sociopolitical precision, it includes every state without a coastline or seaport, save Vermont, and reaches from the Appalachians to the Rocky Mountains. Together, these 25 states cast 223 of the 270 electoral votes needed to elect a President of the United States. In 1968, Nixon carried 21 of the 25 Heartland states. Kindred areas like the Outer South and Southern California (heavily settled from the Heartland) provided the additional margin of victory.

There can be little doubt of the effect that the Negro revolution has had on the Heartland. The old division—the alignment of the Southern-oriented Border and Southwest against the Northern-settled Great Lakes, Farm states and Northern Rockies—is no longer valid. The Heartland is no longer just a spacial concept; it is becoming an ideological entity. Within the House of Representatives, most votes on Great Society issues have straddled the old Civil War division, joining the South, the Farm Belt, the Rocky Mountains, the Border and the Great Lakes against the Pacific, the Middle Atlantic and New England. The old Blue-Gray "Border" is the border no longer. A new ideological fall-line is emerging in the Great Lakes and along the Pacific; its basis is sociology, not history.

During the Great Society days of the Johnson Administration, the forces shaping Heartland unity were fundamentally negative, but a framework of positivism can easily be sketched. Beyond opposition to urban welfarism, the Heartland has many attitudinal ties which command broad support. The insular states share a considerable interest in agriculture, country life and rural redevelopment; they have a bias towards self-help and the Protestant ethic; they have a sense of tradition, religion and history; increasingly they are turning away from indiscriminate internationalism and towards less United States involvement abroad; and they share a historical suspicion of the Megalopolitan Establishment and its policies towards the hinterland. Granted that these are generalizations, some of them unrealizable in the contemporary world; still any new Republican era rooted in the Heartland would reflect some of these predilections, likewise the party's relative orientation in these directions is strengthening Heartland Republicanism.

The Heartland is as heterogeneous as it is huge, and the best way to approach it is region by region. Unlike those of the Northeast, the principal Heartland voting streams can be fitted reasonably well into geographic compartments. The Heartland spans four regions. These regions, however, do not exactly mesh with state boundaries (see Map 29). The Great Lakes states—Michigan, Ohio, Indiana and Illinois—constitute one geopolitical orbit, yet three of the states are also profoundly influenced by Ohio Valley counties lying in the Border region. Probably the best way to structure the Heartland by region is in order of settlement, inasmuch as the historical geography of each region is a major factor in its contemporary political behavior.

The historic Border is just what its name indicates—an area sandwiched between Yankeedom and the Confederacy in the great Civil War which dictated rural political loyalties for the next century. By and large, the Border pivots on the Ohio Valley, the Central Mississippi Valley and the valleys of major tributaries like the Kanawha, Scioto, Wabash, Kentucky, Missouri, Tennessee and Arkansas. In Civil War days, the population was essentially Southern, and although most people opposed secession as a Cotton states parochialism, a majority also opposed the Republicans as a "Yankee" war party. For the next century, the Border—West Virginia, Kentucky, Missouri, Tennessee, Arkansas, Oklahoma, and the Ohio Valley sections of Ohio, Indiana and Illinois—was normally strongly Democratic. This loyalty persisted throughout the New Deal and even into the Great Society era, so that one hundred years after Appomattox, all of the rural lowland districts of the still-countrified Border were represented in Congress by Democrats unsympathetic to their party's social and economic legislation. Today, however, the Border is a border no longer. It is a region of fading tradition and political upheaval.

Just as the Border was settled by Southerners moving west, the Great Lakes region was populated by Yankees—New Englanders, New Yorkers and Pennsylvanians—doing likewise. Map 29 shows how a westward extension of the Mason-Dixon line (the Pennsylvania-Maryland boundary) delineated the approximate frontier between the Border and the Yankee Great Lakes. Michigan and the northern reaches of Ohio, Indiana and Illinois were staunchly pro-Union in the Civil War and Republican thereafter until the Nineteen-Thirties, when the New Deal swung local cities into the Democratic column. Because the Great Lakes is the most urbanized section of the Heartland, the New Deal urban upheaval balanced or overcame the Republicanism of the countryside. Present Democratic strength is centered in the big cities—Chicago, Detroit, Gary-Hammond and Cleveland—long dominated by Irish, Polish, German, Slavic and Italian immigrants who came to the Great Lakes between the Civil War and the early Nineteen-Twenties. Essentially urban, these Catholic voting groups (save for the Farm Belt Germans) are not found in remotely comparable numbers elsewhere in the Heartland. During the mid-Nineteen-Sixties, however, the urban Catholics of the Great Lakes began to turn conservative in response to the liberal Democratic politics reflecting a large influx of poor Negroes from the South. Emerging Negro control of cities like Gary and Cleveland heralds a new era in regional politics.

To the west, the Great Lakes and Border give way to the Farm Belt, pro-Union in the Civil War and generally Republican in later years except for episodes of agrarianism—third-party departures or support for Democrats like William Jennings Bryan. Besides high and low farm prices, the region has also been strongly influenced by the isolationism of its large German American population. Today's principal division is between the heavily Republican Wheat Belt—Kansas, Nebraska and the Dakotas—and the more urbanized and marginal states of Wisconsin, Minnesota and Iowa. The Farm Belt is historically suspicious of the big city East, a trend which jeopardized the Republicans for many years but now menaces the Democrats.

The eight Mountain states constitute the region largest in size but weakest in electoral votes. There is more diversity among the Mountain states than Easterners are wont to think. The eastern plains of Montana, Wyoming and Colorado are basically an extension of the Farm Belt; the immigrant miner-settled Rocky Mountain backbone of the region is a traditional center of progressive politics and labor unrest; and the Southwest is an area of considerable traditional Democratic strength (the Southwest was something of a Civil War "Border" like the Ohio Valley). In recent years, middle-class migration to the "Sun Belt" Southwest has been a major boon to the Republicans and Rocky Mountain economic progressivism has lost relevance in the face of the Negro socioeconomic revolution. Once strongholds of radicalism, the Mountain states are becoming conservative Republican bastions.

MAP 30

The Heartland—Yankee and Southern Settlement Patterns

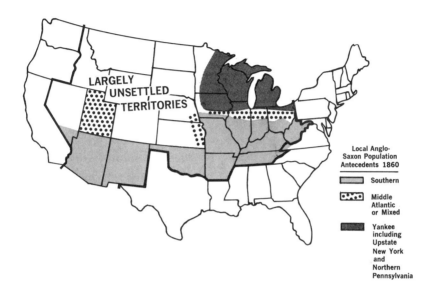

Local Anglo-
Saxon Population
Antecedents 1860

Southern

Middle
Atlantic
or Mixed

Yankee
including
Upstate
New York
and
Northern
Pennsylvania

MAP 31

German Settlement of the Heartland

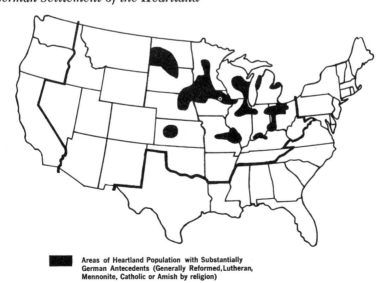

Areas of Heartland Population with Substantially
German Antecedents (Generally Reformed, Lutheran,
Mennonite, Catholic or Amish by religion)

On a non-geographic basis, the Heartland can be analyzed through five major voting streams: Northern Heartland traditional Republicans (mostly Protestant); Southern Heartland traditional Democrats (overwhelmingly Protestant); German Catholics; urban Irish, Southern and Eastern European Catholics; and Negroes. Other groups like the Mormons, Mexicans and Ozark highlanders are much less important.

The loyalties of the old stock population of the Heartland— Northern and Southern Protestants, for the most part—were for many years shaped by Civil War allegiance. This is changing now as sociology supersedes history. Although the Democrats are gaining in Yankee and Scandinavian sections of the northern Heartland, a much greater trend is eroding outdated rural and semi-Southern Democratic voting traditions from West Virginia to Nevada. In balance, more Democratic than Republican traditional support is being re-aligned by the Democratic Party's position on social upheaval.

German American politics have moved in an orbit of sensitivity to foreign policy—to wars against Germany—rather than to American history. German Protestants vote much like their Anglo-Saxon neighbors. German Catholics, however, have generally taken the opposite tack, with the result that the considerable German Catholic population of the Farm Belt and Great Lakes has been normally Democratic (except under wartime stress). More than a quarter of the citizenry of the Heartland is of German origin, and no other group's behavior has been so volatile or so influential in shaping Heartland voting aberrations of the last half century. Teutonic influence is strongest in the Farm Belt, but it is also important in cities like Milwaukee, Chicago, Cleveland, Cincinnati and St. Louis. Chart 87 shows the extent of German settlement in the urban Heartland of fifty years ago.

Prior to the Vietnamese imbroglio, German isolationist opposition to the Democratic "war party" produced three major GOP surges in the Heartland (1920, 1940-44 and 1952). Similar resentment of the war in Vietnam colored the 1968 presidential election. Foreign policy and the ebb of tradition have taken a considerable toll of German Catholic Democratic adherence.

The fastest growing Heartland population group is Negro. Fifty years ago, there were few Negroes outside of the Border, but today, millions of Negroes, mostly Southern-born, constitute a growing

CHART 87

Major Heartland Cities: Population of German Stock, 1910

City	German-Born Population	Native Born Population of German or Mixed Parentage	Total German Stock Population	Total City Population	German Stock Percentage of Total City Population
Milwaukee	64,816	135,106	199,922	373,857	53%
Buffalo (N.Y.)	43,811	98,158	141,969	423,715	33%
Cincinnati	28,425	88,945	117,370	363,591	32%
Detroit	44,674	89,554	134,228	465,766	29%
St. Louis	47,765	138,639	186,404	687,029	27%
Chicago	182,281	319,551	501,832	2,185,283	23%
Cleveland	41,406	78,602	120,008	560,663	22%
Pittsburgh (Pa.)	29,438	70,862	100,300	533,905	19%

percentage—in some case a majority—of the population of Great Lakes cities from Buffalo to Milwaukee. Almost all of these Negroes are Democrats.

Despite the Democratic reliability of the large urban Negro populations, the Negro influx into the Great Lakes cities has not served the party cause because local Italian, Irish, Polish and Slavic voters have responded by turning conservative—often Republican—and moving to the suburbs. In Chicago, Cleveland, Milwaukee, St. Louis, Detroit, Gary and other cities, the Democrats are being troubled by the increasing conservatism of urban white voters and the shrinkage in the percentage of the statewide vote cast by the central cities. In 1968, this trend—a small vote and substantial support for George C. Wallace—reduced Democratic pluralities in most cities.

Across most of the Heartland, the GOP is gaining such strength among hitherto Democratic groups and in heretofore Democratic regions that the 25 interior states—21 of which backed Nixon in 1968—seem to be coming together as the geopolitical fulcrum of a new national Republican era.

A. The Border

American political parlance has long tagged certain states—Kentucky and Missouri, for example—as "Border" states. West of the Appalachians, the Border essentially spans the Central Mississippi-Ohio Basin, historically a cultural watershed between North and South. In order to understand the Border and to know why the present partisan fomentation in the area is crucial to national geopolitics, it is necessary to forget about minimum wage laws, foreign aid and anti-pollution legislation. Forget about Khe Sanh and Con Thien and remember Shiloh and General Morgan's raid; forget about J. William Fulbright and read up on Clement Vallandigham, the Ohio Democratic congressman who led wartime Copperhead (pro-Southern) opponents of Abraham Lincoln. For a century after the peace of Appomattox, the Southern-leaning Border served as a geopolitical fall-line where farmhouses turned from blue to grey; courthouses from Republican to Democratic. Today, a new political era has overtaken the Border states, yet for most of the duration of the 1932-68 political cycle just ended, the region has rested firmly

MAP 32

The Border

in the grip of a partisan alignment precipitated by the sectional animosities of the Civil War.

Geographically, the Border encompasses the area reaching from West Virginia across the Ohio Valley to Missouri, south into Tennessee and Arkansas, and thence into Oklahoma. In Civil War days, these regions were sandwiched between Cavalier and Yankee. Except in a few plantation and mint julep tracts, secessionist sentiments were weak and slaves few; however, most of the inhabitants had Southern antecedents. The Border is essentially one with the network of rivers by which immigrants from Virginia and later Kentucky and Tennessee distributed themselves throughout the basins of the central Mississippi and Ohio. Oklahoma, not admitted to the Union until 1907, was Indian territory during the blue-grey struggle. This did not keep Oklahomans from participating in the war; several units of Creek, Cherokee and Choctaw Indians fought for the Confederacy. When Oklahoma was later opened to settlement, mostly Southerners—Missourians, Arkansans and Texans—flocked in. Oklahoma is the western frontier of the old "Border"; south and west of Oklahoma, one finds the Southwestern states of Arizona, New Mexico and Nevada, cousins to the Border in politics, but carved by a different era.

Nobody can comprehend the vulnerability of the contemporary Democratic Party in the Border without appreciating the extent to which local support has been premised on the coincidence of geography, demography and history rather than empathy (there is not very much) with urban minority group bias in the Great Society vein. The factors which built Democratic hegemony throughout most of the Border a century ago—local traditions of Southern, if not secessionist sympathy—leave today's Democratic Party on sociological quicksand. As the South forswears the Democratic Party, rural Democratic tradition must ebb in the Border.

The underlying key to the political culture of the Border relates back to the last quarter of the Eighteenth Century, when the Anglo-Saxon United States jumped its mountain wall—the Alleghenies, Blue Ridge and Great Smokies—and poured across new frontiers. Yankeedom was busy in the western hinterlands of New York and Pennsylvania (and few areas of Ohio), so that most of the original trans-Appalachian trailblazing was done by Southerners moving west. Virginians trekked into Kentucky and Carolinians into Tennessee; few Yankees moved beyond New York until the completion of the Erie Canal and the Old National Road some years later. To Southerners, though, the Ohio River and its tributaries were a great water turnpike for migrants, especially Virginians, Kentuckians and Tennesseans, to follow into the riverine southern regions of Ohio, Illinois and Indiana. Missouri was settled soon after by similar stock. By 1820, Tennessee, Kentucky, the Ohio Valley areas of Ohio, Indiana and Illinois, and also Missouri had a distinctly Southern orientation. In 1828, they were the core of the "New West" which set a new political cycle in motion with the election of Andrew Jackson as President.

The Border is a creature of Civil War indecision, ambiguity and divided partisanship. One criterion of its genesis was a relatively small Negro population. Where slavery assumed crucial economic importance—as in Tennessee and Arkansas—the Border gave way to the true South. A second criterion was Southern settlement. In mid-Ohio, Indiana or Illinois, the Border ended where Southern-

CHART 88

Negro Population in the Border, 1910-60

State	Negro Share of the Total Population	
	1910	1960
West Virginia	5%	6%
Kentucky	11	7
Missouri	5	8
Oklahoma	8	7
Tennessee	24	16
Arkansas	28	22

sprung populations gave way to Scotch-Irish, Pennsylvania Germans and—especially—Yankees.*

Virginians were the earliest and most prolific settlers of the future Border states. Anyone picking up a map of the eastern United States will see the logic of this: the Ohio Valley and Kentucky lie due west of Virginia, and the post-Revolutionary War "New West" was populated by a movement of extraordinary latitudinalism, i.e., coastal populations moved due west. Actually, Virginian settlement of the Ohio Valley began before the Revolution with the emigration of Daniel Boone and others into the famed Kentucky Bluegrass region. At first, Kentucky was nothing but a Virginian county. It became a state in 1792. When the Revolutionary War was over, Virginians began moving west in greater numbers, and war veterans from the Old Dominion moved into "reserves" in Ohio, Indiana and Kentucky. One must remember that the federal government did not come into being until the ratification of the Constitution in 1789, and in the meantime, the ex-colonies were busy sending their excess population into western lands they claimed by dint of the latitude of their boundaries—which made Virginia the prime force in Kentucky and the Ohio Valley. In Ohio, Virginia's military reserve centered on the Scioto River, where Virginians built the town of

---

*Given the Democratic antecedents of many Pennsylvania Germans and Scotch-Irish, it was often hard to draw a line between their behavior and that of Southerners in states like Ohio or Indiana.

MAP 33

Ohio Valley Settlement Patterns

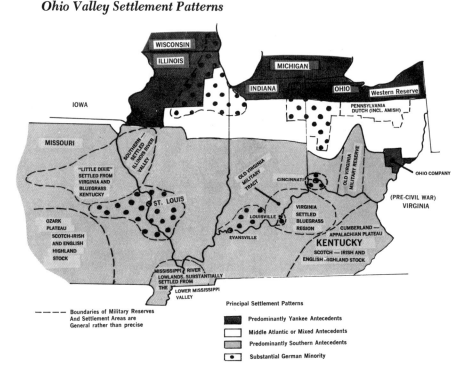

Chillicothe, and in Indiana, where George Rogers Clark and his veterans took up tracts around what is now New Albany, across the Ohio River from Louisville. Around the turn of the century, Virginians pushed into Indiana, following the Wabash and Whitewater valleys north. And in later years, Virginians and Kentuckians followed Daniel Boone west to Boone's Lick Trail in northern Missouri where they carved out a new "Little Dixie." Other Virginians moved into Illinois, pushing up the Illinois River in the vicinity of Springfield. North of the Ohio, Virginian penetration tended to follow a few river valleys. Kentucky and Missouri attracted the largest and most influential concentrations of Virginians.

Not only were Virginians the first settlers of the Border, they were also the most "Southern." The Virginians who emigrated to Missouri, Kentucky and the Ohio Valley came principally from the Piedmont and Tidewater (the Scotch-Irish mountaineers of western

Virginia generally headed for similar highlands). Some brought slaves with them to the new territories and many others were proslavery. In Indiana, Virginian-settled areas led the initial (unsuccessful) agitation to bring the territory into the Union as a slave state.

After the early Virginian settlement of Kentucky and the Ohio Valley, other Southerners—especially backwoods Kentuckians, Carolinians and Tennesseans—began to move through Kentucky into the Ohio Valley sections of Illinois, Indiana and Ohio. Most of these migrants were leaving poor farms to take up minimally better acreage (the unoccupied poor soil lands of the Ohio Valley). This influx, in which the family of Abraham Lincoln participated, was a major factor in the shaping of the Ohio Valley in the first quarter of the Nineteenth Century. It gave the new states of Indiana and Illinois a Southern cast which lasted until Yankee settlers flooded into the Great Lakes in the Eighteen-Thirties and thereafter.* Southern though they were, the trans-Ohio movers were poor and little concerned with Tidewater traditions and institutions like slavery. In a like vein, the large Ozark regions of Arkansas and Missouri, as well as Appalachian Tennessee and Kentucky, were populated by Scotch-Irish and English uplanders apathetic or antipathetic towards slavery.

Beginning in the Eighteen-Thirties, large numbers of Catholic and Protestant Germans came into the Ohio Valley. Cincinnati, St. Louis and Louisville were the principal ports of disembarkation, but other valley towns also received their share of Germans. In Missouri and Kentucky, where the local Anglo-Saxon gentry was Southern and pro-slavery, the Germans generally espoused opposite politics, just as German Catholics settling in the Great Lakes spurned the party of the Yankee ruling class.

As the Civil War approached, the overwhelmingly Southern-settled Border evinced two different brands of Southern politics: the Whig sentiments of the Virginia gentry and the Butternut Democracy, as it was called, of the poor whites.** In Kentucky and Missouri, both dominated by their Virginian regions, the politics of privilege was Southern, but in Illinois and Indiana, Virginia Whigs

*Southern settlement quickly put such a stamp on Indiana that New England migrations largely passed it by. Indiana politics are still colored by a greater Southern influence than affects Ohio or Illinois.

**The Butternut Democrats were so called because they wore homespun clothing usually dyed with the bark of the butternut tree.

were few in number and the political conflict pitted Ohio Valley Butternut Democrats against Great Lakes Yankees—New Englanders, Pennsylvanians and New Yorkers—who had flocked to the northern sections of both states after the completion of the Erie Canal and National Road.* The Butternut Democrats did not care much about slavery, but they could not stand Yankees. To Southern-sprung poor white Baptists and Methodists, the Yankees were a puritanical bourgeoisie out to put the Middle West under its political, cultural and economic thumb. Besides these differences, the Yankee-settled prairielands and dairylands of northern Illinois, Indiana and Ohio were much richer than the poor soils farmed by the Ohio Valley Southerners. Illinois Yankees sneeringly called the southern part of their state "Dark Egypt," only partly in reference to the configurational analogy between the Ohio-Mississippi delta and that of the Egyptian Nile.

The Yankees were Whigs at first, and later became Republicans, while the Ohio Valley Southerners were staunch Democrats. As one would expect, the Yankees took the Union side in the Civil War. Many of the Butternut Democrats became Copperheads, not so much because they cared about secession or the Bonnie Blue Flag as because they did not care about a "Yankee" war. Abraham Lincoln's most belligerent wartime opponents came from the Ohio Valley; congressmen like Clement Vallandigham of Ohio, John Crittenden of Kentucky and Daniel Voorhees of Indiana ("the Tall Sycamore of the Wabash") were less exponents of Dixie's cause than opponents of "puritan" influence over Midwestern culture and politics and of Yankee sacrifice of Middle West interests to serve "Pennsylvania ironmongers and New England manufacturers." Overzealous Yankees jailed Vallandigham and deported him to the Confederacy (where he claimed prisoner of war status), an example of the high-handedness which kept the Middle West so up in ideological arms during the war that Lincoln for a while doubted whether Ohio, Indiana and Illinois would support his reelection in 1864. After the war ended, the Republicans faced an enduring antagonism on the part of many of the Ohio Valley's non-Yankees.

In the slaveholding Border states of Kentucky and Missouri, a very different situation prevailed. Congregationalists and dour New

*In Ohio, there were a few Yankee-settled sections of the Ohio Valley, particularly the Ohio Company lands around Marietta to which New Englanders had come after the Revolutionary War.

Englanders were few in number.* The local upper classes were Southern, predominantly Virginian by ancestry. Although many had been Whigs, that party died in the pre-Civil War sectionalization of politics, with the result that Whigs sympathizing with secession or the South became Democrats. By and large the Virginians of Kentucky and Missouri lined up with the Confederacy. However, both states also had large numbers of German immigrants and mountaineers who liked neither secession nor the Cavalier class propounding it.

Because of the numerical strength of Germans, Ozark Missourians and Appalachian Kentuckians, together with the alertness of local Unionists and the proximity of both states to Northern military reinforcement, Missouri and Kentucky remained in the Union. Nevertheless, there was considerable military maneuvering before the issue was decided. Credit for Missouri's non-secession belonged to the Germans: under Generals Carl Schurz and Franz Sigel, they quickly mobilized, drilled intensively and ultimately fought for the North in large numbers. Because Little Dixie and the leading German settlements were adjacent, they were prone to make military gestures against one another from time to time, raising an interesting sidelight to the war which also helps to give a specific focus to later voting patterns. In few other areas was it so literally true that county marched against county.**

Another Border state, West Virginia, was actually created by the Civil War. Its contemporary character—archetypal rural poverty, shack towns and decaying mining communities—removes much of

---

*Kentucky has no Yankee settlements dating back to pre-Civil War days, but Missouri has. In the northern part of the state, along the Iowa line, there are two Northern-settled counties, Putnam and Mercer. Putnam is the most Republican county in northern Missouri. When the GOP carried no state beyond the Northeast in 1932, Putnam was the only northern Missouri county to back Hoover. Yankee voting is significant, but not too influential in northern Missouri.

**The nation's first land battle of the Civil War was begun by Missouri's Virginians near Boonville in Little Dixie in June, 1861. Much of the local action was well-nigh farcical. When Union militia marched into Little Dixie's Callaway County, they were fooled by four hundred old men and boys and a log painted to resemble a cannon! Just across the Missouri River from Callaway County lies Gasconade County, a German stronghold. Confederate troops tried to capture the Gasconade County seat of Hermann, a cobblestoned, gable-roofed, medieval-balconied bit of Rhineland on the Missouri, but were fooled by six old men who dragged a solitary cannon from hill to hill. All of this happened while the military-aged men of both counties were away in their respective armies. In later days, the two sides voted as they had shot. Little Dixie was the most Democratic section of Missouri, and Gasconade County was the staunchest GOP county north of the high Ozarks.

West Virginia's political behavior from the true Border category, aligning it instead with that of the Black Country of Appalachian southwest Pennsylvania. However, back in Civil War days, other factors than worn-out mines and a need for welfare and kindred federal spending marked West Virginia politics. And like the rest of the Border, although to a lesser degree, West Virginia's Democratic traditions have some Southern overtones.

In 1861, when Virginia—it then reached west to the Ohio River—decided to secede from the Union, the mountainous western part of the state refused to go along. It secured federal protection, and in 1863 was declared by the federal Congress to be an independent state named West Virginia. Although many of the people had Southern antecedents, much of the state was quite primitive and there were few slaves. Local sentiment was not pro-Yankee, but rather indisposed to fighting Tidewater and Deep Southern battles. The more prosperous sections of Virginia seceded with the Mother State, except for the area which is now West Virginia's eastern panhandle. This was tacked onto West Virginia against its will because it included a strategic railway line—the Baltimore and Ohio—which the Union government wanted placed in official Union territory. The three panhandle counties were a controversial piece of Virginia *irridentia* in the years following the war. Jefferson County, the easternmost, was really an extension of Virginia hunt country—its county seat had been laid out by George Washington's brother, Charles, and was named Charles Town—and local ire was aroused at inclusion in *déclassé* West Virginia. For years, Charles Town refused to admit that it was no longer in Virginia, and until 1940, Jefferson County was normally West Virginia's poorest county for any GOP presidential nominee. Such was the persistence of Civil War cleavage.

The highland-lowland polarization of Arkansas and Tennessee has already been described as part of the politics of the Outer South. Inasmuch as the Outer South is a sociopolitical concept and not a geographic region, Arkansas and Tennessee both overlap two regional frameworks—the Heartland (Border) and the South. Both states have the mountaineers of Missouri and Kentucky, but not the Germans, most of whom never ventured south of St. Louis. At the same time, Arkansas and Tennessee have plantation Black Belt lowlands (the Mississippi flood plain), which Kentucky and Missouri largely lack. The last state to join the Confederacy, Tennessee

MAP 34

Missouri Politics as a Mirror of Civil War History

Counties: 1. Yankee-settled Putnam County; 2. Ozark County, one of the banner Ozark mountain counties; 3. Gasconade County, heavily-German Rhineland on the Missouri; 4. Monroe County, the banner county of Virginian-settled "Littie Dixie"; 5. Mississippi County, in the cotton-growing Mississippi flood plain.

All of these counties are rural and small-town, yet local politics, in the century after Appomattox, ignored these ties and reiterated the cleavage of Civil War days.

County	Republican Share of the Total Presidential Vote		
	1920	1940	1960
Putnam	73%	69%	72%
Ozark	80	78	78
Gasconade	90	82	75
Monroe	18	17	28
Mississippi	47	41	41

was also the first ex-Confederate state to vote for a post-Reconstruction Republican President (Harding in 1920). Perhaps Arkansas and Tennessee can be called the border of the old Border. By a yardstick of non-coastal insularity, they are Heartland states, but they reach past the political Heartland into the Deep South. In so doing, they emphasize what the Border is *not*. The old plantation Black Belt around Memphis is no more Border than is Yankee Great Lakes Ohio; its Civil War loyalties were Southern and emphatic, whereas the essence of the Border was division—county against county, stratum against stratum—and ambivalence.

However anecdotal, the settlement patterns, wartime biases and military ventures just sketched are also the crucial underpinning of current Border politics. When the Civil War was over, the Border voted as it had shot: Germans, mountaineers and some others, Republican; the majority of lowland Anglo-Saxons, Democratic. As late as the Eisenhower years, no other counties outside the old Confederacy could match the Democratic percentages of the core areas of Kentucky's Bluegrass and Missouri's Little Dixie, while Republican strength in both states rested on Ozark, Appalachian and German support. In a similar vein, Democratic counties in rural Ohio, Indiana and Illinois mostly followed the riverine probes of remote Southern settlement. (This behavior was already weakening: the concentration of Ohio Democratic strength in the Scioto Valley, for example, had been much clearer in 1924.)

Extraordinary as it may seem, these traditions were still operative a full century after Lee surrendered to Grant. Missouri, Kentucky, Arkansas and Tennessee elected ten Republicans and twenty Democrats to the House of Representatives in 1966. Of these, six of the GOP congressmen represented the six Ozark and Appalachian highland districts, three sat for urban and suburban districts in the German-tinged conurbations of St. Louis and Louisville, and one represented the booming metropolis of Memphis.* *Every* lowland rural district in the four states elected a Democratic congressman, although most were conservatives. So long as the South remained Democratic, Border politics essentially ignored the New Deal, Fair Deal, Square Deal, New Freedom and New Frontier and reiterated the social and geopolitical cleavage imprinted by the fratricide of 1861-65.

---

*While several of these districts were voting Republican for the first time, traditional strength was still the bulwark of victory.

CHART 89

Border Partisanship, 1868-1968

The years in which a Border State voted for the GOP presidential nominee are marked with an "R"

	1868	1872	1876	1880	1884	1888	1892
West Virginia	R	R	—	—	—	—	—
Kentucky	—	—	—	—	—	—	—
Missouri	R	—	—	—	—	—	—
Tennessee	R	—	—	—	—	—	—
Arkansas	R	—	—	—	—	—	—
Oklahoma	*	*	*	*	*	*	*

	1896	1900	1904	1908	1912	1916	1920	1924	1928
West Virginia	R	R	R	R	—	R	R	R	R
Kentucky	R	—	—	—	—	—	—	R	R
Missouri	—	—	R	R	—	—	R	R	R
Tennessee	—	—	—	—	—	—	R	—	R
Arkansas	—	—	—	—	—	—	—	—	—
Oklahoma	*	*	*	—	—	—	R	—	R

	1932	1936	1940	1944	1948	1952	1956	1960	1964
West Virginia	—	—	—	—	—	—	R	—	—
Kentucky	—	—	—	—	—	—	R	R	—
Missouri	—	—	—	—	—	R	—	—	—
Tennessee	—	—	—	—	—	R	R	R	—
Arkansas	—	—	—	—	—	—	—	—	—
Oklahoma	—	—	—	—	—	R	R	R	—

	1968
West Virginia	—
Kentucky	R
Missouri	R
Tennessee	R
Arkansas	**
Oklahoma	R

*Oklahoma was not admitted to the Union until 1907.
**Arkansas supported third-party candidate George Wallace.

Note: The 1860 election was fought in a four-party context; the 1864 election excluded the Confederate states of Tennessee and Arkansas as well as Confederate soldiers from the other states; and even the 1868 election is quite atypical because of the persisting Confederate disenfranchisement, and—in some areas—continuing Northern (Republican) military presence.

Having made this point, it is possible to skip lightly over a long stretch of Border political history. Chart 89 shows how none of the Border states supported Republican presidential candidates in the tightly fought campaigns of 1876, 1880, 1884, 1888 and 1892. German and mountaineer voting never quite turned the trick. The Border was distinctly more Democratic than the nation as a whole because of the predominant Southern influence, thus close national elections invariably saw the Border states cast Democratic electoral votes. The first post-Grant GOP successes in the Border came when the Bryan-McKinley contest eroded some of the Democratic Party's traditional conservative strength, and during the ensuing 1896-1932 era of Republican national dominance, the party often carried several of the Border states. Harding, Coolidge and especially Hoover (who profited from anti-Catholic voting) were quite successful in the Border. In the 1928 election, the Baptist "Bible Belts" of Middle Tennessee and southwest Oklahoma succumbed to vehement religious voting. Al Smith's gains in German Catholic sections of the Border were inadequate compensation.

Paralleling the trends of the rest of the Border, the southern sections of Ohio, Indiana and Illinois were sufficiently Democratic between 1876 and 1892 occasionally to overcome the Republican majorities in the Great Lakes districts of the three states. Indiana voted for Tilden in 1876 and for Cleveland in 1884 and 1892; Illinois left the GOP presidential column only in 1892; Ohio backed all of the Republican candidates, partly because four out of five were Ohioans! Partisanship in each state lay deep in Civil War ruts, so that very little change occurred from one election to the next. Indiana contests were the closest—the parties seesawed between 49 per cent and 51 per cent of the vote—with the result that the state became a favorite vice-presidential selection ground. After William Jennings Bryan dislocated some existing Democratic loyalties in 1896, the Republican task became easier. Between 1896 and 1932, Woodrow Wilson was the only Democratic presidential nominee to win Ohio, Indiana or Illinois.

Although the New Deal soon proved itself to be an essentially urban and labor-oriented impetus, Franklin D. Roosevelt held the rural Border firmly in tow between 1932 and 1944. Some of his programs were unpopular in the Border states, but by and large, the Border had little cause for complaint; the coming to power of the Democratic Party created a leadership role for party leaders, who were able to arbitrate between big city and labor-backed Democrats from the North and Dixie's rural labor-haters and Negrophobes. This was a role tailor-made for the Border. By 1938, when the huge majorities of the New Deal heyday had been lost, the new class of "Border" Democrats established a new hegemony in Washington, assuming a whip hand over the New Deal in the process. Besides Democratic leaders from the old Border, this new set of powerbrokers included men from states like Iowa and Texas, where Civil War loyalties had been quite definite, and others from states like Nevada and Arizona, the Confederate expatriate meccas of the Southwest. An extraordinary number of powerful Washington politicians hailed from these geopolitical areas. Downstate Illinois produced Henry Rainey, Speaker of the House (1933-35), and Scott Lucas, Senate Majority Leader (1949-51). The most prominent Kentuckian was Alben Barkley, Senate Democratic Leader (1937-49) and Vice President (1949-53). Tennessee elected Joseph Byrns, Speaker of the House (1935-36), and Kenneth McKellar, Senate President *Pro Tem* (1945-47, 1949-53). Harry S. Truman, Vice President (1945) and President (1945-53), was Missouri's favorite son. Texas had quite a dynasty: John Nance Garner, Speaker of the House (1931-33) and Vice President (1933-41); Sam Rayburn, Speaker of the House (1940-47, 1949-53, 1955-61); and Senate Majority Leader Lyndon Johnson (1953-61). From Arizona came Carl Hayden, Senate President *Pro Tem* (1957-69), and Ernest McFarland, Senate Majority Leader (1951-53). Nevada contributed Senate President *Pro Tem* Key Pitman, who served from 1933 to 1940. Of course, there were others of lesser title but great importance, but even this list serves to show how the "Border" had more than its share of power beyond the gates of the White House (and even there, in Truman's day) throughout most of the New Deal cycle. The changeover began in 1961, when a Massachusetts Democrat became President, another took the House speakership, and a Montanan took the party reins in the Senate. The vice presidency and subsequent presidency of Texas' Lyndon Baines Johnson in no way restored Border primacy. Quite the contrary.

But to return to the beginning of the New Deal, Franklin D. Roosevelt carried all of the Border states in each of his four election contests, although isolationism (German and mountaineer) narrowed his Missouri majorities in 1940 and 1944. The 1948

Truman-Barkley ticket, an unprecedented Missouri-Kentucky combination, pushed the Democratic vote in the Border states substantially above post-1938 and wartime levels. Truman's politics were quite pleasing to his old neighbors. His liberalism was not of the big city, minority group or urban sweatshop variety, but showed a mild agrarian, nationalist and traditionalist bent.* For these reasons, a considerable majority of Border voters saw Truman as a more appealing candidate than New York Governor Thomas E. Dewey, the aloof candidate of the Northeastern Republican Establishment.

The Border largely shunned another presidential candidate of the year 1948—Dixiecrat Strom Thurmond. The Cotton states' discontent with the Democratic Party, linked to apprehensions over the socioeconomic future of white supremacy, did not sway the Border, where Negroes were few and white supremacy sufficiently assured that Negroes could and did vote. (As of 1960, the Negro population of West Virginia was 6 per cent; Kentucky, 7 per cent; Missouri, 8 per cent; and Oklahoma, 7 per cent.) Not sharing the anxieties of the Deep South, the Border had no reason to bolt from the Democratic Party, especially in light of the way the party served local interests and elevated local leaders to positions of national importance. Thurmond was not even on the ballot in Missouri, West Virginia and Oklahoma, and in Kentucky, where he did run, he garnered only 1 per cent of the total vote. Of course, Thurmond fared much better in Tennessee and Arkansas, actually carrying some counties in the wholly Deep South area around and below Memphis.**

As an Ivy League intellectual, Adlai Stevenson was much less to Border taste than native son Harry Truman. Eisenhower beat Stevenson easily in Oklahoma, defeated him by razor-thin majorities

---

*Samuel Lubell, writing in *The Future of American Politics,* dwells at some length on Truman's representation of the Border mentality. In January, 1938, it seems that then-Senator Truman, nephew of a Confederate soldier, did not want to support the anti-lynching bill before the Senate. He told a leading Southerner: "All my sympathies are with you . . . but the Negro vote in Kansas City and St. Louis is too important." The Border knew Truman too well to be scared by him.

**There is nothing "Border" about the Memphis region, either in Tennessee or lowland eastern Arkansas. Negroes and cotton together mainstayed the local economy for many years. Strom Thurmond carried Shelby County (Memphis), Tennessee in 1948, as well as some other heavily Negro counties (where Negroes by and large could not vote). Because of the weight of the Mississippi flood plain and Memphis, both Arkansas and Tennessee differ from the true Border.

in Missouri and Tennessee, lost by a similarly narrow margin in Kentucky, and failed to carry West Virginia. But in light of the national Republican landslide, Eisenhower's showing in the Border was not particularly strong. The New Deal had eroded Republican strength in urban and mining counties without disturbing Democratic rural hegemony, leaving the GOP weaker than it had been in the Nineteen-Twenties. The pattern of 1952 persisted through 1956 with only minor changes. Eisenhower added West Virginia to his column, but the gain of a few thousand votes which gave him Kentucky's support was balanced by a similar loss in Missouri. In sum, the Eisenhower appeal effected no great change in Border politics, and the partisan alignments of 1956 in Kentucky and Missouri—Germans and mountaineers against Anglo-Saxon low-landers—were substantially similar to those which had prevailed almost a century earlier. Of course, the growth of suburbia made this traditional voting somewhat less influential, but Chart 90 illustrates how the banner rural Little Dixie counties of Missouri and Kentucky remained steadfastly Democratic throughout the Eisenhower era.

CHART 90

Missouri and Kentucky "Little Dixie" Voting Patterns

	Democratic Share of the Total Vote for President				
County	1920	1924	1928	1932	1936
Monroe (Missouri)	80%	81%	78%	89%	87%
Trimble (Kentucky)	85	83	69	89	85
	1940	1944	1948	1952	1956
Monroe (Missouri)	83%	82%	85%	76%	77%
Trimble (Kentucky)	89	87	89	83	78

But while the New Deal did not erode rural Democratic strength in states like Missouri, Kentucky and Oklahoma, where the party was dominated by rural and conservative elements, the Democrats did lose a little ground between 1924 and 1948 in the Ohio Valley. This change was minimal in Southern Illinois and Indiana because both sections retained considerable conservative influence in their state Democratic parties. Ohio, however, proved to be a different case. Prior to the New Deal, there were only a dozen or so rural Democratic counties, and they became increasingly anomalous in a party shaped by its support in Cleveland and the industrial cities. Brown and Holmes counties, 43 per cent and 38 per cent Republican in 1924, both went 49 per cent Republican in 1940, and gave Eisenhower 54 per cent and 65 per cent support, respectively, in 1952.

Most Ohio Valley counties of Ohio, Indiana and Illinois backed Dwight Eisenhower in 1952 and 1956, even though GOP gains were not large. The most striking thing, however, lay simply in the occurrence of Republican majorities in counties which had remained Democratic throughout the Ohio, Indiana and Illinois GOP landslides of 1920-28. Whereas Calvin Coolidge had lost several dozen rural counties in the three states in 1924, Eisenhower failed to carry only a handful. It was little noticed because observers infrequently probed behind Eisenhower's "personal" appeal, but by the Nineteen-Fifties, the Democrats no longer commanded their traditional majorities in the Southern-settled counties of all three Ohio Valley states. This was the price local Democrats were obliged to pay for their new constituencies in Cleveland, Akron, Youngstown, Gary, South Bend and Chicago.

Across the Ohio Valley and the rest of the Border, Protestants—Baptists especially—did not take kindly to John F. Kennedy's Catholicism in 1960, which helped Nixon not only to maintain but occasionally exceed Eisenhower levels. Anti-Catholicism should not be exaggerated—some of the pro-Nixon Ohio and Mississippi Valley counties had voted for Al Smith—but there was considerable religious voting in middle Tennessee and southwest Oklahoma, places where his religion had been a great burden to Al Smith in 1928. At the same time, John F. Kennedy won a considerable Catholic vote in the German Catholic districts of the Ohio Valley and Missouri.* With a few exceptions—counties swayed by religious voting or civil rights reaction—the 1960 election did not

---

*Kennedy's best Kentucky gains came in midstate Nelson and Marion counties (about half Catholic) and in German Catholic Kenton and Campbell counties across the Ohio River from Cincinnati. The sharpest 1956-60 Democratic trend —17 per cent—occurred in Nelson County, the most Catholic, within which typical Baptist precincts went two-to-one Republican while Catholic precincts similar except in religion gave Kennedy 88 per cent support (*U.S. News and World Report*, Dec. 12, 1960). In Missouri, the heaviest Democratic gain came in *ancien régime* French Catholic St. Genevieve County (up 15 per cent), the Missouri River German Catholic counties and greater St. Louis' German Catholic precincts.

rework the pattern of rural Border balloting. Map 34 shows the continuity of traditional Missouri voting in the 1960 election.

The principal 1956-60 Republican trend in the rural Border—spotlighting one geopolitical region—pivoted on the issue of civil rights. Even though the Democrats had not been in power and bore no administrative program opprobrium, they were becoming increasingly identified with the social programs and social revolution of the Northeastern Megalopolis. Upsetting the precedents of a century, the South was more Republican than the Northeast in 1960, and so was the Border. In backing Richard Nixon, Tennessee, Kentucky and Oklahoma cast their first electoral votes for an unsuccessful Republican presidential nominee.

While the civil rights question had not yet focused to the point of re-aligning rural Border partisanship; nevertheless, Nixon's major gains in the Border were clearly attributable to conservative Democratic disenchantment with the leftward drift of their party's social policies. Far from being scattered across areas of fundamentalist Protestant strength, the Kentucky, Missouri, Tennessee and Arkansas counties of Nixon's greatest upsurge were bunched together in a contiguous bloc roughly delineated by geography and strong Negro-engendered Democratic traditions. Spanning a definite multi-state lowland basin, the area included the greatest rural concentrations of Kentucky, Missouri and Tennessee Negroes (the majority of them non-voters). The Arkansas counties, while geographically linked to nearby Missouri, are not the state's black belt. Map 35 shows the area where Nixon's 1960 vote climbed 10 per cent to 20 per cent above 1956 levels, a much more emphatic trend than occurred elsewhere in the Border.

Back in 1928, when Al Smith's candidacy had tested Border loyalties, these counties—too much concerned with the one-party Democratic system and the perpetuation of white supremacy to worry about the Pope—had turned in nearly their usual overwhelming Democratic percentages. Only the Virginian-settled Little Dixie sections matched this adherence to the Democratic nominee. In 1960, it was the new sociological trend of the Democratic Party rather than Kennedy's religion which produced Nixon's gains.*

*In the Deep South—Mississippi, Louisiana and South Carolina especially—the black belts broke to Eisenhower in 1952 and 1956; those of the Outer South did not. By 1960, the black belts of the Outer South and Border were beginning to follow suit.

MAP 35

The Central Mississippi Basin in the 1960 Election

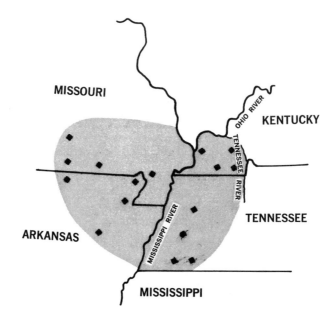

    Within Kentucky, Missouri, Arkansas and Tennessee, the four counties in each state which showed the greatest 1956-60 GOP presidential trend are represented by black dots. All of these counties registered 12 per cent to 20 per cent shifts except for Fayette County, Tennessee, where the GOP share of the total presidential vote rose 31 per cent. The Fayette shift was abnormally high because of the county's 1956 support for a minor party states' rights candidacy. Most of the unmarked counties within the shaded area gave Nixon 4 per cent to 10 per cent greater backing than they had accorded to Eisenhower in 1956.

Consider Fayette County, Tennessee, which showed the sharpest 1956-60 GOP presidential trend in the Border: 49 per cent for Nixon, it had been only 10 per cent Republican in 1928 despite the Catholicism of the Democratic nominee. Many of the other leading Nixon-trend counties likewise had shown no GOP presidential strength or trend in 1928. At the same time that Nixon made these gains in the Border black belts, he made no appreciable strides in the overwhelmingly white, Virginian-settled Little Dixie sections of Missouri and Kentucky, where the race issue was of less direct concern. In retrospect, many of the seemingly religion-prompted GOP gains had origins of a different variety.*

This was also true in Oklahoma, where steady GOP gains reflected a changing intra-state balance of power. During the Nineteen-Fifties, few states swam in a Republican tide comparable to that of Oklahoma. Whereas Dewey had won only 37 per cent of the vote in 1948, Eisenhower won 55 per cent in 1952 and 1956, and Nixon garnered 59 per cent in 1960. Much of this improvement rested in the growth of conservative urban boom towns like Oklahoma City and Tulsa. Whereas in 1920 Oklahoma and Tulsa counties had cast only 12 per cent of the statewide vote, by 1948 they cast 25 per cent, and in 1956, 31 per cent. (With the trend continuing, the two counties cast 35 per cent of Oklahoma's total vote in 1968.) As a result of the statewide balance of power shifting away from Ozark and rural southern Oklahoma, and into urban boom towns comparable to those of the Southwest, Oklahoma began its metamorphosis from a state more Democratic than the rest of the nation into a state more Republican. Anti-Catholic voting swelled Nixon's Oklahoma ballot totals in 1960; however, the changing direction of Oklahoma politics would likely have produced a Republican victory even against a Protestant Democrat.

Another, and different, population trend aided the Republicans in Missouri. In that state, the major cities—long-established, primarily liberal centers like St. Louis and Kansas City—were in the process of steadily losing population. Negroes were flowing into St. Louis from the rural South, but white residents were moving out to the suburbs. Between 1950 and 1960, St. Louis' population dropped considerably, and in a like vein, the share of the Missouri statewide vote cast by the city of St. Louis slipped even farther (from 22 per cent in 1948 to 12 per cent in 1968). In the Border, as elsewhere in the nation, the political influence of the old central cities was on the wane, a factor which definitely worked for the cause of both conservatism and Republicanism.

Despite Richard Nixon's 1960 gains in Deep South-oriented sections of the Border, the basic Democratic loyalties of the rural

*The socioeconomic base of the Nixon trend was not clear at the time, nor was it spotlighted in 1964—indeed it was camouflaged by the fact that these counties trended against Goldwater. The 1960 trend was prompted by an erosion of tradition and by a moderate conservatism, but the 1964 GOP candidacy, revolutionary rather than evolutionary, went too far. In 1968, Democratic strength once again eroded before an evolutionary trend.

Border remained. The cores of the Kentucky Bluegrass and Missouri's Little Dixie, as well as Missouri's "Boot" and the far southwest of Kentucky, voted about two-to-one for John F. Kennedy. But with the election of a Democratic President, a crucial groundwork was laid for changing partisanship..During the years following the 1954 Supreme Court school desegregation decision, the advent of Negro socioeconomic revolution had become more noticeable in the Border, but the Republicans, being in the White House between 1953 and 1961, were not able to profit from local dissatisfaction with Washington's policies. It remained for an innovative Democratic administration committed to social change to antagonize the party loyalty and moderate conservative instincts of the Border.

Across much of the Border, the politics and programs of the national Democratic Party were quite unpopular by 1964. The GOP, however, still proved unable to capitalize on these resentments. Putting the Deep South cart before the Outer South and Border horse, the Republicans mounted a presidential campaign directed towards the never-before-Republican Black Belt, thinking that a breach there would mean victory throughout the entire South and Border. Contrary to these expectations, Barry Goldwater fared badly in the Border, pushing the party presidential vote back past 1948 levels. Chart 91 sets forth the political tides of the Border in 1964.

Goldwater's Border decline was keynoted by heavy losses in Appalachian, Ozark, German "Forty-Eighter," Yankee (Missouri)

CHART 91

The Republican Decline in the Border, 1960-64

State	Republican Share of the Two-Party Vote for President	
	1960	1964
Kentucky	54%	36%
West Virginia	47	32
Missouri	50	36
Oklahoma	59	44
Tennessee	53	45
Arkansas	43	43

and Great Plains (Oklahoma) counties, where the party had hitherto been strongest. In these traditionally Republican and one-time pro-Union voting streams, the Arizona Senator's cotton states ties lessened his appeal. Conversely, the principal 1960-64 GOP gains came in the Deep South sections of Arkansas and Tennessee. The true "Border" went heavily against Goldwater, but in Arkansas and Tennessee, the unprecedented Democratic trends in the Appalachians and Ozarks were partly balanced by GOP gains in the cotton-growing Mississippi flood plain, so that the statewide party fall-off was much less than in West Virginia, Kentucky, Missouri and Oklahoma. The Republicans' Deep South gains did not extend to the Virginian-settled white portico counties of Missouri and Kentucky. These counties, and especially the rich and tradition-soaked Kentucky Bluegrass, spurned the 1964 Republican *entente* with the Cotton States.* Chart 92 shows the Border trends of 1960-64.

As indicated, the political role of the Border has been ambivalence and arbitration between the firebrands of the North and those of the South. It rejected Lincoln and the Republicans in 1860, the vehement secessionists in 1861, the Republican Maine-Vermont axis in 1936, the Dixiecrats in 1948, the Dixie-captivated GOP of 1964 and the Great Society of 1968. The impetus rebuked in 1948 and 1964 was not the moderate conservatism of the Border but the more pointed conservatism of Mississippi, Georgia, Alabama, Louisiana and South Carolina—the same Cotton States bombast that had fired the first shells at Fort Sumter and futilely shed Border blood from Vicksburg to Antietam. However, if the Border is not Dixiecrat, neither is it disposed towards Northeastern establishmentarian liberalism.

---

*The anti-Goldwater trend in the Bluegrass was extremely strong. In Bourbon County, the GOP slipped from 43 per cent to 23 per cent between 1960 and 1964; in Woodford County, from 53 per cent to 29 per cent; and in Franklin County, from 40 per cent to 19 per cent. These are the counties surrounding Lexington, the "Heart of the Bluegrass." The two Little Dixie counties cited in Chart 92 also shunned Goldwater. The Arizona Republican garnered only 18 per cent of the vote in Monroe County, Missouri, and a mere 13 per cent of the vote in Trimble County, Kentucky. Further east in Virginia, Goldwater won a mixed reception. He gained in "Southside" Virginia, and the only two traditionally Democratic rural counties where he fell far below Nixon were those akin to the Bluegrass and Missouri's Little Dixie—horsy-sportsy Loudoun and Fauquier counties (Leesburg, Middleburg, Upperville and Warrenton). Barry Goldwater's Sun Belt and Deep South colors did not suit horse country—in Virginia, Kentucky or Missouri.

CHART 92

Components of the Goldwater Defeat in the Border

County	Republican Share of the Total Vote for President	
	1960	1964
Mountain		
Preston, West Virginia	62%	39%
Ozark, Missouri	78	59
Newton, Arkansas	68	49
Leslie, Kentucky	83	52
Sevier, Tennessee	85	70
German Forty-Eighter*		
Gasconade, Missouri	75	63
Yankee		
Mercer, Missouri	67	45
Putnam, Missouri	72	51
Great Plains		
Alfalfa, Oklahoma	76	59
Little Dixie (Virginian)		
Monroe, Missouri	28	18
Trimble, Kentucky	32	13
Jefferson, West Virginia	40	28
Montgomery, Tennessee	25	22
Mississippi Lowlands		
Fayette, Tennessee	49	53
Ashley, Arkansas	26	56

*The two leading German Catholic counties, Cole and Osage, gave Kennedy abnormally high (religious) support in 1960, and so Goldwater made small gains in 1964.

Negroes are only a small minority throughout most of the Border, and neither their enfranchisement—in some places it was a well-established fact—nor civil rights legislation in general excited Border fears akin to those which moved the white Deep South of 1964. Shortly thereafter, however, the Border drew the line at the socioeconomic planning and subsidies of the Great Society as ratified by the Eighty-Ninth Congress. Passage of this legislation could not have come about except that the 1964 elections disrupted the balance of power in Congress, giving Northern liberals artificial majorities with which to enact extremely liberal social programs over Border opposition. President Lyndon B. Johnson, himself a graduate of the Border brokerage school, ignored history in his haste to make it. Time after time, a majority of Border Democrats in the House of Representatives voted against innovative programs and their appropriations, but usually without success.

The reaction of the Border was readily apparent in the 1966 elections—the first public referendum on the Great Society. Not one staunch anti-Great Society Democratic Congressman from the Central Mississippi-Ohio Basin had trouble at the polls. However, their more liberal colleagues fell or lost ground in patterns correlating with their voting records (see Chart 93). The GOP won a number of new seats in Border state legislatures, elected the first Republican-dominated Kentucky congressional delegation, put the second GOP governor in Oklahoma's statehouse, captured the Arkansas governorship and a Tennessee United States Senate seat for the first time since Reconstruction, produced a large southern Illinois United States Senate majority for Charles Percy and captured four of the five lower Ohio Valley congressional seats held by Ohio and Indiana Democrats.* These were more than mere currents of unrest; they were important breakthroughs foreshadowing re-alignment.

The 1967 Kentucky gubernatorial election—the GOP won for the first time in a quarter of a century—underscored the tides at work. Running on a platform stressing opposition to the Great Society, Republican Louis Nunn lost some previously Republican strength in Louisville's Negro wards, but he garnered huge increments in the traditionally Democratic Bluegrass and southwestern Dixie-leaning lowlands. In many counties which had voted two-to-one against Nunn in the 1963 gubernatorial race, the GOP vote rose by fifteen and twenty percentage points to unprecedented levels.** Few of the reporters milling around in Republican headquarters in the Bluegrass Room of Louisville's Brown Hotel fath-

*The districts captured were the First, Tenth and Fifteenth districts of Ohio (89th Congress) and the Eighth District of Indiana.
**The best 1963-67 Nunn gains came in the lowland counties south of Paducah and west of Bowling Green. This was the most Democratic section of the state, but it was also where Nixon had made his greatest 1960 strides. Nunn's vote confirmed the trend interrupted in 1964.

CHART 93

Impact of 89th Congress Voting Records on 1966 Congressional Elections in the Central Mississippi-Ohio Basin (Lowlands)

Anti-Great Society Congressmen	Congressmen Who Sometimes Suported Great Society	Pro-Great Society Congressmen
Democrats	Democrats	Democrats
HULL (Mo.)	MILLS (Ark.)	FULTON (Tenn.)
ICHORD (Mo.)	NATCHER (Ky.)	EVINS (Tenn.)*
EVERETT (Tenn.)	Shipley (Ill.)	ANDERSON (Tenn.)*
RANDALL (Mo.)	Hamilton (Ind.)	Hungate (Mo.)
JONES (Mo.)	*Chelf* (Ky.)	*Gray* (Ill.)
GATHINGS (Ark.)	*Moeller* (Ohio)	*Grider* (Tenn.)
STUBBLEFIELD (Ky.)	*Murray* (Tenn.)	*Farnsley* (Ky.)
WATTS (Ky.)		*Gilligan* (Ohio)
		Denton (Ind.)
Republicans		
CLANCY (Ohio)		Big City (*St. Louis-Kansas City*)
HARSHA (Ohio)		Democrats
CURTIS (Mo.)		BOLLING (Mo.)
		SULLIVAN (Mo.)
		KARSTEN (Mo.)
		PRICE (Ill.)

Legend
SMITH (Names Capitalized)   —Re-elected by large majority
Smith (Names Not Capitalized)—Re-elected by small margin or with
                            sharply lessened vote
Smith (Names In Italics)   —Defeated in the General Election or
                            Democratic Primary

*Unopposed

omed the full meaning of the returns: throwing aside a century of tradition, the Border was turning Republican.

In 1968, Richard Nixon won four of the six Border States—Kentucky, Tennessee, Missouri and Oklahoma—but his margins of

MAP 36

Wallace Vote in the Border States, 1968

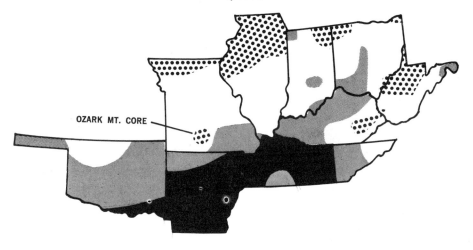

OZARK MT. CORE

Wallace share of total 1968 Presidential Vote (Generalized Contours)

0-8%		8-16%	
16-32%		Over 32%	

victory were not what they might have been. Nixon's edge in the Ohio Valley sections of Ohio, Indiana and Illinois also lagged behind 1960 levels. George Wallace's third-party effort temporarily diverted many of the disgruntled Democratic traditionists who had been shifting towards the GOP, thus reducing the scope of Nixon's victory. Arkansas' conservative Democrats actually carried their state for Wallace, and those in Tennessee came close.* Chart 94 shows the percentages won by the three major candidates in the Border States, and Chart 95 links the trends at work in the Border during the Nineteen-Sixties.

Although national Democratic fortunes ebbed in 1968 throughout the Border, except in Negro precincts and a few northern Appalachia mining counties of West Virginia and Eastern Ken-

---

*Wallace's white support in middle and west Tennessee was large enough for him to have carried Tennessee despite GOP highland solidarity—if only he had run well ahead of Nixon in the Memphis area. Luckily for Nixon, many of the 1948 Dixiecrats who had turned Republican in 1952 stuck by their new allegiance.

CHART 94

Border Presidential Voting, 1968

	Share of the Total Vote for President		
State	Nixon	Wallace	Humphrey
Oklahoma	47%	20%	32%
Kentucky	44	18	38
Tennessee	38	34	28
Missouri	45	11	44
Arkansas	31	39	30
West Virginia	41	10	49

tucky, the party's greatest 1960-68 presidential decline came in Arkansas and Tennessee. The best Goldwater states of 1964, they became the Border's top Wallace states in 1968. As in other Confederate States, however, Wallace's candidacy also captured most white voters who had remained loyal to the Democrats in 1964. Map 36 shows how Wallace's best Border percentages occurred in the Deep South lowland areas of west Tennessee and eastern Arkansas. In general, these sections had led the shift towards the GOP in 1960 (see Map 35) and again in 1964 (see Chart 92). A majority of the Arkansans and Tennesseans who backed Wallace were voters who had backed Democrat John Kennedy in 1960, but

CHART 95

Border Presidential Behavior, 1960-68

State	Democratic Decline, 1960-68	Goldwater Vote Share, 1964	Anti-Democratic Vote, 1968	Wallace Vote, 1968
Arkansas	27%	43%	70%	39%
Tennessee	18	45	72	34
Oklahoma	9	44	69	20
Kentucky	8	36	62	18
Missouri	6	36	56	11
West Virginia	4	32	51	10

most of these—to say nothing of the Republicans who preferred Wallace—would have chosen the GOP candidate in a two-party context.

But the extent of the national Democratic Party's presidential eclipse in Arkansas and Tennessee was more Southern than Border. To the north and west, in Kentucky, Missouri and Oklahoma, 1960-68 Democratic slippage and 1968 Wallace support were much smaller (see Chart 95). In these states, where the 1960-64 Goldwater decline had been considerable, Democratic presidential fidelity was less exclusively based on conservative sectional traditions. Few of the white voters in Tennessee and Arkansas backed Hubert Humphrey, but some 25 per cent to 40 per cent of white Oklahomans, Kentuckians, and Missourians did. Although Humphrey lost all three states, his supporters were predominantly white, and he won pluralities—and a few majorities—in a sizeable number of his party's traditional white rural bastions.

This pattern of fading but by no means extinct white rural Democratic tradition, together with sizeable but not sweeping Wallace support, summed up the behavior of the true Border in 1968. Granted that Democratic support eroded to some extent almost everywhere in Kentucky and Missouri, the only large-scale slippage occurred in the Little Dixie and Mississippi lowland areas of the two states, the sections of peak Wallace penetration. And in Oklahoma, Democratic presidential strength slipped sharply from 1960 levels only in the area around Tulsa. Otherwise, with just a few exceptions, Kentucky, Missouri and Oklahoma voting behavior followed the basic cleavage of 1960. Once again, evolution rather than revolution defined the politics of the Border.

Chart 96 lists the 1960-68 Democratic declines in a cross-section of Border counties. Nixon structured his Kentucky and Missouri victories around GOP strength in the mountain, suburban, Farm Belt and German counties (German Catholics manifested a particularly strong Republican trend from the religion-depleted levels of 1960). Humphrey scored highest in the Negro wards of the stagnating central cities—Louisville, St. Louis and Kansas City—and among rural Negroes, but he also won majorities, albeit somewhat lessened, among the miners of Eastern Kentucky and the white labor unionists of greater St. Louis and Kansas City. From Bluegrass Kentucky to Missouri's Little Dixie, Humphrey captured a respectable minority of the white vote, even though he lost the

CHART 96

The Changing Democratic Position in the Border, 1960-68

	Democratic Share of the Total Vote for President	
County	1960	1968
Missouri Little Dixie		
Monroe, Mo.	73%	59%
Kentucky Bluegrass		
Franklin, Ky.	60	49
Mississippi River Lowlands		
Ashley, Ark.	62	24
Fulton, Ky.	63	31
Mississippi, Mo.	60	43
Suburban		
St. Louis (County), Mo.	51	43
Great Plains		
Alfalfa, Okla.	29	25
German		
Gasconade, Mo.	25	19
Mountain		
Newton, Ark.	31	30
Sevier, Tenn.	15	11
Ozark, Mo.	22	21
Leslie, Ky.	17	23
Yankee		
Putnam, Mo.	28	31
Negro		
Ward 4, St. Louis	83	96

majorities enjoyed by all other post-Civil War Democratic presidential candidates (save Al Smith). In Oklahoma, Nixon swept the cities, suburbs, plains and Ozark foothills, while Humphrey carried only the poor southeastern part of the state, with its large rural Indian and Negro population.

Despite the concentration of George Wallace's Kentucky and

Missouri support in traditionally Democratic sections—the Blue-grass, Missouri's Little Dixie and particularly the Mississippi River lowlands—the Alabaman's vote was amassed principally at the expense of Republican Richard Nixon. Many of the conservative traditional Democrats to whom Wallace appealed had shifted mark-edly towards Nixon in 1960 (see Map 35), and in Kentucky an additional bloc had trended sharply Republican in the 1967 Guber-natorial race. Because of Wallace, however, these traditional Democrats—1960 Nixon supporters and 1967-indicated switchers—were lost to the GOP. For example, Kentucky's McCracken (Paducah) and Daviess (Owensboro) counties had given Richard Nixon a seven hundred vote majority in 1960. In 1968, however, Wallace drew so many of his eleven thousand ballots from prior Nixon adherents that Hubert Humphrey led the GOP nominee by five thousand votes.

As things turned out, Wallace inroads reduced Nixon's 1968 Kentucky majority below 1960 levels, and it would have been lower still except for his recoupment of 1960 religious losses in the German Catholic precincts around Covington, Newport and Louis-ville. Farther west in Missouri, much the same thing occurred. Wallace's appeal to conservative traditional Democrats sidetracked many rural 1960 Nixon backers, and the GOP nominee would have been unable to convert his 10,000-vote statewide deficit of 1960 into a narrow 1968 victory (by a 20,000-vote lead) without a strong pickup among St. Louis-area German Catholics. Specifically, between 1960 and 1968, the Republican standard-bearer turned a 10,000-vote loss in the still quite German area around St. Louis (St. Louis, St. Charles, Osage and Perry Counties) into a 20,000-vote edge. Of course, Nixon's gains in the suburbs of Louisville and St. Louis rested on general suburban as well as German behavior, but rural and urban German movement confirmed the importance of the ethnic factor.

In sum, George Wallace jeopardized rather than facilitated Richard Nixon's success in Kentucky and Missouri. Without Wal-lace, the GOP candidate would have won a much greater victory. Given the prior Republican trend of most Wallace voters, future Republican presidential victories seem assured in a two-party con-test with a northern liberal Democrat. As for Oklahoma, Nixon's handy 1968 triumph should be repeated by GOP presidential can-didates throughout the upcoming cycle.

West Virginia was the only Border state to back Hubert Humphrey. Least favorable to Goldwater in 1964, it gave Wallace his lowest percentage in the Border and produced the region's smallest 1960-68 anti-Democratic trend.* Labor's efforts were a major factor in the Humphrey victory. As indicated in Map 12, most of West Virginia lies within the Black Country of northern Appalachia and behaves in much the same fashion as the steel and coal sections of western Pennsylvania.

North of the Ohio River, the southern sections of Ohio, Indiana and Illinois all backed Richard Nixon, although significant (10 per cent to 20 per cent) support for George Wallace aborted some of the potential Republican majority. As Map 38 shows, balloting for Wallace in the three states principally followed patterns of Southern settlement and kindred conservative Democratic traditions. A few urban Catholic areas—blue-collar sections of Chicago, Cicero, Joliet, Gary, Hammond and Cleveland in particular—also gave the Alabaman substantial percentages. By state, Wallace's top showings came in the Cairo area of Illinois ("Egypt"), the New Albany (onetime Virginia Military Reserve) and Gary sections of Indiana, and the Southern-settled Ohio and Scioto river valleys of the Buckeye State.

Geopolitical patterns have reversed themselves in the half century since the presidential election of 1920. Whereas votes from the river counties and the Cincinnati and Columbus areas once buoyed Democratic victory hopes in Ohio, 1968 Republican majorities in these districts furnished more than the margin of statewide Nixon victory (despite Wallace inroads). And few observers—most are too prone to think of Ohio, Illinois and Indiana as largely Northern, big city states—realize the extent to which the Democratic parties of Indiana and Illinois have been helped by the votes of the Southern-influenced Border country. In 1968, Hubert Humphrey became the first Democratic presidential candidate in history to fail to win a majority of the vote in *any* non-industrial county in all three states, a failure which bodes poorly for future party presidential prospects.

Chart 97 shows how very few of the Southern Pennsylvania Dutch and German Catholic counties that were once Ohio's top

---

*Wallace's minimal vote in some of the poorest counties of West Virginia shatters the notion that low-income, Southern-influenced whites automatically flocked to his standard. On the contrary, he only drew those in the process of forsaking the national Democratic Party.

CHART 97

The Erosion of Democratic Tradition in Rural Ohio, 1863-1968

Ohio's Top 17 Democratic Counties, 1863*	Counties Remaining Among the 17 Best Democratic**				
	1920	1932	1948	1964	1968
German (Substantially Catholic)					
Shelby	X	X	X	X	
Putnam	X	X			
Mercer		X	X	X	X
Wyandot	X	X			
Auglaize		X			
Seneca					
Defiance					
Allen (Lima)					
Pennsylvania Dutch					
Holmes	X	X			
Ashland	X				
Crawford	X	X			
Fairfield	X				
Ohio Valley Southern					
Pike	X	X	X	X	X
Monroe	X	X	X	X	X
Hocking	X	X	X	X	
Butler	X		X		
Franklin (Columbus)					

*Based on the Democratic share of the total vote cast for Governor in 1863; these 17 counties were the only ones to vote for the Democratic nominee.
**Based on the Democratic share of the total vote for President.

Note: Until World War II, the counties giving Ohio Democrats their highest share of the vote were those of German or Southern settlement. In 1940, foreign policy resentments drove many Germans out of the Democratic Party (similar behavior temporarily kept German counties out of the top Ohio Democratic lists in 1920), and the urban, labor and welfare bias of the New Deal era Ohio Democratic Party slowly eroded the fidelity of the Southern-settled rural counties. By 1968, very few of the best Democratic counties of the Civil War period figured among Hubert Humphrey's best.

Democratic strongholds remain so now that the party has switched to a Northeastern and urban orientation. This trend should accelerate as the Ohio Valley Wallace electorate—primarily conservative Democrats shedding obsolescent tradition—shifts to the GOP. The central cities of Great Lakes Illinois and Ohio, instead of strategically thriving on outstate division, are likely to be consistently beaten by increasing outstate solidarity.

From Oklahoma to the Ohio Valley, the Border constitutes a large reach of territory beyond the South, yet reflecting Dixie's re-alignment in its own trends. On its Southern and most heavily Negro fringe—Arkansas and Tennessee—the Border had very few white Democratic presidential voters in 1968, but farther north, an increasing (minority) percentage of whites backed the Democratic nominee. Exactly the opposite was true fifty years ago, when white Democratic fidelity *decreased* as one moved north from the Deep South into the Outer South and Border. The change is a function of the upheaval in Southern politics—and of its (diminishing) outward radiation into adjacent Southern-influenced sections of the nation.

With most 1968 Wallace backers representing a conservative Democratic electorate shifting towards the GOP, and with the Republicans suffering no appreciable slippage among traditional party supporters (except for Negroes), the Border states—with West Virginia as the exception—appear to be taking shape as an important part of the emerging Republican majority.

B. *The Great Lakes*

Not all of the eight states touching the Great Lakes lie wholly within the region's geopolitical orbit. New York and Pennsylvania, for example, are Atlantic-oriented Northeastern states while Minnesota and Wisconsin are basically Farm states. The remaining four states—Michigan, Ohio, Indiana and Illinois—share the essential Great Lakes characteristic of statewide dominance resting in large lakeshore urban and industrial complexes and Northern-settled rural areas. Wisconsin can also be considered with the Great Lakes states, although beyond the Milwaukee area the state is much more akin to the Farm Belt.

Michigan alone lies wholly within the Great Lakes region, epit-omizing trends that sway only sections of Ohio, Illinois and In-diana. Settled from New England, New York and Pennsylvania, the Great Lakes region was overwhelmingly Yankee in the years before the Civil War and Republican thereafter. Michigan was predomi-nantly Yankee and strongly Republican, but until the New Deal modified the traditional politics ingrained by the Civil War, the three lower Great Lakes states were among the principal cockpits of presidential partisan rivalry. Within the three states, the split between the parties was not urban and rural; it was cultural and regional, the opposition of Yankee and Borderer.

No precise line can be drawn through Ohio, Indiana and Illinois to separate Southern-settled areas from those stamped with the Yankee imprint. And the middle-zone concentrations of Pennsyl-vania, New Jersey and Maryland Scotch-Irish and Germans, po-litical in-betweeners, make things even more difficult. Moreover, the occasional hopscotching of settlement produced Yankee and traditionally Republican towns—Athens and Marietta—on the Ohio River, and Virginian-leaning tracts farther north. In Ohio, the preponderance of Southern-populated districts cluster along the Ohio and Scioto rivers, while stereotyped Yankee areas lie in the Northeastern part of the state, especially the Western Reserve, held back by Connecticut when it ceded its lands to the federal government.* The city of Cleveland was also settled by Connecticut men and named for one: Moses Cleaveland. Map 33 illustrates the localities of Yankee settlement.

A more distinct line can be drawn in Illinois and Indiana where

---

*In his book *Lake Erie,* published in 1945, Harlan Hatcher, former dean of Ohio State University, described the pronounced variation in Ohio settlement patterns as follows: "As you travel north across Ohio in the present day from Chillicothe on the Scioto to Painesville on Lake Erie, you feel that you have been trans-ported from Virginia into Connecticut. You leave the Jeffersonian Greco-Roman brick houses with two-story Southern porches along the back wing; you enter a region distinguished by its village greens with graceful white church belfries lifted above the trees, with matching town halls nearby, and green-shuttered white colonial houses spaced neatly around the square. . . . They might have been transplanted without alteration from New England." The northeastern section of Ohio thus settled by Connecticut families was once part of Connecticut, because the original provincial charter granted in 1662 extended Connecticut's boundary to the "Western Sea." After the Revolutionary War, Connecticut ceded most of the state's western lands to the federal government, but kept a "Western Reserve" for emigrants and war veterans. Of course, by the time Ohio became a state in 1803, Connecticut no longer exercised jurisdiction over her onetime reservelands.

the Old National Road (U.S. 40) more or less separates the Yankees from the Borderers, although in both states, the Southern farmers spread somewhat farther north along a few river valleys—the Wabash, Whitewater and Illinois. North of the road, the two states were largely filled up by Northerners and immigrants from Europe, and their politics carried the day.

In the years immediately before the Civil War, the Yankee Great Lakes were second only to New England in their opposition to slavery and Southern culture and in their support of the fledgling Republican Party (founded in 1854 in the New England-settled town of Ripon, Wisconsin). Yankee Ohio nurtured John Brown of Harper's Ferry fame and Michigan disputed Wisconsin's claim to birthing the anti-slavery Republican Party. When it came to the actual fratricide of 1861-65, the Great Lakes were in the front lines. The Michigan (Custer's), Wisconsin and Illinois cavalry were the best in the North, and Great Lakes infantry were often in the van of battle. Pursuing these loyalties, the Great Lakes were bellicosely Republican after the war.

In the years between the Civil War and 1896, Ohio, Indiana and Illinois usually determined which party would occupy the White House. To capture the crucial electoral votes of Ohio, the largest of the three, the Republicans nominated and elected *six* Ohioans to the presidency between 1876 and 1920. Hayes, Garfield, McKinley, Harrison, Taft and Harding all bear witness to Ohio's pivotal position. Between 1868 and 1924, an era during which only two Democrats occupied the presidency, non-Ohio Republicans became President (Arthur, Roosevelt and Coolidge) only through the death of Ohioans! Critics often made reference to an Ohio dynasty paralleling the Virginia dynasty of early Presidents. No presidential election between 1876 and 1892 saw the winner garner a popular vote majority, and this near-stalemate—rooted in Civil War loyalties and the return of the South to the Democratic column after Reconstruction—was invariably resolved in the Ohio Valley, where Yankee Republicans and Butternut Democrats were locked in tight struggles for Ohio, Indiana and Illinois electoral votes. The outcome in Ohio and Indiana was frequently very close; an extraordinary and closely matched number of people were set in Civil War ruts.

Rural conflict in the three-state area was not wholly Anglo-Saxon. German Protestants were much less Republican than the Yankees,

MAP 37

Illinois in the Election of 1860

☐ Counties Giving Lincoln a Majority

■ Counties Casting a Majority Against Lincoln

while German Catholics were even more prone to be Democrats.*
In slave states like Missouri and Kentucky, Germans had often taken
a pro-Union and Republican stance during the Civil War, opposing
the Southern inclinations of the local Anglo-Saxon gentry; but in
Yankee-run upper Mississippi Valley states, the Germans—Catholics in particular—had aligned with the Democrats. (Those in Ken-
tucky-windowing Cincinnati were a major exception.) The reason
is not obscure. Just as the Border German settlers knew themselves to be disliked by the local Anglo-Saxon upper classes, the
German Catholics in Northern states were well aware of—and

*Protestant as well as Catholic Germans constituted a large wing of the Ohio
Democratic Party. A half dozen counties in north central Ohio were settled by
Pennsylvania Dutch (Germans). Like kindred Pennsylvania counties, these
areas opposed Civil War conscription, and from the Civil War through the New
Deal they normally supported Democratic presidential candidates.

reciprocated—the dislike of Yankee elements. And quite naturally, these German suspicions carried over to the Yankee political party—the Republican Party. Moreover, the Republican Party made little attempt to disguise its own sentiments. Many of the foremost Great Lakes leaders of the young movement, such as Schuyler Colfax, Shelby Cullom, Salmon P. Chase and Henry Wilson, were former members of the anti-Catholic "Know-Nothing" Party. Secondly, the Republican Party was heavily larded with Congregationalist clergymen, a New England denomination anathema to Butternut Baptists and German Catholics alike. Thirdly, Republican newspapers, politicians and clergy lost no opportunity to insult German and Irish Catholics. Fourthly, the German and Irish Catholic *proletariat,* for such they mostly were, despised and feared Negroes as job competitors, and thus bridled at Yankee abolitionist fervor. Lastly, the Yankee Republicans sought to use the German Catholics as cannon fodder, imposing unfair draft quotas on certain counties.* Small wonder that the German Catholics of the North supported the Democratic Party in the years after the Civil War. Until the foreign policy strains of European wars dislocated party loyalties, the German Catholic counties of Ohio, Indiana and Illinois contributed essential votes to the occasional statewide Democratic majorities.** And Wisconsin's one Democratic presidential majority between the Civil War and 1932—Grover Cleveland's second-term triumph of 1892—was locally based, like usual statewide party showings, in large-scale German support.

Apart from ethnic behavior, political partisanship in Ohio, In-

---

*In Wisconsin, counties not providing sufficient volunteers were given draft quotas by state authorities. The delinquent counties were, by and large, peopled by immigrants from Bavaria, Saxony, Prussia, the Rhineland and Belgium, many of them refugees from European militarism and conscription and almost all of them disinterested in the war between North and South. Ozaukee and Washington counties, both German, were given larger quotas than bigger Anglo-Saxon counties, and they responded with rioting. The homes of several Yankee politicians were sacked and the Democrats reaped considerable political profit.

**Ohio's German Catholic concentrations group together in the Cincinnati area, which is Republican by tradition, and in the northwestern part of the state (Putnam, Mercer, Auglaize, Shelby and Seneca counties), where pre-New Deal tradition was Democratic. The principal German Catholic concentration in Indiana centers on Dubois County in the southwest, also spreading into Perry and Spencer counties. Local tradition is Democratic. Illinois' German Catholics, those outside Chicago, are most numerous in the area around East St. Louis (Calhoun, Jersey, Madison, St. Clair, Clinton, Washington, Perry, Randolph and Monroe counties, where tradition is likewise Democratic). A second concentration occurs in the Kankakee-Peoria section. See Map 31.

diana and Illinois, from the Civil War to the New Deal, essentially pivoted on the Northern or Southern origins of the local population. These origins—and the Civil War attitudes they nurtured—were the underlying granite of partisanship. The regional opposition of the Great Lakes and Ohio Valley was less than absolute because settlement patterns blurred and overlapped. The noted political analyst V. O. Key has conclusively demonstrated the force of Civil War memories and Yankee or Southern ancestry in later Indiana voting.* In Michigan and Wisconsin the picture was quite clear: the Anglo-Saxon population, being Yankee, was staunchly Republican.

In the years between the Civil War and 1896, the Great Lakes underwent a considerable boom, increasing the population of northern Ohio, Indiana and Illinois relative to the earlier-settled Ohio Valley portions of these states. Some of the new arrivals were Germans, who gravitated towards existing German-American concentrations. Many other new arrivals were also of immigrant stock— Czechs, Irish, Poles, Italians, Finns, Swedes. The majority of these immigrants flocked into the principal Great Lakes cities and into the mining and timber counties of northern Michigan and Wisconsin. The Irish and Germans were inclined to be Democrats. Scandinavian and Anglo-Saxon immigrants usually preferred the Republican Party.

Then in 1896, William Jennings Bryan steered the Democrats into a socio-political posture which changed the balance of power in the Great Lakes.** Not only did Bryan mildly erode Democratic strength in the Ohio Valley sections of Ohio, Indiana, and Illinois, but he buoyed the GOP hegemony in the growing Great Lakes areas to a point where it much more readily dominated the Ohio Valley. Bryan's evangelistic Protestantism disturbed Catholic Democrats, rural Germans and urban workers alike, and his agrarian

---

*"If one plots on the map of Indiana clusters of underground railroad stations and points at which Union authorities had difficulties in drafting troops, he separates, on the whole, Republican and Democratic counties." V. O. Key, Jr., and Frank Munger, "Social Determinism and Electoral Decision: The Case of Indiana," in Burdick and Brodbeck, Eds., *American Voting Behavior* (Glencoe, Illinois), 1959, pp. 281-99.

**The presidential impetus of William Jennings Bryan, which proved so unpopular in the East and Great Lakes, was principally rooted in the Great Plains and Rocky Mountains, and is analyzed in the ensuing subchapters on those regions of the Heartland.

radicalism unnerved Democratic conservatives. Some German Catholic townships voted Republican for the first time since the Civil War. Perhaps more to the point, urban workers feared the economic consequences of Bryanism, especially because quite a few Republican employers had told their men that Bryan's election would mean no more jobs. McKinley's "full dinner pail" carried the day, and sufficient political re-alignment followed, abetted by increasing prosperity, so that Ohio, Indiana and Illinois (and also Wisconsin and Michigan) were normally Republican until the New Deal. Part of this domination rested in cities run by oligarchy-financed GOP machines, able to fasten Catholic immigrant workers into economic and political harness. Chart 98, presenting the Michigan presidential vote between the Civil War and New Deal, proves that the real era of Republican supremacy began in 1896.

By no means all of the Republican urban machines were Establishmentarian; some maintained their appeal with a populism as potent as Tammany's. The municipal fortunes of Roaring Twenties Chicago, for example, lay in the hands of Republican Mayor William Hale "Big Bill" Thompson, who frenzied and enthused local Irish and Germans by promising to hang Britain's King George V if that worthy ever came to the Windy City. A few statistics will convey the importance of the "ethnic" vote: in 1910, 79 per cent of Milwaukee's population was of foreign stock (foreign born or American-born with at least one foreign born parent); 79 per cent of Chicago's; 76 per cent of Cleveland's; and 75 per cent of Detroit's.

CHART 98

Michigan Presidential Voting, 1872-1936

REPUBLICAN SHARE OF THE TWO-PARTY VOTE

1872	1876	1880	1884	1888	1892	1896	1900	1904
64%	54%	58%	56%	53%	52%	55%	60%	72%

1908	1912*	1916	1920	1924**	1928	1932	1936
65%	71%	54%	77%	77%	71%	46%	41%

*Republican-Bull Moose Share of the Three-Party Vote
**Republican Share of the Three-Party (Rep.-Dem.-Prog.) Vote

The scions of the original Yankees still held behind-the-scenes power, but they were vastly outnumbered at the polls.

As late as 1920 and 1924, Republican presidential support in the major Great Lakes cities was substantially greater than in rural areas of Indiana, Ohio and Illinois (see Chart 100). These machine-forged urban majorities safeguarded Republican statewide victories against Ohio Valley Democrats; meanwhile, the cities were growing apace. Obviously, Republican primacy rested on sociological quicksand: the still-Yankee countryside was losing relative power to the immigrant cities. So long as the Democrats ran conservative presidential candidates like those of 1920 and 1924, they could appeal to the Ohio Valley but not to the cities. However, the 1928 Democratic decision to bid for the urban immigrant vote foreshadowed a new chapter in Great Lakes politics.

Al Smith did not carry the Great Lakes states in 1928; as a matter of fact, he ran far behind the Democratic percentages of 1876-92. What he *did* do was set the scene for the breakdown of urban immigrant loyalties to Great Lakes GOP machines. By embracing the urban, immigrant upheaval, the Democrats were giving the foreign-stock, usually-Catholic city dweller a party with which he could identify. Neither the oligarchic Republican Party nor the Southern, Bryanesquely Protestant, Democratic Party had filled the bill. Most of the big city Catholic wards voted for Smith in 1928, even while he was crushed in Appalachian Protestant cities like Flint, Toledo and Akron,* but far bigger Democratic gains were just over the horizon. In 1929, the Great Depression upset the McKinley "full dinner pail," mocked Hoover's "two chickens in every pot" and sent the Grand Old Party reeling into a tailspin.

Still, urban Great Lakes Republican loyalties did not break down all at once. Franklin D. Roosevelt captured all of the Great Lakes states and most of the major cities in 1932, but the GOP continued to fare at least as well in the cities as in the countryside. As it had in the past, rural Ohio split along traditional lines; the Yankee counties were the only ones to give Hoover a majority, just as the Southern-settled counties had been the only ones to give the Democratic presidential nominee 40 per cent or more of the vote

---

*Since the early days of the Twentieth Century, the employment opportunities of heavy industrial cities like Detroit, Flint, Toledo and Akron have lured enough families from the poor hills of Kentucky and West Virginia to give these cities a rather large "hillbilly" element.

CHART 99

The Decline and Fall of the Republican Party in the Urban Great Lakes, 1920-36

State and County	Republican Percentage of the Total Vote for President				
	1920	1924[1]	1928[2]	1932	1936
Illinois	*68%*	*59%*	*57%*	*42%*	*40%*
Cook (Chicago)	71	62	53	42	35
Winnebago (Rockford)	79	71	80	57	46
Indiana	*55*	*55*	*60*	*43*	*42*
Lake (Gary-Hammond)	69	65	60	47	33
St. Joseph (South Bend)	57	58	58	41	37
Ohio	*59*	*58*	*65*	*47*	*37*
Cuyahoga (Cleveland)	64	49	53	45	27
Lucas (Toledo)	59	54	63	41	35
Mahoning (Youngstown)	64	68	64	52	27
Stark (Canton-Massillon)	63	64	71	51	36
Michigan	*72*	*75*	*70*	*44*	*39*
Genesee (Flint)	75	84	79	42	29
Wayne (Detroit)	75	80	62	39	31

1. Sizeable vote cast for LaFollette. The maximum was 42 per cent in Cuyahoga County; the minimum was 6 per cent in Genesee County.
2. Against Al Smith, the GOP vote fell in Catholic cities but held firm or rose in hillbilly towns (Akron, Flint and Toledo) and Scandinavian-German Protestant Rockford.

in the emphatically Republican year of 1924.* And through 1932 at least, some GOP city machines continued to function because if the Republicans had failed, the Democrats had not yet proven themselves. Several Ohio cities voted for Hoover.**

Once the Democrats were in office, however, the urban-welfare-

---

*The counties Hoover carried in 1932, with but a few exceptions, lay in the old Western Reserve, Ohio Company grants, the Miami Valley and immediately adjacent areas—all Yankee-settled. Back in 1924, Democrat Davis scored over 40 per cent of the vote only in the Virginian and German counties, again with few exceptions. The political overlay on a settlement map (Maps 30 and 31) is striking.

**Canton, Youngstown and Columbus.

labor bias of the New Deal gave the Great Lakes cities a positive as well as a negative reason for changing their allegiance and Roosevelt's vote soared in 1936. Ohio's industrial Mahoning County, only 44 per cent for Roosevelt in 1932, gave the President 71 per cent support in 1936. Although anti-New Deal bias caused Roosevelt to drop below his 1932 levels in many Great Lakes rural counties, urban gains far outweighed these losses and the Democratic presidential percentage rose in each state between 1932 and 1936. Nevertheless, the Republicanism of the Great Lakes region was second only to that of the Northeast in both elections, and GOP slippage in the two regions reflected the same urban Democratic trend (sharpest in the Great Lakes because many of the Northeastern cities were already Democratic during the Nineteen-Twenties).

The 1932-36 rural drift back to the GOP accelerated in 1940. Not only was the New Deal unappreciated in the countryside, but the substantial German population of the Great Lakes resented Franklin D. Roosevelt's seeming ambitions to enter the United States in the struggle against Hitler's Germany. This behavior had been hinted at in 1936, when some of the leading German American counties in Ohio and Wisconsin cast 10 per cent to 20 per cent of their vote for William Lemke, the isolationist presidential candidate of the short-lived Union Party. Thirty German Catholic precincts in Wisconsin and Ohio actually cast a plurality of their vote for Lemke; four years later, they voted three-to-one Republican, although they had been three-to-one Democratic in 1932! The sharpest 1936-40 GOP presidential gains in the Great Lakes came in German Catholic counties like Ozaukee and Calumet in Wisconsin, Putnam and Mercer in Ohio, Huron in Michigan and Clinton in Illinois. As in 1920, foreign policy unhappiness gave the Republicans abnormal strength in traditionally Democratic rural German Catholic counties.

With this level of German strength, and with rural Yankee support pretty much back to pre-Roosevelt levels, the Republicans would have swept the Great Lakes had they been able even to approach the level of support which they had enjoyed in Great Lakes urban areas during the Nineteen-Twenties. But that backing was long gone; a new *détente* had developed between the countryside and the cities, and the 1940 presidential race in each Great Lakes state was extremely close. Nor were the Great Lakes states marginal in the way they had been between 1872 and 1896; rural divisions were no longer the key. Chart 100 presents a cross-sectional view of Republican strength in 1940 as opposed to the GOP victory year of 1924. The party was almost as strong in Yankee rural bailiwicks, somewhat stronger in rural Ohio Valley counties, much more powerful in rural German Catholic counties, but greatly weakened in urban and industrial centers.

CHART 100

The Changing Loyalties of Great Lakes Presidential Politics, 1924-40

County	Republican Percentage of the Total Vote for President	
	1924	1940
Major Great Lakes Urban Counties		
Cook, Illinois	62%	44%
Lake, Indiana	65	39
Wayne, Michigan	80	38
Cuyahoga, Ohio	49	38
Great Lakes Mining and Industrial Counties		
Gogebic, Michigan	67	41
Summit, Ohio	65	42
Great Lakes Yankee Rural Counties		
Ford, Illinois	71	65
Jasper, Indiana	64	62
Geauga, Ohio	72	62
Barry, Michigan	71	69
Great Lakes German Counties		
Clinton, Illinois	30	62
Putnam, Ohio	42	71
Ohio Valley Rural Counties*		
Holmes, Ohio	38	49
Brown, Indiana	37	47
Gallatin, Illinois	39	44

*1924 banner traditional Democratic counties of Ohio, Indiana and Illinois

After the first eight years of the New Deal, an urban-rural cleavage was replacing the regionalism which had hitherto distinguished the parties, although the process was by no means complete. As the cities became solidly Democratic and exercised an increasing influence on party policy, rural Democratic traditions slackened. In states where GOP urban majorities had bulked large in the landslides of the Nineteen-Twenties, cigar-chomping politicos learned to do as their Eastern colleagues had done for years; to judge early in the evening whether or not the Democratic big city lead was sufficient to overcome the downstate, outstate or upstate votes.

Chart 101 shows how a few percentage points meant victory or defeat in each Great Lakes state in the elections of 1940, 1944 and 1948. In Wisconsin, the Democratic margin of victory came from Milwaukee; in Michigan, from Detroit; in Ohio, Cleveland; and in Illinois, Chicago. The big city vote was not so dominant in Indiana, but the steel towns of Gary, Hammond and South Bend provided crucial Democratic majorities.

CHART 101

Republican Percentage of the Two-Party Vote for President in the Great Lakes, 1940-48

	1940	1944	1948
Indiana	51%	53%	50%
Michigan	50	50	51
Ohio	48	50	50
Illinois	49	48	50
Wisconsin	49	50	48

Except in Cleveland, where Democratic machines had long prevailed, strong big city Democratic organizations grew up in the Great Lakes during the Nineteen-Thirties to wield their party's growing urban power. One of the least savory was Chicago's Kelly-Nash machine. In 1940, the Democrats held their national convention in Chicago, and the "spontaneous" chant for Roosevelt's precedent-shattering third-term nomination began in the catacombs below the convention hall with a microphone in the hands of the

Kelly-Nash sewers commissioner. (Two decades later, rumor had it that Illinois' electoral votes were won for John F. Kennedy only by the ballot box irregularities of Mayor Daley's Chicago machine.) Not many metropolitan areas can match the machine traditions of Chicago and neighboring Lake County (Gary-Hammond), Indiana; moreover, the Chicago machine has been a major force in Democratic national politics since the Nineteen-Thirties.

Harry Truman's Great Lakes urban pluralities slid below Roosevelt's in 1948, and the Missourian would have lost but for his improved showing in the countryside. The Democrats made considerable strides in German counties, where anti-Roosevelt Democrats returned to their party or lost interest in voting. Farm unrest was also a factor. In the face of a light turnout, Thomas E. Dewey lost three Midwestern states with large German populations—Ohio, Wisconsin and Iowa—which he had carried in 1944. Despite these vagaries, the basic New Deal pattern remained fixed: Democratic cities against GOP suburbs and countryside.

The virtual stalemate of 1940-48 collapsed in 1952 with Eisenhower's landslide victory. In tandem with a 15 per cent gain over Dewey in Farm Belt-trending Wisconsin, the popular General exceeded the New York governor's vote by 6 per cent to 8 per cent in Indiana, Ohio, Illinois and Michigan. Eisenhower's largest gains came in Catholic areas, urban and rural, where anti-communism and resentment of the Korean War were the leading issues.* Nevertheless, the underlying urban-rural division persisted. Stevenson carried the cities of Chicago, Detroit, Gary, Cleveland and Milwaukee with ease, while he lost most of the traditionally Democratic rural counties.

But Eisenhower's strength among the young Irish, Italian and Polish suburbanites was still meaningful. Just as the urban growth of the Nineteen-Twenties had been readying the demise of the GOP quite unknown to party leaders, the demographic trends emerging after the Second World War likewise hinted at the cycle to follow the New Deal: a middle-class era rooted in suburbia. In 1946 and thereafter, young Great Lakes city-dwellers began moving out to

*By far, the biggest Republican gains between 1948 and 1952 came in the German counties where the Korean War and the Democrats' "soft on communism" image nurtured foreign policy sensitivities. In Ohio, the sharpest GOP increase occurred in Putnam County, the leading German Catholic county; likewise Dubois County, Indiana's top German Catholic county, registered the most emphatic GOP gain in that state.

the suburbs, and as a result, the percentage of the Great Lakes vote cast by Chicago, Cleveland, Gary, Detroit and Milwaukee began to slide. As it grew, the new influx of city Democrats diluted suburban Republicanism, although popular GOP candidates like Eisenhower rode the suburban boom to huge majorities. However, the Democratic strength among this prospering lower-middle class was as precarious a support base as the proletarian urban Republicanism of the Nineteen-Twenties. Even as Great Lakes white populations were moving to the suburbs, large numbers of Southern Negroes were leaving Black Belt cabins for city tenements, setting in motion a new ethnic division in regional politics. Chart 102 shows the 1910-70 pattern of Negro population growth in the major Great Lakes cities.

Open Negro-white conflict, being still years away, was not the source of Eisenhower's large 1956 urban Great Lakes gains. When

CHART 102

The Negro Population Growth in the
  Urban Heartland, 1910-70

	Negro Percentage of Total Population			
City	1910	1940	1960	1970 (Est.)
Border				
St. Louis	7%	13%	29%	46%
Indianapolis	9	13	21	29
Cincinnati	6	12	22	31
Louisville	18	15	18	24
Great Lakes				
Detroit	1	9	29	47
Cleveland	2	10	29	40
Buffalo	1	3	13	22
Chicago	2	8	23	33
Toledo	1	5	13	23
Milwaukee	2	2	9	18
Farm Belt				
St. Paul	1	1	3	4
Minneapolis	1	1	2	5
Omaha	2	5	8	12

CHART 103

Republican Share of the Two-Party Vote for
President in Chicago, 1948-56

Ward	1948	1952	1956
Irish			
14th	22%	29%	39%
Italian			
1st	19	26	30
23rd	28	36	47
German			
43rd	44	51	56
Polish			
32nd	23	33	45
Jewish			
5th	48	43	41
50th	63	56	48

the ex-General first captured the White House in 1952, the bulk of his vote had come from the countryside and middle-class or silk-stocking urban and suburban areas, but by 1956, the success of his administration assuaged workers' fears—continually whetted by Democratic campaign oratory—that a Republican President meant hard times. As a result, the President made heavy gains in Irish, Italian, German and Polish low-income precincts, paralleling his strides in similar Northeastern districts.* With their economic fears muted, these voters felt free to respond to the foreign policy (staunch anti-communism) and social conservatism they found appealing in the GOP. Chart 103 shows the 1948-56 GOP upsurge in some of Chicago's principal ethnic wards.

As a result of his much-increased Catholic support, Eisenhower swept the Great Lakes in 1956, winning 56 per cent to 62 per cent of the vote in the five states. Four years later, this transient Republican strength dissipated in the face of Richard Nixon's lesser appeal

*As in the Northeast, Eisenhower lagged behind Dewey among Jews but ran far ahead among Catholics. The trends of the two groups are usually opposite.

and John F. Kennedy's drawing power among his co-religionists. Nixon dropped 20 per cent to 25 per cent below Eisenhower's 1956 levels in Irish, Italian and Polish urban Great Lakes precincts. Outside of the Catholic cities and the few German Catholic rural counties, Nixon did well; in some places he profited from Protestant religious opposition to the Kennedy candidacy.* Nixon carried Ohio and Indiana, where the rural Protestant vote was strongest, and Wisconsin, where rural German Catholics, despite a sharp Democratic trend, remained considerably more Republican than the Irish, Italian and Polish Catholics of the cities. John Kennedy won Michigan and Illinois, the two states with the largest urban Catholic vote. The Illinois victory was extremely narrow—eight thousand votes out of four million—and many observers suspected vote fraud on the part of the Chicago Democratic machine.

Despite Nixon's poor vote in the Catholic cities, the 1960 election was closely fought in the Great Lakes because of the continued high levels of Republican support—only minimally inflated by religion—in the rural areas and suburbs. Generally, the 1960 election reiterated the polarizations of 1940-48. Consider Illinois: Nixon won handily outside of Chicago, but he got only 36 per cent of the vote in that metropolis. Held to such a percentage, Nixon lost Mayor Daley's fiefdom by 456,000 votes. His strong showing in the suburbs and countryside did not quite overcome this deficit and he lost by eight thousand votes statewide.

After Kennedy took office and the Negro socioeconomic revolution gained numerical and political momentum in the urban Great Lakes, some observers began to prognosticate a weakening of Democratic urban loyalties. Notwithstanding the trauma of Ken-

---

*There are some two dozen rural counties in Ohio, Indiana and Illinois, mostly Southern-settled and Methodist or Baptist, where Nixon ran slightly ahead of Eisenhower's 1956 levels. At the same time, religion helped John F. Kennedy in the Catholic strongholds. Augmenting the urban Irish, Italian and Polish swing, Kennedy profited from large gains in the rural German Catholic counties. In Ohio, Indiana and Illinois, Kennedy's best gains came in rural counties—the leading German Catholic county in each state showed the greatest Kennedy trend! The GOP vote dropped from 57 per cent to 38 per cent in Dubois County, Indiana; from 64 per cent to 48 per cent in Clinton County, Illinois; and in Mercer and Putnam counties, Ohio, from 69 per cent and 70 per cent to 50 per cent and 53 per cent. On the more homogeneous township level, Crouch Township, Illinois' First Precinct (almost wholly German Catholic), gave Nixon only 38 per cent of the vote where Eisenhower had won 70 per cent (Howard W. Allen, *Isolationism and German-Americans,* Illinois State Historical Society Journal, Summer, 1964, pp. 143-49). Not only was pro-Catholicism the strongest trend, it probably exceeded anti-Catholicism in voting effect.

nedy's assassination, enough resentment had built up by the spring of 1964 that Alabama Governor George C. Wallace was able to stun local politicians with his protest vote against Wisconsin Governor John Reynolds and Indiana Governor Matthew Welsh, stand-ins for President Johnson in the 1964 Democratic presidential primaries. Wallace won 34 per cent of the Wisconsin vote and 30 per cent of the Indiana vote, carrying Lake County, Indiana, by dint of huge majorities in the white working-class wards of Gary, Hammond and East Chicago. In Wisconsin, Wallace amassed his best ratios in the Polish and Slavic working-class wards of greater Milwaukee.* But as things turned out, this obvious backlash did not carry through into the November elections—or at least not on a large scale.

The 1964 Republican nominee, Senator Barry Goldwater, was largely unable to harness discontent with the national Democratic administration. His farm economics discouraged some farmers, his civil rights position was unpopular with the Yankee Establishment (at least in Ohio and Michigan) and with Negroes, his foreign policy and Vietnamese hawkishness trespassed on Midwestern isolationism and his economic and labor policies were ill-received in working-class neighborhoods. The conservative Arizonian lost all of the Great Lakes states. His largest losses came in the Yankee rural areas of Michigan and northeastern Ohio. Contrary to general public belief, he was not the victim of an urban trend: in most Great Lakes cities, Barry Goldwater ran *stronger* in white urban precincts than Richard Nixon had four years earlier. The 1960 *détente* was revoked, not by GOP failure to make urban gains, but by the disaffection of traditional rural and suburban Republicans, especially the Yankee cousins of the party-bolting voters of New England. As in New England, Goldwater dipped well below 1936 levels in the leading Yankee counties. Chart 104 lists the 1960-64 GOP decline by states and then breaks it down into component voting streams.

Barry Goldwater's defeat was not shaped by white working-class and lower-middle-class urban voters of the Great Lakes, but by the Establishment and its traditional rural outliers. Only in Michigan

---

*The intensity of Polish backlash is doubtless explained by the fact that the Poles are the poorest of the Great Lakes Catholic ethnic groups, and thus also feel most threatened by Negroes. Inasmuch as the Poles normally were the most Democratic of Catholic ethnic groups, their disaffection posed a severe threat.

CHART 104

The 1960-64 Republican Decline in the Great Lakes by States and Voting Groups

Michigan

Rural Yankee County— Osceola	−27%
Silk-Stocking Detroit (Wayne County) Suburbs	−20%
Michigan (Statewide)	−16%
Wayne County (Detroit and Suburbs)	−10%
Working-Class Detroit Catholic Precincts*	−5 to +5%

Indiana

Rural Yankee County— LaGrange	−20%
Indiana (Statewide)	−11%
Lake County (Gary)	−2%
Working-Class Gary Catholic Precincts*	0 to +10%

Change in Republican Share of the Total Vote for President, 1960-64

State	Republican Share of the Total Presidential Vote	
	1960	1964
Indiana	55%	44%
Ohio	53	37
Wisconsin	52	38
Illinois	50	41
Michigan	49	33

*Typical overwhelmingly white precincts

and Ohio, the two states with traditional rural Yankee Republicanism most akin to that of the Northeast, did Goldwater fall below Alf Landon's 1936 levels. In Illinois, Indiana and Wisconsin, the Republican slippage was less severe and the Arizona Senator ran ahead of Landon's percentages. The establishmentarian suburbs of Cleveland and Detroit produced a Republican decline comparable to that in suburban Boston or the Philadelphia Main Line;

but the suburbs of Chicago—seat of the vituperatively anti-Estab-lishment *Chicago Tribune*—turned in a mere 5 per cent loss com-pared with Nixon's 1960 showing. Great Lakes voting behavior in 1964 was not the electorate-wide anti-Goldwater trend it seemed.

Just as the outlines of a new Democratic Party were discernible even in the rubble of Al Smith's 1928 defeat, the 1964 election returns in the Great Lakes suggested a changing GOP. A lesser percentage of the party presidential vote was being drawn from longtime Yankee and silk-stocking bailiwicks, and Ohio Valley German and urban lower-middle-class votes were assuming steadily increased importance. The best two Goldwater states of 1964 were those—Illinois and Indiana—thrusting farthest south.

Quite a comeback awaited the Great Lakes GOP in 1966. Aided by the national reaction against the war in Vietnam, racial violence and the welfarism of the Great Society, the party won all of the gubernatorial races—Wisconsin, Ohio and Michigan—and cap-tured a number of new congressional seats. As a matter of fact, two years after the defeat of Barry Goldwater, the Republican share of the vote for Congress in all five Great Lakes states touched levels unmatched since the Eisenhower sweep of 1956.

But despite these GOP victories, the emerging intra-regional cleavage persisted. Of all the Great Lakes states, Michigan, where the anti-Goldwater trend had been most severe, cast the lowest 1966 Republican share of the congressional vote. Two suburban Detroit districts were the only Great Lakes bedroom areas to elect Demo-cratic congressmen in 1966. And most of the Republican congress-men newly elected in Michigan were liberals. Amidst the re-align-ment of the mid-Nineteen-Sixties, Michigan's Northeastern leanings worked against the national Republican Party they had long suc-cored.

Some of the new Republican success in that state lay in the changing loyalties of the white urban vote. For example, although the Republicans were unable to win any Chicago congressional seats, they appear to have won a majority of the city's white vote, while Negro votes—almost one third of the population—rescued Democratic candidates. Illinois Senator Charles Percy rode white votes to statewide victory; he captured only 19.6 per cent of the total turnout in Negro Boss William Dawson's First Congressional District (black South Chicago). Inasmuch as there is a small white minority in the district, Percy probably won only 15 per cent or so of the Negro vote. On the other hand, he swept Southern-leaning lower Illinois and piled up a majority of the white vote in all save one Chicago congressional district. The same thing happened in Michigan, where Republican Governor George Romney handily won a third term of office, but was badly beaten in Negro neighborhoods. He amassed his large majority in the countryside and white urban and suburban districts. According to the statistics of Michigan precinct voting, Romney won only 18 per cent of the Negro vote. Very like Percy. Beyond any doubt, the Republican tide of 1966 was white and Catholic, not Negro.*

Many of the "backlash" districts where Senator Goldwater had fared reasonably well in 1964, relative to other GOP candidates, were among those sections manifesting the best Republican gains in 1966. During the Nineteen-Fifties, these same districts produced heavy Republican gains which helped build Eisenhower's two landslides. This is logical enough, because the same sociological factors which produced "McCarthyism" and isolationism in the early Nineteen-Fifties—the status apprehensions of the insecure new middle classes—were engendering an antagonism towards a government philosophy of assistance to Negroes which was not extended to white immigrant groups. At any rate, there is a pronounced correlation between rising Eisenhower support during the Nineteen-Fifties and 1966 "backlash" urban Republicanism in Great Lakes white urban districts.

In the summer of 1967, the Great Lakes burst into flame with a series of race riots. Detroit had the worst riot—for days, troops patrolled fire-lit streets under sniper fire—even though many local Negroes held high-paying jobs under United Auto Workers auspices and the city has been a testing ground for liberal urban and social

---

*As moderate-to-liberal Republicans, Romney and (especially) Percy are embarrassed that the statistics of their 1966 victories show little Negro support. Local Democrats, however, are more forthright. An aide to former Senator Paul Douglas, defeated by Percy, described the backlash nature of Percy's victory in a 1967 *Reporter* article. And the candidate George Romney defeated, Michigan State Democratic Chairman Zoltan Ferency, published a devastating analysis of Romney's negligible Negro vote in May, 1967. Ferency's statistics show that Romney won only 18 per cent of the vote in the 75 leading Negro precincts in the cities of Detroit, Highland Park, Hamtramck, River Rouge, Inkster, Ecorse, Saginaw, Muskegon Heights, Flint, Royal Oak, Monroe and Benton Heights. As for Percy, he won only 19 per cent of the vote in the overwhelmingly Negro First Congressional District of Chicago, but 51 per cent to 69 per cent in the Chicago-area arch-backlash districts of Representatives Pucinski, Derwinski and Kluczinski (the Polish GOP trend was the strongest in Illinois).

programs. Scores of other Great Lakes cities experienced lesser disturbances. Milwaukee writhed in a racial cold war as Negroes, led by a militant priest, Father James Groppi, paraded through jeering Polish neighborhoods in demonstrations for open housing.*

The long, hot summer of 1967 also heated up the white backlash, and on the heels of this turmoil, the large Negro populations of Gary and Cleveland enabled black challengers to defeat white Democratic-machine candidates in the two cities' mayoralty primaries. The racial polarization of primary voting spilled over into the general election. Local white Democratic machines, well aware that Negro domination of the party machinery would drive Italian, Irish, Polish and Appalachian whites into the arms of the GOP, all but openly opposed the two Negro candidacies. However, Cleveland's 40 per cent Negro population and Gary's Negro majority bloc-voted for candidates Stokes and Hatcher, who thus won razor-thin victories. The Negro vote went 97 per cent to 99 per cent Democratic and the white vote went overwhelmingly Republican—about 82 per cent in Cleveland and about 90 per cent in Gary—even though white voters were five-to-one Democratic in registration. Chart 105 illustrates the racial polarization of Cleveland voting.

Such as it was, the white vote won by Carl Stokes in Cleveland came substantially from silk-stocking neighborhoods, and many Stokes campaign workers were liberal housewives from rich suburbs like Shaker Heights.** Further evidence of the liberal trend guiding Cleveland's Yankee Establishment was simultaneously occurring in the voting patterns of the Republican congressmen from the one-time Western Reserve, and in the growing support among monied Clevelanders of the 1968 presidential quest of Nelson Rockefeller.*** A comparable trend was at work in Michigan. As the Yankee Northeast moved, so moved Michigan and northeastern Ohio.

*The Negrophobia of Polish Milwaukee was notable. The Sixteenth Street Bridge between the mutually aroused white and black neighborhoods was sometimes called "the longest bridge in the world because it separates Africa and Poland."

**Gary Negro candidate Richard Hatcher had no rich Yankee suburbs to turn to in Lake County, Indiana. However, he received considerable upper-class support and financial backing from the Northeast. Several fashionable soirees were held in Manhattan penthouses to raise money for his campaign.

***During the 89th Congress, the four GOP representatives from Cleveland's suburbs and the rural counties of the Western Reserve—Reps. Bolton, Minshall, Stanton and Mosher—rarely supported any Great Society social programs; they did so frequently by 1968. The old Western Reserve—and Cleveland's Yankee Establishment—provided the backbone of Nelson Rockefeller's Ohio support.

CHART 105

Black and White Bloc Voting in the
1967 Cleveland Mayoralty Election

White Wards	% Negro Population	% Two-Party Vote Cast for Taft (White, Rep.)
1	00.6%	80%
2	00.3%	83%
3	00.9%	78%
4	00.3%	79%
5	00.6%	82%
6	00.8%	83%
7	00.6%	76%
9	00.2%	84%
14	01.4%	87%
15	01.4%	86%
26	01.1%	80%
33	00.3%	79%

Negro Wards	% Negro Population	% Two-Party Vote Cast for Stokes (Negro, Dem.)
10	91.1%	97%
11	91.8%	96%
17	99.0%	98%
20	91.0%	93%
24	92.6%	98%
25	90.9%	98%

In 1968, Richard Nixon carried Ohio, Indiana, Illinois and Wisconsin, losing only Michigan. However, his potential majorities were reduced—and his Michigan defeat was enlarged—by the vote diversions of third-party presidential candidate George Wallace. Four years after scoring his relative successes in the 1964 Indiana and Wisconsin Democratic primaries, Wallace compiled 12 per cent to 18 per cent of the vote in counties round and about the restive cities of Gary, Detroit, Flint and Cleveland. Much as Ohio Valley Wallace backing peaked along contours of Southern settlement and rural Democratic tradition, Great Lakes Wallace support climbed highest in areas where New Deal urban Democratic loyalties were being strained by growing Negro populations, ascending Negro

MAP 38

Wallace Vote in the Great Lakes, 1968

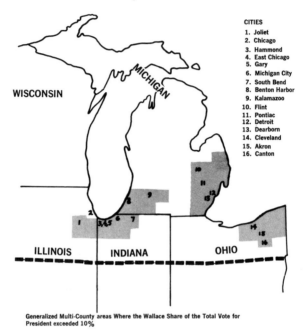

CITIES

1. Joliet
2. Chicago
3. Hammond
4. East Chicago
5. Gary
6. Michigan City
7. South Bend
8. Benton Harbor
9. Kalamazoo
10. Flint
11. Pontiac
12. Detroit
13. Dearborn
14. Cleveland
15. Akron
16. Canton

WISCONSIN

ILLINOIS   INDIANA   OHIO

Generalized Multi-County areas Where the Wallace Share of the Total Vote for President exceeded 10%

(Democratic) political power and severe 1967-68 racial violence (see Map 38). Chart 106 lists the 1968 Nixon, Wallace and Humphrey vote percentages by state.

Granted that this Wallace support principally occurred in normally Democratic areas, it came from 1960 Nixon ranks (in riot-aroused Detroit) or from Republican-trending groups like the blue-collar whites of Cleveland and Gary. Together with the pro-Democratic trends of Negroes, Yankees and silk-stocking voters, Wallace's diversions played a major role in Hubert Humphrey's Michigan victory and close Ohio race. In Illinois and Indiana, Wallace sidetracked potential Nixon conservative Democratic support, but few voting streams were shifting towards the Democrats, and Wallace's vote did not reduce Nixon's 1960 majorities. On the contrary, Illinois switched to the GOP column and Indiana gave Nixon a wider lead than in 1960.

From Wisconsin to Ohio, Catholics—and especially German Catholics—played a major part in Nixon's victory. In each Great

CHART 106

Great Lakes Presidential Voting, 1968

Share of the Total Vote for President

State	Nixon	Wallace	Humphrey
Michigan	42%	10%	48%
Wisconsin	48	8	44
Ohio	45	12	43
Illinois	47	8	44
Indiana	50	12	38

Lakes state, the largest 1960-68 GOP presidential gains occurred in the banner German Catholic counties: Kewaunee (Wisconsin), Clinton (Illinois), Dubois (Indiana), Putnam (Ohio) and Huron (Michigan). Chart 107 shows the extent of the Republican gain.

Spreading into large cities like Milwaukee and Cincinnati, this German Republican tide played a major part in producing Nixon's success in Ohio, Illinois and Wisconsin.* For example, in Ohio's Hamilton County (Cincinnati), the Democratic share of the total presidential vote dropped from 46 per cent in 1960 to just 37 per cent in 1968 while Nixon widened his vote edge from thirty-five thousand to fifty thousand. And Milwaukee's Democratic vote share dropped from 58 per cent in 1960 to 51 per cent in 1968, sharply reducing the party majority. The German trend was little help to Nixon in Michigan, which has a relatively small Teuton population.

In disagreement with the liberal trend of fashionable old-line suburbs, the fast-growing middle-class tracts surrounding Columbus, Cincinnati, Indianapolis, Chicago and Milwaukee gave Nixon better majorities in 1968 than they had in 1960. Easterners may construe Great Lakes suburbia in the image of Shaker Heights, Grosse Point and Winnetka, but these rich towns are no more typical of local suburbs than Scarsdale and Philadelphia's Main Line are of Megalopolitan suburbia. Counties like Cuyahoga

---

*Few observers—Samuel Lubell is the principal exception—have ever understood the important role played in Midwestern politics by the large local German vote. In 1940, the German vote keynoted Republican gains from Ohio to North Dakota. Then in 1948, German Democratic trends helped Truman win surprise victories in Ohio, Illinois and Wisconsin, exactly those Great Lakes states where the German tide was extremely important to Richard Nixon in 1968.

CHART 107

Nixon Gains Among Great Lakes Germans, 1960-68

County	Republican Share of the Major Party Vote for President	
	1960	1968
Kewaunee	48%	63%
Clinton	48	58
Dubois	38	47
Putnam	53	68
Huron	62	70

(Cleveland) and Wayne (Detroit) combine emptying and increasingly-Negro central cities, new subdivisions to house the lower-middle-class white exodus, and stable, rich old-line suburbs.* Like kindred areas in the Northeast, they are not experiencing overall metropolitan growth. While Negroes pour into the major heavy industrial cities, white migration within and into the Great Lakes is focused on new middle-class suburbs, technological and light industrial areas.

Population shifts of this nature help the GOP. For example, Chicago's conservative middle-class environs grew so rapidly between 1960 and 1968 that heavy local support for Richard Nixon—his share of the two-party vote climbed well above 1960 levels—cancelled out most of Hubert Humphrey's majority in the city proper, enabling the Republican nominee to carry Illinois. As a matter of fact, it seems reasonable to suggest that the suburban Chicago upsurge is forging a new balance of statewide power in presidential races. If white conservatives in peripheral Chicago and the Cook County suburbs can offset the Democratic majorities of the central city (lumped together, Wallace and Nixon totals in Cook County equaled Humphrey's in 1968), then Illinois will regularly go Republican by dint of the heavy downstate GOP majorities. The same *détente* could emerge in other metropolitan areas.

Of course, the Republican trend in the middle-class and lower-

*Chart 135 illustrates the population decline in Great Lakes Cities.

middle-class bulk of suburbia is related to—and partially dependent on—the conservative trend of the traditionally Democratic blue-collar and lower-middle-class white electorate of the major urban areas. These voting streams shifted away from the Democrats in 1968, although George Wallace was the principal beneficiary. The Alabaman amassed respectable percentages (5 per cent to 10 per cent) in rural and suburban Great Lakes locales, but his best showing outside the Southern-leaning Ohio Valley centered, as Map 38 shows, on Detroit, Gary and Cleveland, the principal Great Lakes centers of Negro population, political power and violence.*

By and large, Wallace diverted past or potential Nixon support. In Detroit and environs, he pulled his votes principally from Nixon and Goldwater backers; the powerful United Automobile Workers and other unions kept normally Democratic workers in line.** In the Cleveland and Gary areas, Wallace superficially drew most of his strength from 1960-68 Democratic slippage. In actuality, however, Wallace peaked in wards which had trended sharply Republican in 1967 because of opposition to the election of Negro mayors Stokes and Hatcher. Solidly Catholic blue-collar sections of Cleveland generally positioned Humphrey about 10 per cent to 20 per cent behind John F. Kennedy's 1960 strength. Some Catholic wards of Gary and nearby Lake County industrial towns chalked up 1960-68 Democratic presidential declines of 30 per cent or more. Wallace won most of the dissidents, but Nixon also scored an absolute 1960-68 gain in many white neighborhoods. Once the banner Democratic county of New Deal Indiana, Lake gave Hubert Humphrey the lowest vote share of any Democratic presidential nominee since the Republican Nineteen-Twenties. Only slightly more than one third of the white electorate backed the nominee of the party of Franklin D. Roosevelt. Many old-line Lake County Democrats had begun to re-register as Republicans after the 1967 Gary mayoralty upheaval. The moderately pro-Wallace German and Slavic conservative Democrats of Cleveland have a Republican example in their longtime leader, former U.S. Senator Frank Lausche, who bolted to Richard Nixon in 1968.

Abetted by Wallace's diversion of conservative-leaning groups,

---

*Farther south, the substantially Negro and riot-troubled area around East St. Louis was another major center of Illinois Wallace support.
**In Wayne County (Detroit), George Wallace's 10 per cent of the total vote was amassed largely at the expense of Nixon, whose 1960 vote share of 34 per cent fell to a mere 26 per cent in 1968.

the trends of Yankees, Negroes and silk-stocking voters—strongest in Michigan and Ohio—reduced Nixon's two-party vote share in both states below 1960 levels. From Lake Erie to Lake Michigan, Negroes went overwhelmingly for Hubert Humphrey. Richard Nixon appears to have won a mere 2 per cent to 6 per cent of their support, down from his 15 per cent to 20 per cent of 1960. And although the turnout was very poor—heavily Negro wards invariably cast fewer votes than in 1964—the sum total of Negro votes set a local record because Negro migration to the Great Lakes had been so marked during the Nineteen-Sixties. In one respect, this adverse Negro demographic and political trend hurt Nixon, but on the other hand, it paved the way for the breakdown of Democratic loyalties among blue-collar and lower-middle-class whites.

Yankee residents of Michigan, southern Wisconsin, the Western Reserve and old Ohio Company lands of Ohio also trended against Nixon between 1960 and 1968. Yankee counties, mostly in Michigan, were the only rural counties in the Great Lakes to increase their Democratic shares of the total vote between 1960 and 1968. Like upstate New York and rural New England, outstate Michigan voted strongly Republican, but nevertheless showed a Democratic trend. Similar currents swayed the voters of establishmentarian suburbs like Shaker Heights, Pepper Pike, Bloomfield Hills, the Grosse Points and Evanston. And such affluent groves of *academe* as Madison, Ann Arbor and Oberlin joined the pro-Humphrey shift, despite the animosity they had felt towards his pre-convention candidacy only months before. Northeastern-like losses among Yankee and silk-stocking electoral streams hurt Nixon principally in Michigan and Ohio and to a lesser extent in Wisconsin. Illinois and Indiana were minimally affected. Generally speaking, Nixon's worst 1960-68 losses came in those Great Lakes areas where local Republicans had favored Nelson Rockefeller's presidential aspirations. Conservative Democrats were not the only electorate in motion between the parties.

Michigan, which for many years was the most Republican (and Northeastern) of the Great Lakes states, is now clearly the most Democratic. This pattern has been taking shape since the Nineteen-Fifties. Although Richard Nixon and George Wallace together won a majority of Michigan's votes in 1960, hitherto Democratic Appalachian and Catholic white lower-middle-class and blue-collar workers constitute the only conservative-trending group. The state seems to be aligning with the Northeast on the liberal Democratic side.

Ohio, Illinois and Wisconsin were closely fought battlegrounds of 1968, but these states have substantial or dominant Ohio Valley, German and urban Catholic conservative trend groups to offset Yankee, silk-stocking and Negro movement toward the Democrats. Indiana, with its considerable Southern bias and proclivity to parallel the politics of the Border, should be a dependable constituent of the Southern-Heartland *entente*. Although most of the Great Lakes states should usually support coalition presidential candidates, the region is a transition zone between Heartland and Northeastern politics and seems destined to be a major cockpit of the upcoming cycle.

C. The Farm States

The usual Megalopolitan image of the Farm states is one of cow-fodder conservatism, but like most images perceived at a distance, it is inaccurate. First of all, the great majority of Farm-state residents do not live on farms. Second, the conservative strongholds of the Farm states have always been the small towns, not the actual farm precincts. Far from being sedately rustic, the rural sections of the Farm states—not the cities—have traditions of considerable radicalism. North Dakota, perhaps the most agricultural of the Farm states, is about as sedate as a thrusting pitchfork! Among its political favorite sons have been Congressman William "Liberty Bell" Lemke, Father Coughlin's arch-isolationist 1936 presidential candidate; Senator Gerald P. Nye, stalwart in the between-wars congressional investigation of the international munitions business; Senator "Wild Bill" Langer, anti-British opponent of the Marshall Plan and hero of the agrarian radical Non-Partisan League (a major force in state politics for forty years); and sundry other rip-snorters.

Between 1940 and 1952, North Dakota and Vermont were generally paired at the top of the list of the nation's most Republican states, but their dissimilarity can hardly be exaggerated—sociopolitical light years separate the Connecticut River Valley from the Bayerische farmlands southwest of Bismarck. Outside of the Dixiecrat Deep South, the northern Farm Belt is the most volatile stretch of political Americana extant, but whereas the Cotton states are excited by the politics of race, the Farm Belt displays a multiple sensitivity towards foreign wars, low farm prices and the general machinations of the big city Northeast. Wichita, Des Moines, Omaha and Minneapolis-St. Paul, the principal Farm Belt urban centers, are less swayed by these issues than the countryside. The same is true of the small towns, historically the bedrock of Farm states conservatism.

Map 39 illustrates the three major agricultural regions—the Corn Belt, the Wheat Belt and the Dairy Belt—that spread across the Farm states. Kansas, Nebraska, the Dakotas and Iowa are the wheat, corn and livestock states; they are more agricultural and less urban and industrialized than Wisconsin and Minnesota. In the latter two states, dairying is the major farm pursuit, but it is less pervasive than the cash grain and livestock farming of the five deep-

MAP 39

Agricultural Subregions of the Farm Belt

hued Farm states. Moreover, both Minnesota and Wisconsin have mining and industrial areas bordering on the Great Lakes. Except for these Great Lakes heavy-industry concentrations, Farm Belt industry is often related to local agriculture (flour mills, stockyards, packing plants, farm machinery plants), and does not set up a separate culture antagonistic to the countryside, as in the Northeast. Wisconsin and Minnesota are the most populous Farm states, followed by Iowa. The seven Farm states are by no means sharply delineated from their neighbors. To the east, the Corn Belt continues into the Border state of Missouri and the northern part of Illinois. And to the west, the Wheat Belt extends into the eastern parts of Montana, Wyoming and Colorado, although these three states are always put into the Rocky Mountain group. Thus, the Farm Belt does not lend itself to precise definition, but its core area consists of the seven states shown in Map 39.

Within the Farm Belt, there are important population differences to match those of economic geography. North Dakota, Minnesota and Wisconsin contain a higher proportion of German and Scandinavian Americans than any other state in the Union, with the result that they have shown extreme volatility in foreign policy-dominated elections since World War I. Kansas and Nebraska, on the other hand, are the two most strongly Anglo-Saxon states. In the Populist, Granges, and free silver half century after the Civil War, *they* were the fount of political volatility and radicalism.* Today, the politics of vehemence enmesh the urban slums; the Farm Belt is generally uninvolved. However, erosion of Civil War and other obsolescent traditions are causing some re-alignment.

Corn-rich Iowa and southern Wisconsin were the first areas of the Farm Belt to be settled. At first, Iowa was largely filled by Southerners, and it was not until the late Eighteen-Forties that a Yankee influx remade the state character. Large numbers of Yankees entered southern Wisconsin in the Eighteen-Forties; others opened up lower Minnesota during the Eighteen-Fifties. Both Kansas and Nebraska also began to receive population in the Eighteen-

*Kansas, in particular, was a noted center of "isms." For example, there is a small town in south-central Kansas close to the Oklahoma border named Medicine Lodge. Back in the Eighteen-Nineties, Medicine Lodge was the home of two of the leading radicals of the time: "Sockless Jerry" Simpson, leader of the agrarian Populist Party, and Carry Nation, the intemperate temperance advocate who started dozens of riots and took her ax to many a saloon. Times have changed. Kansas is prosperous; the state prohibition law was repealed in 1948; Medicine Lodge is now a reliable bastion of conservative Republicanism.

MAP 40

Major Farm Belt Ethnic Concentrations

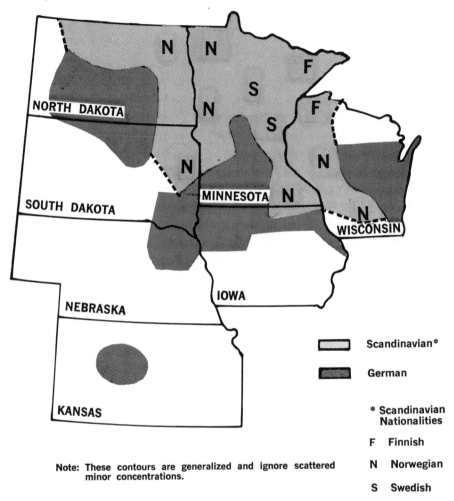

Note: These contours are generalized and ignore scattered minor concentrations.

Scandinavian*

German

* Scandinavian Nationalities

F   Finnish

N   Norwegian

S   Swedish

Fifties. Kansas was a North-South battleground: the abolitionist New England Emigrant Aid Society sent Yankees toting "Beecher bibles" (muskets) to secure the state for the anti-slavery cause, and numerous "Border Ruffians" came across the border from Missouri. As Map 30 shows, Iowa, Wisconsin and Minnesota were the states of pre-Civil War Yankee settlement. In Kansas and Nebraska, not only were persons of foreign stock less numerous, but the Anglo-Saxon population had a substantial Southern element.

After the Eighteen-Thirties, but especially in the wake of the unsuccessful Central European revolutions of 1848, many Germans began to come to the United States. Spurning the East Coast, most of them moved west into the Ohio Valley, Great Lakes and Farm states. The large German urban populations of the Middle West as of 1910 are listed in Chart 87. However, many rural counties in the North Central states were still more Teutonic and remain 80 per cent to 90 per cent German even today. Map 40 shows the major German concentrations. Most of the Germans in Minnesota and Wisconsin dairy country are Catholics. The smaller German populations of Kansas and Nebraska include large numbers of Mennonites and Lutherans. In Iowa and the Dakotas, the substantial German populations are mixed. The distinction between German Protestants and German Catholics is quite meaningful; central Europe did not experience the Thirty Years War for nothing. Farm-state German Protestants have by and large voted as their Anglo-Saxon neighbors—usually Republican—while German Catholics have not.

The second half of the Nineteenth Century also brought large numbers of Scandinavians to the Farm states, especially to northern Wisconsin and Minnesota, where evergreen-encircled blue lakes tugged at Nordic memories. There are many Swedes in Minnesota; Norwegians are important in Wisconsin, North Dakota, Minnesota and northern Iowa; the Lake Superior section of Minnesota has a sizeable Finnish minority; and there is even a colony of Icelanders in the Red River Valley. Minnesota, Wisconsin and North Dakota are simultaneously the most Lutheran (Scandinavian) and most Catholic of the Farm states, in contrast with their more Anglo-Saxon neighbors.

Farm states political behavior has mirrored these demographic patterns. In the era of native agrarianism between the Civil War and World War I, Kansas and Nebraska reflected one behavioral stream and the Yankee-Catholic-Lutheran states another.* This was also the case in the isolationist and religious controversies of the Nineteen-Twenties. Since 1932, as the cleavage in American politics has tended to become an urban-rural one, Kansas, Nebraska and the

---

*To structure an ethnic and religious model of the Farm Belt, Kansas and Nebraska are the strongly Anglo-Saxon Protestant states, while Wisconsin, Minnesota and North Dakota are predominantly Catholic-Lutheran and German-Scandinavian. Iowa and South Dakota fall in between, in both geography and demography.

Dakotas have responded somewhat differently than the more urbanized states of Iowa, Minnesota and Wisconsin. Nevertheless, the political importance of ethnic settlement patterns persists.*

Iowa was the first of the Farm states to be admitted to the Union (1836), and by the time of the Civil War, Wisconsin, Minnesota and Kansas had also graduated from territorial status to statehood. Nebraska followed suit shortly thereafter, but the two Dakotas did not become states until a quarter-century after Appomattox. For the most part, the Farm states were pro-Union during the war, but there were areas of dissidence. Sections of eastern Kansas, partially settled from Missouri in the late Eighteen-Fifties, evinced some Southern sympathy, as did southern sections of Iowa—adjacent to and likewise settled from Missouri. As Map 30 shows, Yankees dominated Minnesota, Wisconsin and most of Iowa by the beginning of the Civil War. They were joined in their loyalties by the large Scandinavian immigrant group. In Wisconsin, Norwegians made up the entire roster of the Fifteenth Infantry Regiment. Its colonel, Hans Heg, commanded ninety men whose first name was Ole, most of whom could not speak English!

Whatever Yankee and Scandinavian sentiment, the war—more exactly, military conscription—was unpopular among the Germans and Irish of Iowa, Wisconsin and Minnesota. Dubuque, Iowa, was a leading center of Middle West German-Irish "Copperhead" opposition to the Lincoln Administration and "New England's war." Heavily German Ozaukee County, Wisconsin, rioted against the military draft; and unrest was rife in other German areas. The Irish shared German animosity towards the draft and Negroes alike— they feared Negro job competition—and Chicago's Irish rioted against military induction on several occasions. When the divisive Civil War was over, the Northern, Yankee and Scandinavian Farm states majority lined up with the Republicans, making Wisconsin and Minnesota among the most regular GOP states in the nation, as Chart 7 shows. Whenever farm revolt threatened, Republican

---

*In *American Panorama,* a collection of articles from *Holiday,* Mark Schorer has described Wisconsin: "Wisconsin's past-in-present character shows clearly in the way its European immigrant groups preserve their national identity. The main groups can be mapped roughly—using climate as a guide—with the Finns and early Poles in the northern timberland, where the winters are sometimes appallingly severe; the Norwegians and Swedes in a loose belt below them where timber shades to grain; the Swiss and Germans in the milder corn and dairy and orchard regions of the central and southwestern prairie; and the southern Europeans and late-coming Poles in the industrial lake cities to the southeast."

orators "waved the bloody shirt" of war memory and raised Union veteran pensions. In similar response to the war, but also to the intermittent nativism of the Protestant and Republican majority (and their pre-war Whig and Know-Nothing forebears), the Catholic German and Irish minority became the mainstay of the Democratic Party. (Ironically, many Border-state Germans became *Republicans* because they supported the Union and disliked the secessionism and later the Bourbon Democratic politics of the Protestant and Anglo-Saxon majority.)

In the century following the Civil War, the two most important fulcrums of political unrest were war and agrarianism. On the one hand, ethnic bitterness caused the Irish and Germans of the Farm states to vote Republican in protest over the two pro-British and anti-German wars fought by Democratic administrations, and on the other hand, the unhappiness of Yankee and Scandinavian farmers over the Northeastern oligarchy-directed economic policies of the Republican Party often superseded Civil War loyalties. Despite these recurring distortions, however, the basic pattern of Farm-state politics for the next century was laid down by the Civil War. True, the New Deal gave the Democrats a new urban bias, yet the fundamental Civil War loyalties of the countryside persisted (witness Missouri's Little Dixie in the heart of the Corn Belt). A hundred years after Appomattox, it remained for the Great Society and the Negro socioeconomic revolution to put rural loyalties on a new basis.

As settlers poured west after the Civil War, Farm-state Republican majorities were little disturbed by agrarian unrest until the Eighteen-Seventies, when a multiplicity of movements protesting low crop prices took shape throughout the region. Cheap money and inflationist sentiments, fanned by enmity towards bankers, railroad barons and milling magnates, keynoted this rural radicalism. And it was justified: tight money *was* throttling the farmer with his own mortgage. To fight the politics and economics of deflation, populist leaders told farmers to "raise less corn and more hell." But for all their economic agitation and advocacy of inflation, most of the agrarian radical movements had a lower-middle-class cultural and religious commitment to the essential conservatism of rural, Anglo-Saxon America.

Agrarian radicalism grew in the Farm states of the Eighteen-Eighties, especially in the Wheat Belt. Finally, in 1892, Kansas forsook the Democratic and Republican presidential nominees to back the Populist candidate, General James Weaver. Nebraska almost did likewise. Elsewhere in the Farm Belt, the Populists commanded less support in the Yankee, German and Scandinavian corn, dairy or timber counties, so that Wisconsin and Minnesota made insufficient cause with the movement. However, because of its large German Catholic Democratic vote, Wisconsin supported conservative Democrat Grover Cleveland in 1892 (rather than Republican Benjamin Harrison, who won the other Farm states).

Populism made its great bid for national power in 1896, when the mortgage-harassed Farm states joined with the Rocky Mountain and Pacific silver mining interests to nominate William Jennings Bryan, an advocate of inflation and free silver—"You shall not crucify mankind upon a cross of gold"—and noted for his florid and fundamentalist oratory. Bryan split the Farm Belt, winning the Protestant cash grain states of Kansas, Nebraska and South Dakota, while losing the states with higher Yankee and foreign stock ratios and more diversified agricultural and industrial bases. Lutherans and Catholics found Bryan's Protestant fundamentalism less than appealing and some Wisconsin German townships voted Republican for the first time since the Civil War. Bryan was a parochial candidate even in the Farm Belt whence he hailed.

The Great Commoner's failure wrote a new chapter in American politics. Bryanesque Democracy offended the staid Eastern middle classes and immigrant working-class groups alike, establishing a new national Republican predominance and breaking a twenty-year near-stalemate. Despite his defeat in 1896, Bryan ran for President twice again, in 1900 and 1908. In 1900 he lost every Farm state, and in 1908 he carried only his home state of Nebraska.

Although he was thrice defeated, William Jennings Bryan was by no means a complete political failure. Many of the programs sought by the farm radicals in 1896 became law in subsequent decades. Agrarian radicalism petered out after 1896, however, for the best of reasons: farm prosperity. Morever, great new quantities of gold were discovered in the years after 1896, stimulating inflation and farm prosperity without resort to the panacea of free coinage of silver. Only the mining interests clung to the free silver issue. The farmers abandoned it and returned to the swelling ranks of the GOP. Today, history books recall the kerosene lamp era of 1900-14 as the golden age of the American farmer. Never before

CHART 108

Farm States Voting Patterns in the Radical Era, 1896-1928

States Ranked by Declining Order of Native Stock Share of the Population, 1920	Bryan Share of the Two-Party Vote 1896 (D)	Harding Share of the Two-Party Vote 1920 (R)	Republican, Democratic & Progressive Vote Shares, 1924			Hoover Share of the Two-Party Vote 1928 (R)
			R%	D%	P%	
Kansas	52%	67%	61%	24%	15%	72%
Nebraska	53	68	47	30	23	64
Iowa	44	73	55	17	28	62
South Dakota	50	76	50	13	37	62
Minnesota	41	78	52	7	41	58
North Dakota	44	81	48	7	45	54
Wisconsin	38	81	38	8	54	55

or since has the farmer's share of national peacetime prosperity equaled that at the turn of the century.

The election of 1912 saw the Farm Belt drop out of the Republican column, although not because of farm dissatisfaction. Democratic presidential candidate Woodrow Wilson was opposed not only by incumbent Republican President William Howard Taft, but by a GOP-vote-splitting "Progressive" candidate, former President Theodore Roosevelt. While Wilson did not win a majority of the vote in any Farm state, he won pluralities in five, losing South Dakota and Minnesota to Roosevelt, whose vote in his beloved Great Plains far exceeded that of President Taft. Four years later, the growing war clouds in Europe had a mixed effect on Farm-state voting behavior. Fearing that Woodrow Wilson's pro-British policies would involve the United States in war against Germany, many traditionally Democratic Germans in Wisconsin and Minnesota broke to the GOP in 1916. On the other hand, Wilson managed to hold the electoral votes of Kansas, Nebraska and North Dakota. essentially by expanding Bryanesque strength. The war issue was not clear-cut in 1916; GOP candidate Charles Evans Hughes was an Eastern internationalist, while Wilson backers claimed of the President that "He kept us out of war." But only weeks after Wilson's second inaugural, the United States *did* go to war.

Disillusionment with the war, the Versailles peace treaty and the League of Nations was rife in 1920, especially among German, Scandinavian and Irish Democrats, and Wilson's record was an albatross around the neck of the party presidential nominee, Ohio Governor James Cox. The isolationist ire of the Farm states in general and German-Scandinavian counties in particular devastated Democratic candidacies from the top of the ticket to the bottom. The GOP presidential vote ranged from a high of 81 per cent in Wisconsin to a low of 67 per cent in Kansas (see Chart 108). Some arch-isolationist counties went Republican by eight-, ten- and twelve-to-one majorities (see Chart 109). Cox garnered his only respectable support in Kansas and Nebraska, where some Anglo-Saxon (Bryan) Democratic traditions still prevailed. Third-party Farmer-Labor and Socialist candidates did almost as well as Cox in the foreign-stock states of Minnesota, Wisconsin and North Dakota.

During the First World War, the Farm Belt prospered and many farmers took out mortgages to expand their operations, leaving

Farm States German and Scandinavian Voting, 1920-68

Leading Foreign Stock Counties	Democratic Percentage of the Total Vote for President												
	1920[1]	1924[2]	1928[3]	1932	1936[4]	1940[5]	1944	1948	1952	1956	1960[6]	1964	1968
German													
Kewaunee, Wis.	18%	9%	72%	85%	74%	47%	39%	42%	23%	32%	52%	62%	34%
Emmons, N.D.	8	4	53	76	58	22	22	34	13	23	54	47	22
Stearns, Minn.	10	8	71	79	57	37	39	59	35	36	58	59	47
Dubuque, Iowa	36	23	67	71	60	49	51	60	44	42	63	70	55
Ellis, Kan.	23	22	66	75	75	48	40	59	34	41	65	69	46
Swedish													
Chisago, Minn.	9	3	23	53	55	43	44	53	39	44	43	63	54
Burnett, Wis.	7	2	24	64	63	49	48	56	39	47	46	65	45
Norwegian													
Nelson, N.D.	14	5	39	77	66	56	56	46	37	50	48	67	47
Norman, Minn.	10	4	29	69	69	63	60	63	44	54	53	69	57
Polk, Wis.	13	4	29	59	54	44	45	56	38	46	45	66	45

1. Wisconsin and Minnesota counties gave Socialist and Farmer-Labor candidates more votes than Democratic nominee was able to win.
2. LaFollette carried most of these counties and won over one third of the total vote in all of them.
3. Catholic Germans voted for co-religionist Smith and Scandinavian Lutherans were the strongest anti-Catholics in the Middle West. No third-party candidacy hurt the Democrats.
4. Lemke won 10 per cent to 20 per cent of the vote in the German counties (except Kansas) and hardly any votes in the Scandinavian counties.
5. Strongest isolationist trend was among Germans, next among Swedes (Sweden was neutral), while isolationism was weakest among Norwegians inasmuch as Hitler had just invaded Norway.
6. German Catholic and Scandinavian Lutheran religious voting occurred on a lesser scale than in 1928.

themselves cruelly vulnerable to the inevitable postwar agricultural depression. Coupled with the isolationist spirit and the post-Versailles bitterness that was abroad in the western United States, these farm problems gave rise to a new agrarianism in the Farm Belt as well as a new coterie of agrarian radical parties. In retrospect, isolationism probably matched economic motivation in producing support for agrarian radical parties. Most of the third-party spokesmen—Wisconsin Senator Robert LaFollette was the best example—had vehemently opposed United States entry into the World War, feeling that the war served only the financial interests while menacing economic reform at home. By these actions, LaFollette and his colleagues earned many of the German and Scandinavian "radical" votes subsequently cast during the Nineteen-Twenties. In states like Wisconsin and Minnesota, the radical parties were strongest in the isolationist German and Scandinavian counties, although German areas were often more prosperous than neighboring Anglo-Saxon counties.*

The economic reform movement of the Ninetween-Twenties flew its colors most boldly in 1924, when Senator LaFollette ran for President as the candidate of the new Progressive Party, challenging orthodox Republican President Calvin Coolidge and Democratic nominee John W. Davis, a conservative corporation lawyer. LaFollette carried his home state of Wisconsin, but lost the other Farm states to Coolidge, albeit the GOP majority was slim in Minnesota and North Dakota, where isolationist voters backed LaFollette heavily.**

To further query the underlying agricultural denominator of 1924 third-party voting, the best Progressive states were those where the populism of 1896 had been weakest. The explanation lies in the different social and cultural impetus of the two movements. The Populist movement, like the Granger movement, was an Anglo-Saxon crusade (replete with fundamentalist religious overtones) in the tradition of the Whiskey Rebellion and other protests of the

---

*Most of the agrarian movements had largely Scandinavian roots, paralleling the cooperative and other agricultural organizations of Scandinavia itself. North Dakota's Non-Partisan League was strongly Scandinavian, as was the Minnesota Farmer-Labor movement. In Wisconsin, LaFollette's Progressive movement (which long had operated in a Republican context) drew most of its strength from Norwegians. German support for these parties was usually premised on their anti-war stance or the past anti-war positions of progressive candidates.

**LaFollette carried all of the key German, Swedish and Norwegian counties in Minnesota and Wisconsin, as well as most of those in North Dakota.

frontier. Backed by the Anglo-Saxon yeomanry, the Populist movement had its greatest strength in the old-stock Farm states—Kansas and Nebraska. On the other hand, LaFollette's Progressive cause, although linked to agricultural issues that won general support throughout the Farm Belt, drew most of its adherents from isolationist and farm cooperative-minded Germans and Scandinavians in the foreign-stock Farm states, particularly Wisconsin, Minnesota and North Dakota. In some ways, the Progressives were akin to the Populists (they both flayed Wall Street), but they struck different cultural chords and won the support of different groups. As Chart 108 shows, the 1924 LaFollette vote correlates very closely with the isolationist inflation of the Republican vote in 1920, and both of these trends were strongest where Bryan had been weakest in 1896.

Further evidence of the pervasive ability of ethnic and religious bias to surmount farm discontent came in 1928. Since 1924, farm furor had increased rather than diminished, and Farm Belt Republicans were up in arms trying to enact farm surplus control legislation. But the "sons of the wild jackasses"—Senate Republicans like Smith Brookhart (Iowa), Henrik Shipstead (Minnesota), Magnus Johnson (Minnesota), George Norris (Nebraska), Lynn Frazier (North Dakota) and Peter Norbeck (South Dakota)—could not sway the Northeastern oligarchy which ran the Republican Party. President Coolidge twice vetoed McNary-Haugen (farm surplus control) legislation, the second time in May, 1928. Herbert Hoover, then Commerce Secretary but slated to be the GOP presidential nominee, was so unpopular in the Farm Belt that the Republican governor of Nebraska called for one hundred thousand farmers to march on the party convention!

Notwithstanding this resentment, Hoover was nominated and the Farm Belt did not bolt. For one thing, the Democratic nominee, New York Governor Al Smith, conveyed no empathy to the farmer; moreover, he refused to take a foursquare position in support of the legislation farmers blamed the GOP for defeating. This reticence directed attention back to Smith's Catholicism. Most Farm Belt Methodists (the local mainstays of the Ku Klux Klan) and Lutherans (historic European antagonists of Catholicism) shrank from voting for a Catholic. Thus, the Democrats failed to realize their true Farm states potential in 1928. Smith's support pivoted on heavy German Catholic backing and partial tolerance on the part of a minority of the anti-Hoover Scandinavian Progressives who had backed LaFollette four years before. Just as one might expect, Smith scored his highest percentages—still short of victory—in Wisconsin, Minnesota and North Dakota. A progressive Protestant Democrat would have done much better. Chart 109 shows the massive pro-Catholic vote in the German Catholic counties and the below-potential Smith vote in the Lutheran LaFollette strongholds.

As shown in Chart 108, there is a surprisingly distinct relationship among the voting patterns of the 1896, 1920, 1924 and 1928 elections. The best 1920 Republican vote came in states where German and Scandinavian isolationist balloting sent party totals soaring. Many of these voters switched to LaFollette in 1924, so that Coolidge was weakest in just those Farm states where Harding had been strongest. The best 1924 GOP levels were reached in the Anglo-Saxon states of Kansas and Nebraska, and Coolidge's backing (as well as that of Democrat John Davis) correlated with 1896 Bryan enthusiasm. The persisting division between the Anglo-Saxon and foreign-stock states was shifting parties, as Bryanesque agrarianism gave way to a new volatility. Then in 1928, Catholic Al Smith garnered most of his votes from formerly LaFollette ranks, and the Republican vote once again followed the Bryan pattern. Hoover's best states in 1928 had been Bryan's best in 1896; and Al Smith's best states in 1928 were those that had been most pro-Harding in 1920 and pro-Lafollette in 1924. All of this underscores the importance of ethnic and cultural factors in voting: in this instance a framework operating for a third of a century.

The Great Depression of 1929 so aggravated farm problems that, to nobody's surprise, the Democrats swept the Farm Belt in 1932. Franklin D. Roosevelt was the Protestant progressive for whom the region had been waiting. Some analysts have suggested that Roosevelt merged the Smith and LaFollette tides, but he did more. By 1932, the Wheat Belt had become a Drought Belt. Roosevelt swept most of the Anglo-Saxon Farm Belt countries and he scored his biggest gain over Smith in parched Kansas, which had overwhelmingly rejected Smith *and* LaFollette. Chart 110 lists Roosevelt's gains over Smith.

Granted that the basic tide of 1932 was an economic one—the plight of the Depression-squeezed farmer—the trends of 1932 were also influenced by the prejudices of 1928. Dubuque County, Iowa, for example, showed a 1928-32 Democratic trend of only 4 per

CHART 110

*Increase in Democratic Share of Major
Party Presidential Vote, 1928-32*

> Kansas—28%
> Nebraska—28%
> S. Dakota—26%
> N. Dakota—26%
> Wisconsin—22%
> Iowa—21%
> Minnesota—21%

cent—not because the Depression spared Dubuque, but because the county was so Catholic that 1928 religious voting had left the Democrats no room for gain. On the other hand, it is easy to find Lutheran, Methodist and Baptist counties where Franklin D. Roosevelt ran 40 percentage points ahead of Smith. The basic rural swing was about 25 per cent; the city trend was much weaker. Main Street was more Republican than the farm precincts in 1932, just as it had been less restive and "Progressive" during the Nineteen-Twenties.* Not many farm counties backed Hoover in 1932; those few that did were strongly Yankee by settlement and heritage.

The New Deal soon reversed the pattern of 1932. In 1936, the Democrats lost ground throughout much of the rural Farm Belt, but Roosevelt wiped out the remaining GOP urban majorities. The political structure of the Farm Belt was beginning to shift: by 1940 and after, foreign-stock population strength would no longer align North Dakota with Minnesota and Wisconsin; the New Deal was carving out an urban-rural division. But this was only hinted at in 1936. The Democrats made some gains in the urban and Great Lakes sections of Wisconsin and Minnesota, and slipped substantially in the rest of the Farm Belt. The best GOP gains came in the rural "Protestant ethic" sections of Kansas, Nebraska and Iowa. Despite these rural Republican gains, Roosevelt held all of the Farm states.

However, Democratic success was threatened by European con-

---

*For example, Hoover lost most rural Iowa counties in 1932—Anglo-Saxon, Scandinavian and (especially) German—but he carried the city of Des Moines. In 1936, Des Moines voted for Roosevelt.

flict resurrecting Farm Belt isolationism. Hitler had remilitarized the Rhineland and taken the anti-Communist (Franco) side in the Spanish Civil War. Once again, Middle West Germans, essential to Democratic majorities, feared United States policies that might lead to war with Germany. Responding to these emotions, North Dakota GOP Congressman William Lemke, supported by radio priest Father Coughlin, ran for the presidency in 1936 on an agrarian, isolationist platform. He won 13 per cent of the vote in North Dakota; he chalked up fair support in German strongholds like Dubuque, St. Paul and Appleton; and he carried dozens of over-whelmingly Teutonic precincts in Ohio, Wisconsin, Minnesota and North Dakota. Irish support enabled Lemke to win 8 per cent of the vote in Boston, but most of the Union Party vote came in the Farm states.

Although Lemke's vote had little effect on the 1936 race, it fore-shadowed a greater trend in the 1940 presidential election, by which time isolationists were much more provoked by the Administration's foreign policy. Franklin D. Roosevelt lost five Farm states in 1940, principally because of isolationist voting. Granted that a general conservative tide had begun to flow in the 1938 congressional elections, Chart 111 structures the 1936-40 GOP presidential gain by ethnic group, and the German coloration of the party tide is manifest. Most of the purely rural and socioeconomic reaction to the New Deal had set in by 1936. The almost wholly Anglo-Saxon counties of Iowa and Kansas, to which one must look for any con-tinuation, showed mere 2 per cent to 4 per cent Republican trends between 1936 and 1940. Some of the leading Norwegian counties of Wisconsin and Minnesota—Hitler had invaded Norway, so pro-German and isolationist outlooks were few—turned in Republican gains of only 3 per cent to 6 per cent.

On the other hand, a massive Republican tide poured out of those same counties, many still German by culture and language, where memories of the First World War and its attendant strains made voters balk at a new and similar war. In the heavily German coun-ties, the Republican vote rose 35 per cent to 45 per cent over Landon's 1936 levels. On a statewide basis, strongly German North Dakota led the way with a 26 per cent trend, and the GOP also won South Dakota, Nebraska, Kansas and Iowa. Notwithstanding such German balloting, Wisconsin and Minnesota remained Democratic because of Scandinavian progressivism and urban New Deal loyal-

Ethnic Voting in the Farm States, 1940 *(Change in Republican Share of the Total Presidential Vote)*

Minnesota

County (ethnic group)	GOP % Gain 1936-40
Sibley (German)	41%
Brown "	41
Stearns "	40
Scott "	36
Carver "	36
Wabasha "	35
McLeod "	32
Wright "	31
LeSueur "	28
Nicollet "	28
Norman (Norwegian)	8
Polk "	8
Marshall "	7
Pennington "	7
Clearwater "	7
Lake (Finn, Swede, Norw.)	7
St. Louis (Finn, Swede, Slav.)	7
Itasca (Finn, Swede, Norw.)	6
Kittson (Swedish)	3
Roseau (Norw., Swede)	3

Wisconsin

County (ethnic group)	GOP % Gain 1936-40
Calumet (German)	41%
Ozaukee "	34
Washington "	34
Dodge "	31
Kewaunee "	30
Manitowoc "	27
Shawano "	26
Fond du Lac "	26
Clark "	26
Marathon "	25
Iron (Finn, Slav.)	11
Ashland (Finn, Slav., Swede)	10
Rock (Yankee)	10
Douglas (Finn, Slav, Norw.)	10
Eau Claire (Norwegian)	9
Florence (Swedish, Polish)	9
Portage (Polish)	9
Bayfield (Finn, Swede, Norw.)	7
Forest (Finn, Polish)	7
Dane (Norwegian)	6

Iowa

County (ethnic group)	GOP % Gain 1936-40
Plymouth (German)	31%
Bremer "	25
Ida "	23
Sioux "	22
Lyon "	21
Dubuque "	21
Crawford "	19
Clayton "	19
Des Moines (Ger., Swede)	19
Carroll (German)	18
Webster (Anglo-Swedish)	4
Dallas (Anglo-Saxon)	4
Marion "	4
Marshall "	4
Warren "	4
Polk "	2
Wapello "	2
Wayne "	2
Davis "	2
Decatur "	2

Note: these counties are those ten in each state showing the *largest* and *smallest* GOP trends (no counties showed Democratic trends).

ties in Minneapolis-St. Paul, Duluth-Superior and Milwaukee.*
Much the same pattern prevailed in 1944 as in 1940, except that
the Republicans also captured Wisconsin.

Several facets of the 1940 vote are worth singling out: (1)
isolationist enmities produced a voter turnout so large that it was
not matched again until the 1952 election and the related stress of
the Korean War; (2) the urban bias and progressive bent of the
New Deal had made Minnesota and Wisconsin into the *best* Democratic Farm states, not the worst as in earlier days; and (3) the
Republican trend did not spread across all ethnic groups but was
overwhelmingly German.

World War II ended in 1945, shortly after the death of Franklin
D. Roosevelt. Many Republican leaders, who had always thought
that only Roosevelt's personal popularity kept them from office,
now looked for victory in 1948. Ignoring the ethnic nature of their
wartime Farm Belt strength, they expected Thomas E. Dewey, the
1948 party nominee, to exceed the levels he had achieved in 1944.
Thus, when Truman ran far ahead of Roosevelt and recaptured
two Farm states lost in 1944, the GOP postulated an "agrarian
uprising," but much of the seeming farm trend was simply a falling-
off of artificial wartime support.

Just as a large vote turnout characterized the 1940 election, a
small one laid down the story in 1948. Enough voters whom the war
had induced to vote Republican stayed home to shrink the electorate as follows between 1940 and 1948: 22 per cent in North
Dakota, 19 per cent in Nebraska, 19 per cent in South Dakota, 14
per cent in Iowa and somewhat less in the other Farm states. (North
and South Dakota, and Nebraska as well, have *never equaled* the
vote they cast in 1940.) When the ballots were tabulated in 1948,
political observers were aghast to find that Iowa, Minnesota and
Wisconsin, the most populous Farm states, had gone for Truman.
The Wheat Belt also rolled up Democratic gains, but not enough to
produce Truman victories.

Although local reluctance to risk the security of New Deal farm
programs by voting for the establishmentarian Republican governor
of New York undoubtedly gave an economic tinge to 1948 shifting

---

*The behavior of these industrial areas—especially the lakeside iron-ore shipping
centers of Duluth and Superior—bears little relation to that of the cash crop
counties of the core Farm Belt. Their trends influence Wisconsin and Minnesota
towards Great Lakes voting patterns. In Des Moines, Omaha or Wichita, industry
has more of an agricultural orientation.

and non-voting (Truman fanned these apprehensions by bombast, alleging that Wall Street treated the South and West as colonies), this does not explain why Governor Dewey had been able to win majorities in Wisconsin and Iowa in 1944 which he could not win in 1948. It is a little foolish to suggest that Dewey menaced farm programs in 1948 because he was expected to win, whereas he had been expected to lose in 1944.

The best answer is that suggested by Samuel Lubell, who states that much of the "farm" revolt against the GOP was a result of non-voting or renewed Democratic voting on the part of isolationist and anti-Roosevelt German Catholics.* Farm Belt election statistics illustrate Lubell's theory. Thirty German precincts in Ohio and Wisconsin that voted for Lemke in 1936 indicated the isolationist nature of much of the Truman tide in the Middle West: only 25 per cent for Roosevelt in 1940, these precincts gave Truman 53 per cent of their vote in 1948. Almost without exception, the leading Middle West German counties showed sharp enough Democratic trends in 1948 to suggest that with 1940 or wartime-level support among German Americans, Dewey would have held Iowa, Ohio, Wisconsin and taken Illinois. The Truman "trend" was not so much actual as numerical. In most of the Farm states, Truman ran behind Roosevelt's 1940 totals, but his percentages ran considerably higher because of the severe fall-off in the GOP vote.

Lost in the shuffle of 1948 was a movement—Henry Wallace's new Progressive Party—for which big things had originally been expected. Before serving as Franklin D. Roosevelt's vice-president (1941-45), Wallace had been the New Deal Secretary of Agriculture and he fancied himself another LaFollette. He hoped to resurrect Farm Belt third-party progressivism in 1948 and he failed utterly. In the first place, the farmers were reasonably happy with the incumbent party. (Earlier Farm-state movements had drawn aim on Northeastern oligarchic Republican administrations and kindred Democratic oppositions.) Secondly, Wallace had an unpopular foreign policy—he was quickly tagged as a gullible friend of the Soviet Union by his speeches and by his roster of fellow-traveling supporters. This latter proclivity was anathema to the German isolationist bloc which had given such meaningful support

*Samuel Lubell, *The Future Of American Politics* (New York, 1952), pp. 142-143. Lubell's discussion of German American isolationism during the New Deal and Fair Deal eras is without peer.

to Senator LaFollette's 1924 Progressive presidential candidacy. Wallace ran best in Minnesota, Wisconsin and North Dakota, just as LaFollette had, but he won only 3 per cent to 4 per cent of the vote. As Chart 112 shows, Wallace's minimal support came from Scandinavians disposed towards agrarian progressivism and not offended by pro-Soviet foreign policies. (Some of it was indeed old LaFollette strength.) German Catholics and Anglo-Saxons shunned Wallace.

It is useful to compare the relative Republicanism of the German Catholic and Scandinavian counties of North Dakota, Minnesota and Wisconsin in 1948, for despite the return of anti-Roosevelt German Democrats to their party, the New Deal and Second World War had moved German Catholic counties to the Right and Norwegian counties (seats of the old LaFollette *economic* tradition) to the Left. Whereas in the typical pre-1936 election, the German Catholic counties had been the most Democratic in their states while the Norwegian areas were GOP strongholds, the situation was in the throes of reversal by 1948. Truman ran better in the strongly Norwegian counties than in the German Catholic bastions. Foreign policy had taken its toll of German Democratic tradition and New Deal progressivism its toll of Scandinavian Republican tradition.

Given the dislocation of ethnic pathologies inherent in fighting two wars against one's ancestral homeland within a single generation, German American isolationist voting did not end with the cessation of hostilities in 1945. The heightened *underlying* Republicanism of the German counties (compared with New Deal and not 1940 totals) was one sign of this, and yet another was the ferocity with which the German counties seized on the rise of postwar Soviet power as proof that their doubts about war with Germany had been justified: Soviet Russia was and always had been the greater enemy. Enmity towards the Russian Bear was old Teuton psychology; moreover such an attitude lent itself to a retrospective view of the ethnic discomfort of 1935-45 as patriotic perception.

As the Cold War emerged, no other Americans outdid the Germans and Irish of the Middle West in vocal anti-communism, but the ex-isolationist bloc was more interested in revising World War Two history than in fighting a new war. The *Chicago Tribune,* apostle of Farm-state isolationism, represented much German opinion in opposing the Korean War, saying that it would have been unnecessary if the militarists and the State Department establish-

CHART 112

The Two Faces of Farm Belt Radicalism, 1936-48

	% of Total Vote Cast for Lemke, 1936	% of Total Vote Cast for Wallace, 1948
State		
North Dakota	13%	4%
Minnesota	7	3
Wisconsin	5	3
South Dakota	3	1
Iowa	3	1
Nebraska	2	0
Kansas	0	1
Minnesota Counties		
German Catholic		
Stearns	20%	1%*
Carver	18	1*
Benton	16	1*
Scott	16	1*
Norwegian Lutheran		
Pennington	3	7*
Clearwater	2	6*
Marshall	2	4*
Kittson	1	4*

*Total Vote Cast for Progressive, Socialist, Socialist Labor and Socialist Worker parties.

mentarians had understood the real menace of the Soviets earlier instead of being preoccupied with crushing Germany. Senator Joseph McCarthy, a native son of Wisconsin's German-American Outagamie County, sounded the isolationist trumpet when he accused Ivy League and Anglophile State Department officials for being "soft on communism" and assailed Franklin D. Roosevelt's "sell-out" to the Russians in Yalta in 1945. Onetime isolationists really soured on the Korean War after Chinese intervention stalled the American advance. Stalemated, the Korean War epitomized Establishment lack of desire to fight communism with the same fortitude used on Germany, and far from mobilizing isolationist support because it was fought against Communists, the war rekindled the foreign policy issues on which isolationist and particularly German American voting pivoted: the politics of revenge, as Samuel Lubell has so aptly put it.

Running against "Communism, Korea and Corruption"—no issues could have better suited the Farm Belt—Eisenhower swept the Farm Belt in 1952, winning lopsided victories in a large turnout. His best improvement over Dewey came in the old isolationist counties, and his biggest statewide gain came in bellwether North Dakota. Throughout the Farm Belt, much of the Republican impetus came from neo-isolationists objecting to the Korean War and bitter against the "war party" Democrats. In the fiercely isolationist Wheat Belt, Eisenhower won majorities (levels of 75 per cent to 90 per cent were common) similar to those chalked up by Harding in 1920. (See Chart 109.)

After the 1952 elections, the Farm states were once again overwhelmingly Republican. (One could almost say that a new "bloody shirt" had replaced the old.) Democratic governors, senators, congressmen and state legislators were few and far between. Mercurial as ever, though, the Farm states soon moved to weaken the GOP

CHART 113

Republican Share of the Two-Party Vote for President and Congress in Selected Farm Belt Precincts, 1952-56

	GOP Share of Presidential Vote 1952	GOP Share of Presidential Vote 1956	GOP Share of Congressional Vote 1952	GOP Share of Congressional Vote 1956
Wisconsin—Sixth District (Dairy Precincts)	83%	75%	86%	76%
Wisconsin—Ninth District (Poorer Dairy Precincts)	64	49	65	38
Iowa—First District (Corn, Hog & Dairy Precincts)	63	52	63	50
Iowa—Eighth District (Corn, Hog & Cash-grain Precincts)	74	58	No Contest	58
South Dakota—First District (Corn, Hog & Range-Cattle Precincts)	64	47	64	38
Minnesota—First District (Corn, Hog & Dairy Precincts)	70	57	73	59
Minnesota—Seventh District (Corn, Hog & Cattle Precincts)	57	43	59	47
Kansas—Fifth District (Wheat Belt Precincts)	78	66	74	43

Source: *U.S. News and World Report,* Nov. 23, 1956.

hegemony. First of all, some of the 1952 GOP voters were isolationist Democrats who returned to their party after Stevenson was
defeated and the Korean War ended. But more important, the
Eisenhower Administration exposed the party's perennial Farm-
state Achilles heel by taking a conservative stance on public power
and agricultural price supports.

Some Farm Belt Republican congressmen, more concerned with
farmers and self-preservation than with party loyalty, spurned the
policies of Secretary of Agriculture Ezra Taft Benson, and many
of those who did not were defeated in 1956 and 1958. Even President Eisenhower lost votes in 1956. Except in Wisconsin, which
behaves much like a Great Lakes state, his majorities were down
from those of 1952. Wisconsin gave him an increased vote share,
not by dint of farm support, but because of gains in the urban
Kenosha-Racine-Milwaukee area (trends akin to his strides in
Catholic districts throughout the Northeast and Great Lakes).*
Chart 113 shows the extent of the 1956 farm revolt against the
Republicans. Further losses occurred in the 1958 congressional
elections. However, the tide turned in 1960.

Among the Farm states, only Minnesota strayed from the Republican column in 1960. In Minnesota and Wisconsin, the two states
with the largest German Catholic and Scandinavian Lutheran
populations, John F. Kennedy's Catholicism lent heavily religious
overtones to voting patterns. These factors were also present in
North Dakota, but not quite to the same extent because many
North Dakota Germans are Protestants (Mennonites and Lutherans) and the German-Scandinavian division lacks the corollary religious denominator found, for example, in Minnesota. Chart 114
illustrates the importance of religious voting to the Farm Belt's 1960
presidential preference. The Scandinavian Lutheran counties
showed a small Republican trend presumably premised on anti-
Catholicism, while the German Catholic counties evinced a much
stronger and pro-Catholic trend. Outside of North Dakota, Wisconsin, Minnesota and Iowa, patches of ethnic volatility can be found,
but they are smaller and less influential.**

---

*Eisenhower also gained in urban Minnesota.
**Nixon did not slip much below Eisenhower in Nebraska, Kansas, South Dakota
   and Iowa, the heavily Protestant states (see Chart 116). Kennedy's major gains
   came in North Dakota, Wisconsin and Minnesota where both Catholics and
   Lutherans indulged in religious voting, but with pro-Catholic behavior dominating.

CHART 114

Religious Voting in the Upper Farm Belt, 1960 (Change in Party Share of the Total Vote for President)

Top four Republican-gain and top four Democratic-gain counties in each state, listing major ethnic group and the 1956-60 party gain

	Wisconsin		Minnesota		Iowa		North Dakota	
Democratic Gain (Catholic)	Brown (German-Belgian)	21%	Stearns (German)	23%	Dubuque (German)	19%	Emmons (German)	31%
	Calumet (German)	20%	Scott (German)	17%	Carroll (German)	14%	Stark (German)	27%
	Kewaunee (German)	20%	Brown (German)	15%	Delaware (German)	9%	Sioux (German)	25%
	Outagamie (German)	20%	Morrison (German)	14%	Jackson (German)	9%	Mercer (German)	21%
Republican Gain (Protestant)	Burnett (Swedish)	2%	Isanti (Swedish)	7%	Marion (Anglo)	6%	Slope (Norwegian)	4%
	Green (Swiss)	2%	Kandiyohi (Swedish)	6%	Decatur (Anglo)	5%	LaMoure (Norwegian, Mennonite)	2%
	Eau Claire (Norwegian)	1%	Kittson (Swedish)	5%	Appanoose (Anglo)	4%	Nelson (Norwegian)	2%
	Jackson (Norwegian)	1%	Roseau (Norwegian, Swedish)	3%	Mahaska (Anglo)	3%	Dickey (Norwegian, Mennonite)	1%

In large measure, the religious trends of 1960 camouflaged the rearranged partisan loyalties of Germans and Scandinavians. During the Eisenhower years, for example, German Catholic counties, captivated by GOP foreign policy, had shunned the farm revolt against Ezra Taft Benson's agricultural economics. German Catholic Farm Belt counties were the most staunchly pro-Eisenhower, while the few rural counties supporting Adlai Stevenson were often Scandinavian. It is safe to say that the large, progressive Swedish, Norwegian and Finnish population is one of the principal reasons why Minnesota is the most liberal and Democratic-minded of the Farm states, although it must be pointed out that, European patterns notwithstanding, there is nothing inherently liberal about Scandinavian Americans. In Minnesota and to a lesser extent in Washington, they have forged a local farmer-logger-fisherman-laborer coalition in the old-country mold, but in New York City, where the residential white middle class is submerged in a sea of minority-group liberal welfarism, the Scandinavian colonies of Bay Ridge, Brooklyn and The Bronx's City Island are centers not just of conservative Republicanism but of the militant Conservative Party.

Four years after Richard Nixon held the farm vote, Barry Goldwater lost it. All seven farm states voted for Lyndon Johnson in 1964. Nor were there any bright spots in the GOP gloom. Most Goldwater strategists were appalled at the low vote the Senator won in the Farm Belt isolationist strongholds. In expecting Goldwater to do well in these areas, his supporters misread the character of Farm-state anti-communism, which was more concerned with World War II revisionism than with contemporary overseas crusades, and ultimately balked at proposals for escalating the Vietnamese war. (Anglo-Saxon nationalism—jingoism, some say—is strongest in the South and in the Southwestern military-industrial complex.) Only a few Great Plains isolationist strongholds backed Goldwater, although 1960-64 losses were very small in the German Catholic counties where religious voting had already shaped large Democratic majorities in 1960.*

Not only isolationists but Scandinavian progressives and farmers

*In Wisconsin, Minnesota and North Dakota, where German Catholic behavior goes contrary to that of liberal Scandinavians, the German Catholic strongholds gave Goldwater some of his best county percentages, but in Kansas, Nebraska and Iowa, where conservatism is Anglo-Saxon, the leading German Catholic counties were Goldwater's *worst* on a statewide basis.

in general refrained from supporting Goldwater. For one thing, his suggestion of a market-place economy was unpopular in farming areas dependent on price supports. Secondly, his campaign's Southern political orientation cost him votes in Yankee-settled farm sections. As Chart 115 shows, the Arizona Senator slid well below Hoover's Depression-year presidential showings of 1932 in the leading Yankee counties of the Farm Belt.

Although Senator Goldwater maintained the general GOP pat-

CHART 115

The Republican Decline in Yankee Farm Counties, 1960-68

	Republican Share of the Total Vote for President				
County*	1932	1960	1964	1968	(**)
Douglas, Kansas	59%	67%	45%	54%	(11%)
Story, Iowa	52	65	40	57	(3)
Lawrence, S. Dakota	54	66	52	60	(5)
Fillmore, Minnesota	48	66	45	59	(4)
Rock, Wisconsin	56	61	42	51	(7)

*These counties are the Yankee strongholds of their states. Douglas County, Kansas, includes Lawrence, a city settled by New Englanders in the years before the Civil War. Pro-slavery Missourians under the infamous Quantrill raided Lawrence in 1862, killing one hundred and fifty people. Douglas County was long the most Republican county in Kansas, and it remained staunchly Republican throughout the depression. The county seat of Lawrence is named for Lawrence, Massachusetts, as is Lawrence County, South Dakota, which in turn was the most Republican county of that state in both 1932 and 1936 (being the only county not to vote for Roosevelt). Both of these counties behaved atypically within their states during the Nineteen-Twenties and -Thirties; they remained steadily Republican, ignoring the agrarian and isolationist vicissitudes of the Scandinavian and German counties. Fillmore County, Minnesota, in the southeastern part of the state, is named for the thirteenth president of the United States, New York Yankee Millard Fillmore, and was the most Republican county in Minnesota in 1932. Rock County, Wisconsin, includes the New England-settled city of Beloit and its college, whence Yankees went forth to all parts of the Middle West in the second half of the Nineteenth Century. Rock County remained solidly Republican in 1924, backing Yankee GOP President Calvin Coolidge, when most Wisconsin counties backed the third party presidential race of Wisconsin Senator Robert LaFollette, and Rock remained Wisconsin's most Republican county in 1932 (being one of two to support Hoover). Story County, Iowa, with its county seat of Ames, commemorates two of the best-known names in Massachusetts jurisprudence, and was Herbert Hoover's best Iowa county in 1932.

**Wallace share of total vote for President is in parentheses.

tern of running worst in the industrial and urbanized Farm states —Minnesota, Wisconsin and Iowa—the sharpest 1960-64 Republican presidential losses occurred in the predominantly old-stock states of Iowa, Kansas and Nebraska, because Wisconsin, Minnesota and North Dakota had already shown religious-based Democratic gains in 1960 (see Chart 114). Johnson carried all but one Farm Belt congressional district—Nebraska's Third—and his statewide percentages almost reached those scored by Roosevelt in peak New Deal years.

Conservative coalition Republicans who had expected the Farm states to support the Goldwater candidacy were stunned by the 1964 elections results. Congressional Republicans were even more stunned—the GOP lost a net eight House seats in Iowa, Nebraska, North Dakota and Wisconsin, most of which had been considered safe. This left the Republicans with only twenty of the thirty-seven Farm states congressmen, a post-New Deal low. But the victors could not maintain their inroads, and shortly after Barry Goldwater's defeat, the Democrats began to instill many of the same old doubts in the Farm Belt electorate with their unpopular farm and foreign policies. By the time the 1966 elections came around, hundreds of thousands of United States soldiers were fighting a stalemated war in Vietnam, while farm prices had declined on an absolute scale and the farmer's share of the national income had plummeted. To the Heartland, the Democrats seemed overly preoccupied with slum dweller and consumer interests, to the detriment of agriculture. In the November balloting, the GOP picked up nine Farm Belt House seats, to restore themselves to a level of strength untouched since the 1952 landslide.

Three Republican gains spotlighted the party's recovery in strongly isolationist areas. Democratic congressmen were defeated in three of the nation's leading German American rural districts—the 1st of North Dakota, the 6th of Wisconsin and the 6th of Minnesota —by GOP challengers Thomas Kleppe, William Steiger and John Zwach. On a lesser scale, the Republicans elected their first state senator in 40 years from Dubuque, Iowa, a 1936 Lemke stronghold and seat of Iowa isolationism.

In the seven Farm states, the 1966 GOP congressional vote climbed 15 per cent to 20 per cent above that won by Goldwater. After this recovery, the Republicans held every congressional district in the Wheat Belt: Kansas, Nebraska and the Dakotas. The

CHART 116

Farm Belt Presidential Voting, 1948-68

State	Republican Share of the Total Vote for President						Share of the Total Vote for President 1968		
	1948	1952	1956	1960	1964		Nixon	Wallace	Humphrey
Nebraska	54%	69%	66%	62%	47%		60%	8%	32%
Kansas	54	69	65	60	45		55	10	35
North Dakota	52	71	62	55	42		56	6	38
South Dakota	52	69	58	58	44		53	5	42
Iowa	48	64	59	57	38		53	6	41
Wisconsin	46	61	62	52	38		48	8	44
Minnesota	40	55	54	49	36		42	4	54

eight seats they lacked elsewhere in the Farm Belt were the major urban districts of Iowa, Wisconsin and Minnesota (Des Moines, Cedar Rapids-Dubuque, Milwaukee, Madison, Minneapolis-St. Paul, Milwaukee and Duluth).

The ingredients of 1966 Republican victory grew even more powerful by 1968. Resentment of the Vietnamese War was so widespread that isolationism regained credibility, prompting the *Chicago Tribune* to urge the academic community to consider whether the isolationists hadn't been correct all along!* Moreover, farmers were enmeshed in severe economic difficulties, yet the Democrats continued to stress the cause of cities and consumers, exacerbating farm anger.** Fear of the government mounted. Lastly, the small but rapidly growing Negro populations of the Farm states touched off racial violence even in out-of-the-way cities and generally stimulated backlash sentiment among white voters. To a majority of Farm-state voters, the Democrats were headed in the old GOP direction of preoccupation with the interests of the establishmentarian Northeast.

On the other side of the coin, Democratic liberalism was gaining strength in former Progressive strongholds like Madison, Wisconsin, acme of Senator Eugene McCarthy's April, 1968, presidential primary triumph. And in Yankee sections of the Farm Belt—the same counties which had given Coolidge, Hoover and Landon their best support—Republicans were rallying around Nelson Rockefeller's effort to capture the 1968 GOP presidential nomination for the party's Northeastern Liberal Establishment. However, these several liberal trends could not match the more powerful tides of conservatism.

In November, 1968, Richard Nixon carried Kansas, Nebraska, the Dakotas, Iowa and Wisconsin, losing to Hubert Humphrey only in Humphrey's home state of Minnesota. Chart 116 shows the

---

*One of the most important political effects of the war in Vietnam (and its failure) has been the resurrection of the isolationist impulse and controversy. The Vietnamese war set up a new internationalist scapegoat for the persistent isolationist voting streams, as witness the *Chicago Tribune* of March 25, 1968: "The fashionable academic literature of a not too bygone day celebrated the virtues of internationalism and excoriated the impulse to isolationism. . . . Judging from the number of backslid internationalists now blowing the trumpet of retreat, these academicians might today sound a different tune."

**Farm costs went up sharply while market prices remained down, putting farmers in a severe cost-price squeeze. Farm parity ratios dropped to the low levels of the Nineteen-Thirties. Realized net farm income (including government payments) dropped substantially between 1966 and 1968.

breakdown of the 1968 presidential vote. Among some groups, notably German Catholics and conservative Kansas and Nebraska Anglo-Saxon Democrats, Hubert Humphrey ran considerably behind 1960 Democratic levels, but he scored gains among Upper Farm Belt Yankees and Scandinavians. As a result of the interaction of these trends, the Farm states showed substantially similar statewide results to those of 1960 and split between the two candidates as in 1960. On each extreme, however, Scandinavian Minnesota produced a meaningful Democratic trend while North Dakota and Nebraska handed the Democrats a sizeable 1960-68 loss.

Predictably, Nixon made his best 1960-68 strides in the Farm Belt's German Catholic counties. Running against a Protestant—unlike 1960—and aided by rising isolationist resentments, the GOP contender bettered his 1960 share of the two-party vote in every major German Catholic county. Extraordinarily volatile Emmons County, North Dakota, turned in the sharpest Democratic decline—32 per cent. In Iowa, Nixon made greatest headway in Dubuque and other German centers. Wisconsin's large bloc of German counties turned in their state's only meaningful 1960-68 Nixon improvements. And even in Minnesota, the GOP candidate scored an absolute gain in archetypal German Stearns County and its peers, despite a statewide slide of 8 per cent. Across the North Dakota-Minnesota-Wisconsin roof of the Farm Belt, where politics and ideology have a German-Scandinavian cleavage, the Teutonic counties not only turned in Nixon's best gains but gave him his highest percentages. Chart 117 enumerates the 1968 behavior of the leading Farm Belt German counties. Heavily German North Dakota was the one state where the Republican candidate actually bettered his 1960 share of the total vote, notwithstanding the third-party inroads of George Wallace.

Besides Germans, the Upper Farm Belt area has sizeable concentrations of Scandinavians and Yankees, the two voting streams which showed pro-Democratic movement between 1960 and 1968. Part of the Scandinavian trend was simply an adjustment of 1960 Lutheran anti-Catholic opposition to John F. Kennedy; part of it represented empathy with Hubert Humphrey's own fractionally Scandinavian antecedents, Democratic-Farmer-Labor Party progressivism and local upbringing. In many of the Swedish and Norwegian counties of the Dakotas, Iowa and Wisconsin, Humphrey

CHART 117

Farm Belt Trends, 1960-68

The counties listed are the five in each state where Richard Nixon's share of the major party presidential vote *increased* and *decreased* the most between 1960 and 1968 (from unofficial 1968 figures)*

Wisconsin

Democratic Gain in Major Party Vote Share	Douglas (Slavic, Finnish, Norwegian)	8%
	Dane (Norwegian)	8%
	Sheboygan (Polish, Mixed)	7%
	Eau Claire (Norwegian)	7%
	Rock (Yankee)	6%
Republican Gain in Major Party Vote Share	Kewaunee (German)	15%
	Brown (German, Belgian)	8%
	Calumet (German)	8%
	Door (German, Belgian)	7%
	Outagamie (German)	6%

Iowa

Democratic Gain	Story (Yankee)	7%
	Marion (Yankee)	7%
	Des Moines (Swede, German)	7%
	Appanoose (Yankee)	5%
	Mahaska (Yankee)	5%
Republican Gain	Dubuque (German)	7%
	Audubon (German, Danish)	7%
	Winneshiek (Ger., Norw.)	7%
	Howard (German)	6%
	Plymouth (German)	6%

Minnesota

Democratic Gain	Chisago (Swedish)	14%
	Lake (Finnish, Slavic)	13%
	Goodhue (Swede, Norw.)	12%
	Carlton (Finnish, Slavic)	11%
	Isanti (Swedish)	11%
Republican Gain	Stearns (German)	8%
	Morrison (German)	5%
	Brown (German)	5%
	Red Lake (Fr.-Canadian)	5%
	Scott (German)	4%

*The varying size and impact of the Wallace vote clouds the meaning of changes in the Republican or Democratic shares of the combined Republican-Democratic vote.

climbed slightly above 1960 Democratic levels despite Wallace's vote diversion, and in Minnesota, he scored considerable gains. Back in 1960, Richard Nixon had carried Hennepin County (Minneapolis) by eleven thousand votes; he lost it by five thousand in 1968. Minneapolis is the state's largest Swedish center, and Humphrey—his relations with Swedes have been intimate—ran particularly well. Swedish counties produced Humphrey's best Minnesota gains (See Chart 117).

Yankee areas also provided dramatic Democratic advances. In Wisconsin, Yankee Rock County, a longtime GOP banner county in the state, turned in one of Wisconsin's top 1960-68 Democratic gains. Iowa's Yankee concentrations stretching from Davenport to Ames and Des Moines—in 1932 they had been Hoover's best counties in the state—produced Humphrey's greatest gains over Kennedy. Polk County (Des Moines) switched from Nixon in 1960 to Humphrey in 1968. As shown in Chart 115, the banner Farm Belt Yankee counties still backed Nixon despite their Democratic trend. The Yankee Democratic trend was most important in Minnesota, Wisconsin and Iowa, the top GOP Farm states of the half century after the Civil War. It was also important in eastern Kansas. On the other hand, Nebraska, southern Iowa, parts of South Dakota and most of Kansas include large non-Yankee Anglo-Saxon populations, some of them Southern or Border states in origin. These are the former strongholds of William Jennings Bryan, and they generally gave Richard Nixon a higher share of the majority party vote in 1968 than they had in 1960. George Wallace compiled his best Farm Belt percentages in such locales.

Opposition to the war in Vietnam was a major factor in Farm Belt voting, but such reaction took two forms. On one hand, ex-progressives and left-leaning war opponents trended sharply Democratic despite their pre-convention opposition to Johnson-Humphrey war policies. Wisconsin's Dane County, which includes Madison, seat of LaFollette progressivism and the liberal state university, gave Humphrey 58 per cent of the *total* presidential vote, up from John F. Kennedy's 52 per cent. With few exceptions, Humphrey did well in the counties—most were substantially Scandinavian— where Henry Wallace had done well in 1948. But if the war did not hurt the Democrats among the Farm Belt progressive anti-war electorate, it definitely did—as indicated above—reduce party support among conservative anti-war (isolationist) German voters.

Thus, while the onetime top counties of Henry Wallace moved towards Hubert Humphrey, the former Lemke counties trended Republican. Both anti-war voting streams saw the unpopular Asian war as they have long seen United States politics: from entirely different psychological points of view.

Generally speaking, the Democrats fared best in the urban Farm states—Wisconsin, Minnesota and Iowa. But even though Democratic strength was centered in urban and industrial areas, urbanization was no more the denominator of the 1960-68 trend than was the generality of opposition to the war in Vietnam. Some Farm Belt urban counties—those including Milwaukee, Green Bay, Dubuque, Omaha, Kansas City and Wichita—gave Nixon a better share of the two-party vote than he had won in 1960, but others—those including Minneapolis, St. Paul, Duluth, Madison, Topeka, Cedar Rapids, and Des Moines—moved in the other direction. Ethnic factors were paramount: Scandinavian, Slavic and Yankee cities produced a pro-Humphrey shift, while German Catholic and non-Yankee Anglo-Saxon cities generally gave Richard Nixon a higher share of the two-party vote than he had won in 1960.

To some extent, agricultural unrest modified this ethnic pattern. Democratic policies were particularly unpopular in the Wheat Belt, and from western North Dakota south to western Kansas, Humphrey took a special drubbing. In Minnesota's wheat-growing Red River Valley, local ire was enough to cancel out any 1960-68 Democratic trend among the Scandinavian farm population.

George Wallace's best Farm Belt counties were traditionally Democratic areas influenced by conservatism. Across the upper Farm Belt, where Scandinavians and Germans are most numerous, the top Wallace counties were usually German Catholic. In the lower Farm Belt—Nebraska, southern Iowa and Kansas—the Alabaman won his best percentages in Anglo-Saxon areas of some conservative Democratic tradition. Eastern and Southern Kansas, especially the counties adjacent to Missouri and Oklahoma, gave Wallace 12 per cent to 15 per cent support. Nebraska's Douglas County (Omaha) and several adjacent Missouri River counties gave Wallace similar backing. Wallace also did well in the (populist) conservative Wheat Belt western sections of the two states. As Map 41 shows, substantial Anglo-Saxon backing for Wallace extended farthest north along the Missouri, Mississippi, Arkansas, Kaw and Platte rivers, all routes whereby Southern and Border settlers moved

MAP 41

Wallace Vote in the Farm Belt, 1968

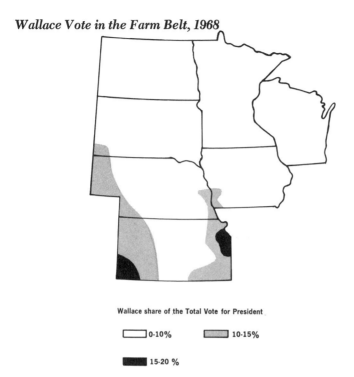

Wallace share of the Total Vote for President

☐ 0-10%   ▨ 10-15%

■ 15-20 %

into the present-day Farm Belt. Both the German Catholic and Kansas-Nebraska Anglo-Saxon Wallace voters belong to groups otherwise shifting into the Republican Party.

Kansas and Nebraska were Nixon's and also Wallace's best Farm states in 1968. Hubert Humphrey won only one third of the vote. These two states, together with the Dakotas, appear solidly Republican. Iowa, Wisconsin and Minnesota are the urbanized and marginal Farm states, and also those where the GOP is most affected by the erosion of Yankee and Scandinavian tradition. Chart 116 sets forth the margins of party victory or defeat in 1968. Iowa, where German and non-Yankee Anglo-Saxon strength is considerable, should be normally Republican. Wisconsin is relatively marginal, but the trend of the large German population and the re-alignment of the substantial Wallace vote augur well for the GOP. To a greater extent than Wisconsin, Minnesota constitutes a political periphery of the Heartland. And as Chart 102 shows, the cities of Minnesota have not received the Negro influx which so dislocates white urban Democratic loyalties, and which has occurred across the Great Lakes and from Milwaukee to Omaha. Already the most Democratic of the Farm states, Minnesota cast the lowest Wallace percentage in 1968 and has few vote groups—Germans alone constitute a large electorate—in motion toward the GOP. Minnesota should be a frequent dissenter from otherwise solid Farm-state participation in the evolving Republican coalition.

D. The Mountain States

Of the four sections of the Heartland, the largest, most sparsely populated and least politically significant is the Rocky Mountain region.* Despite their vast acreage, the eight Mountain states have only thirty-three electoral votes. Nevada and Wyoming, for example, are so thinly settled that they each have only one congressman. Denver and its suburbs make Colorado the most populous of the eight states, but the region's greatest growth is occurring in the Southwest (Las Vegas, Phoenix, Tucson and Albuquerque).

At times, the Mountain states have been rather good reflectors of American political tides. Throughout the last half century, they have usually voted practically *en bloc* for the winning presidential candidate.** However, they are not national bellwethers. On the contrary, they are strongholds of populism and anti-establishmentarianism. No region beyond the South was so strongly for William Jennings Bryan (1896, 1900 and 1908); only the Farm Belt gave higher vote shares to LaFollette in 1924; the Mountain states considerably exceeded Roosevelt's national average in 1936; and in 1964, the eight states posted Barry Goldwater's best non-Southern percentages. Similarly, the eight-state region was Richard Nixon's best in 1968.

Spreading over three quarters of a million square miles, the Mountain states are spanned by three physiographic regions: the Great Plains, the Rocky Mountains and the Western Interior

---

*On the west, the Pacific slope of the Rocky Mountains provides a geographic bond between the Mountain states of Idaho and Nevada and the interior sections of California, Oregon and Washington.

**Colorado missed in 1940; Colorado and Wyoming both missed in 1944; six of the eight states missed in 1960; and Arizona missed in 1964. Otherwise, bellwethers or not, the Rocky Mountain states have voted for the winner since 1916.

MAP 42

Physiographic Divisions of the Mountain States

Plateau. Map 42 illustrates this division, which is worth examination because political differences parallel those of geography.

The Great Plains section of the eight-state region encompasses the eastern portions of Montana, Wyoming and Colorado, where cash grain cultivation (wheat) and cattle ranching are economically dominant. Except for Denver—and at the base of the Rocky Mountains it can hardly be called a Plains city—the only notable urban centers are the relatively small cities of Cheyenne and Billings. There are considerable German populations, also Scandinavian, although neither group is as prominent as in the Farm states. Essentially, the eastern plains of Colorado, Wyoming and Montana are an extension of the Farm Belt, so that the political outlook of the area is by and large quite similar to that which sways the neighboring western (Wheat Belt) sections of Kansas, Nebraska and the Dakotas.

As one progresses west through Colorado, Wyoming and Montana, the Rocky Mountains loom on the horizon and actually rise more or less in the center of each state. Wheat cultivation gives way to mining and industry. As part of the Rocky Mountain range, the western portions of Colorado, Montana and Wyoming have different settlement patterns from the eastern plains. In western Montana— in Anaconda, Butte and Dublin Gulch—Irish mine and smelter workers account for a considerable share of the local population. There are also communities of Slavs and Italians. Another prominent Catholic group consists of the Hispano-Americans who dominate a number of mountain counties in northern New Mexico and adjacent southern Colorado.* Some are small farmers; others are miners and workers; most are poor.

Denver, the Rocky Mountain metropolis, is an old and fashionable city. Besides its growing numbers of young professionals, the city encompasses growing Negro and Mexican communities. Metropolitan Denver includes some prosperous and conservative suburbs, and the oil town of Casper, Wyoming, is another conservative stronghold; but since the New Deal, concentrations of miners, workers and minority group members have given the Rockies a degree of political liberalism not found on either adjacent slope.**

Both slopes of the Rockies are considerably more conservative than the mountain core area—not just the Farm Belt extension to the east, but the western slope which spreads plateau-like across Idaho, New Mexico, Utah, Nevada and Arizona. The first three states are traversed by the Rockies. However, Arizona and Nevada lie wholly to the west. By and large, these states lack the German and Scandinavian populations of the Great Plains or the Catholic

---

*Hispanic northern New Mexico and south-central Colorado constitute a historic and ethnic anomaly with which few Americans are familiar. During the last years of the Sixteenth Century, the Spaniards in Mexico moved settlers north up the Rio Grande into that portion of the valley of the same river straddling the present boundary of New Mexico and Colorado. Others spread into the foothills of the Rocky Mountain range known as Sangre de Christo (Blood of Christ). The area is still mired in the customs, traditions, family structures and church relationships of Eighteenth-Century Spain. Many Hispano-Americans own their own small, uneconomic farms and live far below the poverty level. North central New Mexico is referred to by sociologists as a portion of Latin America occurring in the midst of a typically American state. In New Mexico, the Hispano-Americans dominate a seven-county area (Mora, San Miguel, Taos, Rio Arriba, Santa Fe, Sandoval and Guadalupe) in which about 70 per cent of the population is Spanish or Mexican. Colorado's Hispano-Americans are much less important on a statewide basis, but they are numerous in that portion of the state adjacent to North-central New Mexico. See Map 43.

**Unionized labor is the one major element of yesterday's populism and economic insurgency substantially allied with establishment liberalism.

MAP 43

Ethnic and Religious Minorities of the Southwest

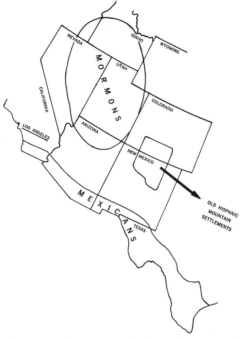

Principal Mexican-American concentrations (persons of Mexican stock) as of 1960: Arizona, 30,000; California, 695,000; New Mexico, 34,000; Texas, 655,000. The number of persons with Spanish surnames, including Mexican-Americans of longer residence and persons missed by the Census, is much greater and has been increasing rapidly. Most of the Mexican-Americans live along the Mexican border or in major Sun Belt cities like Los Angeles. However, a quite different group of Hispano-Americans live in the southern Colorado and northern New Mexico mountains. Although of remote Mexican antecedents, they have lived in their mountains for centuries, eking out a very poor rural living. They are most numerous in New Mexico.

---

concentrations of Rocky Mountain country (mining, industrial or Hispanic communities).* The interior plateau states, though, have a mosaic of their own. Utah and southern Idaho—the Snake and

---

*Northern Idaho is more like the adjacent Rocky Mountain section of Montana and the "Inland Empire" of eastern Washington and eastern Oregon. Southern Idaho, on the other hand, looks towards neighboring Utah. In 1886, Congress passed a bill that would have put northern and southern Idaho in different states, but President Cleveland pocket-vetoed it because of fear that southern Idaho would become a Mormon commonwealth like Utah.

Camas valleys, where the majority of Idahoans live—are heavily Mormon. Arizona, New Mexico and southern Nevada were principally settled by westward migration from the post-bellum South, and many residents have traditionally looked to the South in culture and politics. During the Civil War, the Southwest was something of a "Border" between Rebel Texas and Yankee California. Both Arizona and New Mexico were crossed by Union and Confederate armies and several pitched battles were fought. Nevada, Arizona and New Mexico were long as much "Border" states as Kentucky and Missouri, and for much the same reasons.

Until World War II, the five interior plateau states were basically non-urban, but things have changed. The major Idaho and Utah cities, strongly Mormon Salt Lake City and Boise, have not grown spectacularly. However, there has been a tremendous boom in the Albuquerque-Tucson-Phoenix-Las Vegas "Sun Belt" (which continues west to San Diego and Los Angeles). Such are the all-year climatic attractions (and still others in the case of Las Vegas), that retirees, businessmen and the just-plain-restless have come in droves. These sun-drawn middle classes are quite conservative, as are the Mormons and traditional Democrats of Southern extraction.

Part of the Southwestern population explosion also rests on local agricultural and industrial (defense industry) expansion. The new technology has attracted skilled workers and technicians, while irrigation has facilitated large-scale farming enterprises—cotton, fruit-growing and truck farming—requiring unskilled labor. From the Rio Grande delta at Brownsville and Harlingen, Texas all the way to California's Imperial Valley, the United States-Mexican border zone teems with Mexican agricultural workers. The Mexicans, Negroes and Hispano-Americans of the Southwest do not mix well with the conservative Anglo-Saxons. Ethnic friction is widespread, as it always has been on Anglo-Saxon frontiers.

Thus, the Mountain states are much more geopolitically complex than laymen are wont to think. A rough but useful division can be made between the Mountain-Plains states (Colorado, Montana and Wyoming) with their wheat and cattle; their Germans, Scandinavians and Irish; their isolationists; their agrarian, mine, mill and smelter radicals, and the interior plateau states (Arizona, New Mexico, Nevada, Utah and Idaho) with their booming resorts and retirement towns; their cotton and truck farming; their deserts;

their Mormons, Mexicans, Navajos, Apaches and Southern Democratic traditionalists. These latter states have a sociocultural tension lacking in all-white and small-city states like Wyoming and Montana. Northern Idaho, as indicated, looks to the Inland Empire of the Pacific Northwest rather than south to the interior plateau.

The eight Mountain states were admitted to the Union as follows: Nevada, 1864; Colorado, 1876; Wyoming, 1890; Idaho, 1890; Utah, 1896; New Mexico, 1912; and Arizona, 1912. They first made their political weight felt in 1896 by backing Democrat William Jennings Bryan. Unlike Bryan supporters in the Farm states, the Mountain states were not responding to evangelical Protestantism or to a desire to raise less corn and more hell. The Rocky Mountain silver magnates and miners, understandably pleased by Bryan's pro-silver policies, mobilized in support of inflationary coinage of their favorite metal as the answer to the nation's economic doldrums. With this tangible interest coupled to their basic economic radicalism, the Mountain states were much more pro-Bryan than the Farm Belt whence the candidate hailed. In his first presidential try, Bryan carried Idaho, Montana, Nevada, Utah and Colorado by three-, four- and five-to-one majorities while winning only three of the Farm states, and those by thin majorities. When Bryan ran for President again in 1900, the Farm Belt states all went Republican and the four leading silver states—Colorado, Montana, Idaho and Nevada—cast the only Democratic electoral votes west of the Mississippi (and outside the South). In his last White House bid (1908), the fading populist held only Colorado and Nevada.

Democratic tradition was widespread in the northern Rockies of the late Nineteenth Century. Montana had a large Irish electorate. Mormons were numerous in Idaho—and predominantly Democratic.* Moreover, during the Civil War period, many Southerners, Borderers and Northern draft dodgers had fled to the mines, ranches and navvy gangs of the Rocky Mountain territories. Bourgeois New England Yankees were few and far between. As for those miners, loggers, cattlemen and sheepherders of Northern or recent European origins, such Republican loyalties as they had were often outweighed by progressivism. In the Southwest, a more traditional

---

*Republican denunciations of Mormonism, especially polygamous marriage habits, and efforts to block Utah statehood and keep Idaho Mormons from voting all helped to create many Mormon Democratic loyalties.

pattern prevailed in Mormon Utah and Southern-settled Arizona, New Mexico and Nevada.* It did not require progressive GOP dissatisfaction with the Republican nominee to produce Democratic victories. As a matter of fact, Southwestern Democrats elected to Congress were often more conservative than northern Rocky Mountain Republicans. Until the New Deal, American politics remained in a Civil War orbit, so that the progressive northern Rocky Mountain states were marginal and the conservative Southwest leaned to the Democrats. Chart 118 illustrates some persistent traditional voting in the Southwest. For the first half of the Twentieth Century, Arizona, New Mexico, Nevada and Oklahoma—the Southwestern Heartland—were usually Democratic.

CHART 118

Democratic Presidential Tradition in the Southwest, 1916-68

County	Democratic Share of the Total Vote for President			
	1916	1936	1948	1968
Graham, Arizona	71%	81%	63%	37%
Roosevelt, New Mexico	82	77	76	28
Clark, Nevada	68	81	62	44

The Mountain states all voted for Woodrow Wilson in 1912. None gave the aloof and scholarly Democrat a majority vote, but the non-Wilson vote was fatally divided by incumbent William Howard Taft and former President Theodore Roosevelt, running on a third-party "Bull Moose" ticket. In 1916, however, President Wilson carried all eight states in his re-election bid, despite undivided opposition, by promising not to involve the United States in the war raging across Europe. Progressive elements in the Rocky Mountains strongly opposed American participation in the war, feeling that it would serve only international banking and arman. ts interests while diverting attention from economic reform needed at home. Luckily for Rocky Mountain Democrats, the 1916

---

*New Mexico's traditional Democrats centered in east New Mexico's "Little Texas." The state's Hispano-Americans, usually bloc-voted by a few leaders, were not the major force their numbers would indicate.

GOP presidential nominee was Charles Evans Hughes, an establishmentarian Eastern lawyer (he resigned from the Supreme Court to make the race), who epitomized the oligarchic interests so suspect in the West.

But Woodrow Wilson proved unable to keep his promise. The United States entered the First World War in 1917 over the outspoken opposition of some Mountain states legislators. And after the Peace of Versailles painted the war in just those colors progressives had earlier alleged, the 1920 election saw all eight states cast heavy majorities for the isolationist "Return to Normalcy" espoused by GOP presidential nominee Warren Harding. The Republican tide was strongest in the northern Rockies and weakest in the Southwest, where Democratic nominee James Cox won most of the traditional party vote. Isolationism was not widespread in the Southwest; local Anglo-Saxon, Protestant and Southern-sprung populations did not share the German, Scandinavian, Irish and radical labor views of the northern Rockies electorate.

In 1924, Progressive Party nominee Robert LaFollette appealed to both isolationism and economic radicalism and was able to run ahead of conservative Democratic nominee John Davis in most of the Mountain states, but Republican Calvin Coolidge carried every state with at least a plurality. Throughout the region, Davis' highest vote came in Arizona, Utah and New Mexico, while Senator LaFollette ran best in Idaho, Montana and Wyoming. Four years later, Herbert Hoover, running against Tammany Catholic Al Smith, made his best gains in the traditionally Democratic sections of the Southwest (Eastern New Mexico's "Little Texas," for example), while Smith increased the Democratic vote share in areas which had gone enthusiastically for LaFollette.

Far from being a bastion of conservatism, the Rocky Mountain states were a hotbed of isolationism and economic radicalism for half a century after their admission to the Union. During the Nineteen-Twenties and -Thirties, the mining camps and cities of the Rocky Mountains abounded with socialists, labor union organizers and agitators, and although many regional senators and congressmen were conservative ranchers or business-oriented protectionists like Utah's Senator Reed Smoot of high tariff fame, the statesmen history remembers are the great radicals. Three of the most famous —Senators Burton Wheeler, Montana Democrat; William Borah, Idaho Republican; and Hiram Johnson, California Republican—

were economic progressives and isolationists who staunchly opposed the manueverings of the Eastern Seaboard business and financial community. (They were even more antagonistic to the Southern Pacific Railroad and the Anaconda copper interests, bêtes noires of California and Montana progressive politics.)

With the advent of the Depression, Rocky Mountain economic discontent and animosity towards Wall Street swelled and Roosevelt swept the region in 1932. The Democrats made major gains in the progressive GOP counties, while regrouping their own strength in traditional rural areas. Four years later, the Roosevelt tide continued, except in the Great Plains sections of Wyoming, Montana and Colorado, where GOP gains paralleled those in the Farm Belt. Then in 1940, the lure of isolationism beckoned many voters; leading Senators like Borah, Johnson and Wheeler once again took up isolationist cudgels; and the Republican vote grew large enough for presidential nominee Wendell Willkie to carry Colorado and just miss capturing Wyoming. In 1944, Wyoming also turned against Roosevelt. The isolationist GOP trend was most emphatic in the plains sections of Wyoming, Montana and Colorado, where 1936-40 Republican gains were commonly in the 15 per cent to 20 per cent range. As in 1920, there was much less of a reaction in the Southern-settled areas of New Mexico, Arizona, Nevada, and also Mormon Utah.

But what isolationism had joined together, isolationism subsequently pulled asunder. Many Rocky Mountain isolationist voters of 1940 and 1944 stayed home in 1948, destroying the wartime-inflated GOP majorities in Colorado and Wyoming. Shorn of this Republican strength, the Mountain states voted Democratic in 1948. Truman carried all eight. Dewey's loss of Colorado and Wyoming (he was the candidate both states had supported in 1944) was similar in cause to his loss of Iowa, Wisconsin and Ohio.

The same isolationism which figured so obviously in the Great Plains-influenced Mountain states was relatively unimportant in the Southwest, where Dewey did better in 1948 than he had in 1944. Whereas the number of presidential votes cast declined between 1940 and 1948 in Wyoming, Colorado, Montana and Idaho, it increased in Arizona, New Mexico, Nevada and Utah. The Southwest boomed after World War II, and many of the immigrants were Northern Republicans.

In retrospect, the 1948 election was the last to be fought out in the longtime Mountain states context of economic progressivism in the Northern states and traditional Democratic strength in the Southwest. Times were changing. A middle-class influx was beginning to remake the one-time Spanish Southwest, and another decade would see liberalism begin to shift its orientation towards the Negro socioeconomic revolution and urban ghetto, pushing Northern Rockies economic progressivism towards obsolescence. Of course, this was not apparent in the early Nineteen-Fifties, even though in the Eisenhower era there were clues to the new pattern in the throes of emergence.

In 1952, two major surges—isolationist voting in the Northern Rockies and the middle-class residential boom in the Southwest—enabled Eisenhower to sweep all eight Mountain states. Wheat belt counties in Wyoming, Montana and Colorado gave the General 15 per cent to 20 per cent more of the vote than they had given to the much-suspect Thomas E. Dewey. In the Southwest, the burgeoning greater Phoenix section of Arizona elected its first Republican congressman since the Nineteen-Twenties and simultaneously served up the margin of victory for the first Republican elected to the United States Senate from Arizona in many years, Barry M. Goldwater. Four years later, Northern Rockies voters, no longer concerned with the Korean War, were up in arms against Republican agricultural, public power and resource policies. Hell's Canyon, the name of a power project on the Snake River in Idaho, became both symbol and slogan. Between 1952 and 1956, Eisenhower's vote share fell slightly in Montana, Colorado, Wyoming and Idaho, but the sun trek to the Southwest continued to bolster Republican strength. Phoenix, Tucson, Albuquerque and Salt Lake City all gave Eisenhower a better share of the vote in 1956 than in 1952.

During the Nineteen-Fifties, leading Sun Belt cities like Phoenix, Albuquerque and Tucson gained population at a rate that altered the political complexion of their states. Chart 119 shows the rising percentage of the Arizona-wide vote cast by Maricopa County (greater Phoenix), a trend which has transformed Arizona from a state with a definite Democratic bias to one of the most Republican states in the nation. On a lesser scale, the growth of Bernalillo County (Albuquerque) has had a similar influence on New Mexico.*

---

*One New Mexico trend was hurting the GOP. Prior to the New Deal, the Hispanic counties were more often than not Republican. By World War II, they were Democratic, but their statewide influence was declining in the face of the middle-class Anglo-Saxon influx.

CHART 119

The Phoenix Boom and the Rise of Arizona Republicanism

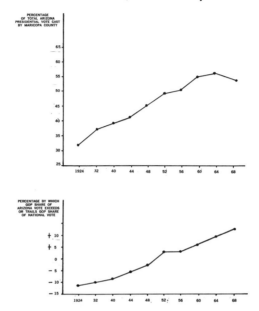

In 1960, Richard Nixon won all of the Mountain states save Nevada and New Mexico, two with strong Democratic traditions, marking the first time since 1900 that a majority of the eight had supported a losing presidential candidate. Part of the explanation lay in local inability to reflect the pro-Catholic voting that tipped the scales to the east, but another trend was also important. Liberalism was turning away from the popular economic progressivism with which Mountain states support had been forged—the Norris-Borah-Wheeler era was over and done with—and was shifting into a welfare establishmentarianism lacking in appeal to the old radical Mountain states (where Northeastern causes are suspect, whether liberal or conservative).

As if to confirm the conservative trend of latter-day populism, the Mountain states were considerably more Republican than the rest of the nation in 1964. Although Goldwater carried only his home state of Arizona, the GOP vote remained roughly at 1948 levels, and the regional Democratic trend was below the national 11 per cent average. In Idaho, Utah, Nevada, Arizona and New

Mexico, Goldwater captured slightly over 46 per cent of the collective vote, down only 7 per cent from Nixon's 1960 levels. No region outside the South showed a lesser Democratic trend. On the other hand, the states of the Great Plains eastern slope of the Rockies —Wyoming, Montana and Colorado—responded much more negatively to the Goldwater candidacy. In these states, large sections of which mirrored negative Farm Belt reactions to the Arizona Senator, only a shade more than 40 per cent of the electorate voted Republican, a sharp dip from the 55 per cent that had supported Nixon in 1960. Thus, the Rocky Mountains constituted a political as well as a continental divide. On the eastern slope, Goldwater's losses approached those he suffered in the Farm Belt, but on the western slope, they were milder. Chart 120 illustrates the 1960-64 GOP decline in a cross-section of major Western urban counties.

Across the interior plateau of Nevada, Idaho, Arizona, Utah and New Mexico, Goldwater ran as well or better than Dewey had in 1948. However, the party showing in the Great Plains dropped to levels untouched since 1936. Together with adjacent Southern California, the Southwest was Goldwater's best region beyond

CHART 120

Decline in the Republican Share of the Two-Party Presidential Vote, 1960-64, Selected Mountain States and Adjacent Urban Counties

Great Plains

Yellowstone (Billings, Montana)	14%
Laramie (Cheyenne, Wyoming)	14%
Denver (Denver, Colorado)	16%

Rocky Mountains

Silver Bow (Butte, Montana)	12%

Interior Plateau

Ada (Boise, Idaho)	4%
Bannock (Pocatello, Idaho)	6%
Spokane (Spokane, Wash.)	8%
Washoe (Reno, Nevada)	7%

Southwest

Clark (Las Vegas, Nevada)	6%
Maricopa (Phoenix, Ariz.)	5%
Pima (Tuson, Ariz.)	7%
Bernalillo (Albuquerque, New Mexico)	11%
El Paso (El Paso, Texas)	7%

Dixie. And as with the South, this represented a considerable about face for a region which had long been more Democratic than the nation as a whole. American politics were breaking out of their Civil War mold and responding to a new socioeconomic conflict.

The 1964 Republican defeat cost the party several Rocky Mountain congressional seats and statehouses. However, by 1966 the tide had turned and these losses were more than recouped. Unpopular Vietnamese, agricultural and Great Society social programs accelerated the basic regional conservative trend. The GOP made sharp gains in the plains sections of Colorado, Montana and Wyoming, but the most emphatic improvement came in the Interior Plateau states, where the patterns of 1960 and 1964 had already hinted at changing partisan alignment. Seven of the eight Mountain states emerged from the 1966 elections with Republican governors; the only exception was Utah, where holdover Governor Calvin Rampton did not have to face the electorate. Perhaps the best evidence of the new Republican era taking shape occurred in the record percentages cast for GOP congressional candidates in several of the Mountain states. Utah, Idaho and Arizona gave Republican House candidates their highest share of the vote since the Nineteen-Twenties, a sign of the emerging party hegemony. Chart 121 demonstrates the 1966 GOP breakthrough in Interior Plateau states congressional voting.

The Republican tide of 1966 continued in 1968, as Richard Nixon swept all eight Mountain states. Farm unhappiness and neo-

CHART 121

Republican Strength in Mountain States
Congressional Races, 1956-66

GOP Share of Two-Party Vote for Congress

	1956	1958	1960	1962	1964	1966
Idaho	54%	48%	45%	47%	51%	60%
Utah	59	51	50	53	47	64
Nevada*	46	33	43	28	37	32
Arizona	48	50	52	51	50	56
New Mexico	47	37	41	42	43	47

*The Democratic congressman from Nevada is the most conservative non-Southern Democrat in the House of Representatives.

isolationist resentment of the war in Vietnam buoyed the GOP among Great Plains voters in eastern Montana, Wyoming and Colorado; conservative Mormons in Idaho and Utah shed Democratic traditions, as did other Southwesterners; and the exploding Sun Belt populations of urban Arizona, New Mexico and Nevada tilted local sentiment in an ever-more-conservative direction. Even Rocky Mountain progressives found it a long way from Hell's Canyon to Harlem. And although the increasing activism of Indians, Mexicans and Hispano-Americans posed a contrary and liberal impetus in Colorado, New Mexico and Arizona, the voting power of these long-dormant groups has been very much diluted by the middle-class Anglo-Saxon influx.*

The sharpest Democratic losses of the 1960-68 period came among the Mormons and Southern-leaning traditional Democrats of the Interior Plateau. Because of these trends, Nixon handily won Nevada and New Mexico, the two Mountain states which he had lost to John F. Kennedy in 1960. Continuing middle-class migration to the Sun Belt metropolitan areas increased Nixon's urban majorities, while George Wallace's third-party candidacy sidetracked large numbers of conservative and populist Democrats. (The Alabaman garnered 12 per cent to 20 per cent of the total vote in New Mexico's Little Texas, southern Idaho and Nevada—Map 2 shows the contours of Wallace strength.) Except in Nevada and Idaho, where the John Birch Society and conservative Republicans were active on Wallace's behalf, most third-party voters were Democrats, though disaffected and Republican-trending ones who would have supported Nixon in a two-party contest. Chart 122 illustrates the sharp 1960-68 decline in the Democratic share of the presidential vote in the Interior Plateau states.

Arizona, Utah and Idaho were three of the nation's six top Nixon states in 1968. The two other Interior Plateau states, Nevada and New Mexico, gave Nixon adequate but not overwhelming victories. On the congressional level, the five states consolidated their Republican bias by electing—after a GOP congressional sweep in New Mexico—eight Republican congressmen, one Southern Democrat

---

*Nixon did fairly well among New Mexico's Hispano-Americans, in part because of the local party's efforts. GOP Governor Cargo, popular among Hispano-Americans because of his Spanish wife, was reelected, and New Mexico elected a Hispano-American GOP Congressman, Manuel Lujan. Across the border in Colorado, Hispano-Americans went overwhelmingly Democratic as did Mexican voters in both Arizona and Colorado.

CHART 122

Mountain States Presidential Voting, 1960-68

State	Percentage of the Total Vote for President				
	Nixon 1960	Goldwater 1964	Nixon 1968	Wallace 1968	Humphrey 1968
Arizona	56%	50%	55%	10%	35%
Utah	55	45	57	6	37
Wyoming	55	43	56	9	35
Colorado	55	38	51	8	41
Idaho	54	49	57	12	31
Montana	51	41	51	7	42
New Mexico	50	40	52	8	40
Nevada	49	41	48	13	39

(Nevada's Walter Baring) and one regular Democrat. There can be little doubt that the Interior Plateau, never a political ally of the Northeastern Establishment, is now a stronghold of the new popular Republicanism.

On the other, eastern slope of the Rockies, the wheat-rich plains of Montana, Wyoming and Colorado went Republican with the same intensity that motivated Kansas, Nebraska and the Dakotas. Nixon handily surpassed his 1960 levels in the wheat granaries of eastern Wyoming, Montana and Colorado, amassing leads which secured his statewide majorities. Counties suggesting a pageant of history with names like Custer, Big Horn, Powder River, Crook, Cheyenne, Kit Carson and Sublette, gave Nixon two, three or four times as many votes as Humphrey. Bellwether Laramie County, Wyoming, which had backed John Kennedy in 1960, switched to the Republican nominee in 1968.

Predictably, the best Democratic percentages in the Rocky Mountain states were cast by the mountain core area itself. One Democratic-trending locale was the city of Denver, increasingly a mecca for both establishmentarian cosmopolitans and local minorities (Negroes and Mexicans). Whereas Nixon had carried Denver by a hair's breadth in 1960, Humphrey won easily in 1968. The Democratic nominee also increased 1960 party levels in the depressed mining city of Butte, Montana, and in substantially Mexican

Pueblo, Colorado. Southern Colorado's Hispano-American counties voted for Humphrey. Colorado was the Rocky Mountain state where Humphrey dipped least—and Nixon dipped most—below 1960 levels. Denver is the oldest major Anglo-Saxon-implanted city in the Rocky Mountains, and it is certainly the center of regional culture, commerce and fashion. Unlike the boom towns of the Southwest, it is beginning to cast fewer votes in succeeding presidential elections and to lose population to its suburbs. (Between 1960 and 1968, Nixon doubled his majority in the four fast-growing suburban counties surrounding Denver.)

Less predictably, George Wallace's best percentages (10 per cent to 20 per cent) in Colorado and Montana were scored in the Rocky Mountain high country. Except for Anglo-Mexican squabbles, racial confrontation is nonexistent in these counties, but the miners and old economic populists of the Rockies constitute a brand of Democrat disenchanted with the party's increasing Northeastern establishmentarian liberalism. After all, these are the counties that cheered and voted six-, eight- or ten-to-one for William Jennings Bryan. In voting for the fiercely anti-establishmentarian Wallace, this Rocky Mountain electorate was simply renewing its populism of yesteryear.

So long as the Democrats remain oriented towards the Northeast, their presidential nominees are not likely to carry the old populist Rocky Mountain states. Not only do the Interior Plateau and Wyoming seem solidly Republican, but the only trend groups in motion are edging towards rather than away from the GOP. Colorado and Montana, the only two states where Humphrey won better than 40 per cent of the vote in 1968, offer the Democrats their best opportunity, but they are not likely to carry *any* of the Mountain states except in presidential years of decisive national victories. Sparsely settled though they may be, the Rocky Mountains have become pillars of the new national Republicanism.

E. A United Heartland

Early this century, British geographer Sir Halford MacKinder propounded a theory that control of the Eurasian land mass rested in the "Heartland" of eastern Europe. His theory did not sit well with British maritime strategists who liked to think that power in

Europe and Asia lay with the British fleet steaming around the hemispheric periphery. Nor does the present day Liberal Establishment of the Northeastern Seaboard much like the idea of the American Heartland's ending its Civil War-ingrained division and uniting to seize political control of the nation. But if the 25 Heartland states join together as they appear to be doing, they command a total of 223 electoral votes, only 47 short of the number required to elect a President.

In support of the proposition that the Heartland is now moving together into one party which it can dominate, a very definite trend can be seen emerging in Heartland political behavior during the last century. As a first phase, the post-Civil War Heartland was divided on a North-South axis paralleling the partisan "vote as you shot" division rooted in the Northeast and South. Subsequently, agricultural unrest turned the plains and the mountains against Bourbon South and industrial Northeast alike, but William Jennings Bryan's Southern-Western coalition fell just short of victory because the Great Lakes and a few Farm states stuck with the Northeast. When this agrarian impetus expired, the Heartland returned to its essential blue-gray cleavage along an extended Mason-Dixon line. From 1920 to 1964, the Heartland, although still divided by Civil War era traditions, overcame the past to the extent of unanimously or nearly unanimously swinging to the winning candidate in eight presidential elections—1920, 1924, 1928, 1932, 1936, 1952, 1956 and 1964. Even in the less decisive years of 1940, 1944 and 1948, a majority of the Heartland states supported the winning side.

Only one election marred this pattern—that of 1960. Two thirds of the Heartland states, the unlikely pair of North Dakota and Tennessee among them, supported a *losing* Republican candidate. In defeat, Richard Nixon carried seventeen of the twenty-five Heartland states, but only nine of the other twenty-five states (a very anomalous GOP showing). The 1960 election, in retrospect, contained the germ of a new era in politics—a new partisan grouping centered on the Heartland. In previous elections, when a nearly unanimous Heartland endorsed a candidate, it did so as a wagging tail to the new President's essential body of strength in his party's regional bastion. Thus, the Harding, Coolidge, Hoover, and Eisenhower Heartland sweeps accompanied well-nigh unanimous GOP electoral-vote triumphs in the traditionally Republican Northeast,

MAP 44

The Changing Map of American Politics

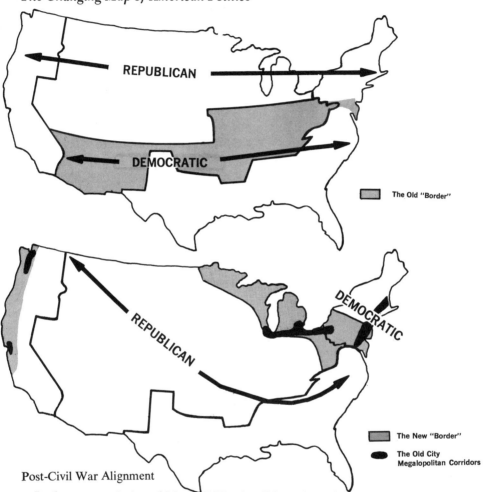

The Old "Border"

The New "Border"

The Old City
Megalopolitan Corridors

Post-Civil War Alignment

In the century during which Civil War loyalties guided American politics, an extension of the Mason-Dixon line cut across Heartland voting patterns. Now a new social and ideological cleavage is redrawing the political map, wiping out the old "Border" and creating another along several fringes of the Heartland (the Great Lakes, the Pacific and Northern Appalachia) and along the southern Potomac-Susquehanna-Chesapeake-Delaware edge of the Megalopolis. The old, stagnant cities of the several megalopolises are the pivot of the Democratic future; GOP majorities rest in the South and Heartland.

Post-Great Society Alignment

while the Roosevelt landslides were cemented by the full support of the South. The 1960 pattern foreshadowed change, and the 1964 election, when the GOP power base shifted to Dixie, confirmed the dissolution of Civil War politics, suggesting that the Heartland might be on the verge of uniting and triumphing in its own right.

This is what happened in 1968. The Heartland provided the muscle of Republican victory—and not as an extension of Northeastern primacy. Evidence of the emerging alignment lay in the fact that states like Tennessee, Oklahoma, Missouri and Arizona joined North Dakota and Idaho in voting more solidly Republican than Michigan, once the most loyal pivot of Heartland Republicanism (in the days when the GOP was rooted in the Yankee Northeast). Twenty-one of the twenty-five Heartland states supported Richard Nixon in 1968, while the other regions of the nation divided less advantageously for the GOP.

As indicated earlier, the Heartland is bound by a number of attitudinal and sociocultural ties. However, these bonds weaken along the frontiers of the Heartland—in the Pacific, across the urban Great Lakes and in northern Appalachia—where the Republican ballot future is also somewhat more doubtful. The Pacific boundary of the Heartland actually falls within California, Oregon and Washington, cleaving where the interior plateau gives way to the coastal ranges. Along the Great Lakes, Heartland orientations fade into lakeward biases in northern Minnesota and Wisconsin, Michigan and northeastern Ohio. In West Virginia, the Heartland shades into the barrens of northern Appalachia. This dissent from the politics of the Heartland suggests a new border—the fringes of the Heartland, as it were—focused on Michigan, Minnesota, West Virginia, Washington and perhaps other states.

The border will no longer be a creature of the first Civil War, although one might suggest that it represents the geography of the *second* civil war. The great political upheaval in the Heartland is a result of the erosion of Southern Democratic traditions, ending the apartheid of the southern Heartland. In addition, the new Republican hegemony in the Heartland is also building on an important trend-base of Germans and Rocky Mountain populists. In comparison, the Democratic shift—and theirs is not very big— among Yankees and Scandinavians poses little threat to the GOP advance.

One can suggest that a pro-Republican norm is emerging. Southern, German, and Rocky Mountain populist counties across the Heartland are shedding obsolescent Democratic voting habits and depressing that party's one-time solid majority support to often a mere third of the total. At the same time, the erosion of purely Civil War traditional support is shrinking two- and three-to-one GOP ratios in Yankee and Scandinavian counties to somewhat narrower victories. But not only is the area of Yankee and Scandinavian settlement less extensive; the Republican Party, as the socioeconomic representative of that America outside the core cities, stands to lose much less—and gain much more—from the Democratic Party's identification with the interests of the urban Northeast. Over the remainder of the century, the Heartland should dominate American politics in tandem with suburbia, the South and Sun Belt-swayed California.

V. THE PACIFIC STATES

⊂⊃ ⊂⊃ ⊂⊃ ⊂⊃ ⊂⊃ ⊂⊃ ⊂⊃ ⊂⊃

N o OTHER REGION IS SO GOOD A MIRROR OF AMERICAN POLITical trends as the Pacific; and behemoth California, now the most populous of the fifty states by dint of immigration from practically everywhere in the Union, is virtually a national sociopolitical microcosm.

For many years, California was atypically dependent on extractive industries—fishing, canning, truck farming, fruit growing, dairying, ranching, logging and mining (as Oregon and Washington still are)—but the great population booms following the two world wars have restructured state social and economic patterns. Unlike the Pacific Northwest, where local cities are not yet badly troubled by Megalopolitan racial and social confrontations, California must bear up under the scars of Watts and Hunters Point, the agitations of radical Left and Right alike and as poignant a cross-section of antipathies—white-black, Anglo-Mexican, white-Oriental, Protestant-Catholic, Christian-Jewish, Okie-Establishment—as any two other states. Not only does California reflect contemporary trends, but the state probably anticipates the future better than any other. The local growth which has made California the largest state in the nation centers in middle-class and blue-collar suburbs (mostly in Southern California), like those housing a steadily increasing segment of the national electorate; and it is just this sort of trend which promises to be typical of the upcoming political cycle. Chart 123 illustrates the accuracy with which California has paralleled national voting trends since the Second World War.

CHART 123

Parallelism Between California and National Voting, 1940-68

GOP Share of the Two-Party Vote for President

	1940	1944	1948	1952	1956	1960	1964	1968
California	42%	43%	50%	57%	56%	50%	41%	48%
United States	45	46	48	55	58	50	39	44

The kaleidoscope of Pacific politics can best be focused by dividing the Pacific into three subregions (see Map 45). This division omits Alaska and Hawaii—two states which, despite their uniqueness, count for little in the game of national politics—and concentrates on large and growing California. Besides reflecting the vagaries of all three subregions, California is the pivot of Pacific—and increasingly American—politics. After the 1970 Census California is expected to have forty-four congressmen, more than any other state in the nation and three times as many as the combined total of Oregon, Washington, Hawaii and Alaska. Already the nation's most populous state, California, like a magnet, continues to attract much of the United States' internal migration.

Cockpit of this population explosion is fabled, eccentric and booming Southern California, which runs from Mexicali and Calexico on the Mexican border through the rich Imperial Valley, Disneyland, the conservative suburbs of Los Angeles, liberal Beverly Hills, the barrios of East Los Angeles, and north to the Tehachapi Mountains and Death Valley in the parched interior. As the result of a massive influx of population, the eight counties of Southern California now cast 60 per cent of the total statewide vote, dominating California politics with a middle-class bias. Futuristically oriented with a myriad of space, electronics, defense and military installations, Southern California also has the greatest per capita concentration of psychiatrists and the highest divorce rate in the country. Not only is Southern California the fastest-growing section of the

MAP 45

Pacific Geopolitical Subregions

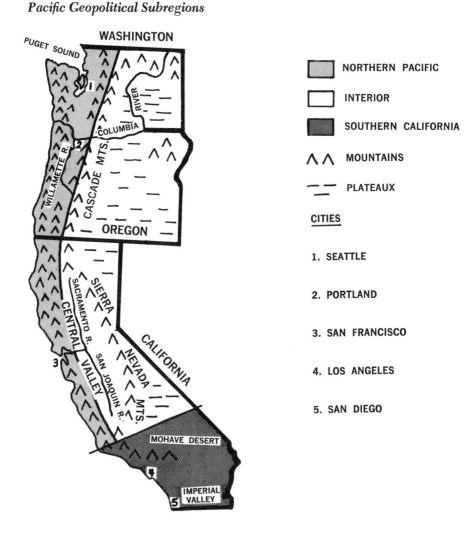

Legend:
- NORTHERN PACIFIC
- INTERIOR
- SOUTHERN CALIFORNIA
- ∧ ∧ MOUNTAINS
- — — PLATEAUX

CITIES

1. SEATTLE

2. PORTLAND

3. SAN FRANCISCO

4. LOS ANGELES

5. SAN DIEGO

Pacific and the nation; it is the hub of Western conservatism, an extension of the Heartland (as regards the origin of local population) and perhaps something of a future-capsule of political Americana.

In most ways, Northern and Southern California might as well be two separate states, and more than once such division has almost come to political fruition. Northern California, with its ethnic heterogeneity, established cities and international outlook is a cosmopolitan far cry from the new, brash and sunny south. The archetypal north lies along the coast. Reaching from the Tehachapi Mountains to the Oregon Border and east to the coastal ranges, the Northern Pacific coastal region includes about a quarter of the state's population, the great bulk of it concentrated in the San Francisco Bay area. The oldest part of the state in terms of Anglo-Saxon settlement, it is also the most liberal area and that to which Northeasterners are instinctively drawn. (San Francisco is the urbane New Yorker's second city, stateside.) And like New York City, it is simultaneously bohemian and establishmentarian. San Francisco is the Pacific outpost of the Northeastern liberal Establishment, but each year its metropolitan area casts a smaller percentage of the California vote. While San Francisco suburbs are growing apace, cities like San Francisco and Berkeley actually declined in population between 1950 and 1960. Here is another analogy to the Northeast.

Northern Pacific currents may no longer sway California, but they still prevail in Washington and Oregon. Only 15 per cent of Oregon's population lives east of the Cascades, and the figure in Washington is about 30 per cent. Oregon's weight lies in greater Portland and the dairy- and orchard-rich Willamette Valley. (Both of these areas—and much of coastal Oregon—have a touch of New England about them.) The balance of power in Washington pivots on the Seattle-Tacoma-Puget Sound area. Like Northern Pacific California, these sections are moderate-to-liberal in political outlook. In many ways, the Pacific Northwest, or at least the coastal area, offers a West Coast parallel to New England (whence several parts of the region were settled).

The third major Pacific subregion can be termed the Pacific Interior. In Washington and Oregon, this section is often called the "Inland Empire" because of its agricultural riches. Only a million people live in the Oregon and Washington interiors, but the agricultural Central Valley of California is much more populous. Extending four hundred miles from Shasta to Bakersfield, this rich valley, together with surrounding mountain ranges, spans about 15 per cent of California's population and plays an important role in state politics. This is "grapes of wrath" country, where Steinbeck's pickers earned five cents a box in the peach orchards. Today, with the help of irrigation, 2 per cent of the nation's cropland produces a third of our fruit and a fourth of our vegetables. Agrarian populism, progressivism and the New Deal all gripped the valley in their day, but Establishment liberalism is less relevant—and less prevalent. Geopolitically, the Pacific Interior is an extension of the Heartland's Rocky Mountain western slope.

CHART 124

Pacific Subregional Congressional Strength, 91st Congress

	Number of Congressional Districts		
	Northern Pacific Coast	Interior	Southern California
Washington	5	2	—
Oregon	3	1	—
California	10	6	22

Chart 124 shows the relative strength (by congressional districts) of each subregion in the three principal Pacific states. California, of course, merits special attention as the confluence not simply of all three subregions but of Pacific political power.*

But first, a brief outline of local political history is in order. California and the rest of the Pacific were not always so "typical." When the Golden State was first admitted to the Union in 1859, the overwhelming majority of American settlers were Forty-Niners—miners and fortune seekers—living in the San Francisco Bay, Sacramento and Sierra foothills sections, and their politics were appropriately hectic. To the north, Washington did not become a state until 1889, but its socioeconomic patterns were no more sedate than those of California. For many years, Pacific voting patterns reflected the radical and tumultuous impetus of grubstake miners, lumberjacks, seamen, sawmill and cannery workers, faro dealers, railway laborers, Oriental coolies and others seeking opportunities not available in more stratified societies.

In contrast with this rich socioeconomic potpourri, Oregon was a relative bastion of conservatism. Early Oregonian settlement had two mainstreams: ranchers and farmers from Texas, Missouri and

---

*To give an example of this tripartite cleavage: the student of California politics finds it necessary to read a Los Angeles, a San Francisco and a Central Valley newspaper. Lesser subcurrents are decidedly secondary.

the Border states; and dairy farmers, tradesmen and townspeople from New England. No sooner had Oregon entered the Union (1859) than a small secession movement took shape, and in 1860, Oregon's ambitious and pro-Dixie Governor Joseph Lane ran for Vice President on the Breckinridge (Southern Democratic) ticket. However, Oregon's New Englanders, concentrated in towns like aptly named Portland and Salem, carried the day and the state voted for Abraham Lincoln. During the latter part of the Nineteenth Century, Oregon's politics followed a two-party traditional pattern, and radicalism was usually weak. More than any other state in the West, Oregon resembled the East.

In 1896, when the Democratic Party embraced William Jennings Bryan and sounded the silver trumpet of populism, the Pacific states responded in mixed fashion. Washington backed Bryan; only the powerful activity of the railroads defeated him in California; but Oregon turned in the best Republican victory west of the Missouri River. All three Pacific states proved to be strong supporters of Theodore Roosevelt in 1904, and when the popular Rough Rider sought to get back into politics as a third-party presidential candidate in 1912, both California and Washington cast "Bull Moose" electoral votes. In Oregon, Republicans divided evenly between Roosevelt and regular party nominee William Howard Taft, enabling Woodrow Wilson to win with traditional Democratic support.

Seeking re-election in 1916, Wilson carried Washington and California—the latter by a very thin margin. The narrow Democratic victory in California is often attributed to progressive GOP Senator Hiram Johnson's dislike for the party presidential nominee, New York's Charles Evans Hughes.* No doubt Wilson would have lost had he not appeared to fit the progressive mold better than Hughes. California was still progressive in 1916; state politics were dominated by Northern California—San Francisco Bay, Sacramento and the Sierra foothills—where the public distrusted the state's avaricious and conservative railroad barons and mineowners. Only staid and establishmentarian Oregon voted for Hughes, giving the New Yorker his sole triumph west of the Farm Belt.

Economic progressivism was the invariable denominator of

---

*With California's electoral votes, Hughes would have won the election. However, his ties to the New York Establishment offended the powerful Hiram Johnson, whose antagonism may well have been the deciding factor. Senator Johnson died thirty years later, shortly after casting one of the two Senate votes against the United Nations. He was an old-line progressive and isolationist to the end.

Pacific politics in the quarter-century prior to World War I and it continued unabated after the war. As indicated, Washington has the most radical political history of all the Pacific states, and in 1920, local voters were sufficiently displeased at the choice between conservative Republican Warren Harding and conservative Democrat James Cox that they cast 19 per cent of their vote for Farmer-Labor Party candidate Parley P. Christiansen. Much of Washington's radicalism can be attributed to the large Scandinavian population of loggers, fishermen, cannery and sawmill workers with ties to Scandinavian political and economic movements in the Farm states and in the old country. Moreover, Washington had—and still has—a large wheat-growing area; and wheat farmers were frequently in the vanguard of agrarian radicalism because of their economic vulnerability to railroads, storage agents, millers and speculators.

Despite the pronounced upsurge in Farmer-Labor and other third-party strength, isolationists and economic progressives in both Washington and California went heavily for Harding in 1920. Many economic radicals were among the most bitter isolationists, feeling that the World War had only served the forces of wealth and reaction. Quiet Oregon, which had been less concerned with economic change and also less ruffled by the war clouds of 1916 and ensuing events, showed much less of an isolationist trend in 1920. Then in 1924, the Progressive Party candidacy of Wisconsin Senator Robert LaFollette once again focused the socioeconomic volatility of the Pacific. Washington and California remained Republican, but LaFollette ran far ahead of the Democratic presidential candidate, Wall Street lawyer John W. Davis. Oregon voted Republican, but LaFollette did less well, running about neck and neck with Davis. During the 1896-1924 radical era of Western politics, the Pacific states moved in an interesting and reliable pattern.

Throughout this period, Oregon led the Pacific in conservatism, and Washington's radical chronology is crystal clear. Without regard to party, Washington invariably voted for economic progressivism or isolationism, two movements which often overlapped during this period. The line-up of Chart 125 altered in 1928 because so many of Washington's radicals were Scandinavian Lutherans who would not support Al Smith, but in 1932, Franklin Roosevelt swept the three Pacific states, running strongest in wild-eyed Washington.

CHART 125

Pacific States Presidential Radicalism, 1896-1924

Ranked By Support of Bryan (D) 1896	Ranked By Support of Roosevelt (P)* 1912	Ranked By Support of Wilson (D) 1916	Ranked By Support of Harding (R) 1920	Ranked By Support of LaFollette (P)* 1924
1. Wash.	1. Wash.	1. Wash.	1. Wash.	1. Wash.
2. Calif.	2. Calif.	2. Calif.	2. Calif.	2. Calif.
3. Oregon	3. Oregon	3. Oregon	3. Oregon	3. Oregon

*Progressive.

CHART 126

Republican Share of the Two-Party Vote for President in the Pacific, 1928-36

	1928	1932	1936
Washington	68%	37%	31%
California	65	39	32
Oregon	65	39	32

The New Deal proved popular in the Pacific, so that in 1936, the Democratic vote continued to climb. Between 1928 and 1936, the Pacific states demonstrated similar voting patterns. (See Chart 126.)

After moving more sharply towards the Democrats than the nation as a whole during the Nineteen-Thirties, the Pacific states showed a considerable GOP trend in 1940, as Willkie won 41 per cent of the vote in California, 41 per cent in Washington and 46 per cent in Oregon. As might have been expected, conservative Oregon showed the greatest disenchantment with the New Deal. In 1944, the GOP share of the presidential vote rose another few percentage points in each state.

Finally, in 1948, the Pacific states split for the first time since 1916; California and Washington staying Democratic while Oregon turned Republican. The old economic radicalism ranking reasserted itself, persisting in 1952 as Eisenhower swept the region.

Somewhat disenchanted with the GOP, particularly with the Administration's conservative agricultural, public power and con-

CHART 127

Republican Share of the Two-Party Vote for President in the Pacific, 1948-52

	1948	1952
Oregon	52%	62%
California	50*	57
Washington	45	54

*Slight Democratic plurality; Progressives also received 5 per cent of total vote.

servation policies (many sensitive Pacific Northwesterners saw them as collusion with utilities and other vested interests), all three states moved towards the Democrats in 1956. Oregon led the pack, notwithstanding the fact that former Oregon Governor Douglas McKay was Eisenhower's Secretary of the Interior. (McKay was defeated in a 1956 U.S. Senate bid, the second Oregon Republican to lose in forty years.) Eisenhower's few Pacific gains came in labor and urban districts around Seattle and San Francisco. In a reversal of the traditional pattern, the Republican vote dropped most (7 per cent) in Oregon, slipped 2 per cent in California and held about steady in Washington.

The Democratic trend in Oregon came as a great shock to the GOP. Like other traditional Republican areas which had kept electing Republicans to state office and Congress during the New Deal, Oregon was disillusioned by the changing cast of the party. (A similar trend was at work in Maine.) As far as Oregon was concerned, unpopular Republican public power and natural resource policies provided a further spark. Republican strength in Oregon plummeted during the Nineteen-Fifties. In 1958, the Republicans also lost their hold on California, as the Democrats won the governorship and a U.S. Senate seat.

Whatever the President's personal popularity, the Eisenhower era did not increase the strength of the Republican Party in the Pacific. Because Eisenhower had not garnered much new Republican support in 1956, there were not so many Eisenhower voters to lose in 1960, as in Catholic New England, for example. Suffering only a moderate decline from Eisenhower levels, Richard Nixon held California, Oregon and Washington by thin majorities. Of the new states, he won Alaska by a few hundred votes and lost Hawaii by a few hundred. Nixon's Pacific states majority marked the first election in which the three major Pacific states unanimously, albeit narrowly, backed the losing candidate. As with the Mountain states, much of the Pacific's Republican bias can be explained by local inability to mirror the exaggerated Catholic swing of the Northeast and Great Lakes.*

Victory in California's Republican presidential primary helped cinch the party nomination for Barry Goldwater in 1964, but the conservative Senator was unable to carry any of the Pacific states in the general election. Chart 128 shows the change in the Republican presidential vote in the Pacific states between 1960 and 1964. The Goldwater decline was very uneven; and analysis of it shows regional politics shifting into a new pattern.

CHART 128

Republican Share of the Two-Party Vote for President in the Pacific, 1960-64

	1960	1964
Oregon	52%	36%
Washington	51	38
California	50	41

Gone were the days of the old "economic progressivism" which pitted "The People" (progressive) against "The Company" (conservative). The liberalism of the Establishment was conjuring up a new populist conservatism—Barry Goldwater was one manifestation—and it fared best in the *old* agrarian populist bailiwicks of the interior and the *new* populist strongholds of Southern California. Establishment liberalism produced its best anti-Goldwater turnout in Northern Pacific coastal precincts from Monterey to Puget Sound. These differences underlay the statewide movements shown in Chart 128. California showed the least anti-Goldwater trend, inasmuch as Southern California's massive vote showed only a 6 per cent Democratic shift between 1960 and 1964, and the Cali-

---

*California includes most of the Catholics on the Pacific Coast, especially the Mexicans of the south and the Italian and Irish concentrations around San Francisco Bay.

fornia interior moved about 12 per cent. Many Northern Pacific coastal counties and silk-stocking precincts showed 15 per cent to 25 per cent Democratic trends. However, such areas do not dominate California. Establishment voting is much more powerful in Oregon, where Portland and the New England-settled Willamette Valley cast two thirds of the state ballots; and thus Goldwater slipped 16 per cent in Oregon. Washington's 13 per cent anti-Goldwater shift was less than that of Oregon because Washington has a more powerful interior. Coastal Washington's forceful Democratic trend was diluted by a minimal (6 per cent to 8 per cent) fall-off in the oldtime populist wheat-growing area of eastern Washington.* Behind the facade of a Republican debacle, the Grand Old Party was shifting its impetus from establishmentarianism to populism.

By 1966, the populist conservative tide was much stronger, sweeping all before it in California. Republican gubernatorial candidate Ronald Reagan rolled up unprecedented GOP majorities in the onetime progressive timber, mining and "grapes of wrath" farm counties, joining them with the ballots of Southern California suburbia to achieve a million-vote majority. San Francisco held out in vain against Reagan, but the coastal regions of Oregon and Washington exercised a much more powerful influence on their states. Oregon elected a few new liberal Republicans to office and Washington—its behavior paralleling that of the liberal Northeast —rejected all of the Republican candidates for congressional seats lost in the 1964 Goldwater defeat.

The 1968 presidential election underscored the cleavage between the Northern Pacific Coastal, Interior and Southern California behavioral patterns. As expected, Richard Nixon slipped below his 1960 levels up and down the Northern Pacific Coast, greatly increasing the Democratic majority in San Francisco and Oakland, and enabling Humphrey to win King County (Seattle), Washington and Multnomah County (Portland), Oregon. These Humphrey Puget Sound gains played a major part in switching Washington—Nixon had eked out a thin victory in 1960—to the Democratic column in 1968. Chart 129 shows the relative strength

---

*It is useful to explain the divergent behavior of the two radical streams in Washington politics. On one hand, the coastal Scandinavian and labor progressivism has meshed effectively with increasing Northeastern Democratic liberalism, while the once-populist wheat farmers of eastern Washington cannot share labor's empathy with an urban and Northeastern-oriented cause.

CHART 129

Pacific Presidential Voting—1960 and 1968

Percentage of the Total Vote for President

	1960		1968		
	Nixon	Kennedy	Nixon	Wallace	Humphrey
Washington	51%	49%	45%	8%	47%
Oregon	53	47	50	6	44
California	50	50	48	7	45

of Nixon and his opponents in the three states in both 1960 and 1968.

Despite the conversion of his 1960 majority in greater Portland into a 1968 deficit of 17,000 votes, together with a lesser slide in rural Yankee areas, Richard Nixon still managed to win Oregon by a bigger edge than in 1960. To offset his Yankee losses, the GOP candidate scored considerable gains in the wheat, timber and ranching areas (where many voters have Southern or populist antecedents). Interior Washington also showed a distinct anti-Democratic trend in contrast to the party strides in the coastal and Puget Sound counties, though many conservative Republicans—especially John Birch Society members—voted for Wallace, fatally reducing Nixon's majorities.

In his home state of California, Nixon won by 225,000 votes, a healthy increase over his 1960 majority of 35,000. Although the San Francisco Bay area gave Humphrey a majority some one hundred thousand votes bigger than it had given Kennedy, Nixon turned the slim 1960 Democratic majority in Interior California into a slight GOP lead and increased his 1960 Southern California majority by a quarter of a million votes. Nixon's top 1968 showing came in fabulous Orange County, the fastest-growing urbanized area—and probably the most conservative—in the United States.

In many ways, California and the Pacific told the political story of the entire nation in 1968. A growing Western, suburban and even partly Southern conservative electorate overcame the strong liberal trend of a once preeminent but now shrinking big city and Northeastern-oriented electorate. The movements of the Pacific geopolitical streams are microcosmic of national re-alignment and the emerging Republican majority.

A. *The Northern Pacific Coast*

In large measure, the Sun Belt has been settled by people from the Midwest, Border and South; twangs and drawls still abound in greater Los Angeles. And while many Northeasterners have also gone to Sun Country, a confirmed Yankee, if obligated to move west, would probably choose to emigrate to San Francisco or the Northern Pacific Coast. The first Anglo-Saxon settlers to come to Washington and Oregon, for example—in addition to the English, Scottish and Canadian fur traders—were New Englanders who found friendly scenery and climate in the lush river valleys. Map 7 shows the agricultural and horticultural kinship of the Pacific Northwest and New England (and by extension Britain and Scandinavia). The entire Northern Pacific Coast has received a considerable migration from northern climes: New England, the Great Lakes, Britain, Canada and Scandinavia. There is also a considerable Oriental population. Although Northern California has its New Englanders—the Mendocino-Westport-Rockport section has a number of salt-box houses built a century ago by Down East Maine men—it also has a haphazard population traceable to gold rush days, the shore leaves of clippers and the building of the transcontinental railways. Many of San Francisco's Irish helped lay the rails which America rode west. Immigrants have been coming to the San Francisco Bay area since the Eighteen Forties, and this influx has encompassed a greater ethnic heterogeneity (although fewer people) than the last half century's middle-class flood into Southern California.

For all these reasons, the social currents that wash Northern Pacific shores are more cosmopolitan than the factors at work in the Sun Belt, where Okies, space technicians and pensioners are squared off against Watts and Beverly Hills. The Northern Pacific Coast is much more liberal. A considerable part of the answer, of course, lies in the relative lack of minority-group confrontation in the Pacific Northwest. Only San Francisco Bay has a large Negro population, and the area also has the only substantial backlash (Italo-Irish) unfolding between Los Angeles and the Canadian line.

Amidst rapid growth in the years after the Civil War, the Northern Pacific Coast invariably backed Republican presidential candidates, although populism and progressivism were strong. (In 1896, most of coastal Washington voted for William Jennings Bryan, who was also strong in Northern California.) During these years of national Republicanism, California's San Francisco Bay, which then cast a much greater percentage of the statewide vote, was a center of Democratic strength, chiefly because of its large working-class Irish population. In Northeastern style, the city's Democratic boss was a saloon-keeper named Chris Buckley.

In politics as in many things, San Francisco-oriented Northern California and Los Angeles-oriented Southern California are traditional opponents. During the Nineteen-Twenties and early Thirties, the cleavage was as follows: San Francisco was substantially Catholic, pro-labor, anti-prohibitionist and usually Democratic, while Los Angeles was predominantly Protestant, nativist, anti-labor, prohibitionist and usually Republican. The partisan division was not hard and fast because Northern California often supported progressive Republicans and Southern California would do the same for conservative Democrats. San Francisco almost voted for LaFollette in 1924 and subsequently did vote for Al Smith in 1928, in contrast to Los Angeles, which shunned both men for the orthodoxy of Calvin Coolidge and Herbert Hoover. Franklin Roosevelt swept California in 1932 and 1936 and won solid majorities in 1940 and 1944; each time, however, he fared better in Northern California than in the south.

Since World War II, Northern California, and especially the San Francisco Bay area, has behaved very much like the Northeast. In 1952, Eisenhower barely carried the San Francisco Bay area, winning most of his statewide majority in Southern California, but in 1956, when GOP agricultural and resources policy cost him votes in most California counties, the San Francisco district was one of the few in the state to buck the Democratic tide. The Italians and Irish of San Francisco, like their compatriots in Jersey City, Pittsburgh and the Bronx, were trending towards the popular President. Along the North Pacific as along the North Atlantic, Nixon fell farthest below 1956 Eisenhower totals in the Catholic urban districts where the GOP had gained in 1956; i.e., San Francisco and environs. The Northern Pacific Coast subsequently displayed the sharpest anti-Goldwater Republican decline among the Pacific subregions in 1964, with the San Francisco suburbs and rural coastal counties in the lead.

Like the Northeast, the Northern Pacific did not produce important Republican gains in 1966. In California, successful GOP gubernatorial candidate Ronald Reagan's worst statewide showings came in the San Francisco Bay area, where he lost San Francisco, Berkeley (70 per cent anti-Reagan, Berkeley was California's banner Democratic city), and Sausalito, the local seaside Greenwich Village. Even the normally Republican suburbs of San Francisco hesitated in their support of Reagan. While he carried them, other GOP candidates ran far ahead.

As any good relief map will show, the part of California fronting the Pacific between San Luis Obispo and the Oregon line is quite distinct from the interior sections lying beyond the coastal ranges. The politics of the two subregions also differ, and the liberal *apartheid* of the coastal counties can be clearly mapped in the context of the 1966 gubernatorial election. Throughout most of California, Reagan won a higher vote share than Eisenhower had amassed in either 1952 or 1956, but not along the Northern Pacific Coast. Almost every coastal county gave Reagan a lower vote share than Eisenhower's maximum. (See Map 46.)

The ideological bent of local congressmen is another index by which the Northern Pacific Coast differs from both Southern California and the interior. Whereas the Republican congressmen from Southern California and the interior are conservatives and many of the Democrats are moderates, up and down the Pacific Coast most of the GOP representatives are establishmentarian moderates (Mailliard, McCloskey and Clausen) and the Democratic congressmen include some of the country's leading ultra-liberals (Edwards, Burton and Cohelan). Not only are the San Francisco area GOP congressmen more liberal than their California party colleagues, but they are also much more internationally-minded, as befits San Francisco's place in the worlds of finance and maritime commerce.

The San Francisco Bay area of California had not liked Richard Nixon very much in 1960, and paralleling the behavior of New England and the silk-stocking areas of greater New York, it liked him considerably less in 1968. Besides the trends of white urban precincts turning Negro, the sharpest 1960-68 Nixon losses came in rich Liberal Establishment bailiwicks like Nob, Russian and Telegraph Hills, as well as the most affluent suburbs of Marin and San

MAP 46

California—Reagan Vote Compared With Eisenhower Vote

Counties where Reagan (1966) won a lower share of the vote than maximum Eisenhower share (1952 or 1956).

Mateo counties. Only a few sections of San Francisco showed Nixon closing the gap on the Democrats. Most were Irish and Italian districts where Wallace garnered 8 per cent to 12 per cent support, another parallel with the Northeast. Chart 130 shows the extent to which the leading Bay Area counties trended against Nixon (despite this shift, the GOP nominee won the state because of southern California support).

Luckily for the Republicans, the Bay area is losing the weight to make its trend felt statewide. Some suburban areas are gaining population rapidly, but San Francisco's share of the total California vote has declined from 16 per cent in 1920 to a mere 4 per cent in 1968.

Unlike California, Oregon is dominated by its coastal section. Roughly 85 per cent of Oregon's population lives in the third of the state which lies between the Pacific and the high Cascades.

CHART 130

Presidential Voting in the San Francisco Bay Area, 1960-68

Percentage of the Total Presidential Vote

	1960		1968		
County	Nixon	Kennedy	Nixon	Wallace	Humphrey
San Francisco	42%	58%	34%	6%	60%
Alameda (Berkeley-Oakland)	46	54	38	7	55
Santa Clara (San Jose)	53	47	46	5	49

Most of the people live in greater Portland and along the nearby Willamette Valley (Salem and Eugene). As has been indicated, this area has a definite New England tint: dairy farms with neat, red barns, lush greenery, wildflowers and berries; well-ordered towns with greens and commons. And so it should, first because of climatic and geographic similarity, and also because this part of Oregon was settled by New Englanders.*

From the Civil War through World War II, Oregon was little troubled by the economic radicalism and isolationism that cut such a broad swath across the rest of the West. First of all, the New England and Southern antecedents of many local citizens gave Oregonian politics a traditionalist coloration. Secondly, relatively few farmers in Oregon (compared with the Dakotas, Montana, Kansas or Washington) were engaged in wheat-growing, and wheat farmers, with their considerable vulnerability to economics and middlemen, were a major force in agrarian radicalism. Furthermore, the state's largely Anglo-Saxon population spared Oregon large-scale Scandinavian progressivism and German or Irish isolationism. For these reasons, Oregon remained aloof from the radicalism so important in other Western states.

This behavior, keynoted then as now by Portland and the Willamette Valley, can be charted with extreme clarity during the years

---

*Oregon's origins are underscored by the story of the naming of the city of Portland: a coin was tossed to decide between naming the new town for Portland, Maine or Boston, Massachusetts. But while New England influence dominated the towns, most of the ranchers were Southern.

between William Jennings Bryan's crusade of 1896 and the La-Follette Progressive candidacy of 1924. While California, Washington, the Rocky Mountain and Wheat Belt states were following the North Star of economic radicalism and isolationism (often connected) from one party to the other, Oregon's settlement and economic patterns served as pro-Establishment and moderating influences on local political life. (See Chart 125.)

In shunning the radicalism of the other Pacific and Rocky Mountain states, Oregon has always showed a unique trans-Mississippi parallelism with the voting trends of rural New England, upstate New York, northern Pennsylvania, northern Ohio and rural Michigan. This is probably the key to Oregon voting behavior. In 1896, Oregon was the worst state west of the Missouri for William Jennings Bryan, the revivalesque voice of the silver interests and over-mortgaged Bible Belt (who painted the Northeast as enemy country). Then in 1916, when the Northeast turned against Woodrow Wilson, so did Oregon. (Oregon was the only state west of the Farm Belt to back New Yorker Charles Evans Hughes, the GOP presidential nominee.) Only four years later, moderate Oregon remained aloof from the isolationist tide that swelled Harding's vote, with the result that Oregon was the *worst* Republican (Harding) state in the entire Farm Belt, northern Rockies and Pacific.

During the New Deal, Oregon always voted for Roosevelt, but otherwise was a pocket of reasonably orthodox Republicanism in a sea of Western progressivism. Throughout the New Deal, the GOP kept both senators from Oregon and the congressman from the Willamette (and usually some others). Maine and Vermont alone share Oregon's record of electing only orthodox GOP senators during the Progressive and Democratic upsurges of the Nineteen-Twenties and Nineteen-Thirties.

The end of World War II saw Oregon remain true to form by turning in the only Republican electoral votes west of the Farm Belt for Republican presidential nominee Thomas E. Dewey—again the extraordinary Oregonian empathy with the Northeast is clear.

Eisenhower carried Oregon easily in both his 1952 and 1956 presidential races, although his share of the vote was lower in 1956 than it had been in the previous contest. Moreover, Oregon began to show a very definite Democratic trend during the Nineteen-Fifties, and here again a strange correlation emerges between the behavior of Oregon and the rural Yankee Northeast.

Kindred Yankee socio-political bias goes a long way to explain the parallel ballot behavior of Pacific Oregon and such Yankee strongholds as Maine and Vermont. Oregon, like the rural Northeast, is a proven behavioral outlier of the Northeastern Establishment which, from Civil War days until World War II, was both Republican and conservative. However, during and after the Second World War, the once-conservative Northeastern GOP Establishment began to turn liberal and internationalist while the old Progressive West took up a conservative stance within the party. This liberal trend within the Northeastern GOP continued during the Nineteen-Fifties; meanwhile liberalism (and eventual Democratic voting) grew in many hitherto Republican areas most loyal to the Establishment. After 1952, the Democrats began to make considerable gains in New Deal era GOP bastions like Oregon, Maine and Vermont. (Oregon elected its first Democratic senators in 1954 and 1956; Maine its first Democratic senator in 1958; and Vermont its first Democratic congressman in 1958.) Eisenhower was personally popular in these states, but local traditionalism was beginning to rebel against party drift towards the Heartland isolationism of Capehart, McCarthy, Bricker, et al. The striking decline in the GOP share of Oregon's congressional vote captures the story of state Republicanism during the Nineteen-Fifties.

CHART 131

Republican Share of the Oregon Congressional Vote, 1952-58

1952—61%   1954—53%   1956—46%   1958—43%

Richard Nixon won Oregon in 1960, capturing 52 per cent of the vote, but Barry Goldwater lost the state, winning only 36 per cent of the ballots cast. The 1960-64 GOP presidential vote decline in Oregon was the sharpest of any state west of the Farm Belt— 16.5 per cent. Once again, Oregon showed its tendency to behave like Maine and Vermont, where the Goldwater decline was extraordinary. The principal Goldwater decline came in the New England-settled Willamette Valley. With GOP 1960-64 declines varying between fifteen and twenty-five percentage points, the thirteen counties of northwestern coastal Oregon, including Portland and the length and breadth of the Willamette Valley, showed the strongest anti-Goldwater trend of any major area west of the

New England-settled sections of Kansas and Iowa. Interior Oregon produced a much weaker reaction against the Arizona Senator.

In 1968, Richard Nixon ratified this pattern by slipping well below his 1960 levels in the counties where Goldwater's losses had been heaviest, and bettering his 1960 levels in the counties where the Arizona Senator had done fairly well. Nixon lost Multnomah County (Portland), which he had carried in 1960, and he gave ground to the Democrats throughout much of the Willamette Valley. The analogy is to New England and upstate New York rather than to the rest of the rural West. It should also be pointed out that Portland is an old city, not any sort of boom town. Multnomah County has cast steadily fewer presidential votes since 1960. Notwithstanding these shifts, however, Nixon carried Oregon.

The fertile valleys of western Washington are much like the Willamette, and Washington also received a considerable early migration from New England, but state political behavior has generally pivoted on other socioeconomic bases. From Washington's statehood year (1889) until the First World War, dairying and fruit growing were of little importance compared to logging camps, sawmills, fisheries, canneries and vast wheatfields. Seattle and Tacoma, now the Megalopolis of the Pacific Northwest, grew up as mill towns to chew the logs floated down to Puget Sound from the Cascades. In 1914, almost two thirds of Washington's payrolls were derived directly from the lumber industry. And while choke-setters and toppers attacked the great stands of pine, fir and spruce, other western Washingtonians netted a rich harvest from rivers and seas. By the beginning of the First World War, Washington ranked fourth among the nation's states in fisheries. Canneries sprang up along Puget Sound to handle Washington's vast catch of salmon, halibut and shellfish; moreover, a considerable canning industry also grew up around the state's fruit and berry production. Before long, there were canneries and saw mills up and down Puget Sound, not just in a few major cities. Washington's labor strength and radical politics were equally decentralized; it was difficult to hold workers under the thumb of powerful millowners or big city machines. The decentralized radicalism of Washington stood in marked contrast to New York State Socialist strength, for example, which in the first quarter of the Twentieth Century was highly concentrated in the Jewish residential ghettoes of Manhattan, Brooklyn and the South Bronx.

In general, the economic impulses of canners, loggers, sawmill workers, sailors and pickers were progressive; ethnic antecedents often supported such tendencies. While many of the loggers and sawmill workers were Anglo-Saxons who had followed their trade from Maine or the Great Lakes, the most influential influx was Scandinavian (often emigrants from timber-stripped Wisconsin and Minnesota). With its mountains and sounds, Washington was even more like the "old country" to Scandinavians than lake-studded Minnesota. Scandinavians brought with them to the Pacific Northwest an empathy for the Social Democratic politics taking shape in Sweden and Denmark, and they felt a kinship with the Farmer-Labor politics developing in Minnesota and Wisconsin. There are considerable numbers of Scandinavians from San Francisco to Portland; however, no Pacific Scandinavian concentration matches that of Washington. This Scandinavian influence along Puget Sound overshadows the more remote New England settlement.

Of the three Pacific states, Washington alone voted for William Jennings Bryan in 1896. The evangelistic free silver advocate carried all of the Puget Sound counties and most of the interior wheat areas, and this was the pattern of economic radicalism and progressivism in Washington politics for many years. When both major parties offered conservative candidates, as in 1920 and 1924, third-party movements could win considerable support in the Puget Sound area. Farmer-Labor candidate Parley Christiansen did not carry any Washington counties in 1920, but he ran ahead of the Democratic presidential nominee in fifteen counties clustered around Puget Sound, populous King (Seattle) and Pierce (Tacoma) counties as well as vividly named Whatcom, Skagit, Snohomish and Kitsap. Such was the Democratic predicament in 1924 that party presidential nominee John W. Davis ran third, behind both Coolidge and LaFollette, in all except two Washington counties. LaFollette carried two Puget Sound labor-stronghold counties and also ran well in Seattle and Tacoma.

In 1928, the Democrats ended their conservative era by choosing Catholic Tammanyite Alfred E. Smith as their presidential standard-bearer, yet this new direction did not remake the party to Puget Sound satisfaction. Tammany Hall was suspect; Scandinavian Lutheranism could not shed its anti-Catholicism; most of the coastal Washington counties gave Herbert Hoover 60 per cent to 70 per cent of the vote. Four years later, Franklin Roosevelt beat Hoover by comparable majorities, although Socialist candidate Norman Thomas was able to amass considerable support.

The New Deal provided Washington radicalism with a home and began a new Democratic era; the labor agitation which had succumbed to the 1919-20 Red scares and the "normalcy" of the Twenties revived. Washington's politics became nationally famous for their circuslike quality. One New Deal United States Senator from Washington, Homer Bone by name, had begun in the Socialist Party, then moved in succession—and in furtherance of the cause of public utilities—to the Progressives, the Republicans and the Democrats. The lieutenant-governor elected in 1932 was a popular band leader who had once campaigned for the Seattle mayoralty by promising a hostess in every streetcar! By 1936, the Democratic state organization had been taken over by the Washington Commonwealth Federation, a motley amalgam of leftists, labor leaders and cause-pleaders, but the WCF was never able to win an election. When Franklin Roosevelt sought re-election in 1936, he swept the counties of coastal Washington by three- and four-to-one majorities, and although a Republican counter-trend emerged in 1940, it was strongest in the isolationist eastern Washington wheat bowl. Roosevelt maintained two-to-one majorities in the Puget Sound area.

Given Washington's eccentric political heritage, it was a state to which strategists of Henry Wallace's 1948 Progressive crusade looked for considerable support. When the ballots were counted, however, the vaguely pro-Soviet Wallace had fallen far short of the strength mobilized by Christiansen or LaFollette in 1920 and 1924, and even Norman Thomas' 1932 vote surpassed Wallace's. Many Puget Sound counties gave Wallace 5 per cent to 10 per cent of their vote, not enough to deprive Harry S. Truman of a solid victory.*

Under the tutelage of the New Deal, coastal Washington's labor impetus had become staunchly Democratic; leftist third parties thereafter proved unable to mobilize the following they had enjoyed in days of conservative national hegemony. When Adlai Stevenson was badly defeated in the Eisenhower landslide of 1952, he nevertheless managed to win a number of coastal counties in Washington.

---

*In the Puget Sound area of Washington, as in Minnesota and Wisconsin, much of the Progressive vote was Scandinavian. No other non-big city electorate showed similar Wallace strength.

This made the area virtually unique in the rural North, save for some kindred Scandinavian Farmer-Labor strongholds of Minnesota. In 1956, Stevenson did a little better.

John F. Kennedy evenly divided that part of Washington west of the Cascades, but he lost the state to Richard Nixon because of Republican strength in the agricultural eastern part of the state. Four years later, Barry Goldwater won less than a third of the vote in the Puget Sound area and captured only 38 per cent of the total statewide vote. The Republicans lost several congressional seats in the Puget Sound area and they were unable to win them back in 1966.

Like upper New England, the Pacific Northwest witnessed minimal Republican gains in the 1966 congressional elections, a trend of considerable importance because it showed that neither area was strongly swayed by opposition to the Democratic Party's Great Society social liberalism, already emerging as the fulcrum of partisan re-alignment. Seattle began to emerge as a center of liberal opinion on the Vietnamese War, and local Democrats gave surprising 1968 support to the presidential nomination quest of Democratic Senator Eugene McCarthy.

Predictably, the Puget Sound area turned in Washington's top Democratic percentages in the 1968 presidential election. Hubert Humphrey carried King County (Seattle), which John Kennedy had lost in 1960. The Democratic nominee scored gains over Kennedy across most of coastal Washington, and these strides were vital in swinging Washington into the Humphrey column. (The Evergreen State was the only Western state Nixon won in 1960 and lost in 1968.) One of the factors which aided Humphrey was his Protestant and Scandinavian background; his antecedents helped him in coastal Washington, whereas John Kennedy's Irish Catholicism had not sat too well with the state's Swedish Lutherans. But while these factors exaggerated the trend at work, there is no doubt that coastal Washington was pursuing a liberal direction at odds with the movement of the great interior bulk of the West.

While the suburban areas around the Northern Pacific metropolitan centers of San Francisco, Portland and Seattle are growing at a fair rate, the central cities themselves are losing population. The Pacific Northwest is not a boom section of the United States, and as far as the one state—California—with rapidly increasing population and political importance, its Northern Pacific coastal area is steadily losing relative power.

B. Southern California

Perhaps no other political impetus in the nation is so important as the middle-class upheaval of the American sun country, and Southern California in particular. Because of the great influx of emigrants from the rest of the United States, California, has become the largest state in the Union and one of the most pivotal—and the key to California is the behavior of its booming, sunny south. Southern California derives its political muscle from a steadily growing share of the state's exploding population. Whereas Los Angeles was a sleepy town of eleven thousand people in 1881, today the population of Los Angeles County is about seven million. Chart 132 sets forth the fantastic growth of Los Angeles, while Chart 133 enumerates the increasing share of the statewide vote

CHART 132

The Southern California Boom

	Population of:			Population of:	
Year	So. California	Los Angeles	Year	So. California	Los Angeles
1860	25,000	5,000	1920	1,347,000	576,000
1870	32,000	6,000	1930	2,933,000	1,238,000
1880	64,000	11,000	1940	3,572,000	1,504,000
1890	201,000	50,000	1950	5,652,000	1,970,000
1900	304,000	102,000	1960	9,031,000	2,479,000
1910	751,000	319,000			

CHART 133

Southern California Share of the Statewide Vote, 1916-68

Percentage of the Major Party Vote for President Cast by the Eight Counties of Southern California (Santa Barbara, Ventura, Los Angeles, San Bernardino, Orange, San Diego, Imperial and Riverside)

1916	1924	1936	1952	1964	1968
38%	47%	54%	56%	58%	61%

cast by Southern California. All of California has boomed, but Los Angeles and environs have led the way.

For some time, Southern California has been more conservative than the state as a whole, but until the Nineteen-Fifties, the disparity was slight. Since then, the human explosion of Southern California, coupled with the conservative leanings of the migrants, has worked to increase sectional Republicanism relative to the rest of the state. Neither Southern California nor its population trend is unique. From the Charleston-Savannah-Jacksonville coastal strip to California's urban south, the conservative "Sun Belt" of the United States is undergoing a massive infusion of people and prosperity. Chart 134 shows how the movement to Sun Country is shifting the balance of presidential voting power. The Southern California phenomenon is simply a part of this overall pattern, albeit California's sun precincts have more influence than most because of their solidifying control over the destinies of the largest state in the Union.

CHART 134

Sun Belt Electoral Vote Strength, 1928-72

THE ELECTORAL VOTE BY SECTIONS

State	1928	1932	1948	1956	1964	1972*
Maine	6	5	5	5	4	4
Massachusetts	18	17	16	16	14	14
New York	45	47	45	43	41	40
Pennsylvania	38	36	35	32	29	27
Northeastern Group Total	107	105	101	96	88	85
Arizona	3	3	4	4	5	6
Texas	20	23	23	24	25	26
Florida	6	7	8	10	14	16
California	13	23	25	32	40	46
Sun Belt Group Total	42	56	60	70	84	94

*Census Projection

1. The Sun Belt Phenomenon

From the colonial days when a growing back country challenged seaboard-run politics from New England to the Carolinas, the movement of population to new frontiers has often remade the map of American politics, throwing up new establishments in place of old ones and infusing the national political ideology with regular dollops of regionalism and populism. All of these human tides have helped to trigger or consummate changing political cycles.

As of the present, another population shift—the huge postwar white middle-class push to the Florida-California Sun country (as well as suburbia in general)—seems to be forging a new, conservative political era in the South, Southwest and Heartland. It is no coincidence that this conservative trend is best exemplified by California, Arizona, Florida and Texas (apart from Nevada, the fastest-growing states in the nation), where the very areas of greatest population explosion are the demonstrated strongholds of Reagan, Goldwater, Gurney and Tower, the vanguardmen of the new conservative sun politics.

Long ago, in the hot valleys of the Tigris, Euphrates and other Near East cradles of civilization, human culture began in the warm womb of a land where people could live without technology, but during later millenniums far greater civilizations evolved in temperate zones where climate, like necessity, mothered progress and invention. Today, however, a reverse trend is afoot. Spurred by high pensions, early retirement, increased leisure time and technological innovation, the affluent American middle class is returning to the comforts of the endless summer, which they can escape at will in swimming pools and total refrigeration.

The persons most drawn to the new sun culture are the pleasure-seekers, the bored, the ambitious, the space-age technicians and the retired—a super-slice of the rootless, socially mobile group known as the American middle class. Most of them have risen to such status only in the last generation, and their elected officials predictably embody a popular political impulse which deplores further social (minority group) upheaval and favors a consolidation of the last thirty years' gains. Increasingly important throughout the nation, this new middle-class group is most powerful in the Sun Belt. Its politics are bound to cast a lengthening national shadow.

From a parochial, Northeastern megalopolitan vantage point, it is easy to ignore the burgeoning power of the sun country and to dismiss its leaders as ideological eccentrics, but the statistics and projections of the Census Bureau affirm that migration within the United States is rapidly dismantling the hegemony of the older urban areas of the nation in favor of the booming cities of the South and Southwest. Chart 134 illustrates how the electoral votes of the Sun Belt will have almost tripled in the half-century between 1920 and 1970, outstripping the declining urban Northeast in the process, and Chart 135 reiterates this impetus by means of another set of statistics showing how the old urban centers—from New York and Boston to San Francisco—lost population between 1950 and 1960, even as the cities of the Sun Belt were doubling and trebling in size. Chart 142 shows how the weight of the old cities has continued to decline since 1960.

The point can be made just as clearly within the boundaries of California. No West Coast city is more liberal than academic and anarchic Berkeley, which voted three-to-one against Barry Goldwater in 1964 and two-to-one against Ronald Reagan. However, Berkeley was one of the handful of California cities which actually lost population between 1950 and 1960. At the other end of the demographic and political spectrum is suburban Anaheim, which went two-to-one for Barry Goldwater and three-to-one for Ronald Reagan. As Berkeley's population was declining, Anaheim's increased sevenfold. At mid-century, Berkeley was eight times the size of Anaheim, but now Anaheim is almost twice as big!

Similar changes have occurred from Miami to Monterey. In states where rural Democrats once held sway, Republican middle-class cities and suburbs are now establishing hegemony. These new cities are not like the old mirrors of European social stratification and heavy industrial development. They have no codfish or other aristocrats, guiltily liberal with money scarcely or remotely earned, and no large, cohesive ethnic communities still half-rooted in Cork, Calabria and Cracow. Instead, the new cities are centers of commerce, light industry, military preparedness, defense production and space-age technology, vocational seedbeds of a huge middle class. Cocoa Beach, Burbank, Cape Kennedy and Space Center Houston, all conservative strongholds, are a century removed from the Allegheny-Monongahela Black Country and the dun-colored mill canyons of the Merrimack.

Urbanization this trend may be, but it is not the sort sympathetic

CHART 135

The Politics of Population Movement

City	Population—1950	Population—1960
Old Liberal Cities		
Boston	801,444	697,197
Fall River	111,963	99,942
Providence	248,674	207,498
New York	7,891,957	7,781,984
Newark	438,776	405,220
Scranton	125,536	111,433
Detroit	1,849,568	1,670,144
Cleveland	914,808	876,050
San Francisco	775,357	740,316
Berkeley	113,805	111,268
St. Louis	856,796	750,026
Sun Belt Conservative Cities		
Anaheim	14,556	104,184
Los Angeles	1,970,358	2,479,015
San Diego	334,387	573,224
Phoenix	106,818	447,414
Tucson	45,454	212,892
Albuquerque	96,815	201,189
Tulsa	182,740	261,685
Oklahoma City	243,504	324,253
Odessa-Midland	51,208	142,963
Dallas	434,462	679,684
Houston	596,163	938,219
Amarillo	74,246	137,969
Shreveport	127,206	164,372
Mobile	129,009	202,779
Savannah	119,638	149,245
Atlanta	331,314	487,455
Fort Lauderdale	36,328	83,648
Orlando	52,367	88,135
St. Petersburg	96,738	181,298
Charlotte	134,042	201,564
Memphis	396,000	497,524

to the sociological spending programs of contemporary liberalism. On the contrary, the new Southwest, behind its wall of total air-conditioning, is as ill-disposed to slum subsidies as the new middle classes marshaled behind the crabgrass curtains of Levittown and Park Forest. Nowhere in the United States are population and urbanization exploding with the exuberance of Florida, California, the Gulf Coast and Southwest, but nowhere is there a stronger conservative trend (excluding the liberalism of local Negro, Latin-American and Jewish minority groups).

The Sun Belt has been quite responsive to the candidacies of America's leading "name" conservatives—Goldwater, Reagan and Tower. By and large, Sun Country was pro-Goldwater in 1964, at least in comparison with the rest of the United States. The Deep South boomtowns backed the Senator, although most Texas and Florida cities did not. Arizona endorsed its native son by a slender majority, the only state outside the old Confederacy to do so. Although Senator Goldwater won only 45 per cent of the vote in Southern California, he did carry the two counties of most rapid population growth, San Diego and Orange.

Between 1964 and 1966, the same middle classes which had hesitated to support Goldwater in 1964 were buffeted and swayed by the San Francisco and Los Angeles (Watts) race riots, Mexican migrant unrest in California's rich Central Valley, unpopular Great Society programs, Vietnik and university (Berkeley) agitation and the multi-faceted controversies surrounding the Vietnamese war. As a result, the conservative stream of 1964 became a torrent in 1966, electing Republicans in Sun Belt upsets from California to Florida.

The epochal conservative triumphs of 1966 followed the general geopolitical outlines which the Goldwaterites had postulated in 1964. Conservative Jacksonville investment banker Claude Kirk lost Florida's liberal and minority-group settled centers of Miami and Tampa, but by dint of heavy majorities in resort, retirement and technology centers (St. Petersburg, Cape Kennedy and Palm Beach, for example), augmented by rural Dixiecrat support in northern and Gulf Coast Florida, he was elected as the state's first Republican governor since Reconstruction. Likewise, John Tower became the first Republican elected to a full term in the Senate from Texas. He lost the Negro and Rio Grande Mexican sections, but swept the white precincts of Dallas, Fort Worth and Houston, as well as rural

East Texas and the oil and ranch counties of the West Texas Plains. Led by the booming cities, Georgia cast its first plurality for a Republican governor, South Carolina elected its first GOP Senator since Reconstruction, and the three principal cities of Alabama reelected conservative Republicans to the House of Representatives. Oklahoma elected its second Republican governor in history, New Mexico its third, largely because of heavy party majorities in the urban explosion centers—Tulsa, Oklahoma City and Albuquerque. Cued by metropolitan Phoenix, Arizona also went strongly Republican. Much of this Sun Belt is traditionally Democratic, and the Republican upheaval of 1966 signaled a new era in national politics.

Undoubtedly the greatest vindication of the basic strategy of 1964 occurred in Ronald Reagan's smashing one million vote gubernatorial majority in California. The onetime movie actor carried every Southern California congressional district except the three in Los Angeles with large Negro, Jewish and Mexican populations. White Christian Southern California voted two-to-one for the spiritual heir of Barry Goldwater. Not only did Reagan sweep the country club, retiree and ex-naval precincts, but he won all of the white working-class suburbs.

Sun Belt conservatism in the 1968 presidential race lived up to the promise of 1966. From Florida, where huge GOP majorities in the boom area from Fort Lauderdale to Cape Kennedy cemented Nixon victory, to Southern California, where heavy Nixon leads in San Diego and Orange counties as well as suburban Los Angeles buried the liberal votes of San Francisco Bay, the Sun Belt showed a strong 1960-68 conservative trend. And quite often, the faster the growth rate—Orange County, California and Brevard County, Florida stand out—the greater the conservative trend. Arizona reelected Barry Goldwater to the U.S. Senate and Florida chose its first Republican Senator since Reconstruction—Ed Gurney. The GOP elected three new Sun Belt congressmen—one in Dallas and two in New Mexico. And in Oklahoma, large Republican majorities in the expanding Sun Belt cities of Tulsa and Oklahoma City sent Republican Henry Bellmon to the U.S. Senate. Even Max Rafferty— whose campaign was marred by mistaken tactics and ideological stridency—barely failed of election to the Senate from California (after winning about half of the vote in Sun Belt Southern California).

George Wallace's Sun Belt showing was somewhat higher than his nationwide average. The Alabaman scored less than 10 per cent of the vote in California, Arizona and New Mexico, but he won 13 per cent in Nevada, 20 per cent in Oklahoma, 19 per cent in Texas, 29 per cent in Florida and considerably more along the Louisiana-Mississippi-Alabama Gulf Coast. By and large, Wallace diverted traditional Democrats *en route* to the Republican Party. His Sun Belt support was primarily gathered at the expense of Richard Nixon. (The best evidence of the Republican inclination of the Sun Belt Wallace vote occurred in the support patterns of the Republican Senatorial candidates in California, Arizona, Oklahoma and Florida.) In Texas, Wallace diverted enough Sun Belt urban conservatives in cities like Dallas, Houston and Odessa-Midland to drive Nixon's majorities below 1960 levels, aborting the potential of 1968 and enabling Humphrey to capture the state's electoral votes with a narrow (41 per cent) plurality. The conservative, Republican future seems bright.

As Chart 134 shows, political power in America is slowly but surely drifting west with the restless millions of migrants to the Sun Belt. In 1970, California, Arizona, Florida and Texas, almost alone among the fifty states, will gain ten new congressmen and electoral votes, principally at the expense of the urban Northeast and Great Lakes. In another generation, the four Sun Belt states will outvote all eleven Northeastern states if present trends continue (and to the extent that Northern cities come under Negro control, the *Drang nach* Sun Belt may accelerate).

The Sun Country is America's new settlement frontier, and like other frontiers of the past, its politics are nationalistic, anti-intellectual and ethnocentric. (Frontier Massachusetts held witch trials, ruthlessly exterminated racial minorities and expelled religious dissenters.) But as the metamorphosis of Ronald Reagan illustrates, these attitudes moderate considerably in confrontation with actual power.

Few Northeasterners realize the new prominence of the South and West or appreciate that a new political era is in the making. Since Roger Williams left Boston in 1634, the center of American life has been moving south and west, and perhaps the most indicative recognition of this fact has come from President Nixon himself. Born in Southern California within sight of orange groves, he gave up his California residence to move to New York in 1963. Shortly after his election as President, however, he announced that he was changing his voting residence from New York to Florida. The political center of power in the United States is shifting away from the Northeast, and the Sun Belt is the principal beneficiary.

2. The Rise of Southern California

A century ago, Southern California was little more than a group of "cow counties" disdained by the populous northern part of the state. In 1880, the eight Southern California counties contained only 8 per cent of the state population. Los Angeles was a cow town; San Francisco was "The City."

Since then, things have changed. Southern California began to undergo its first boom in the Eighteen-Eighties; then another after the turn of the century. Chart 132 illustrates the course of the great influx. Between 1900 and 1930, the population of Southern California increased tenfold. Many of the new Californians came from the Heartland; from the overflowing farmlands of Illinois, Iowa, Missouri and Kansas. One hundred and sixty thousand Iowans alone came to California in the 1900-30 period.* By the mid-Twenties, more than half of the people of California lived south of the Tehachapi Mountains.

Thus swayed by the attitudes of the rural Protestant Heartland, Southern California was strongly Republican during the Nineteen-

---

*It would be difficult to overstate the Middle Western antecedents of Southern California. Carey McWilliams' book, *Southern California Country* (New York, 1946), includes some evocative descriptions. He quotes (page 161) Irvin S. Cobb as saying "At heart, Los Angeles is a vast section of the Corn Belt set down incongruously in a Maxfield Parrish setting." Frank Lloyd Wright is quoted as saying, less kindly, "It is as if you tipped the United States up so all the commonplace people slid down into Southern California." Explaining how the Iowan strain surpasses other Heartland antecedents, McWilliams recounts Southern California's nickname as "the seacoast of Iowa" and notes that during the Nineteen-Twenties, *one hundred and fifty thousand people* attended the more successful of the annual Iowa State Society picnics in Long Beach's Bixby Park. This huge figure indicates more than loyalty—it clearly shows a nostalgia and yearning. A short ditty sums it all up:

> "On the road to old L.A.
> Where the tin-can tourists play,
> And a sign says 'L.A. City Limits'
> At Clinton, Ioway."

Twenties, as well as staunchly prohibitionist, anti-labor and negative towards the presidential candidacy of Catholic Al Smith.* After the Depression broke the bubble of the Nineteen-Twenties, Southern California turned Democratic—and indulged in all kinds of esoteric politics on the side: technocracy, End Poverty in California (EPIC), the Ham and Eggs scheme and others.** Then as now, the uprooted citizenry of Southern California was prey for a multiplicity of causes and "isms."

World War II brought further prosperity and people to Southern California; defense industries and military installations blossomed throughout the region. And in the postwar years, Southern California continued to grow apace. The region voted for Thomas E. Dewey in 1948 and Dwight Eisenhower in 1952 and 1956, displaying a growing middle-class conservatism. Southern California backed Richard Nixon in 1960, enabling him to win a narrow statewide victory despite his loss in Northern California.

The social and racial conflicts of the Nineteen-Sixties stirred California politics into a renaissance of the "ism" politics of the Nineteen-Twenties. Around Northern California's San Francisco Bay, the New Politics thrust leftward, but the "ism" of Southern California was conservatism. And Southern California embodied the state's demographic future. Between 1940 and 1960, the population of the eight counties of Southern California rose from 3.6 million to 9 million. Most of this increment stemmed from immigration, much of it from the Heartland. Many of the uprooted migrants who came to Sun Country were searching for a middle-class promised land; they looked askance on the troubles which emerged during the Nineteen-Sixties—the racial violence of Watts and Hunters Point, the Mexican *bracero* demands of the Central Valley and the student unrest at Berkeley. Part of the attitude was a yearning for bygone, simpler times.*** Quite naturally, Southern California's

---

*Actually, Southern California was sometimes more Protestant, prohibitionist and anti-labor than Republican. During the Prohibition era, Los Angeles usually went Republican, but it was quite capable of going Democratic if the GOP candidate was anti-prohibition (or progressive) and the Democrat was not (William Gibbs McAdoo, for example).

**In 1938, when a $30-Every Thursday initiative was on the California ballot, it won 47 per cent support in Los Angeles.

***To quote Carey McWilliams, *op. cit.,* "Here the alien patrimony is not European, but American. The nostalgia is for an America that no longer exists, for an America that former Kansans, Missourians and Iowans literally gaze back upon."

large retired population was a principal source of this growing conservatism.

Southern California conservatism strode to the fore in 1964 when it triumphed over Northern California liberalism, enabling Barry Goldwater to defeat Nelson Rockefeller in the state's GOP presidential primary—the victory by which the Arizona Senator assured his nomination. But Goldwater could not match his primary success in the general election; not even in Southern California. He won only 45 per cent of the Southern California vote, albeit his total was only 6 per cent below Nixon's, a much smaller drop-off than he experienced in the rest of the nation. And there was something prophetic about Goldwater's few successes: Orange and San Diego, the fastest-growing major urban counties in state and nation, were the only two to back the Arizona conservative.

Most people think of Southern California as little more than metropolitan Los Angeles, but this is not true. Of the eight counties which make up Southern California, two of the fastest-growing—and most conservative—are Orange and San Diego, spanning the distance between Los Angeles and the Mexican border. Before the outbreak of World War II, San Diego was a small navy town; by the late Nineteen-Sixties, its population had reached 800,000, bigger by far than establishmentarian Boston. As one of the most rapidly expanding major urban areas in the United States, San Diego certainly rebuts the stereotyped correlation between urbanization and liberalization. The city's 45,000 Negroes call their city "the Mississippi of the West." If the Southern California boom suggests the future of state politics, Orange and San Diego counties capture the Sun Belt impetus in its least-diluted form. Chart 136 shows how Orange and San Diego are outpacing the other six counties as the centers of Southern California growth.

Southern California conservatism really came into its own in 1966 when it fueled Ronald Reagan's million vote majority gubernatorial sweep. Reagan carried all eight Southern California counties by considerable majorities. He did not carry the city of Los Angeles, although huge suburban majorities—eight- and nine-to-one in some locales—enabled him to carry Los Angeles County. One of the few suburbs that Reagan lost was rich, theatrical and quite Jewish Beverly Hills. Christian suburbs of comparable wealth invariably went overwhelmingly for Reagan; moreover, the overtly

CHART 136

The Changing Makeup of California Sun Belt Growth

	Percentage of Total California Vote for President			
	1920	1940	1964	1968
Santa Barbara, Ventura, Los Angeles, San Bernardino, Riverside and Imperial Counties	33%	49%	46%	47%
San Diego and Orange Counties	5%	6%	12%	14%
Total Southern California	38%	55%	58%	61%

conservative GOP candidate also won virtually every white working-class suburb. The Reagan campaign was massively successful even though the candidate captured only 5 per cent to 10 per cent of the Negro and Mexican vote. These results tend to disprove the argument that minority group support is a mandatory ingredient of Republican victory in a big-city state.

Despite Reagan's ability to win without their support, Negroes and Mexicans constitute a large and growing minority in Southern California. As of the mid-Nineteen-Sixties, some 12 per cent to 15 per cent of the population of Los Angeles County was Mexican or Negro. (Most of this minority-group concentration occurred in the city of Los Angeles.) Elsewhere in Southern California—agricultural areas in particular—Mexicans are the predominant minority. Given the ethnocentricity of white Southern California, the Negro-Mexican population is large enough to provoke white anger and counter-solidarity but seemingly not large enough to achieve a balance of power.

Much of the considerable 1964-66 conservative trend was a response to Watts, Berkeley and the Vietnik-social radicalism syndrome, influences which had been less persuasive in 1964. Further exemplifying the Southern California tide, local Republican congressmen cast five of the non-Southern Republican House votes against the 1967 civil rights bill (federal protection for civil rights workers) and the Southern California Republican House delegation almost unanimously voted to recommit the federal "open housing"

CHART 137

The Southern California Military-Industrial Complex, 1968

Military Facilities in Southern California

Oxnard Air Force Base, Camarillo
Naval Construction Battalion
  Center, Port Hueneme
Pacific Missile Range, Point Mugu
Fort MacArthur, San Pedro
Naval Air Station, Lemoore
Naval Ordnance Test Station,
  China Lake
Edwards Air Force Base, Muroc
Naval Air Station, Miramar
Long Beach Shipyard, Long Beach
Naval Station, Long Beach
Naval Supply Center, Long Beach
Fort Irwin, Barstow
George Air Force Base,
  Victorville
Marine Corps Base, Twenty-Nine
  Palms
Marine Corps Supply Center,
  Barstow
Norton Air Force Base,
  San Bernardino
El Toro Air Station, Santa Ana
Marine Corps Air Facility,
  Santa Ana
Naval Air Station, Los Alamitos
Naval Weapons Station,
  Seal Beach

March Air Force Base, Riverside
Naval Ordnance Laboratory,
  Corona
Coronado Amphibious Base,
  San Diego
Fleet Anti-Air Warfare Training
  School, San Diego
Fleet Anti-Submarine Warfare
  Training School, San Diego
Marine Corps Base, Camp
  Pendleton
Marine Corps Recruit Depot,
  San Diego
Naval Air Station, North Island
Naval Communication Station,
  San Diego
Naval Hospital, San Diego
Naval Public Works Center,
  San Diego
Naval Station, San Diego
Naval Supply Center, San Diego
Naval Training Center, San Diego
Navy Electronics Laboratory,
  San Diego
Ream Field, San Ysidro
Naval Air Facility, El Centro

NASA and AEC

Flight Research Center, Edwards
  (NASA)
Jet Propulsion Laboratory,
  Pasadena (NASA)
Western Test Range, Lompoc
  (NASA)
Reactor Facilities, Santa Susana
  (AEC)

NASA, Pasadena
Western Support Office, Santa
  Monica (NASA)
Reactor Facilities, Canoga Park
  (AEC)

Defense Corporations

Eastman Kodak (military photo supplies), Lompoc, Los Angeles, Whittier and Hollywood

General Electric, Santa Barbara

General Precision Equipment (missiles and components), Los Angeles and Glendale

Harvey Aluminum (ammunition and rockets), Torrance

Hughes Aircraft, Goleta, El Segundo, Los Angeles, Canoga Park, Malibu, Newport Beach and Fullerton

ITT-ITT Gilifillan (electronics), Los Angeles

General Motors (defense research laboratories), Goleta

Raytheon (electronics), Oxnard

Lockheed Aircraft, Los Angeles, Burbank and Ontario

Magnavox (electronics), Torrance and San Diego

Norris Thermador (ammunition), Los Angeles

North American Aviation, Los Angeles, Canoga Park and Anaheim

Northrop (aircraft), Hawthorne, Newbury Park and Anaheim

Radio Corporation of America (electronics), Los Angeles and Van Nuys

Signal Oil and Gas (aviation research), Los Angeles and Torrance

TRW (rockets and components), Redondo Beach

Aerojet-General, Downey, Covina, Azusa and El Monte

Textron (missile components), Whittier and Burbank

Litton (electronics), Canoga Park, Van Nuys and Beverly Hills

McDonnell Douglas (aircraft), Cudahy, Monrovia, South Pasadena, Long Beach and Huntington Beach

Honeywell (missile components), West Covina

Fairchild-Hiller (electronics), Manhattan Beach

Lear-Siegler (electronics), Santa Monica and Anaheim

Ling-Temco-Vought (electronics), Anaheim

Collins Radio (communications), Newport Beach

Ford Motor Company (missiles), Newport Beach

General Dynamics (missiles and electronics), San Diego

Ryan Aeronautical Company, San Diego

On a statewide basis, California is first in the nation in (1) military contract awards; (2) military payroll; and (3) civilian Defense Department payroll.

Fiscal 1967 Military Contract Awards	$6,689,000,000	17.9% of U.S. Total
Fiscal 1967 Military Payroll	$1,149,666,000	12.3% of U.S. Total
Fiscal 1967 Department of Defense Civilian Payroll	$1,327,522,000	16.5% of U.S. Total

bill in April, 1968. Southern Californians have always shown intense opposition to open housing, whether in referenda or otherwise.

The war in Vietnam and the racial conflict in the cities were the two major issues molding Southern California opinion in 1968. Although anti-war sentiments were widespread in greater Los Angeles' liberal and academic circles, the opinion of the man in the street was more hawkish. For one thing, Sun Country in general and California in particular house a vast complex of military bases and defense plants. Defense is one of Southern California's leading industries, and employees of the vast Southwestern Military-Industrial Complex (SMIC) logically tend to support patriotism, pentagon and paycheck. Chart 137 lists the array of defense plants and military bases located in Southern California. Super-patriotism and racial tension were paramount in enabling Alabama's ex-governor George Wallace to mobilize over one hundred thousand registrants, most of them Southern Californians, for his American Independent Party (thus putting his presidential candidacy on the ballot).

In 1968, Richard Nixon carried all eight Southern California counties, including Ventura and Los Angeles, which had both backed John Kennedy in 1960. The GOP nominee carried Southern California by nearly half a million votes, three times his 1960 majority, and this increment was the foundation of his statewide victory. Chart 138 shows the 1960-68 trends of Los Angeles, Orange and San Diego counties. Together, these areas swing most of Southern California's political weight.

CHART 138

Presidential Voting in Southern California, 1960-68

	Percentage of the Total Vote for President				
	1960		1968		
County	Nixon	Kennedy	Nixon	Wallace	Humphrey
Los Angeles	50%	50%	48%	6%	46%
Orange	61	39	63	7	30
San Diego	57	43	57	7	36

The booming San Diego-Orange corridor was the focal point of the 1960-68 Nixon tide in California. Chart 136 shows how this area is the fastest-growing in the state. Between 1960 and 1968, the two counties increased their share of the state vote from 10 per cent to 14 per cent and their Nixon majority increased from 115,000 to 258,000. With the Orange-San Diego corridor leading the way, Southern California raised its share of the statewide vote to 61 per cent in 1968.

Most of this new Southern California growth is middle class, white and suburban. Thus, although the Negro and Mexican populations of the *cities* of Los Angeles and San Diego are growing, the overall regional picture is one of massive white middle-income predominance. Richard Nixon's poor showings in the Negro and Mexican precincts of Los Angeles, San Diego and other cities were swallowed up in the outpouring of conservative whites from Santa Barbara to Chula Vista.

George Wallace did surprisingly poorly in Southern California; witness the figures in Chart 138. The Alabaman ran strongest in lower-middle-income neighborhoods populated by persons of Southern and Midwestern origins or antecedents (especially Oklahomans and Missourians). One of Wallace's best areas was Bell Gardens, a veritable "Little Oklahoma" adjacent to riot-torn Watts, where George Wallace had earlier persuaded a plurality of the electorate to enroll in his American Independent Party. In the vast middle-class tracts of bulldozed orange groves, however, Wallace won relatively poor support (4 per cent to 6 per cent), leaving intact the majorities Nixon needed for victory.

Although most of Wallace's limited Southern California backing appears to have come from conservative Democrats, some also came from conservative Republicans, especially in the John Birch Society stronghold of Orange County. Either way, there was a definite correlation between 1966 Reagan gains and 1968 Wallace backing, which tends to suggest that an overwhelming majority of the Wallace electorate would have moved to Republican Richard Nixon in a two-party contest. The Southern California Wallace electorate was principally an aggregation of conservative blue-collar, lower-middle-class and Southern Democrats in the midst of changing parties.

Chart 139 structures a cross-section of 1968 voting patterns in the Los Angeles area. In Southern California, as in the Texas and

CHART 139

Southern California Voting Behavior (A Profile of Los Angeles County Presidential Voting, 1968)

Locale	Percentage of Total Presidential Vote Cast For:		
	Nixon	Wallace	Humphrey
Upper-Middle-Income White Suburbia			
Palos Verdes Estates	77%	3%	20%
Rolling Hills	80	5	15
San Marino	87	3	10
Middle-Income White Suburbia (Military and Technology Centers)			
El Segundo	60	9	31
Lower Middle-Income White Suburbia (Okie)			
Bell Gardens	50	10	40
Upper-Middle-Income Suburbia (Substantially Jewish)			
Beverly Hills	36	1	63
Mexican-American Urban Neighborhoods*			
East Los Angeles			
Negro Urban Neighborhoods**			
53rd Assembly District of Los Angeles	9	1	90

*Mexican concentrations are split between Assembly Districts. Nixon would appear to have won 15 per cent to 30 per cent support.
**Most of the Nixon and Wallace votes were cast by white stay-behinds.

Note: Most white Southern Californians are lower-middle-income or better in economic status.

Florida reaches of the Sun Belt, Negroes, Latins and Jews constitute the bulwark of the national Democratic Party. White Christian Southern Californians gave Nixon and Wallace twice as many votes as they gave Hubert Humphrey. Because the influx and expansion of this white middle class is the dominant factor in Southern California population growth, there is every reason to surmise that middle-class conservatism should continue to consolidate its hegemony in the Golden State.

C. The Pacific Interior

East of the Cascades and California's coastal ranges, the Northern Pacific Coast gives way to a more insular and less cosmopolitan subregion, the Pacific Interior. Although it encompasses two thirds of the land area of Oregon and Washington and perhaps half that of California, the vast acreage of the interior contains considerably smaller fractions of the three states' population (Washington—30 per cent; Oregon and California—15 per cent). Within the interior, there is considerable mining and logging, but agriculture is paramount, ranging from the orchards and wheatfields of eastern Washington (the rich "Inland Empire") to the vast irrigated stretches of California's great Central Valley. In topography, demography and sociopolitical outlook, the Pacific Interior is an extension of the Interior Plateau section of the Rocky Mountain states. Quite unlike the Northern Pacific Coast (it was settled by different people under different circumstances), the Pacific Interior is virtually a part of the Heartland. Its present ideological thrust is populist conservative.

Like the Rocky Mountains, the Pacific Interior has a tradition of political anti-establishmentarianism. When William Jennings Bryan ran for President in 1896—and again less successfully in 1900 and 1908—his best Pacific levels were achieved in the interior: the Washington wheat bowl (and similar adjacent areas of Oregon), interior mining counties of all three states and the agricultural Central Valley of California. However, only Washington, where Puget Sound radicalism joined with the wheat counties, forged an actual Bryan majority.

The Pacific Interior strongly backed Theodore Roosevelt in 1912, enabling him to beat both Republican President William Howard Taft and Woodrow Wilson, and to win the electoral votes of California and Washington. In 1916, with the specter of war present, the interior areas of all three states supported Woodrow Wilson, who promised progressivism at home and non-intervention abroad, but by 1920 the Democratic record was quite the opposite. Many of Washington's progressive and isolationist-inclined wheat counties reacted so sharply that Democratic presidential nominee James Cox won only 10 per cent to 20 per cent of the vote, and interior Oregon and California were almost as negative.

As the economic difficulties of postwar wheat cultivation mounted, a bevy of radical movements tried to fill the gap. North Dakota's controversial Non-Partisan League began to agitate in the eastern Washington wheat counties, and in 1924, five such counties gave a plurality of their vote to Progressive presidential candidate Robert LaFollette. He also won pluralities in several sections of interior California. The discontent evidenced in 1924 was still highly operative in 1928, but Washington's wheat bowl went strongly Republican. There was little support for Tammany Catholic Al Smith, whose progressivism was of an urban and transcontinental stripe. With the advent of the Depression, farm unhappiness grew, and the wheat counties gave heavy support to Franklin Roosevelt in both the 1932 and the 1936 elections.

Like those in Montana, Colorado and Wyoming, the Washington wheat bowl is the most conservative section of the state. As did wheat-growing areas of the Great Plains, eastern Washington gave considerable support to LaFollette in 1924 and to Roosevelt during the Nineteen-Thirties. However, this behavior was rooted in agrarianism (also isolationism, at least in 1924) rather than the urban and labor orientation which swayed Puget Sound and the mine, mill and smelter sections of the Rocky Mountains. Consequently, the multiple impact of prosperity, isolationism and the emerging non-farm biases of the New Deal helped bring the Washington Wheat Bowl back to the GOP fold in 1940.* By 1944, the minority of wheat counties voting Republican had turned into a majority. Of course, the State of Washington remained Democratic under the primacy of Puget Sound ballots.

To complete the Farm states' parallel, the GOP vote slipped in eastern Washington between 1944 and 1948 because some farmers decided that Democratic agricultural policies should be retained as a hedge against postwar difficulties, while some anti-Roosevelt isolationists stayed home or backed Truman. Nevertheless, the interior of Washington still produced a better Republican vote than

*The wheat country of the Big Bend has a substantial German population, which influenced voting behavior in 1940.

the coast. Then in 1952, the GOP vote soared in the Inland Empire as in the Farm Belt. Interior Washington went heavily for Eisenhower and he carried the state. Although the GOP vote declined in the Wheat Bowl in 1956—the party's farm, resource and power policies were to blame—the eastern counties stayed in the Republican column, as did Washington's electoral votes. Richard Nixon maintained Eisenhower's 1956 strength in the Washington interior and was able to carry the state narrowly, even though John F. Kennedy won Puget Sound and the coast by slim margins. Thus, by 1964, the division within Washington was crystallizing: interior conservatism versus coastal liberalism, empathy with the Heartland versus kinship with the Northeast, Scandinavian Minnesota and Wisconsin.

Barry Goldwater's ideological bluntness accentuated this cleavage. West of the Cascades, his vote slipped almost 15 per cent below Nixon's 1960 levels, but in the east, only 10 per cent or so. The Arizona Senator ran substantially stronger in the east than in the coastal region.

Wheat-rich eastern Washington, fired by low crop prices and the high cost of Vietnam, showed a distinct conservative trend in 1968, giving Hubert Humphrey a generally lower share of the vote than John Kennedy had won. But as in Idaho, George Wallace ran quite well—his support in a number of Washington counties, eastern and western, exceeded 10 per cent—and diverted much of the anti-Democratic trend that otherwise would have helped Richard Nixon. Shorn of this support, Nixon was unable to amass large enough majorities in eastern Washington to overcome liberal Democratic gains in Puget Sound, and Humphrey carried the state. Without Wallace in the race, Nixon would have amassed a winning edge in the Inland Empire. Chart 140 shows the widening ideological split between eastern and western Washington.

Interior Oregon is sparsely populated and does not even amount to an entire congressional district.* In the 1964 election, Barry Goldwater slipped only 3 per cent to 12 per cent below Nixon's levels in the interior counties, while plummeting 15 per cent to 25 per cent below Nixon's percentages in the very dissimilar Willamette Valley and other areas west of the Cascades. By 1968, the conservative

---

*Interior Oregon is somewhat more populous if one includes the logging counties south of Eugene which straddle the Cascades. In the late Nineteen-Sixties, they were conservative-trending areas like the interior.

CHART 140

Washington: The Ideological Division

| | Liberal (Democratic) Share of the Total Vote for President | | |
	1960	1964	1968
Western Washington	50%	64%	50%
Eastern Washington	46	57	42

trend in the interior was considerable. Bellwether Crook County, which has always voted for the winning presidential candidate, switched to Nixon. So did the other interior wheat, ranching and logging counties which had backed John Kennedy in 1960. Gains in these counties—Border and Midwestern voting streams played a part—helped Nixon to maintain his Oregon majority at 1960 levels despite Democratic strides in Portland and the Willamette Valley.*

The California interior, unlike that of Oregon and Washington, is not a wide plateau. Interior California focuses on a four-hundred-mile valley stretching from Shasta to Bakersfield and fenced by high mountain ranges. Almost all of interior California's three million people live in the lush valley and its fringe of foothills. Except where the Sacramento River flows west into San Francisco Bay, the valley—it is called the Central Valley, the Great Valley or sometimes the San Joaquin and Sacramento Valleys after its two major rivers—is completely surrounded by the California coastal ranges on the west and the towering Sierra Nevada on the east.

About 15 per cent of California's people live in the Great Valley, a percentage that used to be much higher. The Forty-Niner goldrush began near present-day Sacramento, and for many years the Valley was traversed by miners heading up into the Sierra foothills. It soon became apparent, however, that the Valley offered other profitable vocations, especially agriculture, and the Sacramento riverlands turned into the breadbasket of California. Agriculture is the prin-

---

*Oregon Yankees have long recognized the difference of the eastern part of the state. In 1875, one complained that the left wing of Confederate General Sterling Price's cavalry was encamped there. (See Rusling, *The Great West and the Pacific Coast*, New York, 1875.) He referred to the number of Missourians.

ciple force in the Valley today. Most people live in the lowlands and in the local urban centers—Fresno, Stockton, Sacramento and Bakersfield—and the Sierra foothills counties have names evoking a romantic past (Sierra, Nevada, Placer, El Dorado) if not a populous present.

Interior California has a political history like similar Western locales: Bryan won most counties in 1896; local voters cheered Hiram Johnson's fight with the Union Pacific and Teddy Roosevelt's "Bull Moose" charge in 1912; conservative Democrats fared poorly against orthodox Republicans in 1904, 1920 and 1924; fifteen California counties, most of them in the interior, gave Progressive Robert LaFollette a plurality in 1924; and Franklin D. Roosevelt swept the Valley from top to bottom in 1932 and 1936.

The Depression of the Nineteen-Thirties played a considerable role in reshaping the politics of the Great Central Valley of California, especially insofar as it helped to spur the westward trek of "dustbowl" Oklahomans, Missourians and others to the fertile promised land of the Golden State. Wave after wave of these migrants caused the Valley's population to mushroom during the Depression decade. At first these people worked as farm laborers and pickers, a style of life which John Steinbeck has immortalized, but eventually the Valley absorbed most of them. Given their states of origin and economic status, most of the migrants were traditional Democrats or New Deal converts and their votes helped to make the Valley into a Democratic stronghold. These attitudes persisted past World War II and the return of prosperity. Thomas E. Dewey was badly beaten in the Valley in 1948, even though he almost carried California. Eisenhower posted thin majorities in the Valley in 1952, only to see them wither away in 1956 as the Valley voiced its objections to GOP agricultural, power and resource policies.

Most California politicians were surprised by Richard Nixon's strong 1960 vote in the Valley. (He ran ahead of Eisenhower in a number of counties.) Normally, when California politicians cannot surpass Nixon's San Francisco and Los Angeles strength evident in 1960, they lose the state, but Nixon won with the help of an abnormal vote in the Valley. In some measure, this represented "Okie" Protestant voting against Catholic John Kennedy, but changing Valley attitudes were also taking hold. Like the Italo-Irish middle classes of the Northeast, which also rose to affluence under the New Deal, Pacific Interior voters began to demonstrate a

CHART 141

Democratic Share of the Total Presidential and Gubernatorial Vote in Selected California Interior Counties, 1936-68

Counties	1936 Pres.	1940 Pres.	1944 Pres.	1948 Pres.	1952 Pres.	1956 Pres.	1960 Pres.	1964 Pres.	1966 Gov.	1968 Pres.
Southern Valley										
Kern (Bakersfield)	75%	62%	56%	56%	44%	48%	49%	59%	37%	41%
Fresno (Fresno)	78	69	64	59	51	56	55	66	46	48
Sierra Mining and Logging										
Shasta	70	68	59	57	43	56	61	68	45	49
Placer	77	68	63	59	49	54	56	66	45	48
Statewide	67	57	57	48	43	44	50	59	42	45

growing lack of empathy with Democratic programs aimed at other regions and socioeconomic groups. Even in 1964, Barry Goldwater barely slipped below 1948 levels in the Valley (although his statewide vote share fell almost 9 per cent below that which Dewey had amassed). Agricultural turmoil, an old story in the Valley, took on a new socioeconomic coloration in 1965 and later years as federal anti-poverty efforts and *bracero* regulations pitted the local white bourgeoisie against the migrant Mexican farm workers. And of course, many of the bourgeoisie of the Nineteen-Sixties were the pickers of the Nineteen-Thirties. Doubtless their attitudes were influenced by memories of picking peaches for five cents a box in days when Northeastern Establishment politicians did not think it fashionable to pose for pictures with the rural disadvantaged. For these and other reasons, Valley and Sierra voters marched to the polls in November, 1966 and cast an unprecedented vote for conservative Republican gubernatorial candidate Ronald Reagan.

As Chart 141 illustrates, the California Interior was considerably more Democratic than the state as a whole during the years between 1936 and 1956, but since the rise of the civil rights and Negro revolutions, the gap has been shrinking. The explanation is simple: the Democratic ideology of the Pacific Interior is geared to progressivism, the New Deal and the Fair Deal—to public power, government agricultural programs and irrigation projects—rather than to the new Establishment liberalism and its preoccupation with urban change and racial integration. Contrary to previous patterns, Nixon and Goldwater ran almost as well in the California Valley as they did in the state as a whole, and in 1966 Ronald Reagan won as much of the vote in the California Interior as he did statewide—a record 58 per cent. Changing Valley attitudes were best shown by the election of a Republican congressman in the onetime "Grapes of Wrath" locale around Bakersfield where Franklin D. Roosevelt had triumphed four-to-one in mid-Depression 1936! (And at the other end of the "dustbowl" trail, southwestern Oklahoma also upset a Democratic incumbent and elected a conservative Republican.)

Aware that the Democratic loyalties of their districts are not attuned to the party's new urban orientation, Pacific Interior Democrats showed occasional disloyalty to the Great Society in the Eighty-Ninth and Ninetieth Congresses. Most of them are little-known Democrats of considerable seniority, and although they rarely gainsaid the party leadership on major issues, they broke ranks on telltale roll calls regarding Adam Clayton Powell, the Mississippi Freedom Democratic Party, home rule for the predominantly Negro District of Columbia, the War on Poverty and rent subsidy appropriations.*

Between 1960 and 1968, the Democratic share of the presidential vote tumbled considerably along the length of the Central Valley and in the nearby foothills and high Sierras. Some of the gain accrued to Richard Nixon, who carried counties that he had lost in 1960, but a substantial part of the anti-Democratic trend took the form of support for George Wallace. The Alabaman garnered considerable support—8 per cent to 12 per cent—in the Okie-settled counties where Reagan had made strong gains in 1966. Profiting from his populism, he also scored 10 per cent to 15 per cent in the mining and logging counties. As Maps 2 and 3 show, California's sharpest Democratic losses and best Wallace showings both came in the Interior.

Obviously, most of Wallace's support in the California Interior came from traditional Democrats; this was the pattern of his strength across most of the nation. Far more important, however, is the Republican-trending nature of this particular electorate. The traditional and New Deal-ingrained Democratic loyalties of Valley farmers from Texas, Sierra miners from Arizona or loggers from Idaho or Georgia are no longer relevant to contemporary partisanship. The size of the 1966 Reagan vote foreshadowed the extent and the underlying cause of conservative Democratic willingness to switch to the GOP.

To a considerable extent, the politics of the Pacific interior represent an extension of Rocky Mountain behavior; and the latter region's reaction to the increasingly Northeastern, establishmentarian and Negro orientation of the Democratic Party has been generally negative. Populist Democratic voting streams rooted in the anti-establishment credos of Bryan and Roosevelt are leaving the party. In some areas, particularly those where a sizeable share of the population has Southern or Border antecedents, George Wallace

*One such congressman was Fresno, California's B. F. Sisk, who helped to hold up the 1968 Civil Rights bill in the House Rules Committee. Born in Texas and educated at Abilene Christian College, Sisk moved to the San Joaquin Valley in 1937 and found more opportunity than in the North Texas dustbowl. He was elected to Congress in 1954. Sentiment for open housing was negligible in Sisk's district, and his Rules Committee hesitancy was well received at home.

captured a good part of this alienated electorate. But there is little doubt that the basic drift of the Pacific Interior, like that of the Interior Plateau of the Rocky Mountains, is towards the new popular conservatism of the Republican Party. In the case of California, GOP majorities in the Central Valley and Sierra will buoy—and guarantee—the statewide predominance of Southern California conservatism.

The Pacific Future

After all is said and done, the political future of the Pacific is essentially that of California. The rest of the Pacific is gaining population at a much slower rate (comparable to that of the country as a whole). The two major forces locked in California political conflict are, of course, the liberalism of the Northern Pacific Coast and the conservatism of Southern and Interior California. The first is a cousin of Northeastern behavior and the second is an impetus akin to that of the Heartland.

Ideologically and demographically, the trend is clearly towards a predominance of Southern California conservatism. Not only is the ideological trend of middle-class California a conservative one, but conservative Southern California is steadily lengthening its population and ballot-box lead over San Francisco Bay-based liberalism. The forces which elected Ronald Reagan, George Murphy and Richard Nixon appear to represent the political future of the most populous state in the Union, in which case California will line up with the conservative coalition of Heartland and South, cementing coalition sway.

What tack Washington and Oregon take is of less significance. However, both states, along with Alaska, the Great Lakes states, and Mason-Dixon Line-straddling Maryland, New Jersey and Pennsylvania, are emerging as something of a border in the new alignment of Heartland and South against the Northeastern Seaboard and the Northern Pacific Coast. By all indications, the Pacific should be a major—and ever more powerful—battleground of the upcoming political cycle. The party able to win a majority of Pacific electoral votes in the quadrennial presidential sweepstakes is also likely to triumph nationally.

VI. THE FUTURE OF AMERICAN POLITICS

ᛜᛜ ᛜᛜ ᛜᛜ ᛜᛜ ᛜᛜ ᛜᛜ ᛜᛜ ᛜᛜ

T HE LONG-RANGE MEANING OF THE POLITICAL UPHEAVAL OF 1968 rests on the Republican opportunity to fashion a majority among the 57 per cent of the American electorate which voted to eject the Democratic Party from national power. To begin with, more than half of this protesting 57 per cent were firm Republicans from areas—Southern California to Long Island's Suffolk County—or sociocultural backgrounds with a growing GOP bias. Some voted for George Wallace, but most backed Richard Nixon, providing the bulk of his Election Day support. Only a small minority of 1968 Nixon backers—perhaps several million liberal Republicans and independents from Maine and Oregon to Fifth Avenue—cast what may be their last Republican presidential ballots because of the partisan re-alignment taking place. The third major anti-Democratic voting stream of 1968—and the most decisive—was that of the fifteen million or so conservative Democrats who shunned Hubert Humphrey to divide about evenly between Richard Nixon and George Wallace. Such elements stretched from the "Okie" Great Central Valley of California to the mountain towns of Idaho, Florida's space centers, rural South Carolina, Bavarian Minnesota, the Irish sidewalks of New York and the Levittowns of Megalopolis. Map 3 shows the locales of Democratic disaffection.

Although most of George Wallace's votes came from Democrats rather than Republicans, they were conservatives—Southerners, Borderers, German and Irish Catholics—who had been trending Republican prior to 1968. As Maps 14, 36, and 41 illustrate, the Wallace vote followed the cultural geography of obsolescent conservative (often Southern) Democratic tradition. There was no reliable Wallace backing among blue-collar workers and poor whites as a class; industrial centers in the Yankee sphere of influence from Duluth to Scranton, Fall River and Biddeford shunned the Alabama ex-governor with a mere 2 per cent to 3 per cent of the vote. Areas of eroding Democratic tradition were the great breeding grounds of Wallace voters.

In the South, Wallace drew principally on conservative Democrats quitting the party they had long succored and controlled. Generally speaking, Wallace's Southern strength was greatest in the Democratic Party's historic (pre-1964) lowland strongholds, while the Alabaman's worst Southern percentages came in the Republican highlands. White voters throughout most sections of the Deep South went two-to-one for Wallace. In the more Republican Outer South, only one white voter out of three supported the third-party candidate. In the South as a whole, 85 to 90 per cent of the white electorate cast Nixon or Wallace votes against the re-aligning national Democratic Party in 1968, an unprecedented magnitude of disaffection which indicates the availability of the Wallace vote to the future GOP.

Four of the five Wallace states had gone Republican in 1964, and although the Alabaman greatly enlarged the scope of Southern revolt by attracting most of the (poor white or Outer South Black Belt) Southerners who had hitherto resisted Republican or States Rights candidacies, much of his tide had already been flowing for Goldwater. Nor does the Nixon Administration have to bid much ideologically for this electorate. Despite his success in enlarging the scope of white Southern revolt, George Wallace failed to reach far enough or strongly enough beyond the Deep South to give his American Independent Party the national base required for a viable future. Republican Nixon won most of the Outer South, establishing the GOP as the ascending party of the local white majority. Having achieved statewide success only in the Deep South, and facing competition from a Southern Republicanism mindful of its opportunity, the Wallace movement cannot maintain an adequate political base and is bound to serve, like past American third parties, as a way station for groups abandoning one party for another. Some Wallace voters were longtime Republicans, but the great majority were conservative Democrats who have been moving—and should continue to do so—towards the GOP.

The linkage of Wallace voting to the obsolescent Democratic loyalties of certain areas and groups can also be proved far beyond the old Confederacy. Map 36 shows how the pattern of Wallace support in the Ohio Valley, instead of standing out in backlash-prone industrial areas, followed rural contours of traditional Democratic strength, moving farthest north along the Scioto River, central Ohio's roadway of Virginia and Kentucky migration. And in New York and Pennsylvania, Map 14 illustrates how certain levels of Wallace support probed farthest north along the Susquehanna, Delaware and Hudson valleys, outliers of traditionally Democratic non-Yankee rural strength. Out West, Wallace percentages were greatest in the Oklahoma- and Texas-settled towns of California's Central Valley, the populist mining and logging counties of the Rocky Mountains, the traditionally Democratic Mormon reaches of Idaho, and in Alaska's long-Democratic sluice and sawmill districts.

In addition to Western or Southern Democrats of conservative or populist bent, Wallace also scored well among Catholics, but only in certain areas. From Maine to Michigan, across most of the belt of Yankee-settled territory where local cleavage, though changing, still pits Protestant Republicans against urban Catholic Democrats, the Catholic trend away from the Democrats was slight. However, in the greater New York area, as well as Gary and Cleveland, where minority group (Negro and/or Jewish) power has taken control of local Democratic machinery, Catholic backing of Wallace was considerable. Here, as discussed in Chapters II and IV, Catholics are leaving the Democratic Party.

The common denominator of Wallace support, Catholic or Protestant, is alienation from the Democratic Party and a strong trend—shown in other years and other contests—towards the GOP. Although most of Wallace's votes came from Democrats, he principally won those in motion between a Democratic past and a Republican future. In the last few weeks of the campaign, labor union activity, economic issues and the escalating two-party context of October, 1968, drew many Wallace-leaning Northern blue-collar workers back into the Democratic fold. Only those fully alienated by the national Democratic Party stuck with Wallace in the voting booth. Offered a three-party context, these sociopolitical streams preferred populist Wallace; a two-party context would have drawn them into the GOP. Three quarters or more of the Wallace electorate represented lost Nixon votes.

A few states—Mississippi or Alabama—may indulge in future third-party or states rights efforts. The Wallace party itself, however, has dubious prospects, being not a broad-based national grouping but a transient 1968 aggregation of conservative Democrats otherwise trending into the Republican Party. Generally speaking, the South is more realistic than its critics believe, and nothing more than an effective and responsibly conservative Nixon Administration is necessary to bring most of the Southern Wallace electorate into the fold against a Northeastern liberal Democratic presidential nominee. Abandonment of civil rights enforcement would be self-defeating. Maintenance of Negro voting rights in Dixie, far from being contrary to GOP interests, is essential if southern conservatives are to be pressured into switching to the Republican Party—for Negroes are beginning to seize control of the national Democratic Party in some Black Belt areas.

Successful moderate conservatism is also likely to attract to the Republican side some of the Northern blue-collar workers who flirted with George Wallace but ultimately backed Hubert Humphrey. Fears that a Republican administration would undermine Social Security, Medicare, collective bargaining and aid to education played a major part in keeping socially conservative blue-collar workers and senior citizens loyal to the 1968 Democratic candidate. Assuming that a Nixon administration can dispel these apprehensions, it ought to be able to repeat—with much more permanence—Eisenhower's great blue-collar success of 1956. Sociologically, the Republican Party is becoming much more lower-middle class and much less establishmentarian than it was during the Nineteen-Fifties, and pursuit of an increasing portion of the Northern blue-collar electorate—an expansion of its 1968 Catholic triumph in greater New York City—would be a logical extension of this trend.

Although the appeal of a successful Nixon Administration and the lack of a Wallace candidacy would greatly swell the 1972 Republican vote in the South, West, Border and the Catholic North, the

1972 GOP may well simultaneously lose a lesser number of 1968 supporters among groups reacting against the party's emerging Southern, Western and New York Irish majority. As discussed in Chapters II, IV and V, Yankees, Megalopolitan silk-stocking voters and Scandinavians from Maine across the Great Lakes to the Pacific all showed a distinct Democratic trend in the years between 1960 and 1968. Such disaffection will doubtlessly continue, but its principal impact has already been felt. Richard Nixon won only 38 per cent of the total 1968 presidential vote on Manhattan's rich East Side; he took only 44 per cent of the ballots in Scarsdale, the city's richest suburb; New England's Yankee counties and towns produced Nixon majorities down 10 per cent to 15 per cent from 1960 levels; fashionable San Francisco shifted toward the Democrats; and Scandinavian Minnesota and Washington state backed Humphrey, as did the Scandinavian northwest of Wisconsin.

As Map 3 shows, all of these locales shifted *towards* the Democrats during the 1960-68 period. Because the local re-alignment pivoted on liberal Republicans rather than conservative Democrats, these areas evidenced little or no support for George Wallace (see Map 2). Beyond the bounds of states that went Democratic in 1968, the Yankee, silk-stocking establishmentarian and Scandinavian trends predominate only in Vermont, New Hampshire and Oregon. Although Northern California, Wisconsin, Ohio's old Western Reserve, central Iowa and parts of the Dakotas are likewise influenced, other conservative trends—those of Southern California suburbanites, German Catholics of the upper Farm Belt and the quasi-Southern Democrats of the Ohio Valley—should keep those states Republican. Yankee, Northeastern silk-stocking and Scandinavian disaffection with the GOP is concentrated in states which the party has already lost, and it menaces only a few states which the GOP won in 1968.

The upcoming cycle of American politics is likely to match a dominant Republican Party based in the Heartland, South and California against a minority Democratic Party based in the Northeast and the Pacific Northwest (and encompassing Southern as well as Northern Negroes). With such support behind it, the GOP can easily afford to lose the states of Massachusetts, New York and Michigan—and is likely to do so except in landslide years. Together with the District of Columbia, the top ten Humphrey states— Hawaii, Washington, Minnesota, Michigan, West Virginia, New

York, Connecticut, Rhode Island, Massachusetts and Maine—should prove to be the core of national Democratic strength. As drawn in Map 4, the new battlegrounds of quadrennial presidential politics are likely to be California, Ohio and Pennsylvania.

Unluckily for the Democrats, their major impetus is centered in stagnant Northern industrial states—and within those states, in old decaying cities, in a Yankee countryside that has fewer people than in 1900, and in the most expensive suburbs. Beyond this, in the South and West, the Democrats dominate only two expanding voting blocs—Latins and Negroes. From space-center Florida across the booming Texas plains to the Los Angeles–San Diego suburban corridor, the nation's fastest-growing areas are strongly Republican and conservative. Even in the Northeast, the few rapidly growing suburbs are conservative-trending areas (see Chart 51). Because of this demographic pattern, the South and West are gaining electoral votes and national political power at the expense of the Northeast. Chart 135 illustrates how the conservative Sun Belt cities are undergoing a population boom—and getting more conservative—while the old liberal cities of the Northeast decline. And Chart 134 shows how the Northeast is steadily losing relative political importance to the Sun Belt.

CHART 142

The Decline in the Big City Presidential Vote, 1960-68

Total Major Party Vote for President
(In Thousands)

City*	1960	1964	1968
New York City	3,081	2,811	2,591
Chicago	1,674	1,607	1,433
Los Angeles	1,053	1,079	1,012
Philadelphia	914	910	826
Detroit	743	681	598
Baltimore	317	317	290
Cleveland	338	302	263
St. Louis	304	268	221
Milwaukee	309	298	256
San Francisco	341	324	272
Boston	292	255	225

*The eleven largest cities of 1960 (excluding Sun Belt Houston); several will no longer be on the list when the 1970 Census is completed.

One of the greatest political myths of the decade—a product of liberal self-interest—is that the Republican Party cannot attain national dominance without mobilizing liberal support in the big cities, appealing to "liberal" youth, empathizing with "liberal" urbanization, gaining substantial Negro support and courting the affluent young professional classes of "suburbia." The actual demographic and political facts convey a very different message.

As Chart 13 suggests, the big city political era is over in the United States. Chart 142 lists the considerable 1960-68 slippage in the presidential vote cast by the leading big cities. With Negroes moving into the cities, whites have moved out. Moreover, white urban populations are getting increasingly conservative. Richard Nixon and George Wallace together won 40 per cent of the vote in liberal New York City. Perhaps more to the point, leading big city states like New York, Michigan and Massachusetts are no longer necessary for national Republican victory.

Youth is important, but voters under 25 cast only 7.4 per cent of the nation's ballots in 1968. And while many Northeastern young people are more liberal and Democratic than their parents— especially the affluent and anarchic progeny of the Establishment— the reverse seems to be true in Southern, Border, Rocky Mountain, Catholic, lower middle class and working-class areas. In these locales, the young electorate's trend against local political tradition helps the GOP, as does resentment of the blyth nihilism of the children of the affluent society.

While urbanization *is* changing the face of America, and the GOP must take political note of this fact, it presents the opposite of a problem. A generation ago, the coming of age of the working-class central cities condemned the Republican Party to minority status, but the new "urbanization"—suburbanization is often a better description—is a middle-class impetus shaping the same ignominy for the Democrats. All across the nation, the fastest-growing urban areas are steadily increasing their *Republican* pluralities, while the old central cities—seat of the New Deal era—are casting steadily fewer votes for Democratic liberalism. No major American city is losing population so rapidly as arch-Democratic and establishmentarian Boston, while the fastest-growing urban area in the nation is Southern California's staunchly conservative Orange County, and the fastest growing cities are conservative strongholds like Phoenix, Dallas, Houston, Anaheim, San Diego and Fort Lauderdale.

Substantial Negro support is not necessary to national Republican victory in light of the 1968 election returns. Obviously, the GOP can build a winning coalition without Negro votes. Indeed, Negro-Democratic mutual identification was a major source of Democratic loss—and Republican or American Independent Party profit—in many sections of the nation.

Chapter II analyzes the alleged suburban "liberal" trend. The liberal and Democratic 1960-68 shifts of a few (now atypical) silk-stocking counties were dwarfed by the conservative trends of the vast new tracts of middle-class suburbia. Actually, the Democratic upswing in a number of rich suburban areas around New York, Boston and Philadelphia is nothing more than an extension of the liberal establishmentarian behavior of Manhattan's East Side, Boston's Beacon Hill and Philadelphia's Rittenhouse Square. Typical suburban behavior is something else again.

Centered in the Sun Belt, the nation's heaviest suburban growth is solidly middle-class and conservative. Contemporary suburban expansion in the Northeast pales next to the spread of the Florida, Texas, Arizona and Southern California suburbs. Rapid, although less spectacular, suburban growth is occurring in the areas around Camden (New Jersey), Washington, D.C., Richmond, Atlanta, Memphis, St. Louis, Chicago, Oklahoma City, Tulsa and Denver. These suburbs are also conservative, often highly so. And even the few fast-growing Northeastern suburban counties—Suffolk, New York; Burlington, New Jersey; Prince Georges, Maryland—are conservative-trending, middle-class sections (see chart 51). The principal exception is Maryland's rich but fast-expanding Montgomery County, liberal seat of the upper echelons of Washington's federal bureaucracy.

From a national perspective, the silk-stocking liberal suburbs of Boston, New York, Philadelphia, San Francisco and (to a lesser extent) Chicago and Washington cast only a minute fraction of the ballots wielded by the preponderance of unfashionable lower-middle- and middle-income suburbs. And because more and more new suburbanites come from lower-middle-income backgrounds, this gap should widen.

The National Commission on Urban Problems, chaired by former Illinois Senator Paul Douglas, has drawn attention to the increasingly powerful shift of blue-collar and lower-middle-class population to suburbia, but surprisingly few establishment liberals under-

CHART 143

*Central City-Suburban Apartheid: The Demographic Projections of
the President's National Commission on
Urban Problems, July, 1968*

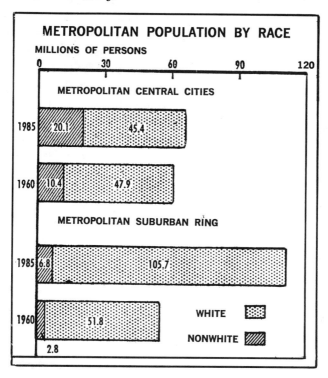

Note—As the chart indicates, the Commission expects the nation's growth over the next twenty years to ignore the cities and focus on suburbia. Indeed, only the urban growth of the South and West will prevent a sharp decline in the nation's central city population based on the steady shrinkage of northeastern central cities.

stand or admit these demographic facts of life. Instead, they typically portray the large conservative majority of Americans as a mere obsolescent and shrinking periphery of society, meanwhile painting their own peer group as the expanding segment of the nation committed to cosmopolitan thinking, technological sophistication and cultural change.

This myopia has considerable precedent. Since the days of Alexander Hamilton and the Federalists, the United States—and the Northeast in particular—has periodically supported a privileged elite, blind to the needs and interests of the large national majority. The corporate welfarists, planners and academicians of the Liberal Establishment are the newest of these elites, and their interests—for one thing, a high and not necessarily too productive rate of government social, educational, scientific and research spending—are as vested as those of Coolidge-Hoover era financiers and industrialists. The great political upheaval of the Nineteen-Sixties is not that of Senator Eugene McCarthy's relatively small group of upper-middle-class and intellectual supporters, but a populist revolt of the American masses who have been elevated by prosperity to middle-class status and conservatism. *Their* revolt is against the caste, policies and taxation of the mandarins of Establishment liberalism.

Granted that the new populist coalition includes very few Negroes—they have become almost entirely Democratic and exert very little influence on the GOP—black solidarity within the Democratic Party is rapidly enlarging Negro influence and job opportunities in many old Northern central cities. In New York, few Negroes have deserted the Democratic Party even to support Republican liberals Rockefeller, Javits, and Lindsay (see Chart 31). These intensely Democratic Negro loyalties are not rooted in fear of the GOP or its promise of a return to law and order, but in a realization that the Democratic Party can serve as a vehicle for Negro advancement—just as other groups have used politics to climb the social and economic ladder of urban America.

Ethnic polarization is a longstanding hallmark of American politics, not an unprecedented and menacing development of 1968. As illustrated throughout this book, ethnic and cultural division has so often shaped American politics that, given the immense midcentury impact of Negro enfranchisement and integration, reaction to this change almost inevitably had to result in political realignment. Moreover, American history has another example of a persecuted minority—the Nineteenth-Century Irish—who, in the face of considerable discrimination and old-stock animosity, likewise poured their ethnic numbers into the Democratic Party alone, winning power, jobs and socioeconomic opportunity through local political skill rather than the benevolence of usually-Republican national administrations.

For a half-century after the Civil War, the regular Democratic fidelity of the unpopular Irish city machines helped keep much of the nation Republican, and it seems possible that rising Negro participation in (national) Democratic politics from Manhattan to Mississippi may play a similar role in the post-1968 cycle. Growing Negro influence in—and conservative Southern, Western and Catholic departure from—the Democratic Party also suggests that Northeastern liberals ought to be able to dominate the party, which in turn must accelerate the sectional and ideological re-alignment already underway.

To the extent that the ethnic and racial overtones of American political behavior and alignment are appreciated, they are often confused or mis-stated. For example, far from being opposed by all non-whites, Richard Nixon was strongly supported by one non-white group—the Chinese. San Francisco's Chinese electorate was more Republican in 1968 than the city's white population. Nor is today's Republican Party Protestant rather than Catholic. In New York City, the party is becoming the vehicle of the Italians and Irish, and in the Upper Farm Belt—Wisconsin, Minnesota and North Dakota—German Catholics are moving to the fore. From the first days of the Republic, American politics have been a maze of ethnic, cultural and sectional oppositions and loyalties, and this has not deterred progress or growth. The new popular conservative majority has many ethnic strains, and portraits showing it as a white Anglo-Saxon Protestant monolith are highly misleading.

The emerging Republican majority spoke clearly in 1968 for a shift away from the sociological jurisprudence, moral permissiveness, experimental residential, welfare and educational programing and massive federal spending by which the Liberal (mostly Democratic) Establishment sought to propagate liberal institutions and ideology—and all the while reap growing economic benefits. The dominion of this impetus is inherent in the list of Republican-trending groups and potentially Republican Wallace electorates of 1968: Southerners, Borderers, Germans, Scotch-Irish, Pennsylvania Dutch, Irish, Italians, Eastern Europeans and other urban Catholics, middle-class suburbanites, Sun Belt residents, Rocky Mountain and Pacific Interior populists. Democrats among these groups were principally alienated from their party by its social programs and increasing identification with the Northeastern Establishment and ghetto alike. Exceept among isolationist Germans, resentment of the Vietnamese war, far from helping to forge the GOP majority, actually produced *Democratic* gains among the groups most affected: silk-stocking Megalopolitans, the San Fran-

MAP 47

The Emerging Republican Majority

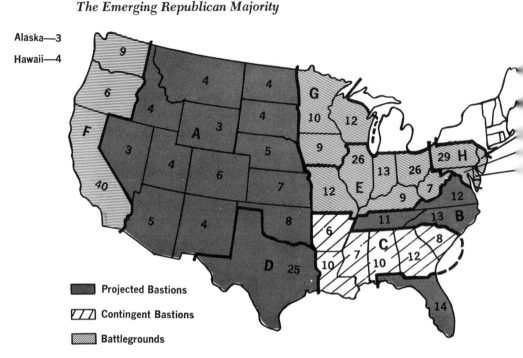

Alaska—3

Hawaii—4

■ Projected Bastions

▨ Contingent Bastions

▨ Battlegrounds

cisco-Berkeley-Madison-Ann Arbor electorate, Scandinavian progressives and Jews. As for the Republican trend groups, nothing
characterizes their outlook so much as a desire to dispel the Liberal
Establishment's philosophy of taxation and redistribution (partly
to itself) and reverse the encroachment of government in the social
life of the nation.

Shorn of power, stripped of vested interests in misleading and
unsuccessful programs, the Liberal Establishment may narrow its
gap between words and deeds which helped to drive racial and
youthful minorities into open revolt. So changed, Democratic liberalism will once again become a vital and creative force in national
politics, usually too innovative to win a presidential race, but inject-
ing a needed leavening of humanism into the middle-class *realpolitik*
of the new Republican coalition.

Because the Republicans are little dependent on the Liberal
Establishment or urban Negroes—the two groups most intimately,
though dissimilarly, concerned with present urban and welfare
policies—they have the political freedom to disregard the multitude

Explanation of Map 47

A. *Plains and Mountain States*—With 61 electoral votes, these constitute the conservative geographical heartland of the emerging Republican majority.

B. *The Outer South*—The states of Florida, Virginia, North Carolina and Tennessee are not only conservative but ever more reliably Republican in presidential elections. Their 50 electoral votes are vulnerable only to Republican Administration policies which keep alive third-party sentiment.

C. *The Contingent South*—The conservative Deep South and Arkansas (totaling 53 electoral votes) will join GOP ranks—by default—against Northern liberal Democrats, provided simply that Republican policies pay sufficient attention to conservative viewpoints to undercut third party movements and create a national Republican vs. national Democratic context.

D. *Texas*—Without third-party interference, Texas (25 electoral votes) will support moderate conservative national Republicanism against Northern Democratic liberalism.

— • —

The South and rock-ribbed conservative sections of the Heartland have 189 of the 270 electoral votes needed to elect a President. *Moderate* conservatism will forge its emerging Republican majority in several battleground areas: The Ohio-Mississippi Valley (93 electoral votes); the Pacific (60); the Upper Mississippi Valley (31); and the non-Yankee Northeast (59).

— • —

E. *The Ohio-Mississippi Valley*—The erosion of Civil War-rooted German and Border Democratic fidelity, together with growing white urban Catholic conservatism from Cleveland to St. Louis should put most of the key 93 Missouri, Illinois, Indiana, Kentucky, Ohio and West Virginia electoral votes into the GOP column.

F. *The Pacific*—California, which casts 40 of the 60 Pacific electoral votes, is becoming more Republican than the nation as a whole in response to the middle-class population explosion of Southern California.

G. *The Upper Mississippi Valley*—The GOP is not on the upswing in Iowa, Minnesota and Wisconsin—old Yankee-Scandinavian party strongholds —but it remains likely to win Iowa's and Wisconsin's share of 31 electoral votes.

H. *The Non-Yankee Northeast*—Of Pennsylvania, New Jersey, Delaware and Maryland, the latter three (30 electoral votes), all pushing below the Mason-Dixon Line, are particularly likely to participate in the emerging Republican majority.

of vested interests which have throttled national urban policy. The GOP is particularly lucky not to be weighted down with commitment to the political blocs, power brokers and poverty concessionaires of the decaying central cities of the North, now that national growth is shifting to suburbia, the South and the West. The American future lies in a revitalized countryside, a demographically ascendant Sun Belt and suburbia, and new towns—perhaps mountainside linear cities astride monorails 200 miles from Phoenix, Memphis or Atlanta. National policy will have to direct itself towards this future and its constituencies; and perhaps an administration so oriented can also deal realistically with the central cities where Great Society political largesse has so demonstrably failed.

When new eras and alignments have evolved in American politics, the ascending party has ridden the economic and demographic wave of the future: with Jefferson, a nation pushing inland from the Federalist seaboard and Tidewater; with Jackson, the trans-Appalachian New West; with Lincoln, the free-soil West and industrial North; with McKinley, a full-blown industrial North feeding from a full dinner pail; and with Roosevelt, the emergence of the big cities and the coming of age of the immigrant masses. Now it is Richard Nixon's turn to build a new era on the immense middle-class impetus of Sun Belt and suburbia. Thus, it is appropriate that much of the emerging Republican majority lies in the top growth states (California, Arizona, Texas and Florida) or new suburbia, while Democratic trends correlate with stability and decay (New England, New York City, Michigan, West Virginia and San Francisco-Berkeley).

Map 47 sketches the emerging Republican majority. The GOP core areas are the Mountain, Farm and Outer South states. The Deep South will become a GOP core area once it abandons third-party schemes. The Democratic stronghold is obvious: New York and New England. Most of the upcoming cycle's serious presidential campaign strategy will relate to three battleground areas: (1) the Pacific; (2) the Ohio-Mississippi Valley (Ohio, Indiana, Illinois, Kentucky and Missouri); and (3) the non-Yankee Northeast (New Jersey, Pennsylvania, Delaware and Maryland). Overall trends favor the Republicans in each of these battlegrounds.

It is doubtful whether either party could turn back the clock, but neither has attempted to do so. The 1968 election returns were barely final before Richard Nixon announced that he was transferring his voting residence from New York to Florida, and picked a cabinet notably short on representatives of the Northeastern Establishment. And the Democrats waited only a little longer to replace Louisiana's Earl Long with Massachusetts' Edward Kennedy as their Senate Whip. A new era has begun.

INDEX